COUNTRY LIVING
MAGAZINE

Guide to Rural England

THE NORTHWEST OF ENGLAND

Cheshire, Lancashire and Cumbria
including the Lake District

By David Gerrard

Published by:
Travel Publishing Ltd
7a Apollo House, Calleva Park
Aldermaston, Berkshire RG7 8TN
ISBN13 9781904434726

First Published: 2003
Second Edition: 2006
Third Edition: 2008

Country Living Guides:

East Anglia	Scotland
Heart of England	The South of England
Ireland	The South East of England
The North East of England	The West Country
The North West of England	Wales

Please Note:

All advertisements in this publication have been accepted in good faith by Travel Publishing and they have not necessarily been endorsed by *Country Living* Magazine.

All information is included by the publishers in good faith and is believed to be correct at the time of going to press. No responsibility can be accepted for errors.

Editor:	David Gerrard
Printing by:	Scotprint, Haddington
Location Maps:	© Maps in Minutes ™ (2008) © Collins Bartholomews 2008 All rights reserved.
Walks:	Walks have been reproduced with kind permission of the internet walking site: www.walkingworld.com
Walk Maps:	Reproduced from Ordnance Survey mapping on behalf of the Controller of Her Majesty's Stationery Office, © Crown Copyright. Licence Number MC 100035812
Cover Design:	Lines & Words, Aldermaston
Cover Photo:	Buttermere, Cumbria © www.picturesofbritain.co.uk
Text Photos:	Text photos have been kindly supplied by the Pictures of Britain photo library © www.picturesofbritain.co.uk and © Bob Brooks, Weston-super-Mare

Foreword

From a bracing walk across the hills and tarns of The Lake District to a relaxing weekend spent discovering the unspoilt hamlets of East Anglia, nothing quite matches getting off the beaten track and exploring Britain's areas of outstanding beauty.

Each month, *Country Living Magazine* celebrates the richness and diversity of our countryside with features on rural Britain and the traditions that have their roots there. So it is with great pleasure that I introduce you to the *Country Living Magazine Guide to Rural England* series. Packed with information about unusual and unique aspects of our countryside, the guides will point both fair-weather and intrepid travellers in the right direction.

Each chapter provides a fascinating tour of the North West of England area, with insights into local heritage and history and easy-to-read facts on a wealth of places to visit, stay, eat, drink and shop.

I hope that this guide will help make your visit a rewarding and stimulating experience and that you will return inspired, refreshed and ready to head off on your next countryside adventure.

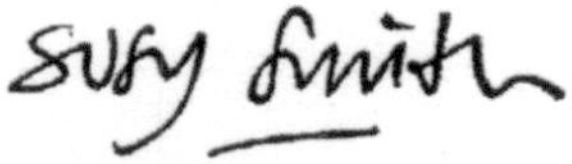

Susy Smith
Editor, Country Living magazine

PS To subscribe to *Country Living Magazine* each month, call 01858 438844

Introduction

This is the third edition of *The Country Living Guide to Rural England - the North West* and we are sure that it will be as popular as its predecessors. Regular readers will note that the page layouts have been attractively redesigned and that we have provided more information on the places, people, and activities covered. Also, in the introduction to each village or town we have summarized and categorized the main attractions to be found there which makes it easier for readers to plan their visit. David Gerrard, a very experienced travel writer has, of course, completely updated the contents of the guide and ensured that it is packed with vivid descriptions, historical stories, amusing anecdotes and interesting facts on hundreds of places in Lancashire, Cheshire and Cumbria, which is home to the wonderful scenery of the Lake District.

The advertising panels within each chapter provide further information on places to see, stay, eat, drink, shop and even exercise! We have also selected a number of walks from walkingworld.com (full details of this website may be found to the rear of the guide) which we highly recommend if you wish to appreciate fully the beauty and charm of the varied rural landscapes and coastlines of the North West of England.

The guide however is not simply an "armchair tour". Its prime aim is to encourage the reader to visit the places described and discover much more about the wonderful towns, villages and countryside of Lancashire, Cheshire and Cumbria. In this respect we would like to thank all the Tourist Information Centres who helped us to provide you with up-to-date information. Whether you decide to explore this region by wheeled transport or on foot we are sure you will find it a very uplifting experience.

We are always interested in receiving comments on places covered (or not covered) in our guides so please do not hesitate to use the reader reaction forms provided at the rear of this guide to give us your considered comments. This will help us refine the content of the next edition. We also welcome any general comments which will help improve the overall presentation of the guides themselves.

For more information on other titles in the *Country Living Rural Guide* series and the full range of travel guides published by Travel Publishing please refer to the order form at the rear of this guide or log on to our website (see below).

Travel Publishing

Did you know that you can also search our website for details of thousands of places to see, stay, eat or drink throughout Britain and Ireland? Our site has become increasingly popular and now receives monthly over 160,000 visits. Try it!

website: www.travelpublishing.co.uk

Contents

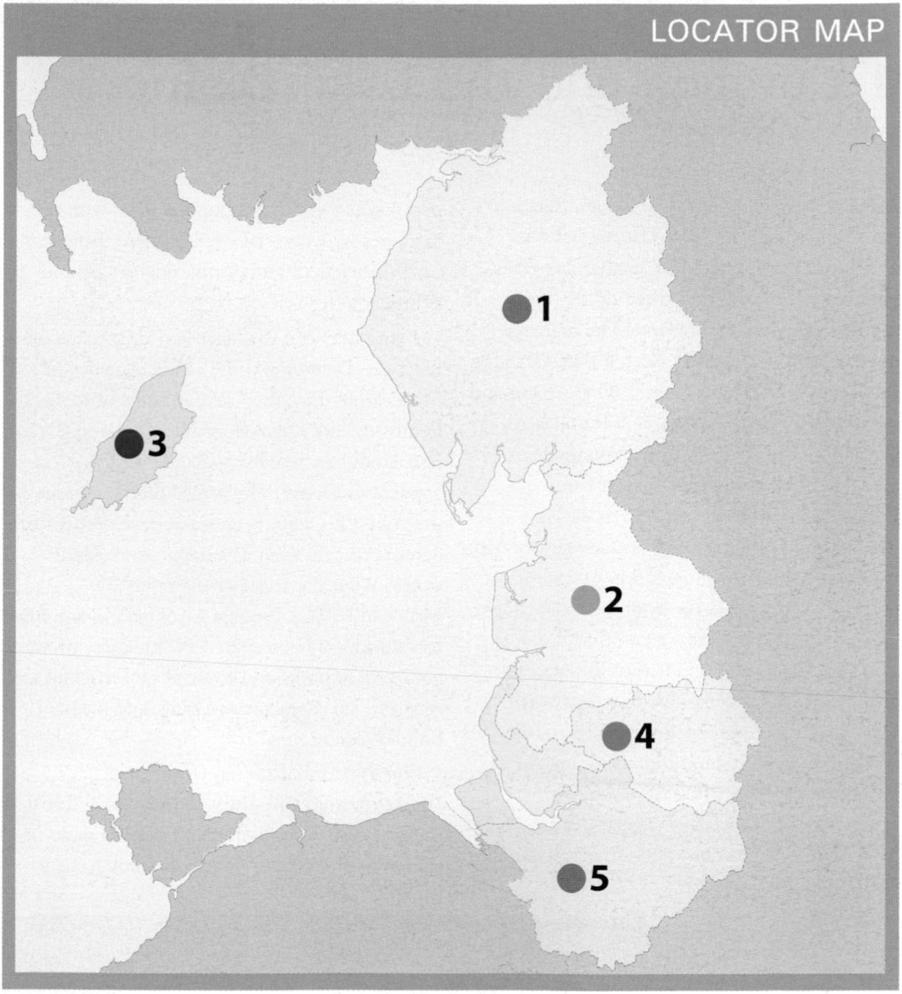

1 Cumbria and the Lake District

Visitors from all over the world are drawn in their millions to the Lake District with its irresistible combination of enchanting lakes, picturesque villages and some of the most dramatic scenery in England. The highest mountain in the country, Scafell Pike (3205ft), the largest and deepest lakes, Windermere and Wast Water respectively, are all found here, along with hundreds of other mountains, another 14 lakes (although apart from Bassenthwaite they are called 'meres' or 'waters'), challenging crags and lovely wooded valleys. Despite the huge influx of visitors, most do not venture far from the main tourist 'honey-pots' so it's still easy to find the peaceful glades and windswept, isolated fells celebrated by the Lake Poets, Wordsworth, Coleridge and Southey. Between them, this lyrical trio transformed the pervading 18th-century perception of the most north-westerly corner of England as an intimidating wilderness into an appreciation of its majestic scenery.

Almost exactly one third of the county's 2636 square miles lies within the boundaries of the Lake District National Park, created in 1951 to protect the area from "inappropriate development and to provide access to the land for public enjoyment". The southeastern corner of the Park is Cumbria's best known and most popular area, with the main resort towns of Windermere, Bowness-on-Windermere and Ambleside set around Windermere itself.

Ullswater, Cumbria

Lying between the lakes and mountains of the Lake District and the sandy estuaries of Morecambe Bay, the Cartmel and Furness Peninsulas are areas of gentle moorland, craggy headlands, scattered woodlands, and vast expanses of sand. The arrival of the railways in the mid-19th century saw the development of genteel resorts such as Grange-over-Sands overlooking the treacherous sands of Morecambe Bay. Grange is still an elegant little town and has been spared the indignity of vast amusement parks and rows of slot machines, retaining its character as a quiet and pleasant holiday centre.

The North Cumbrian coast, from Workington in the south to the Solway Firth in the north, is one of the least known parts of this beautiful county but it certainly has a lot to offer. It is an area rich in heritage, with a network of quiet country lanes, small villages, old ports, and seaside resorts. The coast's largest town, Workington, on the site of a Roman fort, was once a busy port, prospering on coal, iron and shipping. It later became famous for fine-quality steel, and though its importance has declined, it is still the country's largest producer of railway tracks. Further up the coast is Maryport, again a port originally built by the Romans. A short distance inland lies Cockermouth on the edge of the Lake District National Park, a pretty market town with some elegant Georgian buildings. In one of these, the town's most famous son, the poet William Wordsworth, was born in 1770.

Loughrigg Tarn and the Langdale Pikes

The northernmost stretch of coastline, around the Solway Firth, is an area of tiny villages with fortified towers standing as mute witness to the border struggles of long ago. These villages were the haunt of smugglers, wildfowlers, and half-net fishermen. What is particularly special about this coastline is its rich birdlife.

The River Eden, one of the few large rivers in England that flows northwards, rises on the high limestone fells above Mallerstang Common, near the North Yorkshire border, and runs to the outskirts of Carlisle where it turns sharply east and flows into the Solway Firth. For much of its course, the river is accompanied by the famous Settle to Carlisle Railway, a spectacularly scenic route saved from extinction in the 1960s by the efforts of local enthusiasts.

For more than 350 years the area around Carlisle was known as the Debatable Lands, a lawless region where the feared Border Reivers sacked and plundered at will. Every winter, when their own food stocks were almost depleted, armed gangs from across the border would ride southwards to seize the cattle and sheep of their more prosperous neighbours. Stealing and murdering, they wreaked havoc in this area and almost every village would have had a fortified structure, usually a pele tower, where the inhabitants and their animals could hide safely.

This is also the county of Hadrian's Wall, the most important monument built in Britain by the Romans; many stretches of the wall are still visible, and Birdoswald and other centres give an excellent insight into Roman border life.

LOCATOR MAP

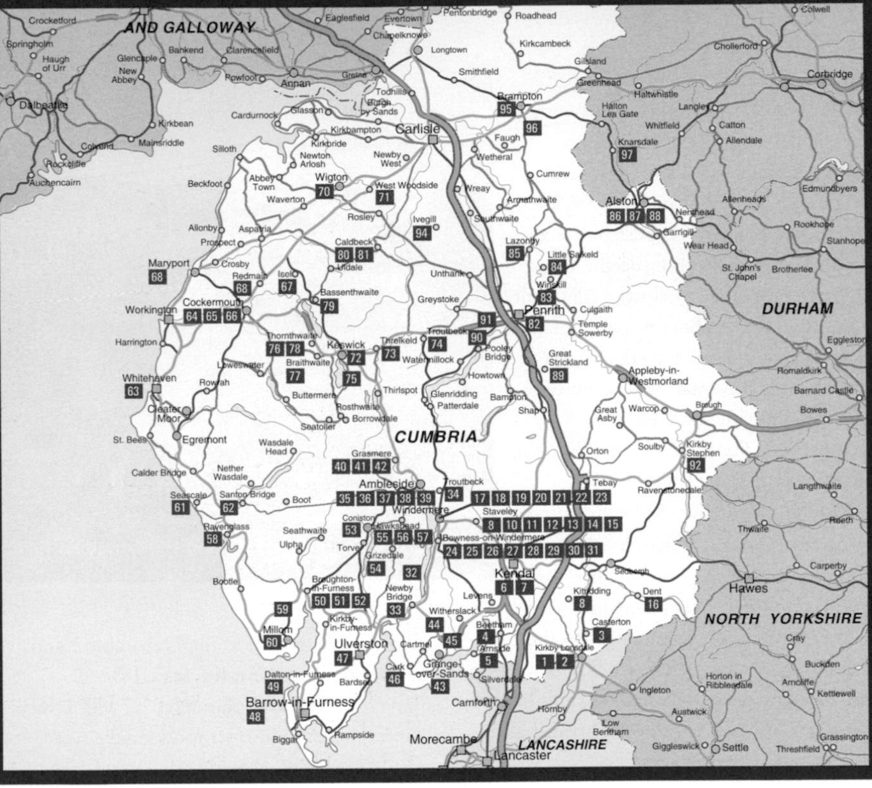

ADVERTISERS AND PLACES OF INTEREST

Accommodation, Food and Drink

historic building | museum and heritage | historic site | scenic attraction | flora and fauna

Activities

Antiques and Restoration

Arts and Crafts

Fashions

Giftware

Home and Garden

Jewellery

Place of Interest

Specialist Food and Drink

Kirkby Lonsdale

Devil's Bridge · Swine Market

St Mary's Church · Victorian Fair

Devil's Bridge, Kirkby Lonsdale

One fine day in 1875, John Ruskin came to Kirkby Lonsdale and stood on the stone terrace overlooking the valley of the River Lune. It was, he declared, "one of the loveliest scenes in England, therefore in the world." He was equally enthusiastic about the busy little market town - "I do not know in all my country," he continued, "a place more naturally divine than Kirkby Lonsdale."

Ruskin had been inspired to visit the town after seeing Turner's painting of that view, and Turner himself had come in 1816 on the recommendation of William Wordsworth. All three of them made a point of going to see the **Devil's Bridge** over the Lune, a handsome, lofty structure of three fluted

CHURCHMOUSE CHEESES

ONLINE SHOP- QUALITY CHEESES DELIVERED RIGHT TO YOUR DOOR

4 Market Street, Kirkby Lonsdale, Cumbria LA6 2AU
Tel: 01524 273005 Fax: 0870 2412581
e-mail: info@churchmousecheeses.com
website: www.churchmousecheeses.com

The winner of the 'Best Independent Cheese Shop in Britain 2007 award', sponsored by Dairy Crest and *The Grocer,* **Churchmouse Cheeses** had an unusual start. Owners John and Julie Natlacen had to cancel their honeymoon when bride-to-be Julie broke her leg. The only suitable celebratory getaway seemed to be a few days in the small Cumbrian village of Beetham. Whilst on a day trip to nearby Kirkby Lonsdale, they spotted an empty 18th-century listed building and it was here that their dream began. John quit his job in the city as a financial adviser, spent a blissful three months travelling around Cumbria sourcing quality produce and opened Churchmouse Cheeses on the 7th of September 2002. Their elegant shop is now an Aladdin's cave of fine cheeses, both local and international, including Blacksticks Blue, Shorrocks Black Bombs, Mrs Kirkham's Lancashire cheeses (and plenty more!), Golden Cross goat's cheese, Cumberland Farmhouse, Swaledale, Ribblesdale, Eppoisses, Brie de Meaux, Picos Blue and much, much more. The shop also sells traditional hand-patted butter, farmhouse cakes, chutneys and pickles, deli meats, antipasto, mouth-watering olives and a wide selection of Cumbrian farmhouse produce.

PARMA VIOLET

52 Main Street, Kirkby Lonsdale, Cumbria LA6 2AJ
Tel/Fax: 01524 272585
e-mail: info@parmaviolet.co.uk
website: www.parmaviolet.co.uk

Parma Violet, together with many other specialist shops, pubs and cafés, is located on the main street of the wonderfully quaint Victorian market town of Kirkby Lonsdale, less than half an hour's drive from the Lake District. We are stockists of Cath Kidston, Emma Bridgewater and Le Creuset, but also pride ourselves on sourcing more unusual and 'one-off' items including vintage and locally crafted products. In short, expect a mix of both beautiful and quirky gifts, toys, homewares, cards and garden items. Not to be missed!

You are also welcome to stay in our brand new holiday apartment situated on the two uppermost floors over the shop (separate entrance). Sleeping 4/6 persons, and with a wealth of original features including a wood-burning stove, complimentary hamper and wine, plus discount voucher for the shop, you will certainly enjoy all that this rather special town has to offer. Attention to detail matters to us, even down to the hand painted mouse hole on the stairs (definitely no residents though!).

See the website for further photos and rates. Short weekend/ midweek breaks also available in addition to full weeks.

arches reputedly built by Satan himself in three days. According to legend, an old woman, unable to cross the deep river with her cattle, had asked the Devil to build her a bridge. He agreed but demanded in return the soul of the first creature to cross, but his evil plan was thwarted by Cumbrian cunning. The old woman threw a bun across the bridge which was retrieved by her dog and thus she cheated the Devil of a human soul.

Kirkby's Main Street is a picturesque jumble of houses spanning several centuries, with intriguing passages and alleyways skittering off in all directions, all of them worth exploring. It's still a pleasure to stroll along the narrow streets bearing names such as Jingling Lane, past the 16th-century weavers' cottages in Fairbank, across the **Swine Market** with its 600-year-old cross where traders have displayed their wares every Thursday for more than 700 years, past ancient hostelries to the even more venerable **St Mary's Church** with its noble Norman doorway and massive pillars. In the churchyard, a late Georgian gazebo looks across to the enchanting view of the Lune Valley painted by Turner.

The town has three times been national winner of the 'Britain in Bloom' competition and also attracts thousands of visitors for its **Victorian Fair**, held on the first full weekend in September, and again in December for the Yuletide procession through streets ablaze with coloured lights and decorated Christmas trees.

THE PHEASANT INN

Casterton, Kirkby Lonsdale,
Cumbria LA6 2RX
Tel: 01524 271230/274267
Fax: 01524 274267
website: www.pheasantinn.co.uk

Idyllically situated in the beautiful Lune Valley, mid-way between the Lakes and the Dales, the peaceful hamlet of Casterton nestles beneath the fells just a mile from the delightful market town of Kirkby Lonsdale. It's here you will find **The Pheasant Inn**, a traditional 18th-century hostelry that is also recommended by the *Good Pub Guide* and the *Which? Pub Guide*.

The Pheasant enjoys a glowing reputation for serving quality food, offering a good choice of imaginative dishes using only the finest local produce. Whether you choose an informal bar meal or dinner served in the attractive oak-panelled dining room, you can be confident of a well-prepared, attractively presented meal. The extensive restaurant menu starts with a wide choice of starters ranging from a home-made soup of the day served with fresh bread, to poached fresh pears with a Stilton dressing. As a main course, how about a Steak tournedos Rossini - pan-fried fillet steak served on fried bread croutons topped with pâté and accompanied by Madeira sauce, or a Supreme of fresh salmon wrapped in smoked salmon and oven-baked in butter and poppy seeds? For vegetarians, the choice includes a tasty Cannelloni stuffed with finely chopped button mushrooms and asparagus spears and topped with a coating of parsley cream sauce. Round off your meal with one of the delicious, freshly prepared homemade sweets and puddings from The Pheasant's kitchen followed by filtered coffee served with mints. In addition to the regular menu, there's also a selection of daily specials available.

If you are planning to stay in this lovely part of the county, The Pheasant has a choice of attractively furnished and decorated guest bedrooms. All bedrooms are individually furnished to the highest standard with central heating, private bathroom, colour TV, tea and coffee making facilities and direct dial telephones. For disabled guests, a twin bedroom is situated on the ground floor. A hearty full English breakfast is included in the tariff.

The Pheasant is open all year round, and has a large car park and easy access. It is within easy reach of the Lake District, Yorkshire Dales and Forest of Bowland, all of which are within half an hour's drive, making the inn an ideal touring base.

Around Kirkby Lonsdale

HALE

7 miles W of Kirkby Lonsdale off the A6

Lakeland Wildlife Oasis

This tiny village surrounded by woodland and close to the Lancashire border is home to the **Lakeland Wildlife Oasis** where a wide range of animals and birds can be seen and a hands-on exhibition tells the evolutionary story. Visitors can drape a snake around their neck, exchange inquisitive glances with a ruffled lemur or a meerkat squatting on its haunches, and admire creatures rarely seen in captivity, such as flying foxes and poison arrow frogs. The tropical hall is the home of numerous free-flying birds, bats and butterflies, and other exhibits range from leaf-cutter ants to pygmy marmosets. The Oasis was established in 1991 by Dave and Jo Marsden, who were keepers at Chester Zoo before setting up this popular family attraction, which is open throughout the year.

BEETHAM

8 miles W of Kirkby Lonsdale on the A6

Church of St Michael and All Angels

Post Office Heron Corn Mill

Museum of Paper Making

Approached through a pergola of rambling roses, the **Church of St Michael and All Angels** dates from Saxon times and, during restoration work in the 1830s, a hoard of around 100 coins minted in Norman times, was discovered inside the building at the base of a pillar. Although badly damaged during the Civil War, when its windows were smashed and effigies broken, a glass fragment depicting Henry IV in an ermine robe has survived the centuries. The village also has an unusual 19th-century **Post Office** with a distinctive black and white studded door.

Just outside the village stands **Heron Corn Mill** (see panel below), a restored and working

Heron Corn Mill

Mill Lane, Beetham, Nr Milnthorpe, Cumbria LA7 7PQ
Tel: 01539 565027
website: www.heronmill.org

Heron Corn Mill on the banks of the River Bela in South Cumbria, close to the Lancashire border, is one of the few working mills in the area. There is documentary evidence to show that a mill existed on the site prior to 1096. In 1220, the Lord of the Manor gave the monks of St Marie's York the right to grind their grain at the mill without multure (payment).

The mill passed through many hands till, in 1927, it came into the hands of W & J Pye, millers of Lancaster. In 1955, they rationalised their business and closed the mill. For the next two decades the mill was unused and decaying. In 1973, Henry Cooke Ltd. leased the mill to the newly-formed Beetham Trust, to rescue the mill for the benefit of the public.

In 1975, the mill was opened by Princess Alexandra and has continued up till the present time to show the mechanics of a water-driven corn mill to the public. It is a unique feature of South Lakeland's industrial heritage.

watermill with fully operational grinding machinery. A fine example of a traditional 18th-century corn mill that served the Westmorland farming area, the mill ceased trading as recently as the 1950s. Visitors to the mill can see an exhibition about its history and view the milling process. Also here is the **Museum of Paper Making**, which was established in 1988 to commemorate 500 years of paper-making in England. The displays illustrate paper making ancient and modern by various means.

ARNSIDE

10 miles W of Kirkby Lonsdale off the B5282

Arnside Knott   Arnside Tower

This quiet town on the Kent Estuary, with its short but elegant promenade, was once a busy port with its own shipbuilding and sea-salt refining industry. As the estuary silted up during the 19th century, a process accelerated by construction of the striking 50-arch railway viaduct, so the port declined. Today, it is a favourite retirement destination and a peaceful holiday resort.

Around Arnside itself there is a wonderful choice of country walks, particularly over and around **Arnside Knott**. This limestone headland, now a nature reserve rich in old woods and wild flowers, is part of the Arnside and Silverdale Area of Outstanding Natural Beauty. Knott comes from the Saxon word meaning 'rounded hill', which, in this case, rises 521 feet above sea level and gives extensive views of the Lakeland fells, the Pennines, and the southern Cumbrian coast. There is a beautiful path around the headland and along the shoreline past Blackstone Point.

THE LITTLE SHOP

36 The Promenade, Arnside, Cumbria LA5 0HA
Tel: 01524 761264
e-mail: biff.mcg@btinternet.com

Located on the Promenade of the peaceful seaside resort of Arnside, **The Little Shop** used to be the village Post Office but now houses a fascinating collection of cards, gifts for all occasions, maps, jewellery, books, gift wrap, relief maps and pictures - a wonderful repository of items to make life easier in the run-up to Christmas especially, but also for presents at all other times. Built in the 1800s, the shop has a prime seafront position in the centre of the village.

The Little Shop is owned and run by Adam Donaldson and Elizabeth McGonagle who enjoy welcoming visitors and helping them to find exactly what they want.

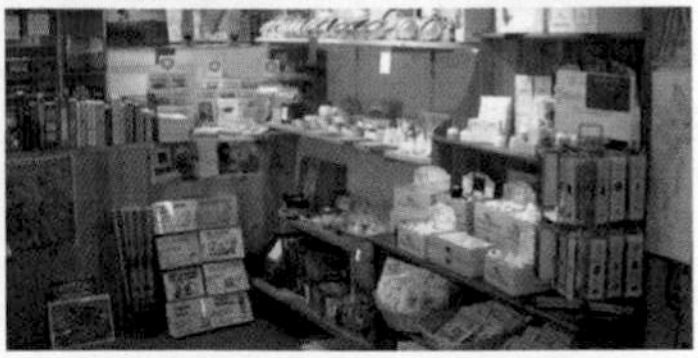

Inland, and found down a quiet lane, is the ruined **Arnside Tower**, one of the many pele towers that were built in the area in the 14th century. This particular tower dates from the 1370s and it may have been part of the chain of towers designed to form a ring of protection around Morecambe Bay.

Kendal

Kendal Bowmen · Kendal Castle
Westmorland Shopping Centre · Elephant Yard
K Village Factory Shopping · Kendal Black Drop
Lakes Leisure Centre · Brewery Arts Centre
Museum of Lakeland Life & Industry
Abbot Hall Art Gallery · Parish Church
Museum of Natural History & Archaeology
Alfred Wainwright · Quaker Tapestry Exhibition

A survey a few years ago by Strathclyde University revealed that the highest quality of life of any town in England was to be found in Kendal, the 'capital' of South Lakeland. That assessment came as no surprise to the residents of this lively, bustling town, which was once one of the most important woollen textile centres of northern England. The Kendal woollen industry was founded in 1331 by John Kemp, a Flemish weaver. It flourished and sustained the town for almost 600 years until the development of competition from the huge West Riding of Yorkshire mills during the Industrial Revolution of the 19th century. The town's motto 'Wool is my Bread' reveals the extent to which the economy of Kendal depended on the wool from the flocks of Herdwick sheep that roamed the surrounding fells. The fame of the cloth was so great that Shakespeare refers to archers clad in Kendal Green cloth in his play *Henry IV*. These archers were the famous **Kendal Bowmen** whose lethal longbows were made from local yew trees culled from the nearby limestone crags. It was these men who clinched the English victories at Agincourt and Crécy and fought so decisively against the Scots at the Battle of Flodden Field in 1513.

Kendal has royal connections too. The Parr family lived at **Kendal Castle** until 1483 - their most famous descendant was Catherine Parr, the last of Henry VIII's six wives. Today, the castle's gaunt ruins stand high on a hill overlooking the town, with most of the castle wall and one of the towers still standing, and two underground vaults still complete. Castle Hill is a popular place for walking and picnicking and in summer the hillside is smothered with wild flowers. From the hilltop there are spectacular views and a panorama panel here assists in identifying the distant fells.

Anyone wandering around the town cannot help but notice the numerous alleyways, locally known as yards, that are such a distinctive feature of Kendal. An integral part of the old town, they are a reminder that the

Kendal Castle

THE AZ BAZAAR

16 New Shambles, Kendal, Cumbria LA9 4TS
Tel: 01539 735728
e-mail: info@azbazaar.com

The Az Bazaar was born out of Lynn Wilson's love for different cultures and artefacts around the world. After spending many years travelling and experiencing many diverse ways of life, Lynn wanted to capture a little of the essence of those experiences. Today, she imports direct from artists throughout Turkey, Egypt, Nepal, Kashmir, Morocco, Chile, the USA and Peru. The variety of the artefacts on display is astonishing. There are ceramics, kilims, Moroccan lights, bespoke ethnic jewellery in semi-precious and handmade beads and silver. There are even belly dancing belts in there somewhere. Lynn believes in trying to support the artisans' efforts towards economic independence and to raise their social standing. "So we try to ensure we have adequate background information about their lifestyles and products", says Lynn. Her shop, in the famous Shambles area of the town, is known to locals as Aladdin's Cave because of its abundant and colourful contents. Incidentally, in Turkish 'Az' means 'small'. The shop may indeed be comparatively small but it is full of riches.

THE COTTAGE KITCHEN

28a Finkle Street, Kendal,
Cumbria LA9 4AB
Tel: 01539 722468
website: www.beautifulcurtains.co.uk

The Cottage Kitchen occupies a rather grand stone building that was once the town's fire station. With its smart royal blue and white décor and outdoor tables, the restaurant looks very inviting indeed. It is owned and run by the mother and son team of Lynn and Mark Robson. Lynn used to be a postal lady before opening the café in the spring of 2006; Mark is the chef and his menu offers a good choice of main meals, snacks, sandwiches, toasties and cakes. For all his cooking, Mark uses locally sourced produce wherever possible, and fresh fish dishes are a speciality of his.

The Cottage Kitchen is open from 8am to 5pm, Monday to Saturday; from 10am to 4pm on Sunday. Private parties of up to 16 people can be catered for.

people of Kendal used to live under a constant threat of raids by the Scots. The yards were a line of defence against these attacks, an area that could be secured by sealing the one small entrance, with the families and livestock safe inside.

Shoppers are spoilt for choice in Kendal. In addition to all the familiar High Street names, the **Westmorland Shopping Centre** and **Elephant Yard**, both in the heart of the town, and the **K Village Factory Shopping** complex on the outskirts, make it easy to shop until you drop. One local product well worth sampling is Kendal Mint Cake, a tasty, sugary confection, which is cherished by climbers and walkers for its instant infusion of energy. Another once-popular local medication, **Kendal Black Drop**, is no longer available. "A more than commonly strong mixture of opium and alcohol", Kendal Black Drop was a favourite tipple of the poets Samuel Taylor Coleridge and Thomas de Quincey.

Kendal's excellent sporting facilities include the **Lakes Leisure Centre**, which offers a one-week tourist pass, the Lakeland Climbing Centre, which is one of the highest indoor climbing facilities in the country, Kendal ski slope, two local golf courses and a driving range. Drama, music and the visual arts are presented in a regularly changing programme of exhibitions, live music, theatre productions and craft workshops at the **Brewery Arts Centre**. The Centre also houses Kendal's cinema, which presents a mixture of mainstream, classic and art house films. The complex also contains a restaurant overlooking a garden, a bar and café.

A number of interesting museums and galleries are located in Kendal. The **Museum of Lakeland Life and Industry**, which is themed around traditional rural trades of the region, and **Abbot Hall Art Gallery** form part of a complex within Abbot Hall park. The museum, in re-created farmhouse rooms, contains a wide variety of exhibits, including Arthur Ransome memorabilia, craft workshops, a Victorian street scene, artefacts from the Arts and Crafts movement, nautical displays and Captain Flint's Locker, a pirate activity area for children and families. The gallery, in an elegant Georgian villa, houses a collection of society portraits by the locally born George Romney and watercolour scenes by Ruskin and Turner, while the 20th century and contemporary scene is represented by Walter Sickert, Ben Nicholson, Lucien Freud and Bridget Riley. The **Museum of Natural History and Archaeology**, founded in 1796, is one of the oldest museums in the country. Based on the collection first exhibited by William Todhunter in the late 18th century, the museum takes visitors on a journey from prehistoric times, a trip which includes an interactive exhibit telling the story of Kendal Castle.

The famous fellwalker and writer, **Alfred Wainwright,** whose handwritten guides to the Lakeland hills will be found in the backpack of any serious walker, was honorary clerk here between 1945 and 1974. Many of his original drawings are on display.

Adjacent to the elegant Georgian Abbot Hall and Museum is the 13th-century **Parish Church** of Kendal, "the Church of the Angels", one of the widest in England, with five aisles and a peal of 10 bells.

Perhaps the most unusual attraction in Kendal is the **Quaker Tapestry Exhibition** at the Friends Meeting House in the centre of the town. This unique exhibition of 77 panels of community embroidery explores Quaker history from the 17th century to the present day. These colourful, beautifully crafted tapestries are the work of some 4000 people, aged between four and 90, from 15 countries. A Quaker costume display, embroidery demonstrations, workshops and courses, and a large-screen colour video combine to provide a fascinating insight into the Quaker movement and its development. The centre also has a shop, garden, tea room and workshop.

Around Kendal

BURNESIDE

2 miles N of Kendal off the A591

Potter Fell

There has been a settlement here since the Stone Age and the remains of a stone circle can be seen close by on **Potter Fell**. By the 15th century, Burneside was a settled agricultural area and a rich variety of mills sprang up along the River Sprint - fulling, corn, cotton, wool, bobbin, and the original rag paper mill at Cowan Head.

The River Sprint, which meets the River Kent just south of the village, has its own remarkably beautiful Longsleddale Valley which curves past Garnett Bridge deep into the high fell country. A bridle path climbs from the head of the valley into Kentmere, another spectacularly beautiful walk.

SEDGWICK

4 miles S of Kendal off the A590

Lakeland Maize Maze

At Raines Hall Farm, the **Lakeland Maize Maze** is the area's first. Designed by Adrian Fisher, the world's leading maze designer, the maze is cut into a nine-acre field of maize with miles of paths creating a devilish puzzle. There's also a Headlong Maze and an Arrow Maze as well as pedal tractors, sandpit, picnic area, giant draughts and a variety of farmyard animals.

LEVENS

5 miles S of Kendal off the A590

Levens Hall   Sizergh Castle

At the southern tip of Scout Scar, overlooking the Lyth Valley and the lower reaches of the River Kent, stands **Levens Hall** with its unique topiary gardens. The superb Elizabethan mansion (described as 'one of the wonders of Lakeland') developed from a 14th-century pele tower and the gardens were first laid out in 1694. They were the work of Colonel James Grahame, a keen gardener, who purchased the hall in 1688 and employed a Frenchman, Guillaume Beaumont, to create the amazing topiary work. (Beaumont also redesigned the gardens at Hampton Court for James II.) The topiary is by no means the only attraction in the grounds, which also include a Fountain Garden created in 1994 to mark the tercentenary of the gardens. The interior of the house is equally rewarding - a wealth of period furniture, fine panelling and plasterwork, a dining room with walls covered in goatskin, and paintings by Rubens, Lely and Cuyp. A major location for the BBC TV serial *Wives and Daughters*, the Hall's other attractions include a collection of working steam engines, a tea room, gift shop and plant centre.

Only a couple of miles north of Levens Hall, just off the A591, is another stately old residence, **Sizergh Castle**, the impressive home of the Strickland family since 1239, although the property is now administered by the National Trust. Originally a pele tower built to withstand border raiders, the house has been added to and altered over the intervening centuries to provide the family, as times became less violent, with a more comfortable home. Now boasting intricately carved chimney mantels, fine oak panelling, and a collection of portraits of the Stuart royal family, the castle stands in well laid out gardens and 1500 acres of grounds, which provide superb views over the Lakeland fells.

STAVELEY

4 miles NW of Kendal off the A591

St James's Church

A pleasant village of grey stone buildings, Staveley is flanked by the rivers Kent and Gowan. It's a popular base for walkers exploring the Kentmere horseshoe and the High Street fells. Its first church was built in

Sizergh Castle, nr Levens

STAVELEY MILL YARD

Back Lane, Staveley, Kendal, Cumbria LA8 9LR
website: www.staverleymillyard.com

Tucked away in the village of Staveley, by-passed now by the main road between Kendal and Windermere, is an artisan estate called **Staveley Mill Yard**. It occupies the Old Wood Mill site and contains an interesting and diverse range of businesses. The main operations here include Wilf's Café, Munx Lakeland Bakery, Hawkshead Brewery & Beer Hall, and Out of the Woods, bespoke furniture makers.

Out of the Woods specialises in making furniture that is both original and specific to the needs of their customers. The craftsmen here excel in working to customers' special requirements so if you have any individual piece, or pieces, of crafted wood furniture in mind, just call them and discuss your requirements. And if you are looking for inspiration, just browse around their showroom at Staveley.

Tel: 01539 822033
website: www.outofthewoodsinteriors.co.uk

Wilf's Cafe, with decking overlooking the River Kent and inside seating that includes a comfy sofa area, offers a varied menu of homemade food, including vegetarian options, gorgeous cakes and daily specials. With a link door through to Hawkshead Beer Hall, it's a great place to start or finish a day in the Kentmere area.

Tel: 01539 822329
website: www.wilfs-cafe.co.uk

Hawkshead Brewery and the **Hawkshead Beer Hall** are showcases for the craft brewery industry. The Beer Hall looks down into the brew house and has a fully stocked bar where Hawkshead beers are available alongside a range of bottled beers from around the world. In 2008, a beer shop will open, selling great beers from here and abroad. Tours of the Brewery are available by arrangement, and the Beer Hall can be hired at night as a function room.

Tel: 01539 822644
website: www.hawksheadbrewery.co.uk

Munx Lakeland Bakery make their bread the traditional way - by hand and with patience. They use the best flour they can get their hands on along with Staveley's natural spring water. The two things that the bakery will never use are artificial flavourings and preservatives.

Tel: 01539 822102
website: www.munx.co.uk

Other businesses on site include a huge cycle warehouse, an engraver's, a local crafts shop, an artist's studio/gallery, a gardening and accessories shop, and a cookery school. The Yard is expanding all the time - and there's plenty of parking. Well worth a visit!

MILL YARD STUDIOS

3 Mill Yard, Staveley, Cumbria LA8 9LR
Tel: 01539 721836
e-mail: millyardstudios @tiscali.co.uk
website: www.millyardstudios.co.uk

Mill Yard Studios was established in 2001 by David Penn and Pam Williamson, two award-winning freelance artists with long and distinguished track records. The studios occupy part of the original wood mill buildings, which boast the longest slate roof in the Lake District and house a number of creative workers.

David's work is principally painting. He has an especial interest in both landscape and life drawing, and the ambiguities of the ground between the two. His recent work has focused on his travel in India (see image right) and most recently in the Falkland Isles, resulting in stunning paintings.

Working in a variety of media, Pam is particularly interested in landscape and its layers of history, both hidden and on the surface. Investigative journeys on foot have provided inspiration and material for her work.

From time to time, Pam and David have worked together to create installations such as the Memory Engine (2004) for the Armitt Museum, Ambleside. Together they curate top-class contemporary exhibitions at the Mill Yard Studios. They also mount displays of their own work and run a variety of workshops throughout the year.

MYRTLE & MACE

Staveley Mill Yard, Staveley, Kendal,
Cumbria LA8 9LR
Tel: 01539 822022
e-mail: info@myrtleandmace.com
website: www.myrtleandmace.com

Myrtle and Mace is a garden shop and online retailer based in Staveley Mill Yard, a former bobbin mill, in the heart of the English Lake District. Here you will find a comprehensive range of garden-related products, featuring the French garden furniture specialist Fermob, along with an extensive range of seeds from the much acclaimed Italian seed company Franchi, Italy's greatest seed company. In addition, we have an excellent choice of garden accessories from many UK companies, including Nutscene and Burgon & Ball.

We care about the impact of our carbon footprint, so sourcing natural and more sustainable products is our top priority, however we feel this shouldn't mean compromising on the design and aesthetics of our products. With this in mind we are proud to promote individual and innovative makers, like our recycled vegetable sack planters from London designer Lucky Bird.

PETER HALL & SON LTD

Danes Road, Staveley, nr Kendal,
Cumbria LA8 9PL
Tel: 01539 821633
Fax: 01539 821905
e-mail: info@peter-hall.co.uk
website: www.peter-hall.co.uk

Peter Hall established his furniture business in 1972, originally working on his own, making simple, Country furniture. The business has now broadened its focus to include interior design, furniture restoration and conservation, upholstery and woodturning.

The showroom of **Peter Hall & Son** displays both the more traditional styles of furniture and contemporary pieces in a light and airy environment. The showroom also provides the opportunity to display beautiful curtains, Jeremy Hall's one-off black and white prints, and lighting from companies such as Rochamp, Chelsom & Artemis. The company's craftsmen also create exquisitely turned bowls and other gift items on the premises - these too are on display. Windows in the corridor allow customers to view the furniture making and furniture restoration workshops and to see the highly skilled craftsmen at work.

The interior design studio has hundreds of fabric books from companies such as Zoffany, Colefax & Fowler and Mulberry, as well as samples of wallpaper, paints, lighting - indeed, everything to make your home feel special.

The quality of the pieces produced at Peter Hall has been recognised by many awards. Jeremy Hall, for example, was presented with a Guild Mark Certificate by the Worshipful Company of Furniture Makers for a corner cupboard in veneered burr walnut with parquetry. The cupboard was made by Head Cabinet Maker Tim Smith and featured a secret compartment containing three drawers and a small cupboard. Another member of staff, Clint Williams, the most recent cabinet-maker out of his apprenticeship, was awarded "Apprentice of the Year" by Herefordshire College of Technology where he impressed his tutors with his drive and skill.

Peter Hall's premises in Staveley have been extended to the full length of the site with the showroom at the front with car parking outside the front door. There is further parking down the yard as you progress past the workshops, heading towards the timber shed where visitors can see the wood being managed and dried.

1388 but only its sturdy tower still stands. It was replaced in 1864 by **St James's Church**, which has a fine stained glass east window designed by Burne-Jones and created by William Morris & Co.

Sedbergh

Howgill Hills | King's Arms Hotel
Sedbergh School | Quaker Meeting House
Firbank Knott | George Fox | Castlehaw
Farfield Mill

In 1974, Sedbergh was brusquely removed from the West Riding of Yorkshire and became part of Cumbria. However, it still lies within the Yorkshire Dales National Park and the surrounding scenery certainly belongs to the Dales with the mighty **Howgill Hills** - great pear-shaped drumlins shaped by glaciers - soaring to more than 2200 feet (670 metres). Winder Hill, which provides a dramatic backdrop to the little market town, is half that height, but with its sleek grassy flanks and domed top, seems much loftier. Four valleys and four mountain streams meet here and for centuries Sedbergh (pronounced Sedber) has been an important centre for cross-Pennine travellers. During the golden age of stagecoach travel, the town became a staging post on the route between Lancaster and Newcastle-upon-Tyne. The complete journey between Lancaster and Newcastle took from 4am to 7pm: 15 hours to cover a distance of about 120 miles, an average speed of eight miles per hour. At the **King's Arms Hotel**, the four horses would be swiftly changed before the equipage rattled off again across the moors to Teesdale, Durham and Newcastle.

In those days, the stagecoach would have been used frequently by the boys attending Sedbergh's famous **Public School**. Its founder was Roger Lupton, a Howgill boy who rose to become Provost of Eton: he established the school because he felt that one was desperately needed "in the north country amongst the people rude in knowledge". In later years, Wordsworth's son studied here and Coleridge's son, Hartley, became a master. The school's extensive grounds, through which visitors are welcome to wander, seem to place the old-world town within a park.

That impression is reinforced by following the path beside the River Rawthay to Brigflatts. Close to where George Fox stayed overnight with his friend Richard Robinson is the oldest **Quaker Meeting House** in the north of England. Built in 1675, and still with its original oak interior, this beautiful, simple building has changed little over the years.

This area is filled with Quaker history and **Firbank Knott,** on nearby Firbank Fell, can be said to be the birthplace of Quakerism, for it was here, in 1652, that the visionary **George Fox** gave his great sermon to inspire a huge gathering from the whole of the north of England. This meeting was to lead to the development of the Quaker Movement. The simple boulder on the fell, from which Fox delivered his momentous words, is marked by a plaque and is now known as Fox's Pulpit.

Sedbergh is a very friendly town. At **St Andrew's Church**, for example, Protestants and Roman Catholics take turns to use the building for their own services, an arrangement believed to be rare in England.

To the east of the town, on a small wooded hill top, stands **Castlehaw**, the remains of an ancient motte-and-bailey castle. Built by the Normans in the 11th century, the castle guarded the valleys of the River Rawthey and the River Lune against the marauding Scots.

Also, just outside town on the A683 Garsdale road, is **Farfield Mill** Heritage and Arts Centre, where spinners, weavers, potters, woodcarvers and other craftspeople use traditional skills to produce high-quality goods, all of it for sale in the shop.

Around Sedbergh

DENT

4 miles SE of Sedbergh off the A684

St Andrew's Church · Dentdale Heritage Centre

Adam Sedgwick

This charming village, the only one in Dentdale - one of Cumbria's finest dales - has a delightful cobbled main street with tall cottages lining the road. Visitors to this tranquil place will find it hard to believe that, in the 18th century, Dent was of greater importance than nearby Sedbergh. The impressive **St Andrew's Church** is Norman in origin though it underwent an almost complete rebuild in the early 15th century. Inside can be seen the Jacobean three-decker pulpit that is still in use and also the local marble that paves the chancel.

Farming has, for many years, dominated the local economy, but knitting, particularly in the village, has also played an important part. During the 17th and 18th centuries, the women and children, on whom this work fell, became known as the 'Terrible Knitters of Dent', which, today, sounds uncomplimentary, but the local use of the word terrible meant quite the opposite (like 'wicked' today!). At the **Dentdale Heritage Centre**, visitors will find a wealth of information about the working lives and social customs of the Dalesfolk. Most of the exhibits are of genuine Dales provenance, a large number of them being taking from the collection of Jim and Margaret Taylor who founded the centre.

Dent's most famous son is undoubtedly the 'Father of Geology', **Adam Sedgwick**. Born the son of the local vicar in 1785, Sedgwick went on to become the Woodwardian Professor of Geology at Cambridge University and a friend of Queen Victoria and Prince Albert. The fountain of pinkish Shap granite in the village centre is Dent's memorial to this great geologist. Dent stone, with no iron pyrites likely to cause sparks, was popular for millstones used in gunpowder works. The little valley of Dentdale winds from the village up past old farms and hamlets to Lea Yeat where a steep lane hairpins up to Dent Station, almost five miles from the village. Dent railway station is the highest in Britain, more than 1100 feet above sea level, and lies on the famous Settle - Carlisle railway line. This is a marvellous place to begin a ramble into Dentdale or over the Whernside.

GARSDALE

6 miles E of Sedbergh on the A684

Baugh Fell

Lying just north of Dentdale, Garsdale is both a dale and a village, overlooked by the dramatic **Baugh Fell**. The River Clough follows down the dale from Garsdale Head, the watershed into Wensleydale, where a row of Midland Railway cottages lies alongside the former junction station on the Settle - Carlisle line. This is now a surprisingly busy little place during the summer months when, from time to time, preserved steam locomotives pause to take on water from a moorland spring.

Windermere

Lakes Line Orrest Head

Claude Glasses

Birthwaite village no longer features on any map, thanks to the Kendal and Windermere Railway Company, which built a branch line to it in 1847. With an eye on tourist traffic, and considering the name Birthwaite had little appeal, they named the station Windermere even though the lake is over a mile distant. In the early days carriages and, in later years, buses linked the station with the landing stages in the village of Bowness on the shores of the lake. As the village burgeoned into a prosperous Victorian resort, it became popularly, and then

Lake Windermere at Dusk

HAISTHORPE GUESTHOUSE

Holly Road, Windermere, Cumbria LA23 2AF
Tel: 01539 443445
e-mail: enquiries@haisthorpe-house.co.uk
website: www.haisthorpe-house.co.uk

A warm welcome awaits visitors from Diana Wilkinson and family at **Haisthorpe Guest House** in Windermere Village. Haisthorpe House is a former gentleman's residence built in 1897 that has now been tastefully converted into a guest house, offering bed and breakfast accommodation.

It is situated in a secluded but central area of Windermere, only a few minutes walk from the village centre and the train/coach station. Diana offers a selection of six comfortable, tastefully decorated bedrooms, one with a jacuzzi bath and four poster bed. All rooms are non-smoking with wireless Internet access and have an en-suite bathroom. Each room is provided with television, radio alarm, hair dryer and hospitality tray including tea, coffee, hot chocolate and biscuits. The king-size room provides accommodation for families of three or can serve as a twin room; the en-suite has a power body shower. Private parking is available at the rear of the building.

Guests at Haisthorpe enjoy free use of Parklands Country Club, a nearby private leisure club where full use of the swimming pool, sauna, steam room, gymnasium, squash and badminton courts, bar and snooker facilities is available.

THE OAK ST BAKERY

1 Oak Street, Windermere, Cumbria, LA23 1BH
Tel: 01539 448284
e-mail: phil@oakstbakery.wanadoo.co.uk

The Oak St Bakery Windermere and the proprietor Phil Eastwood are both something of rarity these days. Many traditional bakeries and skilled bakers have disappeared from the British High Street. Phil and his wife Ruth set up the bakery from scratch eight years ago. A fully trained and experienced baker Phil wanted to bring an open plan bakery into the heart of Windermere. Located in Crescent Road on the corner of Oak Street the bakery is easily found as you follow the delicious aroma of freshly baked bread and cakes! Over thirty different varieties of bread are made here; on any day at least fifteen different breads are available including traditional British breads, Italian, French, Polish, German and more. Extremely popular is the very aromatic Mediterranean Bread, a large tin loaf made with roasted peppers, sun-dried tomatoes, fresh basil, pesto, cheese and extra virgin olive oil. The shop counter is bursting with delicious cakes of all descriptions, sandwiches and savouries.

Next-door is the fabulous new Coffee bar 7, the bakery coffee shop that has all the freshly baked bakery goods on the menu. The décor is contemporary but cosy with a lovely fire for those cooler Lakeland days.

officially, known by the name of its station, while Windermere water was given the redundant prefix of Lake.

The Victorian heritage still predominates in the many large houses here, originally built as country retreats for Manchester businessmen - the railway made it possible for them to reach this idyllic countryside in just over two hours. Hotels, boarding houses, comfortable villas and shops sprang up around the station and spread rapidly down the hill towards the lake until Birthwaite and Bowness were linked together.

Windermere's railway is still operating, albeit now as a single track branch line. The **Lakes Line** is now the only surviving line to run into the heart of the Lake District. Diesel railcars provide a busy shuttle service to and from the main line at Oxenholme. The route, through Kendal, Burneside and Staveley, is a delight and provides a very pleasant alternative to the often crowded A591.

Within a few yards of Windermere Station, just across the busy main road, is a footpath that leads through the woods to one of the finest viewpoints in Lakeland, **Orrest Head**. This spectacular vantage point provides a 360-degree panoramic view that takes in the ten-mile length of Windermere, the Cumbrian hills and even the fells of the Yorkshire Pennines. In Victorian times, visitors wandered through such ravishing scenery carrying, not cameras, but small, tinted mirrors mounted in elaborate frames. Arriving at a picturesque spot, they placed themselves with their back to the view, held the mirrors above them and so observed

CEDAR MANOR HOTEL & RESTAURANT

Ambleside Road, Windermere, Cumbria LA23 1AX
Tel: 01539 443192 Fax: 01539 445970
e-mail: info@cedarmanor.co.uk
website: www.cedarmanor.co.uk

Built in 1854 as a private country retreat, **Cedar Manor Hotel and Restaurant** takes its name from the majestic Indian Cedar tree, said to be 200 years old, which overlooks the mature private gardens, along with fine specimen maples and beautiful flower borders. The hotel is owned and run by the Kaye family who took over here in June 2007 and pride themselves on offering the warmest of welcomes to all their guests, and their personal attention is guaranteed to make your stay an enjoyable and refreshing experience to be savoured to the full.

Comfortably furnished and enjoying a view out across the gardens, the Cedar Manor's lounge provides a welcome haven in which to relax, play board games, read, or enjoy a quiet drink from the well-stocked bar. The hotel's elegant restaurant has recently been awarded an AA Rosette. Head Chef, Alan Dalton, who has lived and worked in Windermere for many years, has designed an enticing menu based on ingredients from the best local suppliers. The interesting and varied choice could include dishes such as Cumbrian fell-bred lamb or Goosenargh Duck, and there's always an imaginative vegetarian option as well - Blue Whinnow Twice Baked Souffle, perhaps, served with sautéed asparagus, baby stem tomatoes, walnut dressed leaves and new potatoes. Don't forget to leave room for one of the sumptuous puddings or a selection of English cheeses.

The accommodation at Cedar Manor maintains the same high standards evident throughout the hotel. Each of the individually designed bedrooms has its own distinct character while remaining in harmony with the overall tasteful style of the rest of the Manor. The rooms range from a full suite to four-poster rooms, and include a twin and exquisite double rooms. Some enjoy fine views of the Langdale Pikes and all are decorated in keeping with the style and tradition of a fine Victorian house. Each room benefits from full en-suite facilities, TV and telephone. There are also two rooms in the Coach House where pets are allowed. At breakfast time, the Manor's Cumberland Grill will set you up for the day, or you could choose Smoked Poached Haddock, or try American-style pancakes with bacon and maple syrup.

HOLLY-WOOD GUEST HOUSE

Holly Road, Windermere, Cumbria LA23 2AF
Tel: 01539 442219
e-mail: info@hollywoodguesthouse.co.uk
website: www.hollywood guesthouse.co.uk

Holly-Wood Guest House is a beautiful Victorian family home built in 1897 and set just a few minutes walk from Windermere village centre. Bowness-on-Windermere with its boat rides is a short stroll down the hill. Holly-Wood is the home of Yana and Ian Miall who extend a warm welcome to all their guests and will do all they can to ensure your stay is pleasant and relaxed. The house has 6 en-suite rooms tastefully decorated and comfortably furnished, comprising of three doubles, a single, a twin and a family room for three people. All the rooms are equipped with shower, colour television, radio alarm clock, hairdryer and hospitality tray with Fair Trade tea, coffee, hot chocolate and biscuits. In the morning, hearty breakfasts, both traditional and vegetarian using locally sourced produce, are served in the spacious dining room between 8.30am and 9.30am. Breakfast can be served earlier if required, please discuss arrangements upon arrival. Well behaved children are welcome from 10-years-old but the Mialls are sorry that they are unable to accommodate pets. Holly-Wood has a small car park at the rear of the property that can accommodate up to three vehicles.

LAKELAND PINE

23 Church Street, Windermere,
Cumbria LA23 1AQ
Tel: 01539 442999
Fax: 01539 443999
e-mail: lynn@lakelandpine.co.uk
website: www.lakelandpine.co.uk

At **Lakeland Pine** you'll find a very extensive range of quality furniture, traditional handmade pieces, unique finishes and a made-to-measure service across a wide variety of products. The family-run business also offers a wide selection of tables, chairs, dressers, beds, wardrobes, chests of drawers, bedside tables, dressing tables, bookcases, office, kitchen and bathroom furniture, dining tables and seating - and much more. In addition to these individual pieces, the company has extensive experience in designing made-to-measure kitchens which are on display in the showroom. Lakeland Pine uses only the best materials but its prices have been set to be extremely competitive.

All major credit and debit cards are accepted and the showroom is open seven days a week. There is an extensive display here but you can also choose from the range on the company's website - it will deliver to any part of the UK.

FIR TREES

Lake Road, Windermere,
Cumbria LA23 2EQ
Tel: 01539 442272 Fax: 01539 442512
email: enquiries@fir-trees.co.uk
website: www.fir-trees.co.uk

Fir Trees is a guest house of considerable character and charm, having been built in 1888 as a Victorian gentleman's residence. The beautiful pitch pine staircase and doors, both original features of special note, are well complemented by fine antique furnishings and prints throughout the premises. Everything fits in handsomely; everywhere is immaculate. The guest bedrooms are lovely, all furnished and decorated to a very high standard and all with private bath or shower room en-suite, tea and coffee-making facilities and television. A few, because of their particularly large size, are especially suitable for families.

Breakfasts are definitely special at Fir Trees, traditionally English in style and cooked to perfection. "Simply scrumptious" is the way one of the guests puts it. Guests receive free use of Parklands Country Club leisure facilities and a free day pass for fly fishing on High Newton; Ghyll Head and reservoir is available to all guests on request. Fir Trees also offers a variety of treatments such as wrinkle relaxing injections and dermal fillers, so you can stay here for a weekend and go home looking 10 years younger!

the view framed as in a painting. The image they saw recalled the romantic landscapes of Claude Lorraine: the mirrors accordingly were known as **Claude Glasses**.

Around Windermere

BOWNESS-ON-WINDERMERE

1½ miles S of Windermere

Windermere | St Martin's Church

World of Beatrix Potter

Blackwell

It is from this attractive, but seasonally very busy town right on the edge of Windermere that most of the lake cruises operate. Lasting between 45 and 90 minutes, the cruises operate daily and provide connections to the Lakeside & Haverthwaite Steam Railway, the Fell Foot Country Park and the Visitor Centre at Brockhole. This centre (also easily reached by road) is idyllically situated in 30 acres of gardens and grounds and has two floors of interactive exhibitions. There are evening wine/champagne cruises during the summer months, and rowing boats and self-drive motor boats available for hire all year round.

Not only is **Windermere** the largest lake in Cumbria, but it is, at 11 miles long, the largest in England. Across from Bowness, the lake is almost divided in two by Belle Island, which is believed to have been inhabited by the Romans. During the Civil War, it was owned by Colonel Phillipson (the Royalist supporter who disgraced himself by riding into Kendal Parish Church). His family had to withstand

STOCKGHYLL COTTAGE

Rayrigg Road, Bowness-on-Windermere, Cumbria LA23 1BN
Tel: 01539 443246 e-mail: welcome@stockghyllcottage.co.uk
website: www.stockghyllcottage.co.uk

A beautiful cottage with lake views, lovely gardens and its own waterfall, surrounded by woods and yet less than quarter of a mile's level stroll from the bustling centre of Bowness-on-Windermere - that's just the start of what **Stockghyll Cottage** has to offer. This idyllically located property is the home of Sue and Ian Alcock who extend a genuinely friendly welcome to all their guests. The house has a 4-star rating from Visit Britain and offers three guest bedrooms, all with en-suite facilities. A double and a twin room enjoy views of the lake; the third has a view into the woods towards the waterfall at the side of the cottage. All the rooms are equipped with TV, clock radio, hair dryer, tissues, and hospitality tray. Fresh towels, liquid soap and shower cream are also provided.

Breakfast at Stockghyll Cottage is definitely something to look forward to. As one guest wrote in the visitors' book: *Thank you again for everything, especially the most wonderful breakfast I have ever had. I am glad I stayed for the sausage alone!!*

Sue & Ian often open their lounge for home made cake and afternoon teas or if you prefer tea and cake can be served outside in one of the pretty seating areas by the stream.

THE WESTBOURNE

Biskey Howe Road, Bowness-on-Windermere,
Cumbria LA23 2JR
Tel/Fax: 01539 443625
e-mail: westbourne@btinternet.com
website: www.westbourne-lakes.co.uk

Enchantingly located in a peaceful area just a 2-minute walk from the local beauty spot 'Biskey Howe', **The Westbourne** is a beautiful, traditionally stone built Lakeland guest house. Resident owners Howard and Amanda offer a warm welcome into their friendly, relaxing home where their upmost concern is that all their guests leave the Lake District refreshed, relaxed and with great memories of their holiday. The Westbourne has a colourful well-tended garden where guests can relax on warm sunny evenings with a drink from the guest bar. In cooler weather, there's the cosy lounge with its log fire on chilly winter evenings. The Westbourne has eight en-suite guest bedrooms, all tastefully furnished to a very high standard, each with its own style and character. Each room is equipped with colour television, hair dryer, radio alarm clock and, in the bathroom, toiletries and fresh towels every day. There are also tea and coffee-making facilities including hot chocolate and biscuits. At breakfast time there's a varied choice including vegetarian and special diets. The Westbourne is just a minute's walk from shops and restaurants, has its own off-road parking, and secure storage for both cyclists and motorists.

THE FAIRFIELD

Brantfell Road, Bowness-on-Windermere,
Cumbria LA23 3AE
Tel: 01539 446565
e-mail: tony&liz@the-fairfield.co.uk
website: www.the-fairfield.co.uk

Situated just above Bowness village and Lake Windermere, **The Fairfield** is set in peaceful secluded surroundings that make it an ideal base from which to explore one of the loveliest areas in Britain. One of Lakeland's original country houses, built more than 200 years ago, The Fairfield now provides both serviced and self-catering accommodation. It stands in half an acre of secluded garden which provides a perfect sense of peace and tranquillity. Inside, guests can relax in the residents' lounge, with a log fire on chilly days, or enjoy a drink in the licensed bar. Breakfasts at The Fairfield, have an enviable reputation with an extensive choice that includes porridge, kippers and a full English breakfast. The staff are always happy to cater for vegetarian and special diets.

Accommodation at The Fairfield comprises single, twin, double, four-poster, deluxe, and family rooms, having views of the garden and surrounding hills. All of the bedrooms have en-suite or private bath/shower rooms and are equipped with colour television, radio alarm, tea and coffee making facilities, assorted toiletries and hairdryer. Also available is a charming self-catering flat, called Claife Heights, which has one en-suite bedroom and a lounge that incorporates a compact kitchenette.

HANNALIN CRAFTS

The Old Antiques Warehouse, North Terrace,
Bowness-on-Windermere, Cumbria, LA23 3AU
Telephone: 01539 442225 e-mail: hannalin@hotmail.co.uk
website: www.hannalincraftscumbria.co.uk

Natural, pure wools from the region are the finest ingredient to our beautiful creations and we invite you to browse our selection. If you love the quality of what you see, you can purchase any of the items, or even a complete Kit that will let you create them for yourself.

We stock felted and knitted bags in a variety of styles and colours, warm hats that work beautifully in any weather, attractive scarves to complement any outfit, as well as superb items for your home or business, like rugs and cushion covers.

Our local wools are the only wools we use and they are of the highest quality. Herdwick, Swaledale and Jacob sheep provide glorious wools in textures that fit so many uses and even local Alpaca now provide beautiful fleeces for our stock or your hobby. Each item is individually handcrafted so that no two are ever the same and we carry this through even to the buttons, each a unique creation made from Larch or Silver Birch – no two can be the same shape. We are stockists of:- Stylecraft, Debbie Bliss, Sirdar wools, American fabrics for patchwork and Husqvarna sewing machines. As members of 'Made in Cumbria', we are proud to be a part of this development initiative by Cumbria County Council to promote the sales of crafts, gifts and local foods. Our membership means that each product conforms to the Trading Standards ruling on the place of origin...Cumbria of course.

an 80-day siege, successfully, while the Colonel was away on another campaign. In 1774, the island was bought by a Mr English, who constructed the round house, which, at the time, caused such consternation that he sold the property and the island to Isabella Curwen, who planted the surrounding trees.

Fishermen, too, find great enjoyment practising their skills on this well-stocked lake. Once considered a great delicacy in the 17th and 18th centuries, the char, a deep-water trout, is still found here - though catching it is a special art.

Cumbrian Mountains across Windermere

Away from the marinas and car parks is the old village where **St Martin's Church** is of particular interest. It has a magnificent east window filled with 14th- and 15th-century glass, and an unusual 300-year-old carved wooden figure of St Martin depicted sharing his cloak with a beggar.

MAGUIRE METCALFE

20 Lake Road, Bowness-on-Windermere, Cumbria LA23 3AP
Tel/Fax: 01539 447291
e-mail: helen@maguiremetcalfe.co.uk
website: www.maguiremetcalfe.co.uk

Anyone convinced that gorgeous boutiques only exist in London should pay a visit to Maguire Metcalfe in Bowness-on-Windermere. This fascinating shop offers a delicious mix of lovely treats from handstitched ribbon corsages to comfortable vintage armchairs....a real treasure trove with interesting finds wherever you look. "It's a real pleasure to source quirky & individual pieces, my customers really appreciate our refreshing different outlook here and always enjoy calling in."

Clothing lines include Avoca (Ireland) St Tropez (Scandanavia) & Lin'n Landry (France) with hand stitched handbags & accessories from Elodie Stitches- (entirely handmade at Maguire Metcalfe). An everchanging selection of vintage furniture & handmade cushions mixed with irresistable home accessories, many from bygone times make it no surprise that Maguire Metcalfe is listed amongst the "English Home" magazines "100 favourite shops"

LOW FELL

Ferney Green, Bowness-on-Windermere,
Cumbria LA23 3ES
Tel: 01539 445612 Fax: 01539 448411
e-mail: louisebroughton@btinternet.com
website: www.low-fell.co.uk

"Simply one of the nicest B&B's we've discovered this side of the Atlantic...great location, lovely house, delicious breakfasts, heavenly beds - and really nice people." So wrote the author of *The American Traveller* enthusing about **Low Fell,** a lovely old Lakeland stone house in the heart of the English Lake District offering luxury bed and breakfast facilities. Quiet, peaceful, and set in an acre of totally secluded and sunny garden, Low Fell is ideally located just a five minute stroll from the shores of Lake Windermere, and the boats and car ferry that ply the lake.

All the guest rooms are en-suite with views either over the garden towards the lake and fells, or over the treetops. The bedrooms have huge comfy 6ft beds with beautiful bed linen, and flat screen television with DVD and radio/CD players. There's even a gorgeous two bedroomed hideaway at the top of the house – ideal for a romantic break or honeymoon, but also perfect for families or friends travelling together.

Delicious Aga breakfasts are served round a big oak table in the family dining room overlooking the garden. The daily menu includes goodies such as warm homemade bread, Aga pancakes with lashings of maple syrup, grilled halloumi cheese, and, of course, a traditional English breakfast.

DENEHOUSE

Kendal Road, Bowness-on-Windermere, Cumbria LA23 3EW
Tel/Fax: 01539 448236
e-mail: denehouse@ignetics.co.uk
website: www.denehouse-guesthouse.co.uk

Built in 1887, **Denehouse** is a beautiful guest house that carefully blends the modern with the traditional. The owners have retained many of the original features of the house whilst ensuring guests are provided with the everyday modern comforts of a 'home from home'.

Denehouse benefits from being in a superb position on the edge of Bowness village with its many pubs and restaurants, and Lake Windermere itself, which is just a three minute walk away. Windermere village is less than a mile away. For your convenience, Denehouse has its own private car parking facilities. The owners of Denehouse pride themselves on their high standards, quality service, fabulous breakfasts and superior accommodation, which has a 4-star gold rating from the AA. After checking into your room, the owners will be pleased to serve you complimentary tea or coffee with biscuits. A choice of freshly prepared breakfasts is served from 8.45am until 9.30am in the bright and airy dining room. Start your day with a light, full or vegetarian breakfast from the extensive menu. Most dietary requirements can be catered for if given notice.

Guests at Denehouse receive complimentary membership of the The Spinnaker Club, with its swimming pool, spa baths, sauna, steam room and trinasium.

World of Beatrix Potter

On the lake shore just to the north of the village the Windermere Steamboat Centre is currently undergoing a major renovation so it is sadly not possible to see its unique collection of Lake Windermere's nautical heritage. The exhibits, mainly Victorian and Edwardian craft, include *Dolly*, the oldest mechanically powered boat in the world, and Beatrix Potter's rowing boat. As we go to press, there is no firm date for re-opening.

Just down the road from the Steamboat Museum is the Old Laundry Visitor Centre, the home of **The World of Beatrix Potter** attraction (see panel below), one of the most popular visitor attractions in the country. Here visitors can enjoy fascinating re-creations of the Lakeland author's books, complete with the sounds, sights and even smells of the

THE WORLD OF BEATRIX POTTER

Old Laundry, Crag Brow, Bowness-on-Windermere LA23 3BX
Tel: 01539 488444
e-mail: info@hop-skip-jump.com
website: www.hop-skip-jump.com

One of the most popular visitor attractions in the country, **The World of Beatrix Potter** is the only authorised Peter Rabbit attraction in the UK. A trip to this magical experience begins with a 4-minute film presentation introducing visitors to the author and her works.

The main exhibition features 3-dimensional scenes from 23 Beatrix Potter stories, with atmospheric lighting and real life sounds and smells taking viewers into the very pages of her stories. After the film, visitors walk into *The Tale of Jemima Puddle-Duck* and continue through a series of scenes featuring much-loved characters such as Squirrel Nutkin, Peter Rabbit, Mrs Tiggy-winkle, Johnny Town-mouse and the Flopsy Bunnies before leaving the main exhibition to join Beatrix Potter on a virtual walk through her beloved Cumbrian countryside.

Round off your visit by browsing through the Beatrix Potter Emporium and enjoying some delicious refreshments in the Tailor of Gloucester Tearoom. The World of Beatrix Potter is open every day from 10am until 5.30pm during the summer months, and from 10am to 4.30pm during the winter. Children under the age of four are admitted free.

countryside. 2002 saw the centenary of the publication of the first *Tale of Peter Rabbit*, and to mark the occasion the Peter Rabbit Centenary springs to life every 15 minutes and features some previously unpublished illustrations from the stories. Visitors can also call on Jemima Puddle-duck in a woodland glade, visit Mrs Tiggy-winkle in her kitchen and follow in Beatrix Potter's footsteps with the virtual walks.

About a mile-and-a-half south of Bowness, **Blackwell** is a treasure trove of the Arts and Crafts Movement. Completed in 1900, it is the largest and most important surviving masterpiece of the architect MH Baillie Scott (1865-1945). Inspired by Lakeland flora and fauna, he designed every last detail of this outstanding house, creating a symphony of art nouveau stained glass, oak panelling, intricate plasterwork and fanciful metalwork. From the gardens there are wonderful views of Windermere and the Coniston fells.

WINSTER

3 miles S of Windermere on the A5074

Arthur Ransome

This charming hamlet has an old post office, originally built in the early 17th century as a cottage, that is much photographed. South from the village runs the Winster Valley, which provided Wordsworth with one of his favourite walks. It was at Low Ludderburn, a couple of miles to the south, that **Arthur Ransome** settled in 1925 and here that he wrote his classic children's novel *Swallows and Amazons*.

While living here, Ransome discovered the peaceful churchyard at Rusland and decided that was where he wanted to be buried. And when he died in 1967 that is indeed where he was interred, joined later by his second wife Eugenia.

NEWBY BRIDGE

8 miles S of Windermere on the A592

Fell Foot Country Park

The bridge here crosses the River Leven, which runs from the southern tip of Windermere to Morecambe Bay. According to geologists, the mass of end moraines seen here show clearly that the village lay at the southernmost point of Windermere since they were deposited by the glacier while it paused having carved out the lake. Today, however, the village is some distance from the water's edge, which can be reached on foot, by car, or by taking the steam train on the Lakeside & Haverthwaite Railway. As the village lies at the junction of two major south Cumbrian roads, it is also a popular tourist destination.

One mile north of the village, **Fell Foot Country Park** (National Trust) is a delightful 18-acre site of landscaped gardens and woodland laid out in late-Victorian times. Rowing boats can be hired at the piers from which there are regular ferries across to Lakeside, and pleasure cruises operate during the summer school holidays.

LAKESIDE

10 miles S of Windermere off the A590

Lakeside & Haverthwaite Railway

Aquarium of the Lakes · Stott Park Bobbin Mill

Located at the southwestern tip of Windermere, Lakeside sits beneath gentle wooded hills. It's the northern terminus of the **Lakeside & Haverthwaite Railway** (see panel on page 34), a four-mile route through the beautiful Leven valley, which was once part of a line stretching to Ulverston and Barrow-in-Furness. Throughout the season, hardworking steam locomotives chug along the track, their

THE KNOLL COUNTRY HOUSE

Lakeside, nr. Newby Bridge, Cumbria LA12 8AU
Tel: 01539 531347 Fax: 01539 530850
e-mail: info@theknoll-lakeside.co.uk
website: www.theknoll-lakeside.co.uk

The Knoll Country House is a beautiful late-Victorian country house set in its own grounds surrounded by unspoilt wooded countryside. The house has many original period features including a lovely ornate staircase with stained glass windows, fireplaces, cornices and picture rails. Owner Jenny Meads has taken great care to decorate and refurbish sympathetically to enhance these attractive features. In addition to its Five Stars, The Knoll is also one of the AA's Premier Collection establishments (the AA's quality award to only 10% of its establishments). The hotel has also achieved success with the AA's breakfast and dinner awards and the Visit Britain's Silver Award for exceptional quality. Guests have the use of a beautifully furnished cosy guest lounge with an open fire, which is always lit on chillier evenings.

The lovely dining room with its well-stocked bar has an original Victorian cast iron fireplace, beautiful carpets and soft furnishings to add to the ambiance of the room. There are eight large en-suite bedrooms, which have all been refurbished with new bathrooms and soft furnishings. All rooms have television, DVD and video player, alarm clock radio, hospitality tray and direct dial telephone with modem access.

departure times set to coincide with boat arrivals from Bowness - a joint boat and train return ticket is available. The locomotives in use include 42073 and 42085, ex-LMR Fairburn 0-6-4 tank engines, and 5643, an ex-GWR 0-6-0 tank. Also present on display or under steam (when not occasionally required elsewhere) is FR20, built for the Furness Railway and Britain's oldest working standard gauge steam locomotive (see also under Haverthwaite page 54).

Nearby lies Britain's only freshwater aquarium, the **Aquarium of the Lakes** with the largest collection of freshwater fish in the UK and also a number of playful otters and diving ducks. A unique attraction for visitors is to walk along a re-creation of Windermere's lake bed in an underwater tunnel.

A mile or so northwest of Lakeside, **Stott Park Bobbin Mill** (English Heritage) is a must for anyone interested in the area's industrial heritage. One of the best preserved in the country, it's a genuine working 19th-century mill and stands in a lovely woodland setting at the southern end of the Lake. Visitors can join the inclusive 45-minute tour, watch wooden bobbins being made as they were 200 years ago, and browse over the informative exhibition.

WITHERSLACK

9 miles S of Windermere off the A590

Latterbarrow Reserve

On the edge of the village is the **Latterbarrow Reserve** of the Cumbrian Wildlife Trust, a relatively small reserve that is home to some 200 species of flowering plants and ferns.

The Lakeside & Haverthwaite Railway

Haverthwaite Station, nr Ulverston, Cumbria LA12 8AL
Tel: 01539 531594

From the Victorian station at Haverthwaite, beautifully restored steam locomotives of the **Lakeside & Haverthwaite Railway** haul comfortable coaches through the Leven Valley. With connections at Lakeside by way of Windermere Lake Cruises, the train offers a unique perspective from which to enjoy the ever-changing lake and river scenery of this picturesque part of the Lake District. This former Furness Railway branch line runs for 3.5 miles, with a journey time of around 20 minutes, giving passengers a leisurely and relaxing trip. Whilst at Haverthwaite, visitors can sample a delicious home-baked scone in the licensed Station Restaurant - an ideal way to start or end the journey.

TROUTBECK BRIDGE

1 mile N of Windermere on the A591

Holehird

Just north of this little village, in the valley of Trout Beck, lies the Lakeland Horticultural Society's four-acre garden at **Holehird**. In 1945, Edward Leigh Groves bequeathed the mansion and the estate "for the better development of the health, education and social welfare services of the County of Westmoreland". Some time later, the Lakeland Horticultural Society took over responsibility for the garden, which is still run by volunteers of that society, whose primary aim is to promote "knowledge on the cultivation of plants, shrubs and trees, especially those suited to Lakeland conditions". Highlights include the borders in the walled garden, the many specimen trees, the summer-autumn heathers and the National Collections of astilbes and hydrangeas.

TROUTBECK

3 miles N of Windermere off the A592

Troutbeck Church Townend

Designated a conservation area, Troutbeck has no recognisable centre, as the houses and cottages are grouped around a number of wells and springs, which, until recently, were the only form of water supply. Dating from the 16th, 17th, and 18th centuries, the houses retain many of their original features, including mullioned windows, heavy cylindrical chimneys and, in some cases, exposed spinning galleries, and are of great interest to lovers of vernacular architecture. **Troutbeck Church**, too, is worthy of a

Townend, Troutbeck

visit as there is a fine east window, dating from 1873, that is the combined work of Edward Burne-Jones, Ford Maddox Brown and William Morris.

However, perhaps the best known building at Troutbeck is **Townend** (National Trust), another enchanting example of Lake District vernacular architecture. Built in 1626, the stone and slate house contains some fine carved woodwork, books, furniture and domestic implements collected by the Browne family, wealthy farmers who lived here for more than 300 years until 1944. Open from April to October, the house runs a regular 'living history' programme, so if you visit on a Thursday you can meet Mr George Browne - circa 1900. Another notable resident of Troutbeck was the 'Troutbeck Giant' - Thomas Hogarth, uncle of the painter William Hogarth.

KENTMERE

8 miles NE of Windermere off the A591

Bernard Gilpin · Kentmere Pottery · Dales Way

This hamlet, as its name implies, lies in part of the valley that was once a lake; drained to provide precious bottom pasture land. A large mill pond remains to provide a head of water on the River Kent for use at a paper mill. Inside St Cuthbert's Church is a bronze memorial to **Bernard Gilpin**, who was born at Kentmere Hall in 1517 and went on to become Archdeacon of Durham Cathedral. Known as The Apostle of the North, Gilpin was also a leader of the Reformation and, in 1558, travelled to London to face charges of heresy against the Roman Catholic Church. During the journey, Gilpin fell and broke his leg but, fortunately, while he was recovering, Catholic Queen Mary died and was succeeded by Protestant Queen Elizabeth. The new queen restored Gilpin to favour and saved him from being burnt at the stake.

Situated in a peaceful riverside location, **Kentmere Pottery** produces fine handmade multi-fired English Enamels. From designs by owner Gordon Fox, the pottery specialises in lamps, individual pieces and unique tableware, all of which are available from the studio showroom only.

The beautiful valley of the River Kent is best explored on foot. A public footpath runs up its western side, past Kentmere Hall, a fortified pele tower that is now a private farmhouse. Following the river southwards, the **Dales Way** runs down into Kendal and on into the Yorkshire Dales.

BROCKHOLE

3 miles NW of Windermere off the A591

Lake District Visitor Centre

The **Lake District Visitor Centre** at Brockhole provides enough activities for a full family day out. Lake cruises depart from the jetty here for 45-minute circular trips and groups of more than 20 can even organise their own private boat. The gardens and grounds were the work of Thomas H Mawson, a Lancastrian who trained in London and set up in business in Windermere in 1885. He soon became fashionable and landscaped the gardens of many wealthy industrialists. Within the beautifully landscaped grounds at Brockhole, visitors can join an organised walk accompanied by one of the gardening team, leave their children in the well-equipped adventure playground, enjoy a lakeside picnic or visit the rare breeds of sheep. A wide variety of events takes place during the season - among them a Medieval Living Weekend, a Taste of Cumbria Food Fair, a Christmas Craft Fair and much more. Brockhole itself is a fine Victorian mansion, originally built for a Manchester silk merchant.

AMBLESIDE

4 miles NW of Windermere on the A591

Market Cross Centre | The Bridge House
Adrian Sankey's Glass Works | Arnitt Collection
Ambleside Sports | Loughrigg Fell
St Mary's Church | Borrans Park
Stagshaw Garden | Homes of Football
Kirkstone Pass

Standing less than a mile from the head of Lake Windermere, Ambleside is one of the busiest of the Lakeland towns, a popular centre for walkers and tourists, with glorious walks and drives radiating from the town in all directions. Ambleside offers a huge choice of pubs, restaurants, cafés, hotels and guest houses, as

Bridge House, Ambleside

LOW WOOD HOTEL

Windermere, Cumbria, England, LA23 1LP
Tel: 01539 433338
Fax: 01539 434072
e-mail: lowwood@elhmail.co.uk
website: www.elh.co.uk

4 star hotel with leisure club and watersports centre on the shores of Lake Windermere

Imagine a place where there is space to relax and unwind, with a choice of restaurants and bars, a Leisure Club, Beauty Salon and Water Sports Centre together with a superb lawned shoreline and one of the finest views across Lake Windermere. At Low Wood Hotel, they offer the ideal holiday venue if you want everything close by.

Low Wood Hotels 4-star rating assures you that each of the hotels 110 rooms offers all the comfort and luxury for a memorable stay. As Low Wood Hotel is in the heart of the lake district, you're also in the ideal place to discover the whole of this timeless lakeland landscape.

Low Wood Hotel is an excellent choice for a short break, special occasion or family holiday, particularly if you want to make the most of the extensive indoor and outdoor leisure facilities. The Low Wood Leisure Club boasts a superb 50ft pool and large spa, extensive gym with personal trainers on hand as well as dance studio, squash court or sauna and steam rooms.

If occasionally you feel the need to escape, a visit to the Beauty Salon could be combined with a short stay at the four star Low Wood Hotel, one of the very special Spa Leisure Days or even just a single hour to refresh and revitalise. The beauty salon offers the haven of a stress free environment for absolute self-indulgence and will not only help make you look great but feel great too!

WATEREDGE INN

Waterhead, Ambleside, Cumbria LA22 0EP
Tel: 01539 432332 Fax: 01539 431878
e-mail: rec@wateredgeinn.co.uk
website: www.wateredgeinn.co.uk

Wateredge Inn occupies an unrivalled position at the very tip of Lake Windermere on the outskirts of the picturesque town of Ambleside at the very heart of the Lake District. The hotel's broad lawns extend to the water's edge on one side, on the other is Borrans Park. This family-run establishment offers so much to visitors. Imagine waking up to the sights and sounds of Lake Windermere, enjoying a hearty breakfast and reading the morning paper by the jetty. Imagine sipping a glass of chilled wine or trying one of the many local real ales in the lake shore garden as the sun is setting over the mountains. Or imagine dining alfresco by the lake enjoying delicious home-cooked food, fine wines or real ales. The bar is open from 11am to 11pm, every day; morning coffee and cakes are served from 10am until noon; a full bar bistro menu and light lunch menus are available from noon until 4pm; and the full bar bistro menu is served from 5pm to 9pm.

Wateredge has 22 bedrooms, many with lake views and all offering the best of Lakeland comfort. All are comfortably and tastefully furnished, each having its own bathroom, colour television and complimentary tea and coffee tray. There's a choice of twins, doubles, king-size doubles, family and single rooms. Guests can choose to stay in one of the pretty bedrooms within the hotel itself, or for added privacy you may prefer a spacious studio room with a balcony or patio. For an extra special occasion, Wateredge also has two luxury suites, Windermere and Fishers Landing both with balconies and a view of the lake. Windermere is a large room with a beautiful hand-painted bed and large bathroom with a commissioned double bathtub and a separate shower. Fishers Landing has a double bedroom, bathroom with bath and separate shower, and a comfortable lounge, with an adjoining area with two single beds.

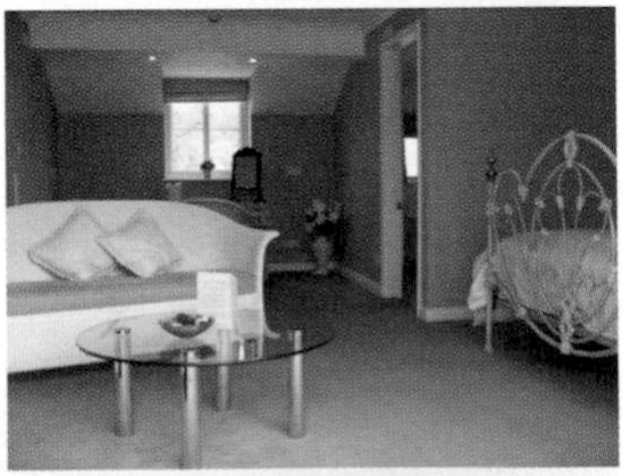

Wateredge is ideally situated for guests to enjoy the villages, scenery and sights of Lakeland. You can take the Steamer from Waterhead Pier, adjacent to the inn and enjoy the views; sail to the Lake District Visitor Centre at Brockhole, or explore Bowness with its bustling shops, The World Of Beatrix Potter attraction, and nearby Steam Boat Museum.

well as art galleries, a two-screen cinema and a mix of traditional family-run shops supplemented by a modern range of retailers in the **Market Cross Centre**. Because of its many shops specialising in outdoor clothing, the town was recently described as 'the anorak capital of the world' and it would certainly be hard to find a wider selection anywhere of climbing, camping and walking gear.

Stagshaw Garden, Ambleside

Many of Ambleside's buildings are constructed in the distinctive grey-green stone of the area which merges attractively with the green of the fields and fells all around. The centre of the town is now a conservation area, and perhaps the most picturesque building here is **The Bridge House**, a tiny cottage perched on a packhorse bridge across Stock Ghyll. Today it's a National Trust shop and information centre, but during the 1850s it was the home of Mr and Mrs Rigg and their six children. The main room of this one-up, one-down residence measures just 13 feet by six feet, so living chez Rigg was decidedly cosy. Close by, at **Adrian Sankey's Glass Works**, visitors can watch craftsmen transform molten material into glass in the age-old way and also purchase the elegant results.

A short walk from the mill brings the visitor to the **Armitt Collection**, which is dedicated to the area's history since Roman times and to two of its most famous literary luminaries, John Ruskin and Beatrix Potter. Among the highlights are Beatrix Potter's early watercolours - exquisite studies of fungi and mosses - and a fascinating collection of photographs by Herbert Bell, an Ambleside chemist who became an accomplished photographer.

The popular panoramic view of Ambleside, looking north from the path up **Loughrigg Fell**, reveals the town cradled within the apron of the massive Fairfield Horseshoe, which rises to nearly 3000 feet. Within the townscape itself, the most impressive feature is the rocket-like spire, 180 feet high, of **St Mary's Church**. The church was completed in 1854 to a design by Sir George Gilbert Scott, the architect of London's St Pancras Station and the Albert Memorial. Inside the church is a chapel devoted to the memory of William Wordsworth and an interesting 1940s mural depicting the ancient ceremony of rush-bearing. The ceremony, dating back to the days when the floor of the church was covered by rushes, is still held on the first Saturday in July. Some 400 children process through the town bearing colourful, decorated

THE APPLE PIE EATING HOUSE & BAKERY

Rydal Road, Ambleside, Cumbria LA22 9AN
Tel: 01539 4 33679 Fax: 01539 431178
e-mail: appleamble@aol.com
website: www.applepieamble.co.uk

Set in the heart of Ambleside, **The Apple Pie Eating House & Bakery** is a family owned bakery/café, which has been serving craft baked products and delicious homemade dishes for over 32 years. Owner David, who previously worked for Warburtons developing tasty recipes, started the business in 1978. The Bakery, on the premises, functions seven days a week and produces delicious breads, cakes and pastries from the finest ingredients sourced locally wherever possible. The shop sells a wide selection of breads, including the very popular olive or sundried tomato rolls. A huge variety of fillings is available for Filled Rolls and there's an extensive selection of apple pies, tray bakes, cream cakes and, the specialty of the house, Bath Buns - a perfect place for fellwalkers to collect a picnic.

The Café has several stylish seating areas including an outside courtyard and serves hearty breakfasts, quality lavazza coffees, wholesome lunches and indulgent afternoon teas. The menu offers local dishes such as Cumberland Sausage & Cider Pie, vegetarian alternatives such as Broccoli & Stilton Pie, soups, salads, hot traditional Cornish pasties, toasties and more. The Bakery and Café are open seven days a week, from 9am to 5pm, except for Christmas Eve.

ROTHAY MANOR

Rothay Bridge, Ambleside, Cumbria LA22 0EH
Tel: 01539 433605 Fax: 01539 4 33607
e-mail: hotel@rothaymanor.co.uk website: www.rothaymanor.co.uk

Rothay Manor is an elegant Regency house built in 1825 as a private summer residence for a prosperous Liverpool merchant and it still retains many original features. The house is a listed building and is set in attractive landscaped gardens a quarter of a mile from the head of Lake Windermere and a short walk from the centre of Ambleside. Fresh flowers and antiques give the feel of a welcoming private house and the lounges are ideal for relaxing over afternoon tea or pre-dinner drinks. Renowned for the comfortable, relaxed atmosphere and efficient yet unobtrusive service, the hotel has been personally managed by the Nixon family for 40 years. The hotel is also widely acclaimed in all the major guides for its culinary expertise, and has a personally compiled wine list with comprehensive coverage of all the wine regions of the world.

With 16 individually appointed bedrooms and three suites - two of which are in the grounds of the hotel, there is accommodation to suit all needs. Families are welcome with rooms and suites available, together with cots, highchairs, baby-listening and an excellent High Tea menu.

Special Interest Holidays are also available from October through to May and offer a range of subjects including: Antiques, Painting, Gardening, Walking, Bridge, Music, Lake District Heritage and Scrabble.

rushes and singing the specially commissioned Ambleside Rushbearer's Hymn.

A few weeks later, the famous **Ambleside Sports** take place, an event distinguished by the variety of local traditional sports it features. In addition to carriage-driving, ferret or pigeon racing, and tugs of war, the Sports include Cumberland and Westmorland wrestling (a little like Sumo wrestling but without the rolls of fat), muscle-wrenching fell racing, and hound trailing.

Another experience not to be missed while staying at Ambleside is a boat cruise on Lake Windermere to Bowness. There are daily departures from the pier at Waterhead, about a mile south of the town. At Bowness, there are connections to other lakeland attractions and, during the summer months, evening wine cruises. Rowing boats and self-drive motor boats can also be hired. Just to the west of the pier is **Borrans Park**, a pleasant lakeside park with plenty of picnic spots, and to the west of the park, the site of Galava Roman Fort. There is little to be seen of the fort but the setting is enchanting. Also well worth a visit is nearby **Stagshaw Garden** (National Trust), a spring woodland garden which contains a fine collection of shrubs, including some impressive rhododendrons, azaleas and camellias. Parking is very limited and vehicular access is hazardous, so it's best to park at Waterhead car park and walk.

Perhaps the most unusual visitor attraction in Ambleside is the **Homes of Football**, described by the *Sunday Times* as a national treasure. It began as a travelling exhibition of football photographs and memorabilia, but now has a permanent home in Lake Road. Photographer Stuart Clarke recorded games and grounds at every kind of venue from the

Premier League down to amateur village teams. There are now 60,000 photographs on file and a massive selection on show, framed and for sale. Some of the memorabilia retail for £200 or more, but a free picture postcard of your favourite soccer ground is included in the modest entrance fee.

From Ambleside town centre, a steep road climbs sharply up to the dramatic **Kirkstone Pass** and over to Ullswater. The pass is so called because of the rock at the top that looks like a church steeple. Rising to some 1489 feet above sea level, the road is the highest in the Lake District and, though today's vehicles make light work of the climb, for centuries the Pass presented a formidable obstacle. The severest incline, known as The Struggle, necessitated passengers stepping out of their coach and making their way on foot, leaving the horses to make the steep haul with just the empty coach.

RYDAL

6 miles NW of Windermere on the A591

William and Mary Wordsworth · Rydal Mount

In 1813, following the deaths of their young children Catherine and Thomas, **William and Mary Wordsworth** were too grief-stricken to stay on at the Old Rectory in Grasmere. They moved a couple of miles down the road to **Rydal Mount**, a handsome house overlooking tiny Rydal Water. By now, the poet was well-established and comparatively prosperous. A salaried position as Westmorland's Distributor of Stamps (a tax official), supplemented his earnings from poetry. Although Wordsworth only ever rented the house, it is now owned by his descendants and has been open to the public since 1970. The interior has seen little change and retains a lived-in atmosphere. It contains first editions of the poet's work and many personal possessions, among them the only surviving portrait of his beloved sister, Dorothy. William was a keen gardener and the four-acre garden remains very much as he designed it.

GRASMERE

7 miles NW of Windermere on the A591

William Wordsworth | Dove Cottage

Heaton Cooper Studio | Grasmere Sports

William Archibald Spooner

In 1769 Thomas Gray described Grasmere as "a little unsuspected paradise". Thirty years later, **Wordsworth** called it "the loveliest spot that man hath ever found". Certainly, Grasmere enjoys one of the finest settings in all Lakeland, its small lake nestling in a natural scenic amphitheatre beside the compact, rough-stone village.

Dove Cottage, Grasmere

For lovers of Wordsworth's poetry, Grasmere is the pre-eminent place of pilgrimage. They come to visit **Dove Cottage** where Wordsworth lived in dire poverty from 1799 to 1808, obliged to line the walls with newspaper for warmth. The great poet shared this very basic accommodation with his wife

WALK | 1

Grasmere

Distance: *3.7 miles (5.9 kilometres)*

Typical time: *180 mins*

Height gain: *305 metres*

Map: *Explorer OL7*

Walk: *www.walkingworld.com ID: 1390*

Contributor: *Jim Grindle*

ACCESS INFORMATION:

Grasmere is north of Ambleside on the A591 Ambleside/Keswick road. There are three large car parks in the village and some smaller ones. Buses from Ambleside to Keswick call in the village.

ADDITIONAL INFORMATION:

A lane gives way to a track rising gradually above the Vale of Grasmere. There are a number of seats and other resting places from which to admire the views so that the walk can be savoured by the slowest walker. The tarn itself is an attractive, quiet spot (although Wainwright didn't like it much). The descent is clear but steeper than the way up and the return is across the beautiful meadows surrounding Grasmere Village.

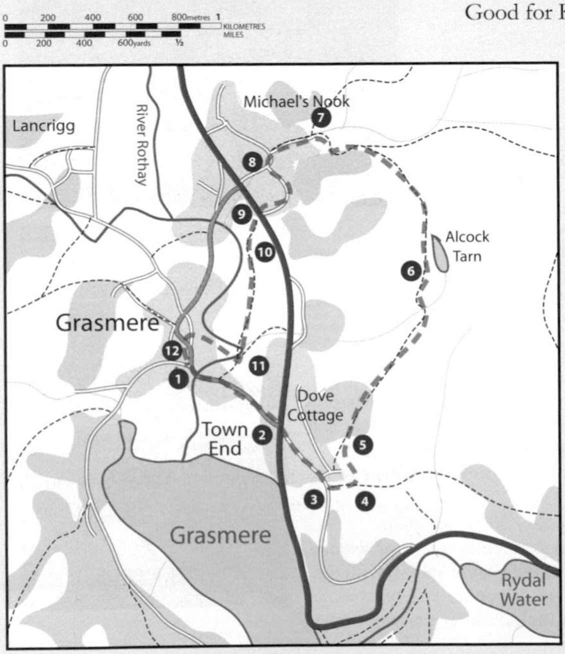

DESCRIPTION:

In the churchyard at Grasmere are the graves of William Wordsworth and his wife. On the main road is Dove Cottage, their home for a number of years and worth a visit. Much of the open land in the area is owned by the National Trust.

FEATURES:

Hills or Fells, Mountains, River, Lake/Loch, Toilets, Museum, Church, National Trust/NTS, Wildlife, Flowers, Great Views, Food Shop, Good for Kids, Public Transport, Tea Shop.

WALK DIRECTIONS:

1 | Start from the Information Centre (now closed). Turn right as you leave the Centre and walk up to the junction by the church. Turn right and go past the main car park to the junction with the main road. Turn left there to find the new crossing point.

2 | Go over and turn right. Just ahead of you a lane branches off from the main road. Follow signs for Dove Cottage. Take the lane, which is a left fork. Past Dove Cottage the lane rises and you come across an open marshy area. At the top the lane forks.

3 | Take the left fork and then watch for a track on the left, signposted to Alcock Tarn.

4 | The seat is another good indicator. In a few moments the track splits and you will see a gate a little below you.

5 | Go through the gate with its National Trust sign onto the track that leads up to the tarn. One track joins from below but there is no other track off. You will know when you are near the tarn because it has a wall around it.

6 | The walk continues on the left of the tarn to a stile in the wall at the far end. Beyond the wall, the track is rougher but still clear. Zigzags lead down until the path is squeezed between a wall on the left and a beck on the right. Don't despair - there is a bridge, on the other side of which is a gate.

7 | Cross the bridge and go through the gate onto a tarmac drive. This drops to a junction with a lane. Turn left and you will come to another lane on the left.

8 | Turn left at this junction and follow the lane down to the main road, where the Church of Our Lady of the Wayside stands on the corner.

9 | Just to the right on the main road is a crossing point. Go over but don't take the footpath by it. Turn left to a gate 50m away. Go along the enclosed track into the field at the end and then follow the field edge on the right to the first of a sequence of gates.

10 | You can always see the next gate and the yellow arrows accurately show the direction. You will reach the Millennium Bridge (non-wobbly). Only the most recent maps will show this bridge.

11 | Cross the bridge and at the far side, turn left. This path will bring you out at the north side of the church, in the centre of the village.

12 | Turn left and take the first turning on the right for the information centre.

Mary, his sister Dorothy, his sister-in-law Alice and, as almost permanent guests, Coleridge and De Quincey. Sir Walter Scott also stayed, although he often sneaked off to the Swan Hotel for a dram since the Wordsworths were virtually teetotallers. Located on the outskirts of the village, Dove Cottage has been preserved intact: next door is an award-winning museum dedicated to Wordsworth's life and works. Dove Cottage, Rydal Mount, another of the poet's homes near Grasmere, and his birthplace, Wordsworth House at Cockermouth, are all owned by the Wordsworth Trust, which offers a discount ticket covering entrance to all three properties.

In 1808, the poet moved to The Rectory (private) opposite St Oswald's Church. In his long poem, *The Excursion*, he describes the house and its lovely garden beside the River Rothay. The church, too, is remembered in the same poem:

Not raised in nice proportions was the pile,
But large and massy, for duration built,
With pillars crowded and the roof upheld
By naked rafters intricately crossed,
Like leafless underboughs in some thick wood.

In 1850, the Poet Laureate was buried in St Oswald's churchyard beneath yew trees he himself had planted. He was joined there by his sister Dorothy in 1885, and his wife Mary in 1889.

Located opposite the village green the **Heaton Cooper Studio** (see panel on page 43) has a changing exhibition of paintings, prints and sculptures from four generations of the Heaton Cooper family, from Alfred Heaton Cooper (1863-1929) to present day members.

In Grasmere town cemetery is the grave of **William Archibald Spooner**, sometime Warden of New College, Oxford. He gave his name to Spoonerisms, in which the initial

LANCRIGG VEGETARIAN COUNTRY HOUSE HOTEL & THE GREEN VALLEY ORGANIC RESTAURANT

Easedale, Grasmere,
Cumbria, LA22 9QN
Tel: 01539 435317
Fax: 01539 435058
e-mail: info@lancrigg.co.uk
website: www.lancrigg.co.uk

Lancrigg Vegetarian Country House Hotel enjoys a setting of timeless tranquillity in 30 acres of gardens and woodland overlooking peaceful Easedale. Starting life in the 17th century as a modest farmhouse, it was later renovated and enlarged with the considerable encouragement of William Wordsworth. The Lake Poets used regularly to meet here, and Charles Dickens stayed here on his trips to southern Scotland.

It was opened in 1985, by Robert and Janet Whittington, as an elegant hotel, serving delicious vegetarian home cooking. The 12 individually designed guest bedrooms all have private bathrooms (some with whirlpool baths), television, telephone and beverage tray. Each bedroom has unique features that reflect the country house and all are cosy and comfortable.

The evening meals, served in a gracious chandelier-lit room that commands fine views across the valley, use the best and freshest natural ingredients. These can be complimented by the extensive list of organic wines, beers and spirits.

The Green Valley Organic Restaurant at Lancrigg is fully certified organic. All the meals, cakes and wholesome breads are baked on the premises. The Restaurant is open to both residents and non residents from 8.30am until 8.30pm. During the day there is a mouth watering choice of light meals, cakes and sandwiches.

letters of two words are transposed, with amusing results. Here are a few of his gems, some genuine, others perhaps apocryphal:

Kinquering Kongs their titles take.

You have hissed all my mystery lessons.

You have deliberately tasted two worms and you can leave Oxford by the town drain.

Yes indeed: the Lord is a shoving leopard.

He spent many holidays in Grasmere with his wife at her house, How Foot.

Like Ambleside, Grasmere is famous for its **Sports**, first recorded in 1852, which still take place in late August. The most celebrated event in the Lake District, they attract some 10,000 visitors and feature many pursuits unique to Cumbria such as Cumberland and Westmorland wrestling, as well as the more understandable, though arduous, fell running.

Collectors of curiosities who happen to be travelling north on the A591 from Grasmere should look out for the vintage black and yellow AA telephone box on the right hand side of the road. Still functioning, **Box 487** has been accorded Grade II listed building status by the Department of the Environment.

Grange-over-Sands

Morecambe Bay · Hampsfell Summit

The Hospice · Cistercian Way

Grange, as it's known locally, is an attractive little town set in a natural sun-trap on the north shore of Morecambe Bay. Much of its Victorian charm can be credited to the Furness Railway Company, which developed the town after building the Lancaster to Whitehaven line in 1857. The railway provided a safe alternative to this hazardous journey. At Grange, the company built an elegant mile-long promenade (now traffic free) and set out the colourful ornamental gardens. Prosperous merchants built grand country homes here and it wasn't long before local residents began referring to their town as the 'Torquay of the North'.

The route to Grange, across the sands of **Morecambe Bay**, is a treacherous one, though it was used not only by the Romans, but also by the monks of Furness Abbey and, later, even by stagecoaches looking to shorten their journey time. Avoiding the quicksands of the bay, which have taken many lives over the centuries, is a difficult task. Back in the 16th century, the Duchy of Lancaster appointed an official guide to escort travellers over the shifting sands and also provided him with a house at Grange. The town still has an official guide who takes groups on a three-hour walk across the bay. The sands are extremely dangerous since "the tide comes in with the merciless speed of a galloping horse". A crossing should never be attempted without the help of a qualified guide.

Away from the hotels, shops, and cafés of the town, there are some lovely walks and none is more pleasant than the path behind Grange, which climbs through magnificent limestone woodlands rich in wild flowers. The path finally leads to the 727-foot **Hampsfell Summit** and **The Hospice**, a little stone tower from which there are unforgettable views over the bay and, in the opposite direction, the craggy peaks of the Lake District.

Grange is also the starting point of the **Cistercian Way**, an exceptionally interesting 33-mile long footpath through Furness to Barrow, which takes in, naturally, many Cistercian sites.

LYMEHURST HOTEL

Kents Bank Road, Grange-over-Sands,
Cumbria LA11 7EY
Tel: 01539 533076
e-mail: enquiries@lymehurst.co.uk
website: www.lymehurst.co.uk

Lymehurst Hotel is a beautiful Victorian building, with many original features, and offers a welcoming, peaceful atmosphere and a spacious airy feel. The staff are committed to making their visitors' stay as enjoyable as they can. The hotel has 10 en-suite rooms: one premier double, four doubles, two large twins and three large singles. Each room is tastefully and individually decorated with comfortable beds with crisp, white linen, fluffy towels, TV, hair dryer and a hot drinks refreshment tray. All the rooms are large and some even have room for sofas and are ideal for longer stays. Two of the rooms are on the ground floor, but there are some steps to the front door. Also on the ground floor of the hotel is a spacious lounge where guests can take afternoon tea, browse through the local information provided, or enjoy a drink from the restaurant bar.In the morning guests are served a hearty Cumbrian breakfast or may have something cooked to order by Master Chef of Great Britain, Kevin Wyper, and his team in the kitchen, who uses only the finest local ingredients. If you have any special dietary needs, please let the hotel know when you make your reservation. Also, when you book, if there is anything you would like for breakfast, just ask and if they can provide it, they will.

Lunch and dinner are served in the Lymestone Restaurant on the lower ground floor. Kevin believes in using the best, freshest, seasonal ingredients, which he sources as locally as possible. He cooks these ingredients with the respect they are due, treats them simply and cooks them with classical methods but gives them a modern twist and "lets the ingredients do the talking". There is always a vegetarian option on the menu and any dietary requirements can be catered for with prior notice.

At Lymehurst they take the matching of food and wine seriously and work closely with their suppliers to offer the best list they can at affordable prices. Several wines are available by the glass and the wine list features an extensive range of wines from around the world.

Lymehurst is a great place for a get-together or special celebration. Currently, the hotel can cater for up to 25 people in each area, but a new restaurant will be added in November 2008 that will accommodate up to 60 people. An outside terrace will also be added, which can be used for pre- and post-dinner drinks.

YEW TREE BARN

Low Newton, Grange-over-Sands, Cumbria, LA11 6JP
Tel/Fax: 01539 531498

Yew Tree Barn is a stunning 19th-century traditional Westmorland barn in the beautiful South Lakeland countryside and home to a unique collection of fascinating businesses. Find inspiration browsing through an eclectic mix of art, antiques, crafts and interiors, watch craftspeople at work in their studios, enjoy delicious food and drink in the café or garden, and wander through the outdoor displays.

WRS ARCHITECTURAL ANTIQUES

Clive Wilson established **WRS Architectural Antiques** over 20 years ago and it is now the foremost reclamation yard in the North West. Specialising in antiques, garden statuary and furniture, reclaimed building materials, traditional ironmongery and door furniture, period fireplaces and multi fuel stoves, oak doors and flooring. From functional to decorative, there is an ever-changing stock of unusual and inspiring ideas for the home and garden. Clive personally sources all artefacts in the yard and can offer expert advice. *website: www.yewtreebarn.co.uk*

THE GALLERY

Discover an exciting range of traditional and modern work in **The Gallery** at Yew Tree Barn. Set within the original beams and whitewashed walls, the relaxed gallery showcases comtemporary art and design-led crafts, including jewellery, paintings, ceramics, textiles and gifts. It offers exceptional style and quality, in a collection to suit both the impulse buy and the considered purchase. The Gallery hosts regular exhibitions and demonstrations, many of which are by *Made in Cumbria* artists.

THE HAT TRICK CAFE

Jane and Sam warmly welcome you to the "must visit" café of South Cumbria. Famous for their own-brand lemonade, a visit to the café is guaranteed to revive the weary traveller. Choose from an imaginative menu of savouries, puddings and cakes.
Tel: 01539 530577 website: www.hattrickcafe.co.uk

LAKELAND PHOTOGRAPHY

Ian Johnson has been selling images of the Lake District since 1993, taken using only natural light. The images are sold as cards and framed or unframed endprints.
Tel: 01539 824345 website: www.lakelandphotography.co.uk

GARY ECCLES

Gary Eccles is the resident **Furniture Maker and Restorer** specialising in 17th- to 19th-century pieces. As well as traditional handmade furniture in reclaimed, new and painted pine, oak, elm and native woods, Gary offers an expert restoration service. Bespoke kitchen pieces are a speciality. *Tel: 07968 735550*

GRAHAM GLYNN

Graham Glynn works from his **Studio Pottery** at Yew Tree Barn, where he produces a wide range of thrown and hand-built pottery, from mugs and bowls to large sculptural pieces for the home and garden. Trade orders and private commissions welcome.
Tel: 01539 530012

SILVER FORGE

Silver Forge produces unique jewellery items that are hand-crafted, easy to wear, and have personality! Jo Dix, studio owner and designer maker, also runs day workshops in jewellery-making, which are open to all. Commissions welcome.
Tel: 01539 530306 website: www.silverforge.co.uk (e-shop and gallery)

Around Grange-over-Sands

LINDALE

2 miles NE of Grange-over-Sands off the A590

John Wilkinson

This small village was the birthplace of a man who defied the scepticism of his contemporaries and built the first successful iron ship. 'Iron Mad' **John Wilkinson** also built the first cast iron barges and later created the castings for the famous Iron Bridge at Coalbrookdale. After his death in 1808, he was buried in an iron coffin (naturally) in an unmarked grave. The lofty Wilkinson Obelisk to his memory that stands near the village crossroads is also cast in iron. The admirers who erected it, however, omitted to provide the iron column with a lightning conductor. A few years later it was struck to the ground by a lightning bolt. The obelisk lay neglected in shrubbery for some years but has now been restored and towers above the village once again. Just outside Lindale, at Castle Head, is the imposing house that Wilkinson built by the River Winster.

CARTMEL

2 miles W of Grange-over-Sands off the B5278

Cartmel Priory | Church of St Mary & St Michael

Racecourse

One of the prettiest villages in the Peninsula, Cartmel is a delightful cluster of houses and cottages set around a square from which lead winding streets and arches into back yards. The village is dominated by the famous **Cartmel Priory**, founded in 1188 by Augustinian canons. Like all monastic institutions, the priory was disbanded in 1537 and several of its members were executed for participating in the Pilgrimage of Grace. Today, substantial remains of the 12th-century Gatehouse (National Trust) survive, but the rest of the Priory was cannibalised to build many of the village's cottages and houses. After the Dissolution, only the south aisle of the **Church of St Mary and St Michael** was still standing but, in 1620, George Preston of Holker began restoring the entire building and the richly carved black oak screens and stall canopies date from this restoration. St Mary and St Michael's has recently been described as "the most beautiful church in the northwest". Inside, in the southwest corner of the church, is a door known as Cromwell's Door. The holes in it are said to have been made by indignant parishioners firing at Parliamentarian soldiers who had stabled their horses in the nave.

Cartmel is also famous for its attractive **Racecourse**, set beside the River Eea, on which meetings are held in May, July and August. Located close to the village, the course must be one of the most picturesque in the country, and it is certainly one of the smallest.

FLOOKBURGH

3 miles SW of Grange-over-Sands on the B5277

Lakeland Miniature Village

An ancient Charter Borough, Flookburgh is still the principal fishing village on Morecambe Bay. Roads from the square lead down to the shore where fishermen still land their catches of cockles, shrimps and (less often nowadays) flukes, the tasty small flat fish from which the village takes its name.

At the **Lakeland Miniature Village** are more than 120 buildings handmade from local

Holker Hall

Cark-in-Cartmel, Nr Grange-over-Sands, Cumbria LA11 7PL
Tel: 01539 558328
e-mail: publicopening@holder.co.uk
website: www.holker-hall.co.uk

Showing the confidence, spaciousness and prosperity of Victorian style on its grandest scale, **Holker Hall** can trace its foundations back to the beginning of the 16th century. Built following the disastrous fire of 1871, its magnificent library and outstanding craftsmanship vie for attention with the Regulator Clock, the Linen Fold Panelling and the Grand, hand-carved, cantilever staircase. Today it is the home of Lord and Lady Cavendish, who welcome visitors of all ages to enjoy a wonderful insight into one of the country's best-loved stately homes.

Holker's gardens are a feast for the eyes. In soft and gentle contrast to the surrounding Lakeland countryside, they feature the evolving inspiration of generations of gardeners who have lovingly tended the shrubs and trees, many of which can be dated back to the 1750s. Rare and exotic plants are a feature, but the gardens are not tied by the designs and ideas of a bygone age. In fact, quite the opposite, as the addition of the magnificent Cascade and many other new features and species means that more has changed in the past three decades than in the 300 years that preceded them.

Coniston slate by Edward Robinson and accurate down to the last detail. In 2005 an oriental teahouse was opened here and overlooks the owner's oriental garden.

CARK-IN-CARTMEL

3 miles SW of Grange-over-Sands on the B5278

Holker Hall · Holker Garden Festival

Lakeland Motor Museum

Cumbria's premier stately house, **Holker Hall** (see panel on page 51) is one of the homes of the Cavendish family, the Dukes of Devonshire. An intriguing blend of 16th-century, Georgian and Victorian architecture, it's a visitor-friendly place with no restraining ropes keeping visitors at a distance. There's a fire burning in the hearth and a lived-in, family atmosphere. There's also an impressive cantilevered staircase, a library with some 3500 leather-bound books (plus a few dummy covers designed to hide electricity sockets), and an embroidered panel said to be the work of Mary, Queen of Scots.

Each year, Holker's 25 acres of award-winning gardens host the **Holker Garden Festival**, which has been hailed as the 'Chelsea of the North'. The gardens are the pride of Lord and Lady Cavendish, who developed the present layout from the original 'contrived natural landscape' of Lord George Cavendish 200 years ago. The Great Holker Lime and the stunning spring display of rhododendrons are among the delights not to be missed. Here, too, are a wonderful rose garden, an azalea walk and a restored Victorian rockery. Lord and Lady Cavendish put their pride into words: "If you gain from your visit a small fraction of the pleasure that we ourselves get from them, then the work of generations of gardeners will not have been in vain."

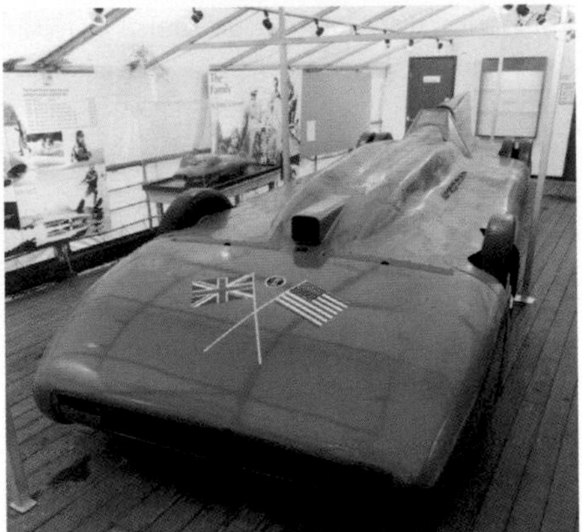

Lakeland Motor Museum, Cark-in-Cartmel

The Holker Hall estate contains a wide variety of other attractions - formal gardens, water features, a 125-acre deer park, picnic and children's play areas, a gift shop and café. Also within the grounds is the **Lakeland Motor Museum**, which houses an extensive and fascinating collection of some 30,000 exhibits, including cars, motorcycles, tractors, bicycles, pedal cars and engines, plus perhaps the largest display of auto memorabilia on public display within the UK - mascots, badges, advertising posters, petrol pumps, globes, enamel signs, pottery and models.

Ulverston

Hoad Hill · Replica of the Eddystone Lighthouse

Stan Laurel · Laurel & Hardy Museum

Church of St Mary · Lakes Glass Centre

Gateway to Furness Exhibition

Ulverston Heritage Centre · Cumbria Way

It was way back in 1280 that Edward I granted Ulverston its market charter; more than seven centuries later, colourful stalls still crowd the narrow streets and cobbled market

Laurel and Hardy Museum, Ulverston

square every Thursday. It's a picturesque scene, but a walk up nearby **Hoad Hill** is rewarded with an even more striking view of the town. The great expanse of Morecambe Bay with a backdrop of the Pennines stretches to the south, the bulk of Ingleborough lies to the east, Coniston Old Man and the Langdale Pikes lie to the west and north. Crowning the hill is a 100ft-high **Replica of the Eddystone Lighthouse**, raised here in 1850 to commemorate one of Ulverston's most distinguished sons, Sir John Barrow. Explorer, diplomat and author, he served as a Lord of the Admiralty for more than 40 years, his naval reforms contributing greatly to England's success in the Napoleonic Wars.

An even more famous son of Ulverston was Stanley Jefferson, born at number 3, Argyle Street on June 16th 1890. Stanley is far better known to the world as **Stan Laurel**. His 30-year career in more than 100 comedy films with Oliver Hardy is celebrated in the town's **Laurel and Hardy Museum** in King Street. The museum was founded in 1976 by the late Bill Cubin, who devoted his life to the famous duo and collected an extraordinary variety of memorabilia, believed to be the largest in the world. Everything is here, including letters, photographs, personal items, and even furniture belonging to the couple. There's also a small cinema showing the duo's films as well as documentaries about them, throughout the day.

The oldest building in the town is the **Church of St Mary**, which, in parts, dates from 1111. Though it was restored and rebuilt in the mid-19th century and the chancel was added in 1903, it has retained its splendid Norman door and some magnificent stained glass, including a window designed by the painter Sir Joshua Reynolds.

Ulverston also boasts England's shortest, widest and deepest canal. Visitors can follow the towpath walk alongside which runs dead straight for just over a mile to Morecambe Bay. Built by the famous engineer John Rennie and opened in 1796, the canal ushered in a half-century of great prosperity for Ulverston as an inland port. At its peak, some 600 large ships a year berthed here, but those good times came to an abrupt end in 1856 with the arrival of the railway. The railway company's directors bought the canal and promptly closed it.

The town's other attractions include **The Lakes Glass Centre**, which features the high-quality Heron Glass and Cumbria Crystal. Also at the Centre is the **Gateway to Furness Exhibition**, providing a colourful snapshot of the history of the Furness Peninsula. There's more history at the **Ulverston Heritage Centre**, which also has a gift shop selling souvenirs and crafts made in Cumbria, while modern entertainment is provided at the Coronation Hall theatre complex and the traditional Roxy Cinema.

The open area to the north of the town, known as The Gill, is the starting point for the 70-mile **Cumbria Way**. The route of the Cumbria Way was originally devised by the Lake District area of the Ramblers Association in the mid-1970s and provides an exhilarating journey through a wonderful mix of natural splendour and fascinating heritage. The first section is the 15-mile walk to Coniston.

Around Ulverston

HAVERTHWAITE

5 miles NE of Ulverston off the A590

Haverthwaite is the southern terminus of the Lakeside & Haverthwaite Railway, a branch of the Furness railway originally built to transport passengers and goods to the steamers on Lake Windermere. It was one of the first attempts at mass tourism in the Lake District. Passenger numbers peaked in the 1920s, but the general decline of rail travel in the 1960s led to the railway's closure in 1967. However, a group of dedicated rail enthusiasts rescued this scenic stretch, restored its engines and rolling stock to working order and now provide a full service of steam trains throughout the season.

SWARTHMOOR

1 mile S of Ulverston off the A590

Swarthmoor Hall · George Fox

Swarthmoor Hall was built in around 1586 by George Fell, a wealthy landowner. It was his son, Judge Thomas Fell, who married

Margaret Askew, who, in turn, became a follower of **George Fox** after hearing him preach in 1652. At that time, many people were suspicious of Fox's beliefs but Margaret was able to persuade her husband to use his position to give Fox protection and shelter, and the hall became the first settled centre of the Quaker Movement. Missionaries were organised from here and the library was stocked with both Quaker and anti-Quaker literature. Judge Fell died in 1658 and, 11 years later, Margaret married George Fox. The hall is open during the summer and it gives a fascinating insight into the history of the early Quakers.

BARDSEA

2 miles S of Ulverston off the A5087

Conishead Priory

The village stands on a lovely green knoll overlooking the sea and, as well as having a charming, unhurried air about it, there are some excellent walks from here along the coast either from its Country Park or through the woodland.

Just up the coast, to the north, lies **Conishead Priory**, once the site of a leper colony that was established by Augustinian canons in the 12th century. The monks from the priory used to act as guides across the dangerous Cartmel Sands to Lancashire. After the Dissolution, a superb private house was built on the site and the guide service was continued by the Duchy of Lancaster. In 1821, a Colonel Braddyll demolished the house and built in its place the ornate Gothic mansion that stands here today. He was also responsible for the atmospheric ruined folly on Chapel Island that is clearly visible in the estuary.

Latterly, the Priory has been a private house, a hydropathic hotel, a military hospital and a rest home for Durham miners; it is now owned by the Tibet Buddhist Manjushri Mahayana Buddhist Centre, which was established here in 1977. During the summer months, visitors are welcome to the house, which is open for tours, and there is a delightful woodland trail to follow through the grounds. A new Buddhist temple was opened in 1998, based on a traditional design, which symbolises the pure world (Mandala) of a Buddha.

GREAT URSWICK

3 miles S of Ulverston off the A590

Church of St Mary & St Michael

Birkrigg Common   Druid's Circle

The ancient village **Church of St Mary and St Michael** is noted for its unusual and lively woodcarvings that were created by the Chipping Campden Guild of Carvers. As well as the figure of a pilgrim to the left of the chancel arch, there are some smaller carvings in the choir stall of winged children playing musical instruments. Also worthy of a second look is the 9th-century wooden cross which, bears a runic inscription.

Lying between Great Urswick and Bardsea, and overlooking Morecambe Bay, is **Birkrigg Common**, a lovely area of open land. Here, on the east side of the common, is the **Druid's Circle**, with two concentric circles made up of 31 stones up to three feet high.

LINDAL-IN-FURNESS

3 miles SW of Ulverston on the A590

Colony Country Store

The **Colony Country Store** combines the aromatic character of an old-fashioned country general store with the cost-cutting advantages of a Factory Shop. There's a huge range of textiles, glassware, ceramics and decorative accessories for the home, but the Colony is also Europe's leading manufacturer of scented candles, supplying millions of scented and dinner candles every year to prestigious stores around the world.

Barrow-in-Furness

Dock Museum Sir James Ramsden

Cistercian Way

Undoubtedly the best introduction to Barrow is to pay a visit to the **Dock Museum** (see panel below), an impressive glass and steel structure that hangs suspended above a Victorian graving dock. Audio-visual displays and a series of exhibits describe how Barrow grew from a tiny hamlet in the early 1800s to become the largest iron and steel centre in the world and also a major shipbuilding force in just 40 years. The museum has some spectacular models of ships of every kind, an art gallery hosting both permanent and travelling exhibitions, and a high tech interactive film show where characters from Barrow's history come to life to tell the town's story. It was **James (later Sir James) Ramsden** who established the first Barrow Iron Ship Company in 1870, taking

The Dock Museum

North Road, Barrow-in-Furness, Cumbria LA14 2PW
Tel: 01229 894444
e-mail: dockmuseum@barrowbc.gov.uk
website: www.dockmuseum.org.uk

One of the very best attractions in the North of England, the **Dock Museum** tells in fascinating detail the story of Barrow and its rapid growth from a small fishing village in the early-19th century to a town famed throughout the world for its industrial production and innovation. It was once the biggest iron and steel centre in the world and a major shipbuilder. Its first iron steamship was lunched here in 1873, and in 1901 the Barrow shipyard built Britain's first submarine – and today it is once again building state-of-the-art subs.

The spectacular modern museum was built over an original Victorian dock, occupying a landscaped waterfront site with walkways linked to the Cumbria Coastal way, a picnic area and an adventure playground. Inside are exciting interactive displays, a range of model ships, film shows, photographs and access to many images from the nationally important collection of glass negatives. It also hosts a vibrant programme of exhibitions and events throughout the year. Visitors can enjoy a wide range of snacks and hot meals in the coffee shop. Parking and admission are free at the Museum, which is open daily except Monday in season (10am to 4.30pm), and Monday and Tuesday out of season (10.30am to 4pm).

advantage of local steel production skills. In 1896, the firm was acquired by Vickers, a name forever linked with Barrow, and for a number of years was the largest armaments works in the world. Sir James was also the general manager of the Furness Railway and the town's first mayor. At the Ramsden Square roundabout is a statue of him, and at the next roundabout is a statue of HW Schneider, one of the men who developed the Furness iron mines and was involved in the Barrow Haematite Steel Company.

Barrow is the western starting point of the **Cistercian Way**, a 33-mile walk to Grange-over-Sands through wonderfully unspoilt countryside.

Around Barrow-in-Furness

GLEASTON

3 miles E of Barrow-in-Furness off the A5087

Gleaston Castle · Gleaston Water Mill

This village is typical of the small, peaceful villages and hamlets that can be found in this part of the peninsula. Here, standing close by the ruins of **Gleaston Castle** is **Gleaston Water Mill**. The present buildings date from 1774, with the massive original wooden gearing still in place. The machinery is operational most days - an 18ft waterwheel and an 11ft wooden pit wheel serviced by an intriguing water course. Evening tours with supper are available by prior arrangement. Also on site is the Pig's Whisper Country Store with thousands of piggy collectables and a Dusty Miller's teashop selling homemade meals and scones.

PIEL ISLAND

5 miles SE of Barrow-in-Furness via foot ferry from Roa Island.

Piel Castle · Knight of Piel Island

Though this tiny island was probably visited by both the Celts and the Romans, its first recorded name is Scandinavian - Fotheray - from the Old Norse meaning 'fodder island'. In 1127 the islands were given to the Savignac Monks by King Stephen and, after the order merged with the Cistercian monks in the middle of the 12th century, the monks of Furness Abbey began to use Piel Island as a warehouse and storage area.

Piel Castle from Walney Island

Piel Castle was originally a house fortified in the early part of the 14th century and at the time it was the largest of its kind in the northwest. Intended to be used as one of the abbey's warehouses and to offer protection from raiders, in later years the castle also proved to be a useful defence against the King's customs men and a prosperous trade in smuggling began. The castle has, over many years, been allowed to fall into ruin and now presents a stark outline on the horizon.

Despite being so small, the island does have a pub. Even more remarkable, the landlord has the authority to bestow the title **Knight of Piel Island** on any of his customers he might wish to honour.

WALNEY ISLAND

2 miles W of Barrow-in-Furness on the A590

North Walney National Nature Reserve

South Walney Nature Reserve

This 10-mile-long narrow island is joined to the Furness Peninsula by a bridge from Barrow docks and is home to two important nature reserves that are situated at either end of the island. **North Walney National Nature Reserve** covers some 350 acres within which are a great variety of habitats including sand dunes, heath, salt marsh, shingle and scrub. As well as having several species of orchid and over 130 species of bird either living or visiting the reserve, there is also an area for the preservation of the Natterjack toad, Britain's rarest amphibian. Unique to the Reserve is the Walney Geranium, a plant that grows nowhere else in the world. North Walney also boasts a rich prehistoric past, with important archaeological sites from mesolithic, neolithic, Bronze and Iron Age times.

Situated on the island's long foot, **South Walney Nature Reserve** is home to the largest nesting ground of herring gulls and lesser black-backed gulls in Europe. It is also the most southerly breeding ground of such species as the oystercatcher, tern and ringed plover and, in all, over 250 bird species have been recorded. A stopover for many migratory birds, the reserve has considerable ecological interest with mudflats, sandy beaches, rough pasture and fresh water. There are waymarked trails around the reserve, with a number of hides.

The island's southernmost tip, Walney Point, is dominated by a 70ft lighthouse, which was built in 1790 and whose light was, originally, an oil lamp.

DALTON-IN-FURNESS

5 miles N of Barrow-in-Furness off the A590

Dalton Castle | George Romney

Drinking Fountain | South Lakes Wild Animal Park

Furness Abbey

Lying in a narrow valley on the part of Furness that extends deep into Morecambe Bay, this ancient place was once the leading town of Furness and an important centre for administration and justice. The 14th-century pele tower, **Dalton Castle**, was built with walls six feet thick to provide a place of refuge for the monks of Furness Abbey against Scottish raiders and it still looks very

Dalton Castle, Dalton-in-Furness

historic building | museum and heritage | historic site | scenic attraction | flora and fauna

CROWN COURT HOUSE

143 Market Street, Dalton-in-Furness, Cumbria LA15 8RQ
Tel: 01229 466097
e-mail: daltonvip@aol.com
website: www.geocities.com/crowncourthouse@aol.com

An imposing stone building, **Crown Court House** was originally built in 1879 as a County Police Station and Court House, complete with cells and a mortuary. It served the then busy mining community of Dalton for almost 50 years before the court heard its last case - a betting offence - in October 1928.

After a series of different owners, this magnificent building was then left empty until one day Tim Bell passed by and immediately saw the potential. He bought the building and set about restoring it, saving or reproducing many original features as he did so. It took almost four years to renovate the ground floor into a fully equipped Coffee Bar with state-of-the-art facilities and catering equipment. It's a cosy, welcoming place with real fireplaces, leather sofas, ambient music and sympathetic lighting effects.

Next door to the Coffee Bar, the former Court Room, with its oak panelled walls and resident invisible pianist, is an ideal setting for parties of up to 20 people. Then there's the Dalton Room, which also seats 20 people, has a relaxing ambience and displays some superb murals of Dalton by local artist Brian Miller. Situated in the historic ancient capital of Furness with it's castle and Abbey, Dalton is home to South Lakes Wild Animal Park and close to magnificent sandy beaches. Car parking in Dalton is free.

formidable. It is now owned by the National Trust and houses a small museum with an interesting display of 16th- and 17th-century armour, along with exhibits about iron mining, the Civil War in Furness, and the life and work of **George Romney**, the 18th-century portrait painter. He was best known in his day for his many portraits of Nelson's mistress, Lady Hamilton, with whom he formed a romantic attachment in spite of having a wife in Kendal. He is buried in the graveyard of the red sandstone Church of St Mary, where his grave is marked with the inscription '*pictor celeberrimus*'.

Visitors to Dalton will find that it is time well spent looking around the many fascinating facades in and close to the market place, such as the unique, cast-iron shop front at No 51 Market Street. In the market place itself is an elegant Victorian **Drinking Fountain** with fluted columns supporting a dome of open iron work above the pedestal fountain. Nearby stands the market cross and the slabs of stone that were used for fish-drying in the 19th century.

From the mostly pedestrianised Tudor Square, visitors can board a bus to the award-winning **South Lakes Wild Animal Park**, which has been designated the Region's Official Top Attraction by the Cumbria Tourist Board. It's the only place in Britain where you can see rare Amur and Sumatran tigers (the world's biggest and smallest tigers). At feeding time (2.30pm each day) they climb a 20ft vertical tree to 'catch' their food. Ring-tailed lemurs wander freely through the park, visitors can walk with emus and hand-feed the largest collection of kangaroos in Europe.

RING HOUSE COTTAGES

Woodland, Broughton-in-Furness,
Cumbria LA20 6DG
Tel: 01229 716578 Fax: 01229 716850
e-mail: info@ringhouse.co.uk
website: www.ringhouse.co.uk

Ring House Cottages are set in beautiful and unspoiled Woodland Valley, close to both Coniston and Broughton-in-Furness yet retaining an unrivalled atmosphere of calm and peace in a rural setting. There are five charming properties in all, ranging from the secluded and private Stablecroft Cottage, which has spacious accommodation for two people, to Church Cottage, the oldest part of the 18th-century farmhouse, which can sleep up to six people. The other three properties, Latter Rigg Cottage, Farm Cottage and Fell View Cottage, all accommodate up to four guests. All the cottages are fully equipped - even washing up liquid, dish cloths and scourers are provided - and all electricity, gas, logs and coal are included in the price.

The amenities at Ring House include ample parking space, payphone, laundry room and a library of guide books, games and videos. Bicycles can be rented locally and there's ample, lockable storage space for them at Ring House. The nearest village, Broughton-in-Furness, has a first class grocer's and butcher's shop, a bakery, post office, newsagents, several pubs, two cafés and an excellent restaurant. The owners of Ring House, Stuart and Chris Harrison, also run the Vintage Traction Engine Experience - see below.

VINTAGE TRACTION ENGINE EXPERIENCE

Ring House Farm, Woodland, Broughton-in-Furness,
Cumbria LA20 6DG
Tel: 01226 716578
e-mail: steam@ringhouse.co.uk
website: www.steam-traction.co.uk

The father and son team of Stuart and Chris Harrison who run Ring House Cottages (see above) also own and run the **Vintage Traction Engine Experience** where visitors can step back in time and drive the 1912 Traction Engine *Western Star* for a day. The Traction Engine is based at Muncaster Castle near Ravenglass and the courses start at 9am. The engine is prepared, the fire is lit and then there's a general discussion while the steam is being raised. Having raised steam and become familiar with the controls, a short drive is taken to Ravenglass Station where there's an opportunity to look at the steam engines there before having lunch at the Ratty Arms. After lunch, the party sets off for an approximate eight-mile drive during which participants will be able to take the controls under the supervision of Stuart or Chris. The course ends at around 5pm when the engine is 'put to bed'. The courses are ideal for one or two people as there are two jobs to do on the engine. The instructor, who is on the footplate at all times, supervises. The courses are available from March until the end of October.

The 17 acres of natural parkland are also home to some of the rarest animals on earth, among them the red panda, maned wolves and tamarin monkeys, as well as some 150 other species from around the world, including rhinos, giraffes, tapirs, coatis and the ever-popular meerkats. In 2005, pygmy hippos, mandrills and penguins were added to the menagerie. Other attractions include a safari railway, adventure play area, many picnic spots, a gift shop and café.

To the south of the town lies **Furness Abbey** (English Heritage), a magnificent ruin of eroded red sandstone set in fine parkland, the focal point of south Cumbria's monastic heritage. Furness Abbey stands in the Vale of Deadly Nightshade, a shallow valley of sandstone cliffs and rich pastureland. The abbey itself was established in 1123 at Tulketh, near Preston, by King Stephen. Four years later it was moved to its present site and, after 20 years, became absorbed into the Cistercian Order. Despite its remoteness, the abbey flourished, with the monks establishing themselves as guides across the treacherous sands of Morecambe Bay.

BROUGHTON-IN-FURNESS

19 miles N of Barrow-in-Furness on the A595/ A593

Clocktower Gallery · Branwell Brontë

Broughton House · Swinside Circle

The Coleridge Trail

At the heart of this attractive, unspoilt little town is the Market Square with its tall Georgian houses, commemorative obelisk of 1810, village stocks, fish slabs and some venerable chestnut trees. The old Town Hall, occupying the whole of one side of the square, dates back to 1766 and now houses the town's Tourist Information Centre and the **Clocktower Gallery**, which exhibits paintings, ceramics, mirrors and glassware. On August 1st each year, Broughton's Lord of the Manor comes to the Square to read out the market charter granted by Elizabeth I, while councillors dispense pennies to any children in the crowd.

One of the town's famous short-term residents was **Branwell Brontë,** who was employed here as a tutor at **Broughton House**, a splendid double-fronted, three-storey town house just off the Square. Branwell apparently found time to both enjoy the elegance of the town and to share in whatever revelries were in train.

Wordsworth often visited Broughton as a child. Throughout his life he loved this peaceful corner of Lakeland and celebrated its charms in some 150 poems; his 20th -century poetical successor, Norman Nicholson, was similarly enchanted.

Some of the Lake District's finest scenery - the Duddon Valley, Furness Fells, Great Gable and Scafell, are all within easy reach, and about three miles west of the town is **Swinside Circle**, a fine prehistoric stone circle, some 60 feet in diameter, containing 52 close-set stones and two outlying 'portal' or gateway stones.

Swinside Stone Circle, Broughton-in-Furness

THE SQUARE CAFÉ

The Square, Broughton-in-Furness,
Cumbria LA20 6JA
Tel: 01229 716388
e-mail: info@thesquarecafe.biz
website: www.thesquarecafe.biz

At the centre of Broughton-in-Furness is a fine Georgian square where Annan House - **The Square Café** - is located. Annan House also offers comfortable bed and breakfast accommodation and has an interesting display of framed original photographs by John Rousseau.

The café is a comfortable and friendly place to be whether you want a late breakfast, a bowl of warming homemade soup or a more substantial lunch, a snack, or coffee with a generous slice of organic cake, you will be given a warm welcome. Most of the food is made on the premises from first-rate ingredients, and owner Jane Rousseau is proud of the fact that she has a strong following of local people. Meals are tailored to the seasons of the year and the café is open from 10.30am to 5pm every day.

The comfortable accommodation at Annan House comprises three guest rooms on the first floor. Two have double beds and one has twin beds. One of the double rooms has an en-suite bathroom; the other two rooms have washbasins and share a large bathroom on the same landing. Two of them have views over the Square, and the other a view of gardens to the rear.

About three miles north of the town, the peaceful hamlet of Broughton Mills will attract followers of the **Coleridge Trail**. During the course of his famous 'circumcursion' of Lakeland in August 1802, the poet stopped to refresh himself at the Blacksmith's Arms where he "Dined on Oatcake and Cheese, with a pint of Ale, and two glasses of Rum and water sweetened with preserved Gooseberries". The inn, built in 1748, is still in business and barely changed since Coleridge's visit.

Coniston and Southwest Cumbria

Three distinct areas lie within the southwest quarter of Cumbria. The enchanting scenery around Coniston Water and its environs is very much on the tourist trail, and also has strong literary connections. John Ruskin, the 19th-century author, artist, and critic made his home at Brantwood on the shore of Coniston, and the lake is also the setting for many of the adventures recounted in *Swallows and Amazons* as told by Arthur Ransome. Wordsworth went to school in Hawkshead where the desk he defaced with his name can still be seen. But probably the most popular of Coniston's literary denizens is Beatrix Potter who, after holidaying at Near Sawrey as a child, later bought a house at Hill Top as well as many acres of farms, which she later bequeathed to the National Trust. Further west is Cumbria's 'Empty Quarter', a vast terrain of magnificent mountains and desolate fells beloved of climbers and walkers. England's highest mountain, Scafell Pike, rises here; the country's deepest lake, Wast Water, sinks to a depth of some 200 feet and is surrounded by sheer cliffs soaring up to 2000 feet, and the village of Wasdale Head claims to have the smallest church in England.

Bordering this untamed landscape is the narrow coastal strip, stretching from Whitehaven down to Millom, which has its own identity as well as a quiet charm. The coastline is dominated by small 18th- and 19th-century iron mining communities set between the romantic outline of the Lakeland fells and the grey-blue waters of the Irish Sea.

Coniston

Beatrix Potter · John Ruskin · Arthur Ransome

Sir Donald Campbell · Old Man of Coniston

Ruskin Museum · Brantwood

Beatrix Potter, John Ruskin, Arthur Ransome, Sir Donald Campbell - all of them have strong connections with Coniston Water, the third largest and one of the most beautiful of the central Cumbrian lakes. **Beatrix Potter** lived at Sawrey near Lake Windermere, but she also owned the vast Monk Coniston estate at the head of Coniston Water. On her death, she bequeathed it to the National Trust, a body she had helped to establish and to which she devoted much of her time and fortune.

John Ruskin came to Coniston in 1872, moving into a house he had never seen. **Brantwood**, on the eastern side of the lake, is open to the public and enjoys superb views across the water to the great crumpled hill of the **Old Man of Coniston**, 800 metres high. From its summit there are even more extensive vistas over Scotland, the Isle of Man, and on a clear day as far as Snowdonia.

Arthur Ransome's *Swallows and Amazons* has delighted generations with its tales of children's adventures set in and around the Lake District. As a child he spent his summer holidays near Nibthwaite at the southern end of the lake and recalled that he was always "half-drowned in tears" when he had to leave. Later he bought a house overlooking Coniston Water and many locations in his books can be recognised today.

Sir Donald Campbell's associations with the lake were both glorious and tragic. In 1955 he broke the world water speed record here; 12 years later, when he was attempting to beat his own record, his boat, Bluebird, struck a log while travelling at 320mph. In March 2001, his widow was present as the tailfin of the boat was at last hauled up to the surface. For 34 years the 15 feet rear section had lain on a bed of silt, 140 feet down and right in the middle of the lake. Bluebird's tailfin is now on display at the Ruskin Museum. Sir Donald's body was later recovered and was buried on September 12th 2001 in the village cemetery - an event that was comparatively little covered by the media, who were obviously more concerned with the tragic events in New York and Washington the day before.

Nowadays, boats on Coniston Water are restricted to a 10mph limit, which is an ideal speed if you're travelling in the wonderful old steamship, the *Gondola* (see panel on page 64). So called because of its high prow, which enabled it to come in close to shore to pick up passengers, *Gondola* was commissioned by Sir James Ramsden, General Manager of the Furness Railway Company and first Mayor of Barrow, and was launched on Coniston Water in 1859. She was retired in 1936, but found a new career as a houseboat in 1945. Abandoned after a storm in the 1960s, she

Coniston Gondola

Gondola NT Bookings Office, The Hollens,
Grasmere, Cumbria LA22 9QZ
Tel: 01539 463831
website: www.nationaltrust.org.uk

The original steam yacht ***Gondola*** was first launched in 1859 and now, completely rebuilt by the National Trust, provides a passenger service in its opulently upholstered saloons. This is the perfect way to view Coniston's spectacular scenery. *Gondola* carries up to 86 passengers and can comfortably accommodate large groups. Enjoy a round trip of 45 minutes. A buffet lunch or tea can be provided if Gondola is privately hired.

was saved by a group of National Trust enthusiasts and restored and rebuilt by Vickers Shipbuilding. Coniston Launch also offers lake cruises in its two timber launches, and at the boating centre craft of every kind are available to rent.

Coniston village was once an important copper mining centre with the ore being mined from the Old Man of Coniston and some of the surrounding hills. Mined from the days of the Romans, the industry's heyday in Coniston was in the 18th and 19th centuries but, with the discovery of more accessible deposits elsewhere, the industry went into decline and the village returned to pre-boom peacefulness. At 2631 feet, the Old Man of Coniston is a considerable climb, but many make the effort and the summit can be bustling with fell walkers enjoying the glorious views.

Coniston's most famous inhabitant was John Ruskin, the 19th-century author, artist, critic, social commentator and one of the first conservationists. He lies buried in Coniston churchyard and the **Ruskin Museum** nearby contains many of his studies, pictures, letters, photographs and personal belongings, as well as his collection of geological specimens. Here, too, is his funeral pall made of Ruskin lace embroidered with wild flowers. The lace was so called because Ruskin had encouraged the revival of flax hand-spinning in the area. Lace pieces made to his own designs and based on the sumptuous ruffs worn by sitters in portraits by Titian, Tintoretto and Veronese were attached to plain linen to make decorative cushions, table covers and bedspreads - many of these are on display.

Brantwood House, Coniston

From the jetty at Coniston, a short ferry trip takes visitors to John Ruskin's home, **Brantwood** which occupies a beautiful setting on the eastern shores of Coniston Water. It was his home from 1872 until his death in 1900. When he arrived for the first time he described the house, which he had bought for £1500 without ever seeing it, as "a mere shed". He spent the next 20 years extending the house, by adding another 12 rooms, and laying out the gardens. The view from the Turret Room he had built was, Ruskin declared, "the best in all England". Sadly, Ruskin's later years were blighted by mental illness: "He was," said a biographer, "at times quite mad."

Visitors today can wander around rooms filled with Ruskin's watercolours, paintings by Turner (who was one of his heroes), see his study which is lined with wallpaper he designed himself, and watch a 20-minute video that provides a useful introduction to his life and works. There's also a well-stocked bookshop, a craft shop, an excellent tea room, restaurant and 250 acres of grounds with well-marked nature trails and where a theatre season is held during the summer.

Around Coniston

GRIZEDALE

3 miles SE of Coniston off the B5285

Grizedale Forest | Tree Sculptures

The village lies at the heart of the 9000-acre **Grizedale Forest**, which was acquired by the Forestry Commission in 1934 and is famous for its theatre and sculpture. The Commission's

POPPI RED OF HAWKSHEAD

Main Street, Hawkshead,
Cumbria LA22 0NT
Tel/Fax: 01539 436434
e-mail: info@poppi-red.co.uk
website: www.poppi-red.co.uk

Wander gently into the picturesque Lakeland village of Hawkshead and one of the first welcoming sights to greet you is **Poppi Red,** a fantastic display of pink and scarlet among the whitewashed cottages, slate roofs and cobbled streets. You are drawn in by the fantastic colours, seductive sounds of jazz swing, and the enticing smell of freshly ground coffee.

Poppi Red is a "pamper emporium" of pottery, jewellery, scarves, knitwear, cushions, unusual books and cards - unique ideas to delight friends, loved ones and, of course, yourself. Often in the shop you'll be met by Kim Merrick, proprietor, buyer and inspiration behind Poppi Red. Bright, bubbly, incredibly hospitable - if ever a business were created in its founder's image, this is it. Poppi Red offers the ultimate shopping experience, with cheery staff - all local from the village - and service as it used to be in a beautifully laid out shop. You can meander around and see something different every time you visit.

Partners can relax in the café with a drink and a fresh sandwich or scrummy cakes baked in a local farmhouse. The café is licensed, so on warm days have a glass of wine, beer or a refreshing Pimms; in the winter, enjoy a warming gluhwein.

POPPI RED'S BATH TO BED

Tel/Fax: 01539 436248 (mail order)
website: www.poppi-red.co.uk

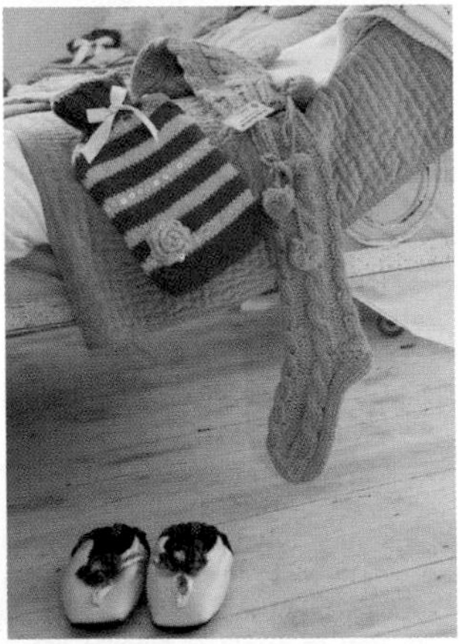

New to Hawkshead is the beautiful **Poppi Red's Bath to Bed**. Kim has sourced fabulous gift ideas for bathrooms and bedrooms - soft velvet cushions, floral robes, knitted hot water bottle covers and matching slippers. Local toiletries handmade in Ambleside, "Pure Lakes" include soothing creams and lotions designed with tired walkers' feet in mind. Bath House's men's range of Spanish Fig shaving products are wonderful and very popular - the cologne has proved irresistible to both men and women! Matilda M is a fabulous French range that Kim discovered in Paris. These seductive fragrances and soft cream ceramics make perfect gifts. Kim and her staff make up all their hampers and gift packs to your choice and are happy to take orders for these by phone or on their website.

original intention of chiefly cultivating the forest for its timber met with much resistance and, over the years, many pathways have been opened and a variety of recreational activities have been encouraged. The Visitor Centre vividly illustrates the story of the forest as well as showing how the combination of wildlife, recreation, and commercial timbering can work together hand-in-hand. The forest, too, is famously the home of some 80 **Tree Sculptures** commissioned since 1977.

HAWKSHEAD

3 miles E of Coniston on the B5285

Beatrix Potter · Beatrix Potter Gallery

William Wordsworth · Esthwaite Water

Hawkshead Grammar School

Church of St Michael & All Angels

There are more **Beatrix Potter** connections in the enchanting little village of Hawkshead. Her solicitor husband, William Heelis, worked from an office in the Main Street here and this has now been transformed into **The Beatrix Potter Gallery**. The gallery features an exhibition of her original drawings and illustrations alongside details of the author's life.

Hawkshead has specific **Wordsworth** connections, too. **Hawkshead Grammar School** was founded in 1585 by Edwin Sandys, Archbishop of York, and between 1779 and 1787 the young William Wordsworth was a star pupil. The earliest of his surviving poems was written to celebrate the school's 200th year. The school is open from Easter to September and visitors can inspect the classrooms during the summer holidays, see the desk where William carved his name and have a look around the headmaster's study. Ann Tyson's Cottage, where Wordsworth lodged while he attended the school, has also survived. It stands in Wordsworth Street and is now a guest house.

Situated at the head of Esthwaite Water, enjoying glorious views of Coniston Old Man and Helvellyn, Hawkshead is a delightful village of narrow cobbled lanes with a pedestrianised main square dominated by the Market House, or Shambles, and another square linked to it by little snickets and arched alleyways that invite exploration. The poet Norman Nicholson observed that, "The whole village could be fitted into the boundaries of a large agricultural show; yet it contains enough corners, angles, alleys and entries to keep the eye happy for hours."

The **Church of St Michael and All Angels**, with its massive 15th-century tower, seems rather grand for the village, but it too was built at a time when Hawkshead was a wealthy town. Inside, there are some remarkable wall paintings from the late 1600s, and also look out for the "Buried in Woolen" affidavit near the vestry door. In 1666 the Government had decreed that corpses must not be buried in shrouds made from "flaxe, hempe, silke or hair, or other than what is made of sheeps wool onely". The idea was to help maintain the local woollen industry and this was one way of ensuring that even the dead got to help out. The church is the focal point of the annual Lake District Summer Music Festival and a popular venue for concerts and recitals. In the churchyard is a war memorial erected in 1919 and modelled on the ancient runic cross at Gosforth.

Some lovely walks lead from Hawkshead to Roger Ground and **Esthwaite Water**, possibly the least frequented of the Lakes, and also to the nearby hamlet of Colthouse where there's an early Quaker Meeting House built

Hawkshead

Distance: *5.0 miles (8.0 kilometres)*

Typical time: *180 mins*

Height gain: *50 metres*

Map: *Explorer OL7*

Walk: *www.walkingworld.com ID: 3277*

Contributor: *Mark & Tracey Douglas*

ACCESS INFORMATION:

Hawkshead is 6 miles south west of Ambleside. Buses are either Stagecoach 505 Windermere-Coniston or the Cross Lakes Shuttle from Bowness, April-Oct. Tel: 01539 445161 for details. There is a large pay and display car park in the centre of Hawkshead.

DESCRIPTION:

Hawkshead is one of the most beautiful small villages in the Lakes. An ancient township that has flourished since Norse times and belonged to Furness Abbey until the 12th century. Much loved by Beatrix Potter and William Wordsworth, the village is home to the Beatrix Potter Gallery, The Grammar School where Wordsworth was educated, and the fashion label that bears the village name. Hawkshead is surrounded by beautiful scenery, much of which is owned by the National Trust. Cars are even banned from the village centre (cars park in the large car park where the walk starts).

This pleasant, undulating walk starts in the village centre and heads across pastureland, woodland and meadow, skirting Blelham Tarn to reach the National Trust Property of Wray Castle on the banks of Windermere and returning over open farmland.

ADDITIONAL INFORMATION:

There are numerous pubs, shops, tearooms etc in Hawkshead including the Hawkshead store home of the famous high street label. This store is opposite the car park at the start of the walk. Wray Castle is owned by the National Trust. The grounds are open to the public and are well worth visiting for the sake of the specimen trees - wellingtonia, redwood, gingkoa, weeping lime and varieties of beech. There is a mulberry tree planted by William Wordsworth in 1845. Watbarrow Wood is the wooded bank between the castle and the lake, and has several pleasant paths leading through it to the water's edge. There are spectacular views across Windermere. The castle is not currently open to the public.

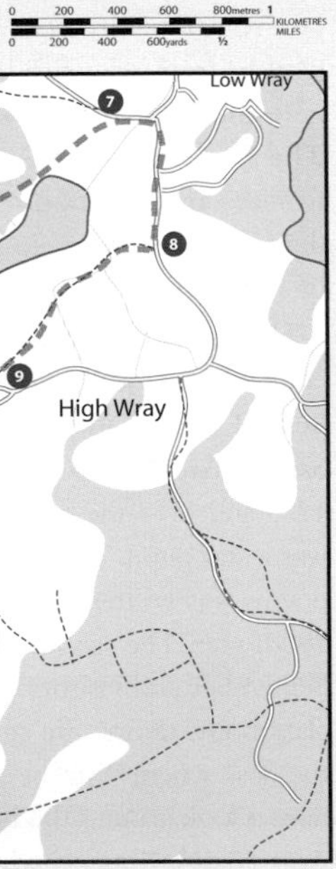

FEATURES:

Hills or Fells, Mountains, Lake/Loch, Pub, Toilets, Museum, Church, Castle, National Trust/NTS, Wildlife, Birds, Flowers, Great Views, Butterflies, Café, Gift Shop, Food Shop, Good for Kids, Industrial Archaeology, Mostly Flat, Public Transport, Nature Trail, Restaurant, Tea Shop.

WALK DIRECTIONS:

1 | From the car park turn right out onto North Lonsdale Road, and then turn left, as the road bears left, cross the road and turn right down a track, with a high wall on your right, turning right down a track to reach a small footbridge. Cross the footbridge and turn left following the stream and then almost immediately cut across the field to reach a kissing gate. Continue through the fields following the Footpath waymarks (taking the left hand path at a finger post) to reach a narrow lane. Turn left along the lane looking for a kissing gate on your right.

2 | Go through the kissing gate and continue straight ahead up the field on a stony path with the fence on your right. Pass through a couple of gates/stiles to reach a double gate at a metalled public road at Loanthwaite Farm.

3 | Pass through the gate onto the metalled road and turn left. Continue through the farm buildings and after the house turn right into a narrow lane/ bridleway.

4 | Look out for a stile almost immediately on your left and cross the field and pasture into woodland, heading by a tall marker/gatepost. Keep ahead in the same direction to reach the gate at the rear of the Outgate Inn.

5 | Pass through the gate and at the main road turn right past the front of the Inn and continue along the road for 300m ignoring the first footpath sign to reach a bridleway on your right.

6 | Head down the bridleway, through woodland to reach Blelham Tarn within 1km. Keep straight ahead with the tarn on your right to eventually reach on old iron gate at a public road.

7 | For safety, a permissive path has been created down the field to avoid the road. Turn right with the fence on your left to reach a gate, and then turn right down the road and keep straight ahead (ignoring the road to the left signposted Low Wray Campsite). The road will gently ascend and pass the main gate of Wray Castle (visit the gardens if open, and you have time). Keep ahead on the road past the lodge, church and the old vicarage, and as the road descends look out for a gate on the right.

8 | Go through the gate and follow the path with a hedge on your left down to cross a stone footbridge and through the trees into a field where the path follows a fenceline on your left. Rising gently the path becomes a clear farm track at a gate, follow the farm track to reach Hole House. Pass through the houses and buildings and on reaching the road keep straight ahead ignoring the roads on your left and right. Look out for a turn-off down to the right within 200m.

9 | Heading right down the lane into High Tock How Farm/B&B, turning left before reaching the buildings, and follow the fence and waymarkings to a gate on the hilltop. Pass through the gate and turn left (signposted Loanthwaite and Hawkshead) keeping in the same general direction before crossing the field diagonally down to a gate in the far corner. Pass through the gate heading straight ahead, before turning left across the field to a gate in front of a line of trees. Pass through the gate and straight ahead with the line of trees on your right through another two gates to reach the gate at the bridleway at Waymark 6.

10 | Pass through the gate onto the road and turn left through the farm buildings at Loanthwaite and retrace your initial steps back to Hawkshead.

LAKELAND HIDEAWAYS COTTAGES

The Square, Hawkshead, Cumbria LA22 0NZ
Tel: 01539 442435 Fax: 01539 436178
e-mail: bookings@lakeland-hideaways.co.uk
website: www.lakeland-hideaways.co.uk

Hawkshead, with its whitewashed cottages, cobbled yards and floral displays, has been described as "the prettiest village in the Lake District" and right in the heart of this charming little village are the offices of **Lakeland Hideaways Cottages.** The company was formed in 1989 by Ruth and Gary Thomason with the aim of bringing the personal service back into letting holiday homes. They pride themselves on knowing their cottages inside and out, able to describe everything from the view from the windows to the easiest walk to the pub. All their properties are in the village and the surrounding vales of Esthwaite and Grizedale in the area so loved by Wordsworth and Beatrix Potter - her farm, Hill Top, is just a couple of miles away.

Whether you prefer a traditional Lakeland cottage, or a barn conversion; a location in the village of Hawkshead, or overlooking the beautiful Lakeland fells; close to local pubs and restaurants, or beside a lake, they are confident that they will have a property to suit your taste and your pocket. Many of their properties offer free fishing and welcome pets, and all of them are listed on the Hideaways website with full details, pictures and online booking. Bookings are usually from Saturday to Saturday, but short three or four night breaks are available and can be tailored to your holiday dates. If you can get to Hawkshead, Hideaways will be glad to welcome you at their office and, subject to availability, show you around the cottages and answer any queries.

Hawkshead's location is idyllic. It nestles in the rolling countryside between the lakes of Windermere and Coniston Water, with the mountains only a short drive away. Whether you are wanting a walking holiday, cycling or just relaxing and touring the lakes and villages, Hawkshead provides the perfect base for exploring this beautiful area.

GRAHAMS OF HAWKSHEAD

Main Street, Hawkshead,
Cumbria LA22 0NT
Tel: 01539 436600
Fax: 01539 436992
e-mail: sales@grahamsofhawkshead.co.uk
website: www.grahamsofhawkshead.co.uk

Located in the heart of this appealing Lakeland village, **Grahams of Hawkshead** is full to bursting with an astonishing range and variety of gifts of every kind.

The business has been established for more than 30 years and is now owned and run by Jane Robinson and Diane Ireton who have gathered together an alluring collection of quality items. There are gifts for babies, gifts for senior citizens, and gifts for everyone between.

One of the shop's specialities is the range of Beatrix Potter gifts but they also offer children's toys, an amazing range of dolls, crystal ware from Cath Kitson and Moorcroft, ceramics, kit for outdoor games and a selection of locally-made chocolates and fudge.

Whether you are looking for a gift for friends or family, or indeed something eye-catching to enhance your own décor, you can be certain of finding just the right thing here.

Hawkshead itself is a delightful place to explore with its narrow cobbled lanes, little snickets and arched alleyways. It stands at the head of Esthwaite Water and enjoys wonderful views of Coniston Old Man and Helvellyn. The village has strong connections with Beatrix Potter whose solicitor husband worked from an office in the main street which now houses the Beatrix Potter Gallery which contains an exhibition of her original drawings and illustrations.

Hill Top, Near Sawrey

around 1690. Esthwaite Water was much loved by Wordsworth, as he shows in *The Prelude*:

My morning walks were early;
oft before the hours of school
I travelled round our little lake, five miles
Of pleasant wandering. Happy time!

NEAR SAWREY

4 miles E of Coniston on the B5285

Beatrix Potter | Hill Top | Tarn Hows

After holidaying here in 1896, the authoress **Beatrix Potter** fell in love with the place and, with the royalties from her first book, *The Tale of Peter Rabbit*, she purchased **Hill Top** in 1905. After her marriage in 1913 to a local solicitor, she actually lived in another house in the village and used the charming 17th-century cottage as her study. Oddly, she wrote very little after the marriage, spending most of her time dealing with the management of the farms she had bought in the area.

Following Beatrix Potter's death in 1943, the house and the land she had bought on the surrounding fells became the property of the National Trust. In accordance with her will, Hill Top has remained exactly as she would have known it. One of the most popular Lakeland attractions, Hill Top is full of Beatrix Potter memorabilia, including some of her original drawings. The house is very small, so it is best avoided at peak holiday times. **Tarn Hows**, part of the 4000-acre Monk Coniston estate bought and sold on to the National Trust, was created to resemble a Swiss lake and is very rich in flora and fauna - it has been designated a Site of Special Scientific Interest.

GREAT LANGDALE

9 miles N of Coniston on the B5343

Dungeon Ghyll

One of the most dramatic of the Lake District waterfalls is **Dungeon Ghyll**, which tumbles 60 feet down the fellside. The

Millbeck, Great Langdale

'dungeon' is actually a natural cave. Nearby is the well-known Old Dungeon Ghyll Hotel, which makes an excellent starting point for walks in this spectacularly scenic area where the famous peaks of Crinkle Crags, Bowfell and the Langdale Pikes provide some serious challenges for hikers and ramblers.

SEATHWAITE

5 miles W of Coniston off the A593

Dunnerdale · William Wordsworth

Rev Robert Walker

A mere five miles or so from Coniston as the crow flies, by road Seathwaite is nearly three times as far. It stands in one of the Lake District's most tranquil and least known valleys, **Dunnerdale**. Little has changed here since the days when **William Wordsworth**, who knew the area as Duddon Valley, captured its natural beauty in a sequence of sonnets. In his poem *The Excursion*, he wrote about the **Rev Robert Walker**, the curate of Seathwaite. 'Wonderful Walker' as Wordsworth referred to him, served the church here for some 67 years though he also filled various other jobs such as farm labourer and nurse, as well as spinning wool and making his own clothes.

Fell walkers and hikers who prefer to escape the crowds will delight not only in the solitude of this glorious valley, but also in the wide variety of plant, animal and birdlife that have made this haven their home.

HARDKNOTT PASS

5 miles W of Coniston off the A593

Hardknott Fort

Surrounded by the fell of the same name, this pass is one of the most treacherous in the Lake District, yet it was used by the Romans for the road between their forts at Ambleside (Galava) and Ravenglass (Glannaventa). Of the remains of Roman occupation, **Hardknott Fort** on a shoulder of the fell, overlooking the Esk Valley, is the most substantial and also provides some of the grandest views in the whole of the Lake District.

BOOT

8 miles W of Coniston off the A595

Ravenglass & Eskdale Railway

Hardknott Fort, Hardknott Pass

Lying at the eastern end of the **Ravenglass and Eskdale Railway**, this is a wonderful place to visit whether arriving by train or car. A gentle walk from the station at Eskdale brings you to this delightful village with its pub, post office, museum, waterfall and nearby St Catherine's Church in its lovely secluded riverside setting.

ESKDALE GREEN

10 miles W of Coniston off the A595

Eskdale Mill

One of the few settlements in this beautiful and unspoiled valley, the village lies on the route of the Ravenglass and Eskdale Railway. Further up the valley stands a group of buildings that make up **Eskdale Mill** where cereals have been ground since 1578, when it is recorded that the brothers Henry and Robert Vicars were the tenants, paying an annual rent of eight shillings (40p). Approached by a picturesque 17th-century packhorse bridge, the Mill contains original machinery for grinding oatmeal and is in full working order.

Ravenglass

Glannaventra · Ravenglass & Eskdale Railway

Muncaster Castle · World Owl Centre

Muncaster Water Mill

Lying as it does at the estuary of three rivers - the Esk, the Mite, and the Irt - as well as enjoying a sheltered position, it is not surprising that Ravenglass was an important port from prehistoric times. The Romans built a naval base here around AD78, which served as a supply point for the military zone around Hadrian's Wall. They also constructed a fort, **Glannaventra**, on the cliffs above the town, which was home to around 1000 soldiers. Little remains of Glannaventra except for the impressively preserved walls of the Bath House. Almost 12 feet high, these walls are believed to be the highest Roman remains in the country.

One of the town's major attractions is the 15-inch narrow gauge **Ravenglass and Eskdale Railway**, which runs for seven miles up the lovely Mite and Esk River valleys to the foot of Scafell. Better known to locals as "La'al Ratty", it was built in 1875 to transport ore and quarried stone from the Eskdale Valley and opened the following year for passenger traffic. Since then the railway has survived several threats of extinction. The most serious occurred at the end of the 1950s when the closure of the Eskdale granite quarries wiped out the railway's freight traffic at a stroke. However, at the auction for the railway in 1960 a band of enthusiasts outbid the scrap dealers and formed a company to keep the little railway running.

Today, the company operates 12 locomotives, both steam and diesel, and 300,000 people a year come from all over the world to ride on what has been described as "the most beautiful train journey in England". There are several stops along the journey and at both termini there is a café and a souvenir shop. At Ravenglass Station there is also a museum that brings to life the history of this remarkable line and the important part it has played in the life of Eskdale.

A mile or so east of Ravenglass stands **Muncaster Castle** (see panel opposite), which has been in the ownership of the Pennington family since 1208. In 1464 the Penningtons gave shelter to King Henry VI after his defeat at the Battle of Hexham. On his departure, Henry presented them with his enamelled glass drinking bowl, saying that as long as it remained unbroken the Penningtons would survive and thrive at Muncaster. Apart from the many treasures, the stunning Great Hall, Salvin's octagonal library and the barrel ceiling in the drawing room, Muncaster is also famous for its gardens. The collection of rhododendrons is one of the finest in Europe, gathered primarily from plant-hunting expeditions to Nepal in the 1920s, and there are also fine azaleas, hydrangeas and camellias as well as many unusual trees. For many visitors the chief attraction is the **World Owl Centre**, where endangered owl species are bred. Snowy owls have become great favourites on the back of the Harry Potter craze, and ther have been many enquire about keeping them as pets. The staff at the Centre have to point out that the snowy owl is a mighty predator with a five-feet wingspan. Mighty as he is, he is not the mightiest of the owls at the Centre: that honour goes to the European eagle owl, whose full splendour can be seen at the daily demonstrations. Muncaster's latest attraction is the Meadow Vole Maze. These little creatures are the staple diet of barn owls, and visitors can find out what it's like to be a vole on the run from a hungry owl.

Originally part of the Muncaster Castle Estate, **Muncaster Water Mill** can be traced back to 1455, though it is thought that this site may be Roman. The situation is certainly idyllic, with the mill race still turning the huge wooden water wheel and the Ravenglass and Eskdale Railway running alongside. In November 1996, Pam and Ernie Priestley came to the mill and Ernie put his years of engineering experience to use as the miller. Until January 2008 the mill was open every day, working just as it has done for hundreds of years. Sadly, it is currently not open to the public.

Around Ravenglass

SILECROFT

10 miles S of Ravenglass off the A595

Perhaps of all the villages in this coastal region of the National Park, Silecroft is the perfect example. Just a short walk from the

CUMBRIAN HEAVY HORSES

Chappels Farm, Whicham Valley, nr Millom, Cumbria LA18 5LY
Tel: 01229 777764
e-mail: annie@horseridinglakedistrict.co.uk website: www.horseridinglakedistrict.co.uk

Set amidst the stunning landscape of the Lake District, **Cumbrian Heavy Horses** offers the ultimate horse riding experience. The UK's only specialised Heavy Horse Riding establishment, this is a small, professional, family-run Equestrian Centre unique in its use of magnificent Clydesdale and Shire horses for riding. The courses are suitable for riders of varying ability, with steadier rides and mounts for the nervous novice and forward-going, fluent Clydesdale horses for those wishing to experience the thrill of riding a REAL horse!!!

Annie Rose started West Highland Heavy Horses many years ago on the Isle of Skye with the firm belief that heavy horses required a future without the traditional perception of them being a bygone relic. Her passion has led to the business's growth over the past 10 years from a two-horse dray outfit to a vibrant and friendly yard with BHS Approved Riding School status using only Clydesdales and Shires for riding. Annie loves developing the business, but her first love, that of directly working with these beautiful horses, is still what she calls "her driving passion (pardon the pun!)". Annie runs Cumbrian Heavy Horses with partner in life and in business, Tim Ancrum, who is an excellent ride leader loving adventure and long routes.

The Centre offers a variety of rides. There are farm rides run in several ways, either as a beginner/novice, a mixed ability group, or as a fast ride for experienced riders. The ride is through local farmland comprising of fields, tracks and stream crossings, all with fantastic Whicham Valley views. For more experienced riders/ groups who are able to walk, trot and canter in full control of their horse, there's a ride that takes you from the Chappells Farm Base, along the Whicham Valley, and on to the nearby Irish Sea Coastline, which offers miles of sand and sea for you to enjoy. An amazing riding experience...

The Centre also offers horse riding holidays, work experience holidays, carriage driving instruction as well as regular riding lessons and tuition.

The horses are also available for weddings, shows and other events. The Centre is open seven days a week but booking ahead is essential.

heart of the village is the beach, which extends as far as the eye can see. On the horizon lies the distant outline of the Isle of Man. There is also a Site of Special Scientific Interest close by, a tract of coastal scrubland that provides the perfect habitat for the rare natterjack toad.

MILLOM

13 miles S of Ravenglass on the A5093

Millom Folk Museum RAF Millom Museum

Norman Nicholson Hodbarrow

Hodbarrow Beacon

This small and peaceful town stands at the mouth of the River Duddon with the imposing Black Combe Fell providing a dramatic backdrop. Originally called Holborn Hill, the present-day name was taken from nearby Millom Castle, which is now a private, working farm. Like many neighbouring towns and villages in Furness, Millom was a small fishing village before it too grew with the development of the local iron industry. **Millom Folk Museum** tells the story of the town's growth and also has a permanent memorial to **Norman Nicholson** (1914-1987) who is generally regarded as the best writer on Lakeland life and customs since Wordsworth himself. Nicholson's book *Provincial Pleasures* records his affectionate memories of Millom, the town where he spent all his life. Other displays include a full-scale reproduction of a drift and cage from nearby Hodbarow mine.

South of Millom, at Haverigg, is the **RAF**

THE STATION HOTEL

Salthouse Road, Millom, Cumbria LA18 5AD
Tel: 01229 772223
Fax: 01229 773223
e-mail: stationhotelmillom@hotmail.co.uk
website: www.stationhotelmillom.co.uk

The largest pub/hotel in Millom, **The Station Hotel** is a friendly drinker's pub which hosts music sessions twice a month and also holds regular karaoke evenings. The hotel's welcoming bar has the usual amenities of pool, darts and sports coverage. On tap are lagers including Foster's, Kronenberg, ciders and mild, and bar snacks and basket meals are also available.

The hotel has six guest bedrooms(four family rooms; one double and one single) and can take group bookings of up to a maximum of 16; reduced rates are available with maximum occupancy. If payment is made by credit or debit card 2% of the booking value is charged. All bedrooms have an en-suite shower room and are furnished to a high standard with all the comforts of home. The hotel's breakfast facilities are run on a self service basis with the fully equipped residents kitchen available to guests 24 hours a day.

The hotel provides an ideal base from which to explore the Central Lakes and the unspoilt beauty of the Western Coast, a firm favourite with both walking and rambling groups.

Millom Museum situated in the former Officers Mess. Visitors to the site will find a fascinating collection of more than 2000 photographs of the wartime activities of the RAF in the area, various artefacts connected with the period and a number of items recovered from local crash sites. The museum also has a fine collection of aero engines including a Rolls Royce Merlin, a Westland Whirlwind helicopter, the cockpit section of a De Havilland Vampire jet trainer and an example of the HM14 or Flying Flea.

The Duddon Estuary is an important site for wildlife, and the RSPB site at **Hodbarrow** is home not only to birds but to many kinds of flora and fauna. **Hodbarrow Beacon**, which still stands, was built in 1879 as a lighthouse to assist vessels taking iron ore from the mines to destinations in Europe.

DRIGG

2 miles N of Ravenglass on the B5343

Drigg Dunes

The main attractions here are the sand dunes and the fine views across to the Lakeland mountains and fells. There is an important nature reserve, **Drigg Dunes**, on the salt marshes that border the River Irt, but take note, adders are common here. The reserve is home to Europe's largest colony of black-headed gulls.

SEASCALE

4 miles N of Ravenglass on the B5343

Victorian Wooden Jetty

Sellafield Visitors Centre

One of the most popular seaside villages in Cumbria, Seascale enhanced its resort status in

NEATE CRAFTS

39 Santon Way, Seascale, Cumbria CA20 1NG
Tel: 01946 727131
e-mail: neates@onetel.net website: www.neatecrafts.co.uk

Neate Crafts is owned and run by Susan Neate who trained as a Fine Artist and is an extremely versatile professional artist and craftswoman. A former designer at Bramall Hall and Artist-in-Residence at Muncaster Castle, she paints and draws in pencil, pastel, watercolour and acrylic in many styles - from realistic to abstract, in any size from miniature to mural, and on any surface including canvas, paper, wood, silk and glass.

Susan creates hand-illustrated and painted cards and prints, as well as producing pyrographic (wood-burning) decoration on thimbles, egg cups, key rings, leather bookmarks, house signs and much more. Her other accomplishments include designing and producing jewellery, patchwork items and creating knitted creations, sewing decorative and practical items including herb sachets, catnip mice, cushions and so on. Then there are hand-painted items such as plant pots (any size, shape or design), furniture, ceramics and glassware; and signs that are hand-painted or pyrography (pokerwork) on sycamore and beech plaques. These can be practical (We are in the Garden) or humorous - Susan has 250 sayings so far!

Susan works from a shed at the bottom of her garden so do not expect any frills, however you can expect quality, original and unique items. In addition to her wide range of handcrafted items, Susan also accepts commissions from individuals and companies (in the UK and overseas). Mail order is available. View by appointment only.

2000 by restoring the **Victorian Wooden Jetty** to mark Millennium Year. Stretching out into the Irish Sea, it is the focal point for fishing, beach casting, wind surfing and water-skiing, and also provides the starting point for many walks, including the Cumbrian Coastal Way which passes along the foreshore. Two Victorian buildings stand out: the Water Tower, medieval in style and with a conical roof, and the old Engine Shed, which is now a multi-purpose Sports Hall.

A couple of miles north of the village is the **Sellafield Visitors Centre** where you can get switched on to the debate about electricity and nuclear power through a range of interesting exhibits, interactive features and presentations.

GOSFORTH

5 miles N of Ravenglass on the A595

Viking Cross · Chinese Bell · Gosforth Pottery

Wasdale Church

On the edge of this picturesque village, in the graveyard of St Mary's Church, stands the tallest ancient cross in England. Fifteen feet high, the **Viking Cross** towers above the huddled gravestones in the peaceful churchyard. Carved from red sandstone and clearly influenced by both Christian and pagan traditions, the cross depicts the crucifixion, the deeds of Norse gods and Yggdrasil, the World Ash Tree that Norsemen believed supported the universe. The interior of the church also contains some interesting features. There's a **Chinese Bell**, finely decorated with Oriental imagery, which was captured in 1841 at Anunkry, a fort on the River Canton, some delightful carved faces on the chancel arch and a collection of ancient stones the most notable of which dates from Saxon times and depicts the Lamb of God trampling on the serpents of pagan faith.

A major attraction in this appealing village is **Gosforth Pottery**, where Dick and Barbara Wright produce beautifully crafted work and also give pottery lessons.

To the east of Gosforth runs Wasdale, the wildest of the Lake District valleys but easily accessible by road. The road leads to **Wast Water**, which is just three miles long but is the deepest lake in England. The southern shores are dominated by huge screes some 2000 feet high that plunge abruptly into the lake, and they provide an awesome backdrop to this tranquil stretch of water. A lake less like Windermere would be hard to find, as there are no motorboats ploughing their way up and down; this is very much the country of walkers and climbers and from here there are many footpaths up to some of the best fells in Cumbria.

Viking Cross, Gosforth

Wasdale Head, just to the north of the lake, is a small, close-knit community with an inn that has provided a welcome refuge for walkers and climbers since the mid-1800s. **Wasdale Church** is claimed to be the smallest in England - although this title is hotly disputed by Culbone in Somerset and Dale Abbey in Derbyshire. The church was built in the 14th century and it is hidden away amidst a tiny copse of evergreen trees. Local legend suggests that the roof beams came from a Viking ship and it is certainly true that until late Victorian times the church had only an earth floor and few seats.

As well as the deepest lake and the smallest church, Wasdale also boasts the highest mountain, Sca Fell Pike (3205ft) - and the world's biggest liars. This latter claim goes back to the mid-1800s when Will Ritson, "a reet good fibber", was the publican at the inn. Will enthralled his patrons with tall stories of how he had crossed foxes with eagles to produce flying foxes and had grown turnips so large he could hollow them out to make a comfortable residence. In the same spirit, the 'World's Biggest Liar' competition takes place every November, usually at the Bridge Inn at Santon Bridge.

SANTON BRIDGE

3 miles NE of Ravenglass off the A595

'World's Biggest Liar' Irton Church

The churchyard of **Irton Church**, reached from Santon Bridge via an unclassified road, offers the visitor not only superb views of the Lakeland fells to the west, but also the

SANTON BRIDGE GIFT SHOP & WOODLANDS TEA ROOM

Santon Bridge, nr Holmrook, Cumbria CA19 1UY
Tel/Fax: 019467 26281
e-mail: nancyhogge@aol.com
website: www.santonbridge.co.uk

If you go down to the woods today, you're sure of a big surprise. The **Woodlands Tea Room** nestles in a delightful setting in the Woodlands of Santon Bridge near Wasdale. The surprise is two-fold - not only are you able to sample some of the tastiest home-made snacks, meals and cakes available anywhere in the district, you can then go next door for a leisurely browse around one of the most innovative craft and gift shops in the west of the country.

The Craft Shop has been on site since 1954 and in those days hot drinks were sold from a flask. Since then things have evolved - the craft shop has turned into a veritable institution. Quality leather goods and sheepskin are synonymous with the **Santon Bridge Craft and Gift Shop**. In addition to the quality leather there are charming gifts including Pilgrim Jewellery, Beatrix Potter, Border Fine Arts, children's toys, outdoor clothing, ceramics, glassware and much much more .....Shop assistants Lorna & Barbara have worked for over 30 years apiece at the Gift Shop. Considering what a lovely place it is, that's the only thing that's not a big surprise!

opportunity to see a beautiful Anglican Cross, in excellent condition, that is certainly 1000 years old. The Bridge Inn here plays host each November to the **'World's Biggest Liar'** competition when contestants from all over the country vie in telling the most prodigious porkies.

"When I was a lad", Egremont

CALDER BRIDGE

7 miles N of Ravenglass on the A595

Calder Abbey · Monk's Bridge

From this small, grey 19th-century settlement there is an attractive footpath to **Calder Abbey**. It was founded by monks from Savigny in 1134 but amalgamated with the Cistercians of Furness Abbey after it was ransacked by the Scots a few years later. Following the Dissolution, the monastery buildings lapsed slowly into the present-day romantic ruin. To the northeast of the village, the River Calder rises on Caw Fell. **Monk's Bridge**, the oldest packhorse bridge in Cumbria, was built across it for the monks of Calder Abbey.

EGREMONT

12 miles N of Ravenglass on the A595

Egremont Castle · Florence Mine Heritage Centre

Crab Fair · World Gurning Championship

Lowes Court Gallery

This pretty town is dominated by **Egremont Castle** with walls 20 feet high and an 80 foot tower. It stands high above the town, overlooking the lovely River Eden to the south and the market place to the north. The castle was built between 1130 and 1140 by William de Meschines on the site of a former Danish fortification. The most complete part still standing is a Norman arch that once guarded the drawbridge entrance. Nearby is an unusual four-sided sundial and the stump of the old market cross dating from the early 13th century.

Egremont's prosperity was based on the good quality of its local red iron ore, and jewellery made from it can be bought at the nearby **Florence Mine Heritage Centre**. Visitors to the mine, the last deep working iron ore mine in Europe, can join an underground tour (by prior arrangement) and discover why the miners became known as the Red Men of Cumbria. The museum here also tells the story of the mine, which was worked by the ancient Britons, and there is a re-creation of the conditions that the miners endured at the turn of the 20th century.

In September every year the town celebrates its **Crab Fair**. Held each year on the third Saturday in September, the Fair dates back more than seven centuries - to 1267 in fact, when Henry III granted a Royal Charter for a three-day fair to be held on "the even, the day and the morrow after the Nativity of St Mary the Virgin". The celebrations include the Parade of the Apple Cart, when a wagon loaded with apples is driven along Main Street with men on the back throwing fruit into the crowds. Originally, the throng was pelted with crab apples - hence the name Crab Fair - but these are considered too tart for modern taste so nowadays more palatable varieties are used. The festivities also feature a greasy pole competition (with a pole 30 feet high), a pipe-smoking contest, wrestling and hound-trailing. The highlight, however, is the **World Gurning Championship** in which contestants place their heads through a braffin, or horse collar, and vie to produce the most grotesque expression. If you're toothless, you start with a great advantage!

Lowes Court Gallery, in a listed 18th-century building, holds fine art exhibitions throughout the year. The premises also house a gift shop selling Made in Cumbria gifts, and a Tourist Information Centre.

Whitehaven

The Beacon · Weather Zone · Harbour Gallery

The Rum Story · Haig Colliery Mining Museum

St James' Church · St Begh's Church

Mildred Gale · Harbour Pier · Tom Hurd Rock

The first impression is of a handsome Georgian town, but Whitehaven was already well established in the 12th century as a harbour for use by the monks of nearby St Bees Priory. After the Reformation, the land was acquired and developed by the Lowther family in order to expand the coal industry. By the mid-1700s, Whitehaven had become the third largest port in Britain, its trade based on coal and other cargo business, including importing tobacco from Virginia, exporting coal to Ireland, and transporting emigrants to the New World. When the large iron-steamships arrived however, the harbour's shallow draught halted expansion and the port declined in favour of Liverpool and Southampton. For that reason much of the attractive harbour area - now full of pleasure craft and fishing smacks - and older parts of the town remain largely unchanged.

The harbour and its environs have been declared a Conservation Area and located here is **The Beacon** (see panel opposite) where, through a series of innovative displays, the history of the town and its harbour are brought to life. The displays reflect the many aspects of this harbour borough with a collection that includes paintings, locally made pottery, ship models, navigational instruments, miners' lamps, and surveying equipment. The Beilby 'Slavery' Goblet, part of the museum's collection, is one of the masterpieces of English glass-making and is probably the finest example of its kind in existence.

Also here are the **Harbour Gallery**, with an ongoing arts programme, and the **Weather Zone**, where visitors can monitor, forecast and broadcast the weather. They can also learn about the "American Connection" and John Paul Jones' attack on the town in 1778. John Paul Jones had been an apprentice seaman at Whitehaven before going to the New World, where he became well-known in the War of Independence. In 1777 he became Captain of the privateer *The Ranger* and led a raid on Whitehaven with the intention of firing on the ships in the harbour. Thwarted by light winds, the party raided the fort and spiked the guns, then managed to damage only three ships before retreating under fire. The Beacon also has a cinema that presents vintage footage of Whitehaven in times past.

There's more history at **The Rum Story**, which tells the story of the town's connections

The Beacon

West Strand, Whitehaven, Cumbria CA28 7LY
Tel: 01946 592302
e-mail: thebeacon@copelandbc.gov.uk
website: www.copelandbc.gov.uk

Situated on Whitehaven's attractive harbourside, **The Beacon** is home to the town's museum collection. It traces the social, industrial and maritime heritage of the area, using local characters, audio-visual displays and fascinating museum pieces. The Met Office Weather Gallery, where you can monitor, forecast and broadcast the weather, offers panoramic views of the town and coast. Also, don't miss the Harbour Gallery, which offers free entry to the changing exhibitions; our gift shop and café. Guided heritage walks are available through the town and over the headland to Haig Colliery Mining Museum. Disabled access and facilities.

with the Caribbean. The display is housed in the original 1785 shop, courtyards, cellars and bonded warehouses of the Jefferson family, the oldest surviving UK family of rum traders. Visitors can learn about the various processes involved in the making of rum, travel through realistic re-creations of far-off villages, and experience the sights, sounds and smells of life on board the slave ships.

In Solway Road, Kells, the **Haig Colliery Mining Museum** features the world's only Bever Dorling Winding Engines, various displays about the mining industry and exhibits on mining disasters. Haig Colliery was the last deep coal mine worked in the West Cumberland coalfield. Sunk between 1914 and 1918, it closed in 1986 and was later sold for restoration.

As well as the elegant Georgian buildings that give Whitehaven its air of distinction, there are two fine parish churches that are worth a visit. Dating from 1753, **St James' Church** has Italian ceiling designs and a beautiful Memorial Chapel dedicated to those who lost their lives in the two World Wars and to the local people who were killed in mining accidents. The younger **St Begh's Church**, which was built in the 1860s by EW Pugin, is striking with its sandstone walls. In the graveyard of the parish church of St Nicholas is buried **Mildred Gale**, the grandmother of

Haig Colliery Mining Museum

George Washington. In 1699, a widowed mother of three, Mildred married George Gale, a merchant who traded from Whitehaven to Maryland and Virginia. Her sons were born in Virginia but went to school in Appleby. When their mother died they returned to Virginia; one of them, Augustin, became the father of George Washington, first President of the United States of America.

Whitehaven is interesting in other ways. The grid pattern of streets dating back to the 17th century gives substance to its claim to be the first planned town in Britain. Many of the fine Georgian buildings in the centre have been restored and Lowther Street is a particularly impressive thoroughfare. Also of note is the **Harbour Pier** built by the canal engineer John Rennie, and considered to be one of the finest in Britain. There is a fascinating walk and a Nature Trail around **Tom Hurd Rock** above the town.

Around Whitehaven

ST BEES

3 miles S of Whitehaven on the B5343

St Bees Head · Coast to Coast Walk

Church of St Mary & St Bega

St Bees Head, a red sandstone bluff, forms one of the most dramatic natural features along the entire coast of northwest England. Some four miles long and 300 feet high, these towering, precipitous cliffs are formed of St Bees sandstone, the red rock that is so characteristic of Cumbria. Far out to sea, on the horizon, can be seen the grey shadow of the Isle of Man and, on a clear day, the shimmering outline of the Irish coast. From St Bees the 190-mile **Coast to Coast Walk** starts on its long journey across the Pennines to Robin Hood's Bay in North Yorkshire.

Long before the first lighthouse was built here in 1822, there was a beacon on the headland to warn and guide passing ships away from the rocks. The present 99ft high lighthouse dates from 1866-7, built after an earlier one was destroyed by fire.

St Bees Head is now an important Nature Reserve and the cliffs are crowded with guillemots, razorbills, kittiwakes, gulls, gannets and skuas. Bird watchers are well-provided for with observation and information points all along the headland. There is a superb walk of about eight miles along the coastal footpath around the headland from St Bees to Whitehaven. The route passes Saltam Bay and Saltam Pit, which dates from 1729 and was the world's first undersea mineshaft. The original lamp house for the pit has been restored and is now used by HM Coastguard.

St Bees itself is a delightful place to explore, with its main street winding up the hillside between old farms and cottages. The Priory at St Bees grew in size and importance until it was destroyed by the Danes in the 10th century: the Benedictines later re-established the priory in 1129. **The Priory Church of St Mary and St Bega** is all that is now left and although it has been substantially altered there is still a magnificent Norman arch and a pre-Conquest carved Beowulf Stone on a lintel between the church and the vicarage, showing St Michael killing a dragon. The most stunning feature of all is much more modern, a sumptuous art nouveau metalwork screen. In the south aisle is a small museum.

Close by the church are the charming Abbey Cottages and St Bees School with its handsome clock tower. The school was founded in 1583 by Edmund Grindal,

Archbishop of Canterbury under Elizabeth I, and the son of a local farmer. The original red sandstone quadrangle bears his coat of arms and the bridge he gave to the village is still in use. Among the school's most famous alumni is the actor and comedian Rowan Atkinson, creator of the ineffable Mr Bean.

CLEATOR MOOR

3 miles SE of Whitehaven on the B5295

Kangol Factory Shop

Cleator developed rapidly in the 19th century because of the insatiable demand during the Industrial Revolution for coal and iron ore. As the Cumbrian poet Norman Nicholson wrote:

From one shaft at Cleator Moor
They mined for coal and iron ore.
This harvest below ground could show
Black and red currants on one tree.

Cleator is surrounded by delightful countryside and little evidence of the town's industrial past is visible. But there is a thriving business nearby - the **Kangol Factory Shop** in Cleator village, which stocks a huge range of hats, scarves, bags, caps and golf wear.

ENNERDALE BRIDGE

7 miles E of Whitehaven off the A5086

Ennerdale Water

The bridge here crosses the River Ehen, which, a couple of miles upstream, runs out from **Ennerdale Water**, one of the most secluded and inaccessible of all the Cumbrian lakes. The walks around this tranquil lake and through the quiet woodlands amply repay the slight effort of leaving the car at a distance. The Coast to Coast Walk runs the whole length of Ennerdale and this section is generally considered to be by far the most beautiful.

Cockermouth

Wordsworth House · William Wordsworth

Cockermouth Castle · Castlegate House

Toy and Model Museum · Jennings Brewery

Kirkgate Centre · Printing House Museum

Percy House Gallery

Lakeland Sheep & Wool Centre

A market town since 1226, Cockermouth has been fortunate in keeping unspoilt its broad main street, lined with trees and handsome Georgian houses, and dominated by a statue to the Earl of Mayo. The earl was Cockermouth's MP for 10 years from 1858 before being appointed Viceroy of India. His brilliant career was brutally cut short when he was stabbed to death by a convict at a prison settlement he was inspecting on the Andaman Islands.

But Cockermouth boasts two far more famous sons. Did they ever meet, one wonders, those two young lads growing up in

Wordsworth House, Cockermouth

NEO'S BOOKSHOP CAFÉ GALLERY

25-31 Market Place, Cockermouth,
Cumbria CA13 9NH
Tel: 01900 829900
e-mail: info@neo-bookshop.co.uk
website: www.neo-bookshop.co.uk

In recent years, the area around Cockermouth's Market Place has developed into something of a cultural enclave. A flourishing arts centre - The Kirkgate Arts Centre - is located here and there are four independent galleries situated 'on or over the bridge', which spans the River Cocker. The most recent of these is Debbie Taylor and Ryan Griffiths' excellent **Neo's Bookshop Café Gallery**, which opened in July 2004 and has come to be thought upon as a venue. Neo's sell inspiring books with an emphasis on the arts, design and humanities. The owners love beautiful books and, alongside well-known publishers' titles, are ever-sourcing out-of-the-ordinary titles that you wouldn't easily find on the high street. These include collectables like 'Artist's Books'; rare and out-of-print books and books from small, independent presses. Some of the books on sale are secondhand. The range of quality publications is increasing all of the time to include books on fantastic architecture, Japanese illustration, interior design, garden and landscape design, photographic portfolios and poetry and prose collections.

Books aside, Neo's also sell cards and stationery, ever-sourcing new and original cards and postcards with the aim of promoting the work of contemporary artists and designers. Notwithstanding cards and postcards, Neo's don't sell mass-produced prints or reproductions of images, which are, in actual fact, posters. Rather, they sell original printmaking that has been handmade. They also have a selection of music from small, independent labels.

Neo's Gallery hosts regularly changing exhibitions of original art, but workshops, evening events and not-for-profit events in collaboration with local and nationwide organisations also take place during the summer and autumn.

The Market Place itself, taking in the Castlegate and Kirkgate areas too, is an ideal meeting place for cultural activities and events precisely because of the cluster of galleries, the Arts Centre, and other social meeting places such as wine bars, pubs and restaurants. "There is a really fantastic community of people here," says Debbie. "It is a friendly and supportive area, and all of these aspects signify the creative and cultural dynamic of this unique town."

Cockermouth in the 1770s, both of them destined to become celebrated for very different reasons? The elder boy was Fletcher Christian, who would later lead the mutiny on the *Bounty;* the younger lad was William Wordsworth, born in 1770 at Lowther House on Main Street, an imposing Georgian house now maintained by the National Trust. Now known as **Wordsworth House**, it was built in 1745 for the Sheriff of Cumberland and then purchased by the Earl of Lowther; he let it to his land agent, John Wordsworth, William's father. All five Wordsworth children were born here, William on 7th April 1770. Many of the building's original features survive, among them the staircase, fireplace, and fine plaster ceilings. A few of the poet's personal effects still remain; costumed actors provide insights into what life was like then. The delightful walled garden by the River Cocker has been returned to its Georgian splendour. The garden is referred to in *The Prelude*.

Built in 1134 by the Earl of Dunbar, **Cockermouth Castle** saw plenty of action against Scottish raiders (Robert the Bruce himself gave it a mauling in 1315), and again during the Wars of the Roses; in the course of the Civil War it was occupied by both sides in turn. Mary, Queen of Scots, took refuge at the castle in 1568 after her defeat at the Battle of Langside. Her fortunes were so low that she was grateful for the gift of 16 ells (about 20 yards) of rich crimson velvet from a wealthy merchant. Part of the castle is still lived in by the Egremont family; the remainder is usually only open to the public during the Cockermouth Festival in July.

ANNABELLES

80 Main Street, Cockermouth, Cumbria CA13 9LU
Tel: 01900 825338

High-fashion ladies' clothes, shoes and accessories from leading designers can all be found at **Annabelles,** a stylish shop on Cockermouth's Main Street. It's owned and run by Anne Trafford who has gathered together a huge range of absolute 'must-have' items. There's cashmere knitwear from Magaschoni, Escada sportswear, Lejaby underwear and beautiful creations from Crea Concept, Michael Ambers, Marina Auraam, Frank Usher, Betty Barclay, Mariella Rosati, Kapalua and Caractere. There's also a wide choice of accessories including jewellery, scarves and belts.

Friendly and helpful staff add to the pleasure of shopping here. Annabelles is actually two shops with Anne's mother and father running David's Shoes where you'll find another amazing collection, this time of shoes from all around the world. There are shoes for fashionable occasions, shoes for comfort, shoes for the working day. Taken together, Annabelles and David's Shoes can kit you out completely!

Opposite the castle entrance, **Castlegate House** is a fine Georgian house, built in 1739, which hosts a changing programme of monthly exhibitions of the work of mostly Northern and Scottish artists - paintings, sculptures, ceramics and glass. To the rear of the house is a charming walled garden, which is open from time to time during the summer.

Just around the corner from Castlegate House is the **Toy and Model Museum**, which exhibits mainly British toys from around 1900 to the present day. There are many visitor operated displays including 0 and 00 gauge vintage tinplate trains, Scalextric cars, Lego models and even a 1950s helicopter that can fly. There are prams and dolls' houses, and a working railway in a garden shed.

Almost next door, **Jennings Brewery** offers visitors a 90-minute tour, which ends with the option of sampling some of their ales - Cumberland Ale, Cocker Hoop or the intriguingly named Sneck Lifter. The last independent brewing company in Cumbria, Jennings have been brewing traditional beers since the 1820s and today there are more than 100 Jennings pubs across the north of England.

A short walk from the Brewery brings you to the **Kirkgate Centre**, which is housed in a converted Victorian primary school. Run by volunteers, the Centre offers a wide range of events and activities including live music, amateur and professional drama, films, dance, workshops, exhibitions of art and local history.

The **Printing House Museum** occupies a building dating back to the 16th century and follows the progress of printing from its invention by Johann Gutenberg in 1430 to the end of the letterpress era in the 1960s, when computers took over. On display is a wide range of historical presses and printing equipment, the earliest being a Cogger Press dated 1820. Visitors are offered the opportunity to gain hands-on experience by using some of the presses to produce cards or keepsakes.

Another ancient building is Percy House in the Market Place. It was built in 1598 for Henry Percy, 9th Earl of Northumberland. Many of the original features still remain including the flagged stone floor, oak beams and fireplaces. The house is now home to the **Percy House Gallery**, which has an interesting collection of arts and crafts on display. These include jewellery, textiles, glassware, ceramics, metalware, paintings and photographs.

Located just south of the town, the **Lakeland Sheep and Wool Centre** provides an introduction to life in the Cumbrian countryside with the help of a spectacular visual show, 19 different breeds of live sheep and a wide variety of exhibits. The Centre also hosts indoor sheepdog trials and sheep-shearing displays for which there is a small charge. The Centre has a large gift shop selling sheepskins and various 'sheepy' gifts, and a café.

Around Cockermouth

BRIDEKIRK

2 miles N of Cockermouth off the A595

Carved Font

The village church contains one of the finest pieces of Norman sculpture in the country, a **Carved Font** with a runic inscription and a mass of detailed embellishments. It dates from the 12th century and the runic

HUDDLESTONE COTTAGE AND THE HAYLOFT

Redmain House, Redmain, Cockermouth, Cumbria CA13 0PZ
Tel: 01900 825695 e-mail: chris@lakesnw.co.uk
website: www.lakesnw.co.uk/hudcot

Huddlestone Cottage and The Hayloft are the appealing names chosen by owner Christine Neale for her two self-catering cottages located in a quiet rural hamlet within the Lake District National Park. These charming properties have been converted from stone barns attached to a traditional Cumbrian long house dating from the 1690s. Redmain House and the cottages stand in three acres of grounds and landscaped gardens that rise gently behind the house to give wonderful views over the Cockermouth valley towards Skiddaw and Grassmoor.

Huddlestone Cottage has a large open-plan living, dining and kitchen area with open log fire and some original stone walls. There's a downstairs shower and cloakroom. A pine staircase leads upstairs where there is a spacious master bedroom with king-size bed, exposed beams and stone wall with window seat. A second large bedroom has twin beds. There is also another full bathroom. The Hayloft has a separate split barn door with stairs leading to a very attractive large open-plan living room with kitchen on one side, separate bedroom with another king-size bed and separate bathroom. French doors look out directly to the garden. These properties have bags of country atmosphere with all mod cons and the wildlife friendly garden is a real treat with picnic areas, bbq's, woodland copse, flower borders, herb garden, small orchard and extensive vegetable garden.

inscription states that:

Richard he me wrought
And to this beauty eagerly me brought.

Richard himself is shown on one side with a chisel and mallet. Not only is this a superb example of early English craftsmanship, but it is exceedingly rare to find a signed work from this period. Ancient tombstones stand round the walls of this cruciform church and inside it has an unusual reredos of fleur-de-lys patterned tiles.

LINSKELDFIELD

6 miles NE of Cockermouth off the A595 or A591

Linskeldfield Tarn Nature Reserve

Opened in 2005, **Linskeldfield Tarn Nature Reserve** is home to a great variety of birds including goldeneye, European widgeon, shovellers, pintail, little grebe, whooper swan and cormorant. With Skiddaw as a backdrop, the six-acre site of peat and wetland also shelters otters, red squirrels and carp. There's a custom-built 12-person birdwatching hide and free parking. The tarn is easily accessible from the nearby osprey watching centre at Dodd Wood.

HIGH & LOW LORTON

5 miles SE of Cockermouth on the B5289

There is a yew tree, pride of Lorton Vale... wrote Wordsworth in his poem *Yew Trees*, and astonishingly it's still there behind the village hall of High Lorton. It was in its shade that the Quaker George Fox preached to a large gathering under the watchful eye of

Cromwell's soldiers. In its sister village, Low Lorton, set beside the River Cocker, is Lorton Hall (private), which is reputed to be home to the ghost of a woman who carries a lighted candle. Less spectral guests in the past have included King Malcolm III of Scotland, who stayed here with his queen while visiting the southern boundaries of his Kingdom of Strathclyde of which this area was a part.

EAGLESFIELD

2 miles SW of Cockermouth off the A5086

John Dalton

The most famous son of this small village is **John Dalton**, who was born here in 1766. The son of Quaker parents, Dalton was teaching at the village school by the time he was 12. Despite having had no formal education himself, he became one of the most brilliant scientists, naturalists and mathematicians of his age, and was the originator of the theory that all matter is composed of small indestructible particles called atoms. He was also the first to recognise the existence of colour blindness. He suffered from it himself and in medical circles it is known as Daltonism. A memorial to this remarkable man now marks the house where he lived in Eaglesfield.

BRIGHAM

2 miles W of Cockermouth off the A66

St Bridget's Church   Fletcher Christian

St Bridget's Church, which was probably founded as part of a nunnery, contains many interesting features, including pre-Norman carved stones, a rare 'fish window' and a window dedicated to the Rev John Wordsworth, son of William and vicar of Brigham for 40 years. One of the tombs in the graveyard is that of Charles Christian, the father of **Fletcher Christian**, the *Bounty* mutineer. Fletcher himself was baptised in the church on the day of his birth as it was thought unlikely that he would survive.

Workington

Workington Hall   Mary, Queen of Scots

Helena Thompson Museum

Church of St John the Evangelist

Harrington Reservoir Nature Reserve

The largest town on the Cumbrian coast, Workington stands at the mouth of the River Derwent and on the site of the Roman fort of Gabrosentum. Its prosperity was founded on the three great Cumbrian industries - coal, iron and shipping. In later years, Workington became famous for its fine quality steel, especially after Henry Bessemer developed his revolutionary steel making process here in 1850.

The seat of the Curwen family for more than 600 years, **Workington Hall** has an interesting history. Originally built around a 14th-century pele tower, the hall was developed over the years with extensive alterations being made in the 18th century by the then lord of the manor, John Christian Curwen. Now a stabilised ruin, it has several commemorative plaques that give a taste of the hall's history. The most famous visitor was **Mary, Queen of Scots** who sought refuge here when she fled from Scotland in 1558. She stayed for a few days during which time she wrote the famous letter to her cousin Elizabeth I bemoaning her fate, *"for I am in a pitiable condition.... having nothing in the world but the clothes in which I escaped"*, and asking the queen *"to have compassion on my great misfortunes"*. The letter is now in the British Museum.

Just across the road from Workington Hall is the **Helena Thompson Museum**, which tells the story of Workington's coal mining, ship-building, and iron and steel industries for which the town became internationally renowned. The Georgian Room gives an insight into the variety of decorative styles that were popular between 1714 and 1830, with displays of beautiful cut-glass tableware, porcelain from China, and period pieces of furniture. Bequeathed to the town by the local philanthropist Miss Helena Thompson, the museum was opened in 1949 and contains some of her own family heirlooms. One particularly interesting exhibit is the Clifton Dish, a locally produced 18th-century piece of slipware pottery, while further displays demonstrate the links between this local industry and the famous Staffordshire pottery families.

Fashionistas will be interested in the display of women's and children's dresses from the 1700s to the early 1900s, together with accessories and jewellery.

Workington's **Church of St John the Evangelist** is a very grand affair built at enormous expense in 1823 to give thanks for the defeat of Napoleon at Waterloo. It is a copy of St Paul's, Covent Garden, and its walls were built with stones from the local Schoose and Hunday quarries. The interior was splendidly restored by Sir Ninian Comper in 1931. St Michael's is the ancient parish church, restored after a fire in 1994.

Workington is at the start of the C2C (Coast to Coast) cycle route that runs to Sunderland and Newcastle. A short distance south of town is **Harrington Reservoir Nature Reserve**, a haven for wildlife with a rich variety of wild flowers, insects, butterflies, birds and animals.

Around Workington

MARYPORT

6 miles NE of Workington on the A596

Senhouse Roman Museum | Maritime Museum

Lake District Coast Aquarium

Dramatically located on the Solway Firth, Maryport is a charming Cumbrian coastal town rich in interest and maritime history. The old part is full of narrow streets and neoclassical, Georgian architecture, which contrast with sudden, surprising views of the sea. Some of the first visitors to Maryport were the Romans, who built a clifftop fort here, Alauna, which is now part of the Hadrian's Wall World Heritage Site. The award-winning **Senhouse Roman Museum** tells the story of life in this outpost of the

Maritime Museum, Maryport

empire. Housed in the striking Naval Reserve Battery, built in the 1880s, the museum holds the largest collection of Roman altars from a single site in Britain.

Modern Maryport dates from the 18th century when Humphrey Senhouse, a local landowner, developed the harbour at what was then called Ellenport to export coal from his mines, and named the new port after his wife, Mary. Over the next century it became a busy port as well as a ship-building centre; boats had to be launched broadside because of the narrowness of the harbour channel. The town declined, along with the mining industry, from the 1930s onwards. It nevertheless attracted the artist LS Lowry, who was a frequent visitor and loved painting the harbour. Today, Maryport is enjoying a well-earned revival, with newly restored Georgian quaysides, clifftop paths, sandy beaches and a harbour with fishing boats.

The town's extensive maritime history is preserved in the vast array of objects, pictures and models on display at the **Maritime Museum** overlooking the harbour. Housed in another of Maryport's more interesting and historic buildings, the former Queen's Head public house, the museum tells of the rise and fall of the harbour and docks. Other exhibits include a brass telescope from the *Cutty Sark* and the town's connections with the ill-fated liner, the *Titanic*, and with Fletcher Christian, instigator of the mutiny on the *Bounty*. The *Titanic* was part of the fleet of the White Star Line, which was founded by a Maryport man, Thomas Henry Ismay; Fletcher Christian was also more or less a local man, being born at nearby Brigham in 1764.

Close by is **The Lake District Coast Aquarium** (see panel below), where a series of spectacular living habitat re-creations

The Lake District Coast Aquarium

South Quay, Maryport, Cumbria CA15 8AB
Tel: 01900 817760
e-mail: info@ld-coastaquarium.co.uk
website: www.lakedistrict-coastaquarium.co.uk

The Lake District Coast Aquarium was built in 1997 using private funding with support from the European Regional Development Fund. It has a wonderful position on the South Quay of Maryport Harbour, affording views out across the Solway Firth to Scotland on most days. The harbour area has received substantial public investment from the mid-1980s onwards as part of a regeneration programme following the closure of local coal mining, steel making and shipbuilding, and tourism was seen as having a vital part in this.

The 45 displays that make up the live exhibition all contain local or Irish Sea species, as well as a wide variety of shellfish and invertebrates. It is rated as being one of the best places to go to see native sealife now that most other aquariums have diversified into being eclectic selections of world-wide species. In order to broaden the appeal of the attraction, and make it possible to stay all day, there is a highly rated integral café overlooking the harbour, a well stocked gift shop, a 12-hole crazy golf course, a radio control boat pool and water cannon game, and an extensive adjacent free adventure play park.

introduces visitors to the profusion of marine life found in the Solway Firth - thornback rays (which can be touched), some small sharks, spider crabs and the comically ugly tompot blenny among them. Also on site are a Harbourside Café, Gift Shop, radio-controlled model boat pool and miniature golf.

DEARHAM

9 miles NE of Workington off the A594

Lakeland Heavy Horse Centre

The **Lakeland Heavy Horse Centre** provides an opportunity of getting close to these magnificent beasts, learn about their lives and witness some of the work they do. Breeds on show here include Clydesdales, Shires, Percherons, Ardennes and the very rare Suffolk Punch. Cart and trap rides are available, there's a café and gift shop, pets' corner, an attractive play area and playground equipment, and picnic facilities.

ASPATRIA

14 miles NE of Workington on the A596

Memorial Fountain | Sir Wilfred Lawson

Norman Church

Lying above the shallow Ellen Valley, Aspatria's main interest for most visitors lies in the elaborate **Memorial Fountain** to 'Watery Wilfred', Sir Wilfred Lawson MP (1829-1906), a lifelong crusader for the Temperance Movement and International Peace. According to one writer, "No man in his day made more people laugh at Temperance meetings". Also worth a visit is the much restored **Norman Church** that is entered through a fine avenue of yew trees. Inside are several ancient relics including a 12th-century font with intricate carvings, a Viking hogback tombstone, and a grave cover with a pagan swastika engraving.

ALLONBY

11 miles N of Workington on the B5300

Allerdale Way

This traditional Solway village is backed by the Lake District fells and looks out across the Solway Firth to the Scottish hills. Popular with wind-surfers, the village has an attractive shingle and sand beach, which received a Seaside Award in 1998. The **Allerdale Way** and the Cumbrian Cycle Way both pass close by, and the village is also on the **Smuggler's Route** trail. Smuggling seems to have been a profitable occupation around here - a government enquiry into contraband trade reported in 1730 that "the Solway people were the first working-class folk to drink tea regularly in Britain".

In the early 1800s, Allonby was a popular sea-bathing resort and the former seawater baths, built in 1835 and now Grade II listed buildings, still stand in the old Market Square. In those days, the upper floor was in regular use as a ballroom for the local nobility. Allonby still keeps much of its Georgian and early Victorian charm with cobbled lanes, alleyways, and some interesting old houses. It was also an important centre for herring fishing and some of the old kippering houses can still be seen.

HOLME ST CUTHBERT

14 miles N of Workington off the B5300

Tarns Dub

This inland hamlet is also known as Rowks because, in the Middle Ages, there was a chapel here dedicated to St Roche. Northeast of the hamlet, and enveloped among low hills, is a lovely 30-acre lake known as **Tarns Dub**, which is a haven for birdlife. A couple of miles to the southwest, the headland of

Dubmill Point is popular with sea anglers. When the tide is high and driven by a fresh westerly wind, the sea covers the road with lashing waves.

MAWBRAY HAYRIGG

14 miles N of Workington off the B5300

The Gincase

This small village is home to **The Gincase**, a family attraction with a Children's Rare Breed Farm Animal Park where children can pet the animals, walk through the large parrot aviary, let off steam in the indoor and outdoor playgrounds and release more energy on the pedal go-carts. The site also has a Craft Barn selling quality handmade Cumbrian crafts, an Art Gallery that mounts regular exhibitions of work by Cumbrian artists, and a Farmhouse Tearoom serving delicious homemade food.

BECKFOOT

16 miles N of Workington on the B5300

Bibra Bank Mill Experience

At certain times and tides, the remains of a prehistoric forest can be seen on the sand beds here. To the south of the village is the site of a 2nd-century Roman fort known as **Bibra**. According to an inscribed stone found here, it was once occupied by an Auxiliary Cohort of 500 Pannonians (Spaniards) and surrounded by a large civilian settlement. The small stream flowing into the sea was used in World War I as a fresh water supply by German U-boats.

A mile or so south of Beckfoot is the **Bank Mill Experience**, which promises a great day out for all the family. The site contains a Tropical Butterfly House, home to the largest number of species of butterfly and moth in the world; a lizard house with species from all around the world; and a Nature Reserve that provides a refuge for the endangered natterjack toads. Foxes and badgers can also be seen and there's a hide for birdwatchers. Also on site is a coffee shop, a licensed restaurant open evenings only, and a plant nursery.

SILLOTH

18 miles N of Workington on the B5300

Solway Coast Discovery Centre

This charming old port and Victorian seaside resort is well worth exploring and its two-mile-long promenade provides wonderful views of the Solway Firth and the coast of Scotland. With the coming of the railways in the 1850s, Silloth developed as a port and railhead for Carlisle. The Railway Company helped to develop the town and had grey granite shipped over in its own vessels from Ireland to build the handsome church that is such a prominent landmark. The region's bracing air and low rainfall helped to make Silloth a popular seaside resort. Visitors today will appreciate the invigorating but mild climate, the leisurely atmosphere, and the glorious sunsets over the sea that inspired Turner to record them for posterity. The town remains a delightful place to stroll, to admire the sunken rose garden, the pinewoods and the busy dock where local fishermen offload their catches of Solway shrimps.

Silloth's 18-hole golf course was the 'home course' where Miss Cecil Leitch (1891-1978), the most celebrated woman golfer of her day, used to play. Another keen woman golfer was the great contralto, Kathleen Ferrier, who stayed in the town for part of her tragically short life. One of the most popular attractions is the **Solway Coast Discovery Centre**, where Auld Michael the Monk and Oyk the Oystercatcher guide visitors through

10,000 years of Solway Coast history. There's also a mini-cinema presenting a film tour of the Solway Coast Area of Outstanding Natural Beauty.

Wigton

Olenacum

For centuries, Wigton has been the centre of the business and social life of the Solway coast and plain, its prosperity being based on the weaving of cotton and linen. It has enjoyed the benefits of a Royal Charter since 1262 and the market is still held on Tuesdays. Horse sales are held every April (riding horses and ponies) and October (Clydesdales, heavy horses and ponies). Today, most of the old town is a Conservation Area and, particularly along the Main Street, the upper storeys of the houses have survived in an almost unaltered state. On street corners, metal guards to prevent heavy horse-drawn wagons damaging the walls can still be seen.

One mile south of Wigton are the scant remains of the Roman fort of **Olenacum**; most of its stones were removed to rebuild Wigton in the 18th and 19th centuries.

Around Wigton

ABBEYTOWN

5 miles W of Wigton on the B5302

Abbey of Holm Cultram Church of St Mary

As its name suggests, Abbeytown grew up around the 12th-century **Abbey of Holm Cultram** on the River Waver and many of the

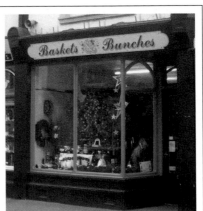

JEWELLERY BY MICHAEL KING

West Woodside, nr Wigton, Cumbria CA7 0LP
Tel: 01697 345889
e-mail: angela@angelaking9.wanadoo.co.uk
website: www.kingjewellery.com

At **Jewellery by Michael King** in the village of West Woodside, visitors will find a display of exquisite craftsmanship and design in gold, silver and precious stones.

Michael was born in Kent and trained at Medway College of Art before working for the internationally acclaimed designer/silversmith Christopher Lawrence. A Fellow of the Institute of Professional Goldsmiths, Michael has been working in Cumbria since 1982. In 2001, he opened his spacious gallery showcasing a wide range of gold and silver pieces.

During the past 20 years Michael has completed many important commissions. Among them have been a series of ornate weapons recalling the wonderful workmanship of the early Britons for the film *The Lost Kingdom*, commissioned for the Rheged Centre near Penrith, Cumbria. He was more recently commissioned to copy the beautiful cross of St Cuthbert, kept in the treasury of Durham Cathedral, for a film about the life of the saint.

Wedding and engagement rings and decorative jewellery form a basis of much of Michael King's work and Celtic art has been a strong influence. His showroom is open from 10am to 5pm, Monday to Friday, and from 10am to 2pm on Saturdays. Other times by appointment.

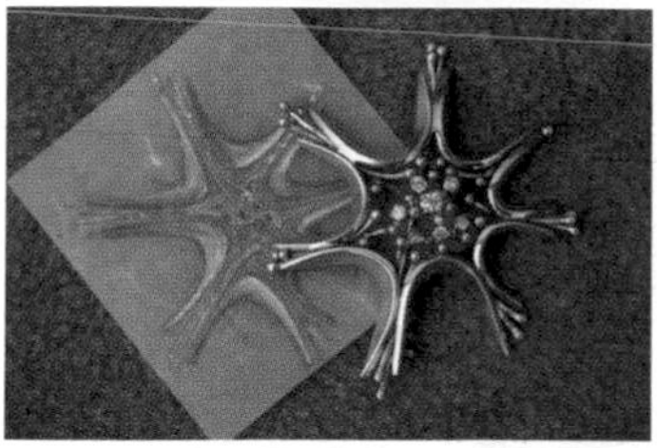

town's buildings are constructed of stone taken from the abbey when it fell into ruins. The red sandstone **Church of St Mary** is still the parish church and was restored in 1883, a strange yet impressive building with the original nave shorn of its tower, transepts and chancel. The east and west walls are heavily buttressed, and a porch with a new roof protects the original Norman arch of the west door. Within the church buildings is a room, opened by Princess Margaret in 1973, which contains the gravestones of Robert the Bruce's father. Nearby, there are some lovely walks along the River Waver, which is particularly rich in wildlife.

SKINBURNESS

11 miles W of Wigton off the B5302

Allerdale Ramble   Grune Point

A lively market town, in the Middle Ages, Skinburness was used by Edward I in 1299 as a base for his navy when attacking the Scots. A few years later a terrible storm destroyed the town and what survived became a small fishing hamlet. From nearby Grune Point, the start of the **Allerdale Ramble**, there are some tremendous views over the Solway Firth and the beautiful, desolate expanse of marshland and sandbank. **Grune Point**, which was once the site of a Roman fort, now forms part of a designated Site of Special Scientific Interest notable for the variety of its birdlife and marsh plants.

NEWTON ARLOSH

5 miles NW of Wigton on the B5307

Fortified Church

Situated on the Solway marshes, the village was first established by the monks of Holm Cultram Abbey in 1307 after the old port at Skinburness had been destroyed by the sea. The village church is one of the most delightful examples of a Cumbrian **Fortified Church**. In the Middle Ages, there was no castle nearby to protect the local population from the border raids and so a pele tower was added to the church. As an additional defensive measure, the builders created what is believed to be the narrowest church doorway in the country, barely two feet seven inches across and a little over five feet high. The 12-inch arrow-slot east window is also the smallest in England. After the Reformation, the church became derelict but was finally restored in the 19th century. Inside, there is a particularly fine eagle lectern carved out of bog oak.

Newton Arlosh Church

Keswick and the Northern Lakes

For many visitors this part of the county is classic Lakeland, the scenery dominated by the rounded, heather-clad slopes of the Skiddaw range to the north of Keswick, and the wild, craggy mountains of Borrowdale, to the south. Yet, despite this area's popularity, there are still many hidden places to discover and many opportunities to leave the beaten track.

The major town, Keswick, on the shores of Derwent Water, is a pleasant Lakeland town that has much to offer the visitor. The lake too, is interesting as, not only is it in a near perfect setting, but it is unusual in having some islands - in this case four. It was the view over the lake from Friar's Crag that formed one of John Ruskin's early childhood memories. The area is also rich in history, from prehistoric times through Roman occupation to the period of industrial growth.

The Lakeland Fells are home to Herdwick sheep, one of the country's hardiest breeds. Their coarse fleece cannot be dyed, but Herdwick sheep of various ages yield wool in a variety of subtle shades of grey and black which produces an unusual and very durable tweed-like weave.

Keswick

- Castlerigg Stone Circle · Moot Hall
- Museum and Art Gallery · Rock, Bell & Steel Band
- Cumberland Pencil Museum
- Keswick Mining Museum · The Teapottery
- The Puzzling Place · Cars of the Stars
- Theatre by the Lake · Derwent Island House
- Friar's Crag

For generations, visitors to Keswick have been impressed by the town's stunningly beautiful setting, surrounded by the great fells of Saddleback, Helvellyn and Grizedale Pike. Tourism, now the town's major industry, actually began in the mid-1700s and was given a huge boost by the Lakeland Poets in the early 1800s. The arrival of the railway in 1865 firmly established Keswick as the undisputed 'capital' of the Lake District, with most of the area's notable attractions within easy reach.

The grandeur of the lakeland scenery is of course the greatest draw but, among the man-made features, one not to be missed is the well-preserved **Castlerigg Stone Circle**. About a mile to the east of the town, the 38 standing stones, some of them eight feet high, form a circle 100 feet in diameter. They are believed to have been put in place some 4000 years ago and occupy a hauntingly beautiful position. Beautiful, but forbidding, as evoked by Keats in his poem *Hyperion*:

A dismal cirque of Druid stones, upon
a forlorn moor,
When the chill rain begins at shut of eve,
In dull November, and their chancel vault,
The Heaven itself, is blinded throughout night.

Keswick old town developed along the banks of the broad River Greta, with a wide main street leading up to the attractive **Moot Hall**, which now houses the town's and the National Park's tourist information centres. A little further south, in St John's Street, the church of that name was built in the very same year as the Moot Hall and its elegant spire provides a point of reference from all around the town. In the churchyard is the grave of Sir Hugh Walpole, whose once hugely popular series of novels, *The Herries Chronicle* (1930-33), is set in this part of the Lake District.

In the riverside Fitz Park is the town's **Museum and Art Gallery**, which is well worth a visit not just to see original manuscripts by Wordsworth and other lakeland poets, but also for the astonishing **Rock, Bell and Steel Band** created by Joseph Richardson of Skiddaw in the 19th century. Variously described as a stone dulcimer, rock harmonicon or geological piano, it's a kind of xylophone made of 60 stones (some a yard long), 60 steel bars and 40 bells. Four 'musicians' are required to play this extraordinary

Castlerigg Stone Circle

MIMOSA

22 Station Street, Keswick,
Cumbria, C12 5HF
Tel: 01768 780332
Fax: 01768 780233
e-mail: tracy@mimosaflorists.co.uk

Tracy Baker developed her talent for an eye-catching display as a window dresser for a fashion chain store before deciding to train as a florist over 10 years ago. Tracy's work for a variety of florists since then, has eventually led her to opening up her own shop, '**Mimosa**'.

Located in Station Street, not far from the busy centre of the town, this sensational shop is overwhelmingly colourful and fragrant with blooms and plants of all imaginable colours, sizes and varieties. You are greeted with warmth and a personal service that comes only from a true love of creating something beautiful for the pleasure of others.

A very interesting and creative approach to flower design and arrangement is taken at Mimosa. In addition to the more traditional displays, much of Tracy's work has a continental flavour to it resulting in a range of unique floral tributes that will appeal to the tastes of all.

Mimosa can boast the full compliment of florist services including displays, bouquets and buttonholes for weddings, providing flowers for hotels and businesses and ensuring that all your special occasions can be remembered with a handmade bouquet brought personally to your door by the exceptional delivery service.

However, the shopping experience isn't limited simply to flowers. Mimosa also offers a wide variety of quality giftware some of which has been carefully selected from the continent. Other items available include handmade jewellery, prints and paintings from locally based artists, vases, handmade greeting cards and many different gifts from local craftsmen.

Another string to the bow of Mimosa is the fantastic range of organic fruit & vegetables available. You can enjoy the fresh, seasonal produce safe in the knowledge that it is wholesome, healthy and supports independent growers.

instrument. The instrument was once taken to London where performances were given to Queen Victoria.

Surrounded by a loop of the River Greta to the northwest of the town is a museum that must be pencilled in on any visit to Keswick. This is the **Cumberland Pencil Museum**, which boasts the six feet long 'Largest Pencil in the World'. The 'lead' used in pencils (not lead at all but actually an allotrope of carbon) was accidentally discovered by a Borrowdale shepherd in the 16th century and Keswick eventually became the world centre for the manufacture of lead pencils. The pencil mill here, established in 1832, is still operating although the wadd, or lead, is now imported.

At the **Keswick Mining Museum** nine rooms are filled with exhibits portraying Cumbria's mining history from the Stone Age to the present day. For an additional small fee, visitors can try their hand at panning for gold. The museum also has a shop selling new and second-hand books on topics related to mining.

Other attractions in the town centre include the **Cars of the Stars Museum**, home to such gems as Laurel and Hardy's Model T Ford, James Bond's Aston Martin, Chitty Chitty Bang Bang, Batman's Batmobile, Lady Penelope's pink Rolls-Royce FAB 1, the Mad Max car, Mr Bean's Mini and Harry Potter's Ford Anglia. There are film set displays and vehicles from series such as *The Saint*, *Knightrider*, *Bergerac* and *Postman Pat*, and Del Boy's 3-wheel Reliant from *Only Fools and Horses* is there, too.

The Teapottery makes and sells a bizarre range of practical teapots in the shape of anything from an upright piano to an Aga stove. Keswick's most recent visitor attraction to open is **The Puzzling Place**, an ingenious display of mind-bending illusions, including computer video clips, three-dimensional holograms and an anti-gravity room where everything you've learned about gravity will be turned on its head as you watch water flow uphill and other impossibilities. There's also a large selection of puzzles, brain-teasers and associated novelty goods on sale.

A short walk from the town centre, along Lake Road, leads visitors to the popular **Theatre by the Lake**, which hosts a year-round programme of plays, concerts, exhibitions, readings and talks. Close by is the pier from which there are regular departures for cruises around Derwentwater and ferries across the lake to Nichol End where you can hire just about every kind of water craft, including your own private cruise boat. One trip is to the National Trust's **Derwent Island House**, an Italianate house of the 1840s on an idyllic wooded island. Entry is by timed ticket only.

Another short walk will bring the visitor to **Friar's Crag**. This famous view of Derwent Water and its islands, now National Trust property, formed one of John Ruskin's early childhood memories, inspiring in him "intense joy, mingled with awe". Inscribed on his memorial here are these words: "The first thing which I remember as an event in life was being taken by my nurse to the brow of Friar's Crag on Derwentwater." The Crag is dedicated to the memory of Canon Rawnsley, the local vicar who was one of the founder members of the National Trust, which he helped to set up in 1895.

Keswick is host to several annual festivals, covering films, Cumbrian literature, jazz and beer. And on the first Sunday in December a colourful Christmassy Fayre is held in the Market Place.

Around Keswick

THRELKELD

3 miles E of Keswick off the A66

Blencathra | Threlkeld Quarry & Mining Museum

From Keswick there's a delightful walk along the track bed of the old railway line to the charming village of Threlkeld, set in a plain at the foot of mighty **Blencathra**. The village is the ideal starting point for a number of mountain walks, including an ascent of Blencathra, one of the most exciting of all the Lake District mountains. Threlkeld is famous for its annual sheepdog trials, though its economy was built up on the several mines in the area and the granite quarry to the south. At **Threlkeld Quarry & Mining Museum** (see panel below) visitors can browse through the collection of vintage excavators, old quarry machinery and other mining artefacts, wander through the locomotive shed and machine shop, or join the 40-minute tour through a re-created mine. The museum has interpretive displays of Lakeland geology and quarrying and is used as a teaching facility by several university geology departments.

MATTERDALE END

8 miles E of Keswick on the A5091

This tiny hamlet lies at one end of Matterdale, a valley that is an essential stop on any Wordsworth trail: it was here, on April 15th 1802, that he and his sister saw that immortal

Host of golden daffodils,
Beside the lake,
beneath the trees,
Fluttering and dancing in the breeze.

Threlkeld Mining Museum

Threlkeld Quarry, Keswick, Cumbria CA12 4TT
Tel: 01768 779747/01228 561883
website: www.threlkeldminingmuseum.co.uk

The Threlkeld Quarry & Mining Museum is situated three miles east of Keswick, in the heart of the breathtaking Lake District in Cumbria. The quarry and museum have been lovingly run by knowledgeable and dedicated staff for more than 10 years, and the site continues to expand through the dedication of the staff and volunteers. The quarry itself is a RIGS site and displays contacts between the "Skiddaw Slate" and the granite intrusion, as well as other fascinating features.

The museum now has a new mining section, which has been developed with the help and cooperation of the Cumbria Amenity Trust Mining History Society and a number of individuals. The Mining Room contains artefacts, plans and photographic records of explorations of many local mines, which, in this area, exploited copper, iron, lead, zinc, tungsten, graphite, barites and fluorite. A representative display of local minerals can be seen and there is a new section on lighting, drilling and explosives.

The museum offers activities for all the family, from budding geologists to hopeful prospectors, including an underground tour of a realistic mine, a quarry site with a unique collection of machinery and mineral panning. There is ample free parking, a shop and refreshments available. Open seven days a week from Easter to October.

THIRLMERE

4 miles S of Keswick off the A591

Helvellyn

This attractive, tree-lined lake, one of the few in the Lakes that can be driven around as well as walked around, was created in the 1890s by Manchester Corporation. More than 100 miles of pipes and tunnels still supply the city with water from Thirlmere.

The creation of the huge Thirlmere Reservoir, five miles long, flooded the two hamlets of Armboth and Wythburn. All that remains of these places today is Wythburn chapel towards the southern end. Overlooking the narrow lake is **Helvellyn**, Wordsworth's favourite mountain and one that is very popular with walkers and climbers today. At 3116 feet, it is one of just four Lakeland fells over 3000 feet high and the walk to the summit should not be undertaken lightly - but those reaching the top will be rewarded with some spectacular views. The eastern aspect of the mountain is markedly different from the western as it was here that the Ice Age glaciers were sheltered from the mild, west winds.

BORROWDALE

Runs South from Keswick via the B5289

Lodore Falls | Bowder Stone | Honister Pass

Honister Slate Mine

"*The Mountains of Borrowdale are perhaps as fine as anything we have seen,*" wrote John Keats in 1818. Six miles long, this brooding, mysterious valley, steep and narrow with towering crags and deep woods, is generally regarded as the most beautiful in the Lake District. Just to the south of Derwent Water are the **Lodore**

ASHNESS FARM

Borrowdale, Keswick, Cumbria, CA12 5UN
Telephone: 01768 777361 e-mail: enquiries@ashnessfarm.co.uk
website: www.ashnessfarm.co.uk

Come and stay in our 16th Century farmhouse & experience the charm of Lakeland from within a working fell farm. We have five en-suite double rooms (two can be twin) three have bath and shower and two have a shower only. All come with central heating and a magnificent view across Derwentwater. We want your stay at **Ashness Farm** to be an unforgettable experience and we always aim to extend our family welcome to make your stay a special occasion. From waking to the stunning view across the lake to star-gazing in truly unspoilt night skies we're sure you will be moved by the visual delights to be seen from your room. That said, we can't guarantee perfect weather and it wouldn't be the Lake District if it didn't rain from time to time! Breakfast is served the traditional way in our separate dining room. All of the food we provide is home produced wherever possible including the freshest of eggs from our own free range hens. We are more than happy to provide continental style breakfasts and special diets can be catered for by arrangement. We enjoy nothing more than to share our love of such a beautiful place and many of our guests from around the globe return to us again and again. We take great pleasure in extending our welcome to make our home your home for the duration of your stay.

As well as being our beautiful home, Ashness Farm is a working Lakeland fell farm. We encourage our visitors to come & appreciate Cumbrian family farm life from close-up & share in a little of what means so much to us.Ashness Farm has a long and notable history and in keeping with its tradition many of our farming practices are centuries old. The use of Belted Galloway Cattle a natural and effective way of controlling bracken and successive shrubs.In addition to our pedigree herd of cattle, we also breed Gloucester Old Spot pigs, Swaledale and Herdwick sheep. Even the eggs we use in our traditional farmhouse breakfasts are laid by our own genuine free range, naturally fed hens and the traditional Cumberland sausage is made from our own herd of pigs. You are welcome to bring your wellies and find out what we are doing out on the farm, children often like to help collect the eggs and feed pet lambs. Whether you are a guest enjoying the comforts of our home or just a walker passing through, you are welcome to enjoy the beautiful scenery from the specially created walks which pass through the heart of Ashness Farm.

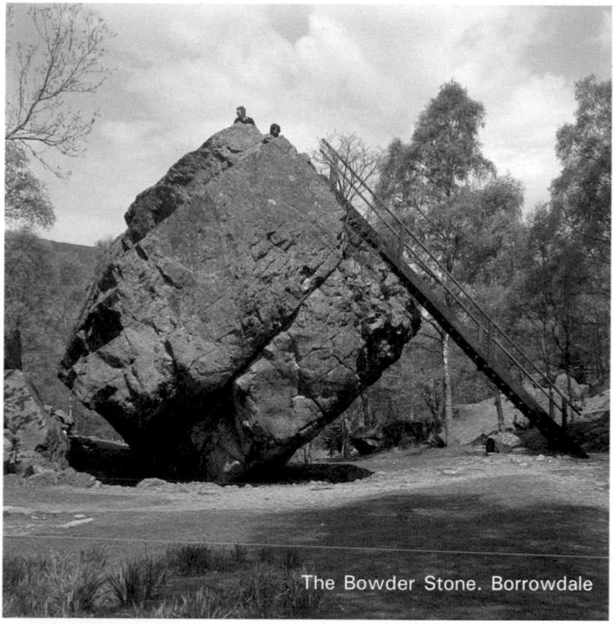
The Bowder Stone, Borrowdale

Falls, where the Watendlath Beck drops some 120 feet before reaching the lake. Further along the dale, in woodland owned by the National Trust, stands the extraordinary **Bowder Stone** which provides an irresistible photo-opportunity for most visitors. A massive 50-foot square and weighing almost 2000 tons, it stands precariously on one corner apparently defying gravity. Just south of Rosthwaite the road turns westwards to the village of Seatoller where there's a National Park Information Centre, and a minor road turns off to Seathwaite, which enjoys the unenviable reputation of being the wettest place in England with an average of 131 inches a year. From Seatoller, the B5289 slices through the spectacular **Honister Pass**, overlooked by dramatic 1000-foot-high Honister Crag. At the top of the pass, the 18th century **Honister Slate Mine** has been re-opened and is once again producing the beautiful green slate that adorns so many Lakeland houses and is famous throughout the world. Buckingham Palace, The Ritz, New Scotland Yard and RAF Cranwell are among the prestigious buildings donned with this stone. Helmets and lights are provided for a guided tour through great caverns of the mine to show how a mixture of modern and traditional methods is still extracting the slate, which was formed here some 400 million years ago.

BUTTERMERE

8 miles SW of Keswick on the B5289

Buttermere Lake Church of St James

Half the size of its neighbour, Crummock Water, **Buttermere** is a beautiful lake set in a dramatic landscape. To many connoisseurs of the Lake District landscape, this is the most splendid of them all. The walk around Buttermere opens up superb views of the eastern towers of Fleetwith Pike and the great fell wall made up of High Crag, High Stile, and Red Pike.

Standing above the village is the small, picturesque **Church of St James**, where the special features of interest include an antique organ and a memorial to fellwalker and author Alfred Wainwright.

CRUMMOCK WATER

9 miles SW of Keswick on the B5289

Fed by both Buttermere and Loweswater, this is by far the largest of the three lakes. In this less frequented part of western Cumbria, where there are few roads, the attractions of Crummock Water can usually be enjoyed in solitude. Best seen from the top of Rannerdale Knotts, to the east, the lake has a footpath running around it though, in places, the going gets a little strenuous.

Whinlatter Forest Park

BRAITHWAITE

3 miles W of Keswick on the B5292

Whinlatter Pass · Whinlatter Forest Park

Lake District Osprey Project

This small village lies at the foot of the **Whinlatter Pass**, another of Cumbria's dramatic routes. The summit of this steep road, the B5292, is some 1043 feet above sea level. On the westerly descent, there are magnificent views over Bassenthwaite Lake.

MAPLE BANK COUNTRY GUEST HOUSE

Braithwaite, Keswick, Cumbria CA12 5RY
Tel: 01768 778229
e-mail: enquiries@maplebank.co.uk
website: www.maplebank.co.uk

Standing within a well-tended acre of garden, **Maple Bank Guest House** is a handsome Edwardian stone-built residence now converted to a friendly and welcoming Country Guest House. It occupies a superb location, commanding uninterrupted views across the Derwent Valley towards the lofty Skiddaw and the smaller Latrigg. The owners of Maple Bank, Rhona and Tommy Duncan Brown, moved from a small guest house in Ayr, Scotland, to Maple Bank for a larger venture. From the Guest House visitors can look to see the various weather conditions on Skiddaw, one of England's highest mountains, which overlooks the Derwent Valley.

The accommodation at Maple Bank comprises seven guest bedrooms (four of which overlook Skiddaw), which have been tastefully refurbished in a style sympathetic with the house's origins, with the addition of en-suite facilities, hospitality trays, and colour TVs. Included in the price is a full Cumberland breakfast using local produce where possible. As well as the comfortable guest rooms, there is also a residents' dining room and lounge to relax in.

A large car park is provided at the rear of the house, affording ample parking for all guests, some of whom leave their cars here while exploring the local fells. We have a cycle store and drying facilities. There are four eating establishments in Braithwaite a short walk from Maple Bank, all serving fine food and local beers. For the more active guest Braithwaite is a perfect base. There is a range of recreations - including fishing, golf, riding, sailing and fell walking - and for the more passive guest, the chance to explore the historic part of Keswick and Cockermouth and their interesting museums, or just enjoy a picnic by Derwentwater.

The village of Braithwaite is just a few minutes drive from the market town of Keswick, midway between the lakes of Derwentwater and Bassenthwaite. Maple Bank is situated 30 yards along the road to Thornthwaite, on the northern edge of Braithwaite.

THWAITE HOWE

Thornthwaite, Keswick, Cumbria CA12 5SA
Tel: 01768 778744
website: www.thwaitehowe.co.uk

Thwaite Howe was built of local stone in the 1860s and stands in its own attractive grounds of one acre. Thornthwaite Forest provides a stunning backdrop to the rear, and the house occupies an elevated position looking across the Derwent Valley to the magnificent mountain views of Skiddaw, Blencathra and Helvellyn.

This beautiful house of much character is spacious enough for those seeking solitude and rest, yet sufficiently small and informal to cater for those who enjoy the company of their fellow guests. Owners Adrian and Nicola place great emphasis on creating an atmosphere of friendliness and informality, offering value for money and a hearty Cumbrian Breakfast prepared from the freshest of local produce, which can be enjoyed in the comfortable dining room that commands panoramic views of the surrounding Lakeland Fells.

The accommodation at Thwaite Howe comprises eight bedrooms, all of which have en-suite bathrooms, colour television, radio, tea and coffee making facilities, hairdryers and radiator thermostats to control the room temperature. Thwaite Howe provides an excellent centre from which to explore the whole of the Lake District, any part of which is easily accessible by car in the day. Nature lovers will enjoy seeing the red squirrels and a huge variety of birds, including woodpeckers, nuthatches, goldcrests, treecreepers and many other species, which can regularly be seen from our dining room window.

The road runs through the **Whinlatter Forest Park**, one of the Forestry Commission's oldest woodlands, which has a Visitor Centre, trails and walks for all ages and abilities, an orienteering course, adventure playground, viewpoints, gift shop and a tearoom with a terrace overlooking the woodlands and valley. Many of the record numbers who visit the centre come to see live footage of the Lake District ospreys beamed to a viewing facility, or to see the birds through high-powered telescopes at the Dodd Wood viewing point. **The Lake District Osprey Project** is a partnership of the Forestry Commission, the Lake District National Park Authority and the RSPB whose aim is to protect the nesting ospreys and to encourage others to settle and breed in other suitable locations.

LOWESWATER

10 miles W of Keswick off the B5289

Reached by narrow winding lanes, Loweswater is one of the smaller lakes, framed in an enchanting fellside and forest setting. Because it is so shallow, never more than 60 feet deep, Loweswater provides an ideal habitat for wildfowl, which also benefit from the fact that this is perhaps the least visited lake in the whole of Cumbria. To the east of the lake lies the small village of the same name, while to the north stretches one of the quietest and least known parts of the National Park, a landscape of low fells through which there are few roads or even paths.

BASSENTHWAITE LAKE

4 miles NW of Keswick on the A66

Trotters World of Animals

Church of St Bridget and St Bega Mirehouse

Here's one for the Pub Quiz: Which is the only lake in the Lake District? Answer: Bassenthwaite, because all the others are either Waters or Meres. Only 70 feet deep and with borders rich in vegetation, Bassenthwaite provides an ideal habitat for birds - more than 70 species have been recorded around the lake. Successful breeding is encouraged by the fact that no power boats are allowed on the lake and some areas are off limits to boats of any kind. Also, most of the shoreline is privately owned, with public access restricted mostly to the eastern shore where the Allerdale Ramble follows the lakeside for a couple of miles or so.

At the northern end of the lake, at Coalbeck Farm, **Trotters World of Animals** is home to many hundreds of animals - rare breeds, traditional farm favourites, endangered species, birds of prey and reptiles. It has the only Canadian Lynx in the UK, the largest of all monkeys - the mandrills - and the smallest otter in the world, as well as a cat that likes to swim - the Asian Fishing Cat. In addition to the ring-tailed lemurs, wallabies, racoons and gibbons, there are also rough-coated lemurs, lechwe antelope, red, fallow and sika deer and guanaco. Visitors to the 25-acre site can bottle-feed baby animals, cuddle bunnies, meet Monty the python, take a tractor trailer ride, watch the birds of prey demonstrations, find a quiet picnic spot or sample the fare on offer in Trotters Tea Room. And for the smaller children there's an indoor soft play climbing centre.

Rising grandly above Bassenthwaite's eastern shore is **Skiddaw**, which, ever since the Lake District was opened up to tourists by the arrival of the railway in the 19th century, has been one of the most popular peaks to climb. Although it rises to some 3054 feet, the climb is both safe and manageable, if a little unattractive lower down, and typically takes around two hours. From the summit, on a clear day, there are spectacular views to Scotland in the north, the Isle of Man in the west, the Pennines to the east, and to the south, the greater part of the Lake District.

Also on the eastern shore is the secluded, originally Norman, **Church of St Bridget and St Bega**, which Tennyson had in mind when, in his poem *Morte d'Arthur*, he describes Sir Bedivere carrying the dead King Arthur:

to a chapel in the fields,
A broken chancel with a broken cross,
That stood on a dark strait of barren land.

This then would make Bassenthwaite Lake the resting place of Excalibur but, as yet, no one has reported seeing a lady's arm, "clothed in white samite, mystic, wonderful", rising from the waters and holding aloft the legendary sword.

Set back from the lakeside, **Mirehouse** is a 17th-century building that has been home to the Spedding family since 1688. Literary visitors to the house included Tennyson, Thomas Carlyle and Edward Fitzgerald, the poet and translator of *The Rubaiyat of Omar Khayyam*. As well as some manuscripts by these family friends, the house also has a fine collection of furniture, and visitors can wander around the wildflower meadow, the walled garden and the lakeside walk, or sample home-cooked Cumbrian food in the tearoom.

Dodd Wood

Distance: *2.5 miles (4.0 kilometres)*

Typical time: *90 mins*

Height gain: *80 metres*

Map: *Explorer OL4*

Walk: *www.walkingworld.com ID: 933*

Contributor: *Craig Lannigan*

ACCESS INFORMATION:

There is a regular bus service, stopping at Mirehouse from Keswick. Parking is limited and costs approximatley £1.50 for the day.

DESCRIPTION:

You commence this walk from the car park at Mirehouse. There are toilet, tea and tourist facilities at the stone building at the far end of the car park. The walk takes you past many nature trail signposts and over a weir. A gently ascending path leads you to junctions with forest tracks and through Dodd Wood itself. The wood in places is imposing and can be eerie if you are a lone walker. Sounds are echoed and the path underfoot is soft with pine needles that crunch at every step.

As you continue to ascend gently you will notice the vegetation around becoming less dense, allowing you intermittent views over the lake. Very quickly, you emerge from the wood and onto the foothills of Ullock Pike. To your left is the striking Bassenthwaite Lake and to your right the summit of Skiddaw. Continuing onwards, the path begins to descend, ultimately to the A591. A short section of road-walking reveals another path, heading towards the shore of the lake through fields and over stiles. The route takes you back to another section of the A591 which is again crossed. A forest path now follows above the line of the main road and leads to a lay-by and a tarmacked track up to the car park building from whence you came.

ADDITIONAL INFORMATION:

Additional routes around Dodd Wood are well worth the effort, particularly as this route will take under two hours to complete. The nature trails are well marked out and enjoyable.

FEATURES:

Hills or Fells, Mountains, Lake/Loch, Toilets, Great Views, Food Shop, Moor, Nature Trail, Woodland.

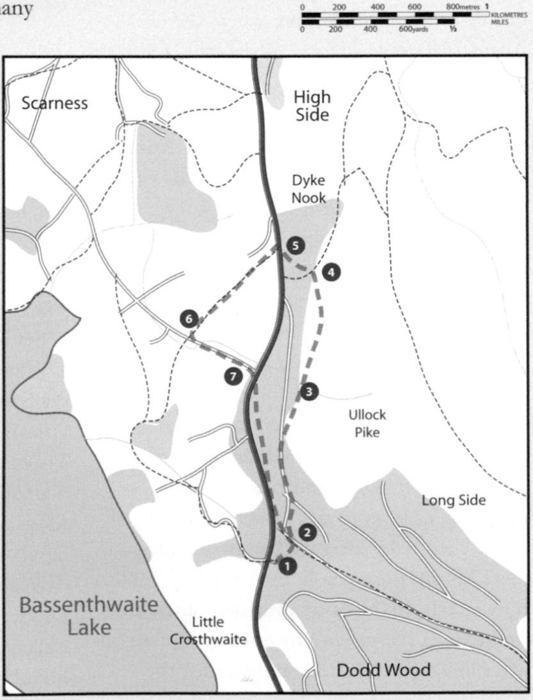

WALK DIRECTIONS:

1 | Begin the walk from the car park at Mirehouse. Use the shop and/or toilet facilities available at the stone building at the far end of the car park. Looking to your right, you will see a series of available forest walks as depicted with a wooden bridge just behind. Walk past the advertised walks and across the bridge, following the footpath that gently rises ahead until you come to a junction with a forest track. At the junction turn left and begin walking downhill for approximately 40 metres.

2 | The path now splits into a lower and higher path. Take the right-hand side path that is less defined and rises uphill. Follow this path for 1km through some lovely isolated pine-canopied aisles that rise gently, teasing you with intermittent views of Bassenthwaite Lake. Be very careful not to pass by the next change of direction. The path ahead takes you to a later waypoint but misses the spectacular views of the lake. Turn right at the pictured junction and follow the path that gently rises ahead.

3 | Continue along the path for about 300 metres, again through tree-lined aisles that are blanketed with pine needles, making it unusually soft underfoot. The path ahead becomes less defined and greatly covered with vegetation. You will follow this for another 300 metres and every metre forward reveals a striking comprehensive view of Bassenthwaite Lake and the fells beyond. It is certainly worth dwelling on this section of the walk as it provides maximum views with minimum effort. To your right, if you can pull yourself away from the views left, you will see the summit of Skiddaw beyond Ullock Pike. This path comes to an end after a small descent and the path double backs on itself to the left. Contine along the gently descending gravel track for 200 metres. Bassenthwaite Lake is now on your right-hand side and begins to disappear behind the looming trees in the foreground of your view.

4 | The path ends in another notable double back as pictured and this path is to be followed until you reach the main A591, which is only another 200 metres away. When you reach the road turn right towards the hotel, which stands back a little. Walk along the front of the hotel grounds until both entrances to the grounds have been passed.

5 | Cross over the road and you will notice in front of you a bus stop next to a series of stone steps descending along a dry-stone wall. This is the onward route. Follow this path, which bears to the right, and cross the stile in front of you. You will be faced with an open field headed by a small wire fence. Head for the centre of the field and walk towards the centre of the fence, where you will see another stile. Go over the stile. Follow the path ahead, which takes you towards a copse of trees. The path then bears to the left and takes you over another three stiles in quick succession. After the third stile you will find yourself once more on the road. Turn left and head towards the junction with the A591 again.

6 | When the Keswick sign appears in front of you, turn right and cross over the road. The entrance to a path, which runs alongside the main road for just over 1km, will soon appear. This a lovely low-level forest section with lots to see.

7 | The path ends at a small lay-by for cars and a path leading ahead towards a gate. Follow this rising path for 150 metres and you will come to the path junction that takes you down to the bridge you first walked over. Another 50 metres and you are in the car park once again.

BASSENTHWAITE LAKESIDE LODGES

Scarness, Bassenthwaite, Keswick, Cumbria CA12 4QZ
Tel: 01768 776641 Fax: 01768 776919
e-mail: enquiries@bll.ac
website: www.bll.ac

Located on the edge of Bassenthwaite Lake, at the foot of Skiddaw in the Lake District National Park, **Bassenthwaite Lakeside Lodges** offer exceptional self-catering accommodation in an exclusive, privately-owned holiday park. Almost all the lodges enjoy views across the lake, as well as natural landscaping that blends perfectly with the surrounding woodland. Such is the care lavished on the environment here, Bassenthwaite Lakeside Lodges has been awarded the coveted David Bellamy Gold Award. Here, visitors can share the woods with red squirrels, the waterside with the wildfowl and the lake with the reflected sky. Tranquillity surround the visitor in this verdant woodland setting, whilst across the lake, the mountains and fells seem to march down to meet the water, crating a vista of unique timeless beauty.

Bassenthwaite is one of the most unspoiled of Cumbria's magnificent lakes and has been designated a National Nature Reserve. It provides the perfect setting for the beautifully appointed timber lodges, some of which are available for holiday hire and short breaks; others are privately owned as a weekend or anytime retreat.

The centrally heated and double-glazed lodges offer every comfort and modern convenience, from the extensively equipped kitchens, to colour televisions and music centres. Some also have spa whirlpool baths. Bedrooms are provided with warm duvets, crisp linen and soft towels, and each lodge has a private balcony complete with gas barbecue to allow visitors to make the most of those idyllic summer evenings.

The reception centre has a small family pool and sauna, and visitors can enjoy boating, sailing, windsurfing and fishing on the lake. Within easy reach there are facilities for horse riding, cycling, tennis, golf and, of course, for walkers the freedom to roam the fells. The Lakeland area also offers a rich heritage of historic houses, gardens, castles, monuments and museums, as well as some fascinating craft shops and galleries.

ULDALE

11 miles N of Keswick off the A591

Northern Fells Gallery

To the northeast of Bassenthwaite Lake stretches the area known locally as the 'Land Back of Skidda', a crescent of fells and valleys constituting the most northerly part of the Lake District National Park. This peaceful region is well off the tourist track and offers visitors a delightful landscape of gently undulating bare-backed fells and valleys sheltering unspoilt villages such as Uldale. The village boasts a friendly traditional pub, The Snooty Fox, and a Victorian school, which now houses the **Northern Fells Gallery & Tea Room** where a wide range of work by Cumbrian artists - watercolours, jewellery, copperwork, ceramics, knitwear and woodcarvings - can be seen, all available to buy. This tranquil village has one small claim to fame: it was the daughter of an Uldale farmer who eloped with and married the legendary huntsman John Peel (see Caldbeck).

CALDBECK

13 miles N of Keswick on the B5299

John Peel Priest's Mill The Wool Clip

The Howk

Caldbeck is perhaps the best-known village in the northern Lakes because of its associations with **John Peel**, the famous huntsman who died in 1854 after falling from his horse. His ornate tombstone in the churchyard is decorated with depictions of hunting horns and his favourite hound. Also buried here are John Peel's wife Mary and their four children.

SWALEDALE WATCH

Whelpo, Caldbeck,
Cumbria CA7 8HQ
Tel/Fax: 01697 478409
e-mail: nan.savage@talk21.com
website: www.swaledale-watch.co.uk

Swaledale Watch is a busy working sheep farm just outside the picturesque village of Caldbeck. The farm offers comfortable bed and breakfast accommodation in peaceful, unspoilt surroundings. There's a choice of bedrooms - twin, double or family - and all have en-suite bath and shower. The cosy bedrooms are well equiped with everything necessary for a comfortable stay such as colour TV, clock/radio, hair dryer and hospitality tray. Guests have the use of a spacious lounge with plenty of books, games and jigsaws with open fire for chilly evenings.

Guests are also welcome to roam the farm's 300 acres of land and owners Nan and Arnold Savage, who know the area very well, are happy to guide guests to its many attractions. Badger watching evenings are popular. Caldbeck is centrally situated for touring or walking, being equidistant from Carlisle (Border City), Penrith (Ullswater), Cockermouth (Wardsworth) and Keswick (Derwentwater).

John Peel was Master of Hounds for more than 50 years and was immortalised by his friend John Woodcutt Graves, who worked in a Caldbeck mill making the grey woollen cloth mentioned in the song, "D'ye ken John Peel with his coat so grey?" The tune itself is based on an old Cumbrian folk song adapted by William Metcalfe, a chorister and organist at Carlisle Cathedral.

A few paces from Peel's tomb lies 'The Fair Maid of Buttermere', whose grave bears her married name, Mary Harrison. With its picturesque church, village green, cricket pitch, pond and blacksmith's forge, Caldbeck has all the ingredients of a picture postcard village. Some 200 years ago, Caldbeck was an industrial village with corn mills, woollen mills and a paper mill, all powered by the fast-flowing 'cold stream' - the Caldbeck. **Priest's Mill** (see panel for the Watermill Café on page 113), built in 1702 by the Rector of Caldbeck, next to his church, was a stone grinding corn mill, powered by a water wheel that has now been restored to working order. It is open to the public and has an accompanying Mining Museum, a collection of old rural implements and an excellent tea room. Also at the mill is **The Wool Clip**, the retail outlet for a local cooperative of farmers and craft workers producing high quality items using wool from local sheep.

About a quarter of a mile outside the village is the limestone gorge known as **The Howk**, a popular beauty spot where the Caldbeck rushes past the restored ruins of one of the old bobbin mills.

HESKET NEWMARKET

13 miles N of Keswick off the B5305

Hesket Newmarket Brewery

Set around a well-kept village green, this pleasing little village used to have its own market, as the name suggests, and much earlier there was probably also a racecourse here since that is what Hesket meant in Old Scandinavian. It could well be the reason why the village's main street is so wide. Although the market is no longer held, Hesket hosts two important agricultural events each year: an Agricultural Show and Sheepdog Trials. There's also a vintage motor cycle rally in May. In a converted barn at the back of the Old Crown pub, **Hesket Newmarket Brewery** was set up in 1988 and beer sales, which were at first limited to the pub, soon spread across Cumbria. Many awards have come the way of Hesket Newmarket beers, which include Skiddaw Special Bitter, the nearly black Great Cockup Porter and the pale but potent Catbells Pale Ale.

In and Around Penrith

Ullswater

Penrith is the most historic of Lakeland towns and was almost certainly settled long before the Romans arrived. They quickly appreciated its strategic position on the main west coast artery linking England and Scotland and built a fort nearby, although nothing visible remains today. Most of the town's oldest buildings have also disappeared, victims of the incessant Border conflicts down the centuries. Penrith today is a busy place, its location close to the M6 and within easy reach not only of the Lakes but also the Border Country and the Yorkshire Dales making it a hub of this northwestern corner of England.

Only a few miles from the town, **Ullswater**, eight miles long and the second longest lake in Cumbria, is also one of its most beautiful. The area around Penrith has some interesting old buildings, notably Shap Abbey and Brougham Castle, as well as two outstanding stately homes, Hutton-in-the-Forest where the Inglewood family have lived since 1605, and Dalemain, a fine mixture of medieval, Tudor and Georgian architecture. Sadly, Greystoke Castle, which according to Edgar Rice Burroughs was the ancestral home of Tarzan, is not open to the public.

Penrith

Penrith Castle | St Andrew's Church

Giant's Grave | William Wordsworth

Penrith Museum | Rheged | Beacon Hill Pike

Cowraik

In Saxon times Penrith was the capital of the Kingdom of Cumbria, but after the Normans arrived the town seems to have been rather neglected - it was sacked several times by the Scots before **Penrith Castle** was finally built in the 1390s. Richard, Duke of Gloucester (later Richard III) strengthened the castle's defences when he was Lord Warden of the Western Marches and was responsible for keeping the peace along the border with Scotland. By the time of the Civil War, however, the castle was in a state of ruin. The Cromwellian General Lambert demolished much of what was left and the townspeople helped themselves to the fallen stones to build their own houses. Nevertheless, the ruins remain impressive, standing high above a steep-sided moat. A short walk from the castle leads to the centre of this lively town with its charming mixture of narrow streets and wide-open spaces.

THE GEM DEN

31 King Street, Penrith CA11 7AY
Tel: 01768 899989
e-mail: info@thegemdenco.uk
website: www.thegemden.co.uk

Ever thought of making a pet of a trilobite? As Sue Kane of **The Gem Den** points out, "They're lovable and easy to care for!" At Sue's 'treasure trove of gems' there are plenty of other striking and unusual items. She always stocks large crystal display pieces as well as small tumbled stones and collectors' specimens. Amongst the jewellery items are many pieces in sterling silver set with beautiful semi-precious stones. Sue also enjoys experimenting with shapes and colours to create pieces such as earrings or a necklace to match your own clothes - some can even be made for you while you visit the town.

The Gem Den also has vast stocks of stones and beads, and work in silver or gold, wind chimes, eggs, globes, wands, bowls, coasters, equipment and gifts. Sue is happy to accept commissions - recently creating a hallmarked silver pendant incorporating an ammonite. The Gem Den is located on King Street, the main road (A6) into Penrith and is open from 10am to 5pm, Monday to Saturday except for Bank Holidays. Penrith itself is just off the M6 at junction 40.

Penrith has a splendid Georgian church in a very attractive churchyard, surrounded by a number of interesting buildings. The oldest part of **St Andrew's Church** dates from Norman times but the most recent part, the nave, was rebuilt between 1719 and 1772, possibly to a design by Nicholas Hawksmoor. Pevsner described it as "the stateliest church of its time in the county". Of particular interest is the three-sided gallery and the two chandeliers, which were a gift from the Duke of Portland in 1745, a reward for the town's loyalty during the Jacobite Rising. A tablet on the wall records the deaths of 2260 citizens of Penrith in the plague of 1597.

The church's most interesting feature however, is to be found in the churchyard, in the curious group of gravestones known as **Giant's Grave** - two ancient cross-shafts, each 11 feet high, and four 10th-century hogback tombstones, which have arched tops and sharply sloping sides. According to a local legend, the stones mark the burial place of a 5th-century King of Cumbria, Owen Caesarius. Also buried somewhere in the churchyard is Wordsworth's mother, but her grave is not marked.

Overlooking the churchyard is a splendid Tudor house, bearing the date 1563, which is now a restaurant but was at one time Dame Birkett's School. The school's most illustrious pupils were **William Wordsworth**, his sister Dorothy, and his future wife, Mary Hutchinson. William is also commemorated by a plaque on the wall of the Robin Hood Inn stating that he was a guest there in 1794 and again in 1795.

Occupying a listed building erected in 1670 for the education of poor girls, **Penrith Museum** features the archaeology, art, social, cultural and natural history of the area.

About a mile west of Penrith, on the A66, **Rheged Discovery Centre** dedicates itself to "a celebration of 2000 years of Cumbria's history, mystery and magic - as never seen before". Named after Cumbria's Celtic Kingdom, this extraordinary grass-covered building is also home to Britain's only exhibition dedicated to mountains and mountain adventure. It also has a giant cinema screen, speciality shops, pottery demonstrations, an artists' exhibition, restaurants and a children's play area.

Penrith is dominated by **Beacon Hill Pike**, which stands amidst wooded slopes high above the town. The tower was built in 1719 and marks the place where, from 1296, beacons were lit to warn the townsfolk of an impending attack. The beacon was last lit during the Napoleonic wars in 1804 and was seen by the author Sir Walter Scott who was visiting Cumberland at the time. Seeing it prompted Scott to hasten home to rejoin his local volunteer regiment. It is well worth the climb from the Beacon Edge, along the footpath to the summit, to enjoy a magnificent view of the Lakeland fells. It was on top of this hill, in 1767, that Thomas Nicholson, a murderer, was hanged. The gibbet was left on the summit and so was Nicholson's ghost, seen in the form of a skeleton hanging from the noose. The red sandstone from which many of Penrith's Victorian houses were built was quarried along the escarpments of Beacon Edge, and one of the old quarries, at **Cowraik**, is now a local nature reserve and is a Site of Special Scientific Interest for the geological interest of the quarry faces.

Around Penrith

ARMATHWAITE

10 miles N of Penrith off the A6

Eden Benchmarks · Eden Valley Woollen Mill

Set on the western bank of the River Eden, the village has a particularly fine sandstone bridge from which there is a splendid view of Armathwaite Castle (private), the home of the Skelton family, one of whose forebears was Poet Laureate to Henry VIII. Close by is the **Eden Valley Woollen Mill**, where visitors can see traditional looms rattling away, and browse through a huge range of knitwear produced from the finest wools and mohair. Also worth seeking out in Coombs Wood to the south is one of the **Eden Benchmarks**. Entitled *Vista* and created by Graeme Mitchison, this remarkable sculpture seems to make the Lazenby Sandstone flow into liquid shapes.

EDENHALL

4 miles NE of Penrith off the A686

Church of St Cuthbert · Plague Cross

Luck of Eden Hall

An old tradition asserts that in the 8th century the monks of Jarrow, fleeing from Viking invaders with the body of St Cuthbert, stopped here briefly. As a result, the village church is dedicated to the saint. Part of the **Church of St Cuthbert** appears to be pre-Norman, but most of the structure dates from the 1100s. Close to the church is the **Plague Cross**, which stands where there was once a basin filled with vinegar. This acted as a disinfectant into which plague victims put their money to pay for food from the people of Penrith. A visitation of the plague in the 16th century killed a quarter of the village's inhabitants.

Edenhall is particularly famous for the story of the **'Luck of Eden Hall'**, a priceless glass cup which, according to legend, was stolen from some fairies dancing round the garden wall by a butler in the service of the Musgrave family back in the 15th-century. Despite the fairies' entreaties, the butler refused to return the six-inch high glass to them. As he departed with the precious goblet, the fairies laid a curse upon it: "If ever this cup shall break or fall, Farewell the luck of Eden Hall." On inspection, the glass was identified as a 13th-century chalice of enamelled and gilded glass that is thought to have come from Syria and may well have been brought back by a Crusader. It was a treasured heirloom of the Musgraves for many generations and is now in the Victoria & Albert Museum in London. The goblet is still intact but Eden Hall has long since disappeared.

LANGWATHBY

5 miles NE of Penrith on the A686

Eden Ostrich World

Langwathby has a huge village green where maypole dancing takes place on the third Saturday in May. The green is medieval in origin and would once have been surrounded by wood and mud houses, perhaps to protect cattle but also for defence against border raids. After the Civil War and the growth in prosperity in the late 1600s, these wattle and daub cottages were replaced by stone buildings. West of the village, at Langwathby Hall Farm, **Eden Ostrich World** (see panel below) offers visitors the chance to see these splendid birds in a farm setting in the heart of the Eden Valley. The farm is also home to rare breed sheep, cattle and pigs, donkeys, deer, wallabies, alpacas and many other creatures from around the world. Also on site are an adventure playground, a pre-school play area, a maze, riverside walk, gift shop and tea room.

LITTLE SALKELD

7 miles NE of Penrith off the A686

Watermill Long Meg and her Daughters

Lacy Caves

Little Salkeld boasts Cumbria's only fully operational **Watermill** producing stone-ground organic flours by water power (see panel opposite). Tours are available daily except on

Eden Ostrich World

Langwathby Hall Farm, Winskill, Penrith, Cumbria CA10 1PD
Tel: 01768 881771

Have a fun day out at **Eden Ostrich World**, set in the beautiful Eden Valley. It is a working farm with a difference, with many rare breed animals as well as a large flock of African Black Ostrich, and one of Britain's most unusual species, a Zebroid, a Shetland/zebra cross. There are lots of organised events, which include meeting some of our smaller animals, a bouncy castle and tractor and trailer rides. Other features include adventure and pre-school play areas, including a large children's outdoor maze, and indoor heated soft play area. Visit the well-stocked gift shop and Hayloft Gallery or treat yourself in the delightful tea room. Not to be missed is the milking of the sheep daily at 2pm. It's a fun and educational day out for young and old, open seven days a week.

THE WATERMILL

Little Salkeld, nr Penrith, Cumbria CA10 1NN
Tel/Fax: 01768 881523
e-mail: organicflour@aol.com
website: www.organicmill.co.uk

Restored in 1975 by Ana and Nick Jones, **The Watermill** is Cumbria's only fully operational watermill and is committed to the production of high quality flour using British grain. Currently it is producing a wide range of bio-dynamic and organic stone-ground flours milled the traditional way using clean, self-renewing waterpower.

In the Mill Shop you'll find an exciting range of organic flours, porridge oats, oatmeals, dried fruit, nuts, pasta, tea, coffee, chocolate, homemade chutneys, jams and marmalade, and books. All produce is also available though The Watermill's online shop. The tearoom at The Watermill is famous for its delicious vegetarian cooking, wonderful bread, cakes and scones. Everything is organic and local where possible. Enjoy morning coffee or a Miller's Lunch overlooking Sunnygill Beck, or afternoon tea and scones in the Gallery, which is a showcase for weaving and knitting (hats, jerseys, and gloves) by Ana Balfour.

Tours of the Mill are available daily except for Wednesdays and Saturdays, and regular courses in baking and cooking are held here. Member of the Traditional Cornmillers Guild.The Watermill is open daily from 10.30am to 5pm (dusk in winter) from mid-January to Christmas.

Wednesday and Saturday, and there's a mill shop selling a wide range of organic foods.

A lane from the village leads to **Long Meg and her Daughters**, a most impressive prehistoric site and second only to Stonehenge in size. Local legend claims that Long Meg was a witch who, with her daughters, was turned to stone for profaning the Sabbath, as they danced wildly on the moor. There are more than 60 stones in the Circle (actually an oval), which is approximately 300 feet across. The tallest, Long Meg, is a 15 foot column of Penrith sandstone, the corners of which face the four points of the compass. Cup and ring symbols and spirals are carved on the stone which is over 3500 years old. The circle is now known to belong to the Bronze Age but no one is certain of its purpose. It may have been used for rituals connected with the changing seasons since the midwinter sun sets in alignment with the centre of the circle and Long Meg herself. The brooding majesty of the site was perfectly evoked by Wordsworth:

A weight of awe, not easy to be borne,
Fell suddenly upon my spirit – cast
from the dread bosom of the unknown past,
When first I saw that family forlorn.

In 1725 an attempt was made by Colonel Samuel Lacy of Salkeld Hall to use the stones for mileposts. However, as work began, a great storm blew up and the workmen fled in terror believing that the Druids were angry at the desecration of their temple. It was the same Colonel Lacy who gave his name to the **Lacy Caves**, a mile or so downstream from Little Salkeld. The Colonel had the five chambers carved out of the soft red sandstone, possibly as a copy of St Constantine's Caves further down the river at Wetheral. At that time it was fashionable to have romantic ruins and grottoes on large estates and Colonel Lacy is said to have employed a man to live in his caves acting the part of a hermit.

River Eden, Lazonby

KIRKOSWALD

8 miles NE of Penrith on the B6413

Church of St Oswald · Kirkoswald Castle

The College · Nunnery Walks

The village derives its name from the **Church of St Oswald**. Oswald was the King of Northumbria who, according to legend, toured the pagan north with St Aidan in the 7th century. The church is unusual in having a detached bell tower standing on top of a grassy hill some 200 yards from the main building, which is in a valley, so the bells could not be heard by the villagers.

This once thriving market town still retains its small cobbled market place and some very fine Georgian buildings. There's also a striking ruined 12th-century **Castle**, formerly the home of the Featherstonehaugh family.

One of Kirkoswald's most splendid buildings is the **College**, its name recalling the days when St Oswald's was a collegiate church. The two-storey house with its sloping-ended roof was originally built as a pele tower and converted into the college for priests in the 1520s. The manor house opposite has a particularly attractive entrance front in sandstone, which was added in 1696.

Just to the northwest of Kirkoswald are the **Nunnery Walks**, which start at a Georgian house built in 1715 on the site of a Benedictine Nunnery founded during the reign of William Rufus. Narrow footpaths have been cut into the sandstone cliffs along the deep gorge of Croglin Beck and they pass through beautiful woodland to reveal exciting waterfalls. The walks are open to the public during the summer months.

MELMERBY

9 miles NE of Penrith on the A686

Melmerby Hall

Melmerby nestles at the foot of Hartside Pass, its spacious village green dissected by a beck. Even today, every householder in Melmerby has grazing rights on the green. Horses are grazed more commonly now, but in the past it would have been more usual to see flocks of geese - indeed, there was once a cottage industry here making pillows and mattresses from goose feathers. Overlooking the 13-acre village green is **Melmerby Hall**, a defensive tower that was extended in the 17th and 18th centuries. It is now divided into rented apartments. The village church, with its tower, is a Victorian building, but the first known rector of the church on the site came here in 1332.

A curious meteorological feature here is what is known as the Helm Winds, localised gusts that sweep through the valley with the force of a gale while the surrounding countryside is perfectly calm.

From Melmerby, the main road climbs out of the Eden Valley to the east and the landscape changes suddenly. The road passes Fiend's Fell, close to the highest point in the Pennine Chain, the summit of Cross Fell. Early Christians erected a cross on the highest point of the fell to protect travellers from the demons who haunted the moors. Today, a cairn marks the spot where the cross once stood.

ALSTON

20 miles NE of Penrith on the A689/A686

Market Cross | Oliver Twist's Alston Trail
Gossipgate Gallery | South Tynedale Railway
The Hub | Alston Moor | Nenthead Mines

England's highest market town sits 1400 feet up on the North Pennines, reached by the A686, which is acknowledged as one of the most scenic routes in the world. Alston has a cobbled main street and, from the picturesque **Market Cross**, narrow lanes radiating out with courtyards enclosing old houses. Many of the older buildings still have the outside staircase leading to the first floor - a relic from the days when animals were kept below while the family's living accommodation was upstairs. This ancient part of Alston is known as The Butts, a title acquired by the need of the townspeople to be proficient in archery during the times of the border raids.

Because the town centre has changed so little since the late 1700s, it proved to be an ideal location for ITV's 1999 reworking of Charles Dickens' *Oliver Twist* scripted by Alan Bleasdale. The town council has created an **Oliver Twist's Alston Trail** with each of the 24 sites featured in the series marked by a picture of Mr Bumble.

An unusual feature of Alston is the number of watermills in and around the town, and the mill race was once the central artery of the old town. The tall spire of St Augustine's Church is a well-known local landmark and its churchyard contains a number of interesting epitaphs, as well as affording wonderful views of the South Tyne Valley.

Alston supports an astonishing diversity of shops and pubs and is home to a wide variety of craftspeople, ranging from blacksmiths to candlemakers, wood turners to potters. **Gossipgate Gallery**, housed in a converted congregational church built 200 years ago and with its original gas lights still intact, is the premier centre in the North Pennines for contemporary art and craft. A programme of exhibitions runs non-stop from February to December, and in the gallery shop there is a huge range of artefacts for sale, including original watercolours and prints, jewellery, glass, ceramics, sculpture and striking turned wooden bowls made from native woods.

Alston is the southern terminus of the **South Tynedale Railway** and its restored Victorian station, complete with vintage signal box, has featured in many television and film period productions. The narrow gauge (2ft) steam railway runs regular services during the summer months travelling through the beautiful South Tyne Valley. At the northern

JUST GLASS

Cross House, Market Place, Alston, CA9 3HS
Tel: 07833 994648

Situated between Hadrians wall and the Lake District is the town of Alston, the highest market town in England. Ideally located in the centre of this Market town, nestled behind the Market Cross is a quaint 17th-century cottage that is home to '**Just Glass**'.

The owner, Margery Graham, developed a passion for all things glass many years ago and what began as a hobby eventually transformed itself into this beautiful and unique shop. For over eight years now, 'Just Glass' has been overflowing with a large and varied collection of glass collectables and antiques.

Margery's collection dates from the late 1700s to the 1930s, giving an amazing insight into the history of glass production and development of different styles through the years. Stepping inside, you are instantly struck by the veritable rainbow spectrum of twinkling glass curiosities occupying every surface of the cosy interior. From the red Cranberry Decanters, yellow Vaseline wine glasses and Bristol Blue fruit bowls, to the North East and Pressed glass, there truly is something for everyone.

Whether you are a serious collector looking for an essential piece, looking for that special gift for a loved one or simply browsing, 'Just Glass' is an unforgettable experience for all.

LOVELADY SHIELD COUNTRY HOUSE HOTEL

Alston, Cumbria CA9 3LX
Tel: 01434 381203 Fax: 01434 381515
e-mail: enquiries@lovelady.co.uk
website: www.lovelady.co.uk

Lovelady Shield Country House Hotel is an elegant Georgian building that stands on the site of a 13th-century convent on the banks of the River Nent. It is surrounded by three acres of secluded gardens in which guests can sit and relax whilst enjoying the unspoilt views of the Cumbrian countryside. The hotel retains the ambience of a private residence and guests are warmly welcomed by the owners, Peter and Marie Haynes. They believe that, "If you've been disappointed at the impersonal and faceless hotels which pride themselves on their four and five star ratings, you will find Lovelady Shield a refreshing change". We want you to feel 'at home' in our home".

The hotel has an intimate cocktail bar along with a library and lounge with log fires. The highlight for many guests is dinner, which is served in the elegant dining room. The menu varies daily and is imaginatively prepared by Master Chef Barrie Garton. Barrie's menus are inspired and varied using mostly local produce. He describes them as being "British with continental excursions". To complement your meal, the hotel has a wine list of more than 100 wines which, in 2002 was awarded North West Wine List of the Year by Les Routiers.

terminus of the 2½-mile long track travellers can join a stretch of the Pennine Way that runs alongside the River South Tyne. Alston station has a shop and refreshment room and just across the road is **The Hub**, an exhibition of historic vehicles together with a wealth of local images and the stories that bring them alive.

To the south of the town is **Alston Moor**, 50 square miles of superb open landscape. The moor was once at the centre of an extremely important lead mining region, one of the richest in Britain. Lead and silver were probably mined on the moor by the Romans, but the industry reached its peak in the early 1800s when vast quantities of iron, silver, copper and zinc were extracted by the London Lead Company. A Quaker company, it was a pioneer of industrial welfare and also built the model village of Nenthead to house the miners. Here, not only were the workers and their families provided with a home, but education was compulsory and there were some public baths. **Nenthead Mines** is a 200-acre site high in the hills that tells the story of the lead and zinc mining industry. One of the main visitor attractions is 'The Power of Water', an impressive interactive area that looks at the technology used, including three working water wheels that drive model machinery. Another is the Brewery Shaft with its 328-feet drop and amazing virtual stone feature. The site also has a gift shop and tea room.

BROUGHAM

1 mile SE of Penrith off the A66

Brougham Castle · Mayburgh Earthwork

Tarquin · King Arthur's Round Table

St Ninian's

About a mile southeast of Penrith, the substantial and imposing remains of **Brougham Castle** (English Heritage) stand on the foundations of a Roman fort. The castle was inherited in the 1640s by the redoubtable and immensely rich Lady Anne Clifford, whose patrimony as Countess of Pembroke, Dorset and Montgomery also included another six northern castles. She spent a fortune restoring them all in medieval style and when told that Cromwell had threatened to destroy them replied, "As often as he destroys them I will rebuild them while he leaves me a shilling in my pocket."

Brougham Castle

Brougham was her favourite castle and she died here in 1676 at the age of 86. From the castle there's a delightful riverside walk to Eamont Bridge and the circular **Mayburgh Earthwork**, which dates from prehistoric times. Close to the village, on the banks of the River Eamont, is Giant's Cave, the supposed lair of a man-eating giant called Isir. This local tale is linked with the legend of **Tarquin**, a giant knight who imprisoned 64 men in his cave and was eventually killed by Sir Lancelot. Some people also claim that Uther Pendragon, King Arthur's father, lived here and that he too ate human flesh. A nearby prehistoric earthwork has been known as **King Arthur's Round Table** for many centuries. Lady Anne also rebuilt the chapel that stands on a hill above the castle, next to Brougham Hall. The old parish church of Brougham is the remotely located **St Ninian's**, also known as Ninekirks, which contains some family box pews that are screened so that they look almost like cages.

CLIFTON

3 miles S of Penrith on the A6

Clifton Moor · Wetheriggs Country Pottery

One of the last battles to be fought on English soil took place at nearby **Clifton Moor** in December 1745. Bonnie Prince Charlie was in retreat and his exhausted troops were easily routed by the English forces. Eleven soldiers were killed and are buried in Clifton churchyard, but some of the wounded Highlanders were hanged from the Rebels' Tree on the outskirts of the village. The tree is a sorry sight nowadays with its gaunt, dead branches, but it is still a place of pilgrimage for the Scots.

To the southeast of the village is **Wetheriggs Country Pottery**, which was founded in 1855. Visitors can try their hand at the often messy business of throwing a pot, paint a pot, paint on glass and make a candle, and also take a conducted tour of the steam-powered pottery, the only one of its kind in the UK. The pottery was scheduled as an Industrial Monument in 1973, and its steam engine was restored by none other than Fred Dibnah, the famous steeplejack. Also on site are some craft shops and a tea room.

ASKHAM

3 miles S of Penrith off the A6

Toy Works · Askham Fell

Askham is a pleasant conservation village set around two greens. In the centre of the village is one of its most interesting shops, the **Toy Works**, which combines a traditional toy shop with a toymaker's workshop. **Askham Fell**, which rises to the west, is dotted with prehistoric monuments including one known as the Copt (or Cop) Stone, which is said to mark the burial site of a Celtic chieftain.

LOWTHER

4 miles S of Penrith off the A6

Lowther Castle · Lakeland Bird of Prey Centre

St Michael's Church

Lowther Castle is now only a shell, most of it having been demolished in 1957, but it was clearly once a grand place; after one visit Queen Victoria is reputed to have said that she would not return to the castle as it was too grand for her. The ancestral owners of the castle were the illustrious Earls of Lonsdale, a family of statesmen and sportsmen. The most famous is perhaps the 5th Earl (1857-1944), known as the Yellow Earl because of the colour of the livery used on his private carriage. He was the first President of the Automobile Association and permitted his family colours to be used by that organisation. The earl was also a patron of amateur boxing and the Lonsdale Belt emerged from his interest.

Within the castle park is the **Lakeland Bird of Prey Centre**, a sanctuary for a large collection of hawks, eagles, falcons and owls from around the world. There are daily flying demonstrations at 2pm and 4pm, weather permitting, and the site also has a tea room and gift shop.

THE STRICKLAND ARMS

Lowther village itself was built in the 1680s by Sir John Lowther, who moved his tenants here to improve the view from the new house he was building. He also built **St Michael's Church** where several generations of the Lowthers are buried in a series of magnificent tombs beginning with a medieval style alabaster monument to Sir Richard who died in 1608.

BAMPTON

8 miles S of Penrith off the A6

Hugh Curwen   Haweswater   High Street

For several hundred years this small village was well-known for its Grammar School, two of whose pupils rose swiftly in the church hierarchy. One was **Hugh Curwen,** who as a Protestant became Chaplain to Henry VIII, as a Catholic under Queen Mary was elevated to the Archbishopric of Dublin, and then prudently re-embraced Protestantism when Elizabeth succeeded to the throne. Another Bampton boy was less pliable: Edmund Gibson was baptised in the church here in 1669 and later became a fiery Bishop of London who repeatedly denounced the degenerate morals of the age - with little apparent effect.

A couple of miles south of Bampton, **Haweswater** is the most easterly of the lakes. It is actually a reservoir, created in the late 1930s to supply the growing needs of industrial Manchester. Beneath the water lies the village of Mardale and several dairy farms for which Haweswater Valley was once famous. By 1940, the lake had reached its present extent of four miles and Manchester Corporation set about planting its shores with conifers. Today the area is managed as a nature reserve. Walkers have a good chance of seeing woodpeckers and sparrow hawks, buzzards and peregrine falcons, and with luck may even catch sight of golden eagles gliding on the thermals rising above Riggindale. An observation is manned throughout the breeding season if the eagles are nesting.

Above Haweswater runs the **High Street**, actually a Roman road, which is now one of the most popular fell walks in the Lake District. It overlooks the remote and lovely Blea Tarn and the lonely valley of Martindale, a cul-de-sac valley to the south of Ullswater, where England's last remaining herd of wild red deer can often be seen.

SHAP

10 miles S of Penrith on the A6

Shap Fell | Shap Abbey

This small village on the once congested A6 enjoys some grand views of the hills. In coaching days, Shap was an important staging post for the coaches before they tackled the daunting climb up **Shap Fell** to its summit some 850 feet above sea level. Much earlier, in medieval times, the village was even more significant because of nearby **Shap Abbey**, constructed in the local Shap granite which has been used in many well-known buildings, St Pancras Station and the Albert Memorial in London among them.

The Abbey stands about a mile to the west of the village, just inside the National Park, and it's well worth seeking it out to see the imposing remains of the only abbey founded in Westmorland; the only one in the Lake District mountains; the last abbey to be consecrated in England (around 1199), and the last to be dissolved, in 1540.

Shap Abbey

ORTON

15 miles S of Penrith on the B6260

Great Asby Scar | Petty Hall | Orton Hall

Kennedys Chocolates | Keld Chapel

By far the best approach to Orton is along the B6260 from Appleby to Tebay. This scenic route climbs up onto the moors, passing Thunder Stone, some mighty limestone bluffs and the pavements of **Great Asby Scar**, the setting for BBC TV's *The Tenant of Wildfell Hall.*

A pretty village now, for centuries Orton was a market town of some consequence with a charter granted in the 13th century by Edward I and a licence to hold fairs accorded by the puritan Oliver Cromwell. Today, the only market is a farmer's market held on the second Saturday of every month. More than

40 local farmers, growers, producers and artisan craftsmen offer a tremendous variety of high quality and speciality local produce and crafts.

There are reminders of Orton's former importance in the noble church tower, completed in 1504; in the attractive proportions of **Petty Hall**, an Elizabethan house at the lower end of the village (a private residence, incidentally); and in the grandeur of **Orton Hall**, built in 1662 and now converted into holiday apartments. Orton's most famous visitor was Bonnie Prince Charlie who stayed in the village on his way northwards after the crushing defeat of his troops at Derby.

Orton's former school now houses **Kennedys Chocolates**, a small enterprise producing handmade chocolates. There's a factory shop and a coffee house with viewing windows overlooking the production areas.

The village stands below **Orton Scar**, on which a beacon was lit to warn people to seek safety from advancing Scottish raiders. The village church, in common with many in the Eden Valley, has a massive 16th-century tower that was built for defensive purposes and was one place where the villagers sought shelter. Its features include an ancient oak parish chest and a stained glass window by Beatrice Whistler, wife of the American artist James McNeill Whistler.

From the church there's a pleasant walk of well under a mile to Keld, a tiny village of just 17 houses. So quiet today, in medieval times Keld was a busy little place servicing the monks of Shap Abbey nearby. It was the monks of Shap Abbey who built the village's oldest building, the early-16th-century **Keld Chapel** (National Trust).

DALEMAIN

3 miles SW of Penrith off the A592

Dalemain

Dalemain House (see panel below) is one of the area's most popular attractions - an impressive house with a medieval and Tudor

Dalemain Historic House & Gardens

Penrith, Cumbria CA11 0HB
Tel: 01768 486450 Fax: 01768 486223
e-mail: admin@dalemain.com

Dalemain has been a much-loved family home since 1679, and is set against the grandeur and picturesque splendour of the Lakeland Fells and Parkland. Behind the impressive façade you will discover the surprise of Dalemain - its sheer variety. In the Georgian part of the house, the grand public rooms include the breathtaking Chinese Room with its original 18th-century Chinese hand-painted wallpaper. Much of the house dates from Tudor times and here you will find a glorious confusion of winding passages, quaint stairways and unexpected rooms including the Fretwork Room with its magnificent 16th-century plaster ceilings and oak panelling.

The gardens at Dalemain are a pure delight with a series of differing themes including a rose garden, a Tudor knot garden and a wild garden. A glorious woodland walk takes you high above Dacre Beck while other footpaths lead you by the walls of 14th-century Dacre Castle or to Pooley Bridge.

core fronted by an imposing Georgian façade. The house has been home to the same family since 1679 and over the years they have accumulated fine collections of china, furniture and family portraits. The grand drawing rooms boast some very fine oak panelling, while in the Chinese Room is some beautifully preserved 18th century Chinese wallpaper and a rococo chimneypiece by Nathaniel Hedges in Chinese Chippendale style. Visitors also have access to the Nursery (furnished with toys from all ages) and Housekeeper's Room. The Norman pele tower houses the regimental collection of the Westmorland and Cumberland Yeomanry, a troop of mounted infantry that the family usually led, while the 16th-century Great Barn contains an interesting assortment of agricultural bygones. The extensive grounds include a medieval herb garden, a Tudor-walled knot garden with a fine early Roman fountain, a wild garden alongside Dacre Beck, a deer park, and woodland and riverside walks. There is also a tearoom selling home-baked lunches and teas.

DACRE

4 miles SW of Penrith off the A66

Dacre Church Dacre Castle

There is much of historic interest in this village. The **Church** occupies a site of a former monastery, which was mentioned by the Venerable Bede in his accounts of Cumberland in the 8th century. A later reference shows that in 926 the Peace of Dacre was signed between Athelstan of England and Constantine of Scotland. Fragments of masonry are reputed to have come from the monastery, and the four weather-beaten carvings of bears in the churchyard are probably of Anglo-Viking origin. The bears are shown, respectively, sleeping, being attacked by a cat, shaking off the cat and eating the cat. A 14th-century pele tower, **Dacre Castle** (private) is a typical example of the fortified house or small castle that was common in northern England during the Middle Ages. This was the seat of the Dacre family, Catholic Earls of Cumberland, and its turrets and battlements have walls that are eight feet thick.

POOLEY BRIDGE

5 miles SW of Penrith on the B5320

Ullswater Holly House

In Wordsworth's opinion **Ullswater** provides "the happiest combination of beauty and grandeur, which any of the Lakes affords", an opinion with which most visitors concur. The poet also noted the curious fact that the lake creates a sextuple echo, a natural phenomenon that the Duke of Portland exploited in the mid-1700s by keeping a boat on the lake equipped "with brass guns, for the purpose of exciting echoes".

The charming village of Pooley Bridge stands at the northern tip of Ullswater, and there are regular cruise departures from here during the season, stopping at Glenridding and Howton. Rowing and powered boats are available for hire, and since Ullswater is in effect a public highway, private boats can also be launched. A speed limit of 10mph applies over the whole of the eight-mile-long serpentine lake.

The oldest building in Pooley Bridge is part of **Holly House**, which dates back to 1691, while the Bridge of the village's name dates from 1763 when the elegant structure over the River Eamont was built at a cost of £400.

lakeside villages. Lake cruises depart from here, rowing boats are available for hire and there's plenty of room for waterside picnics.

PATTERDALE

15 miles SW of Penrith on the A592

St Patrick's Well

It is this village's magnificent setting that makes it such a popular tourist destination. Close to the head of Ullswater and with a series of fells framing the views, the scenery is indeed splendid. On the north side of the village is **St Patrick's Well**, which was thought to have healing properties. The medieval chapel dedicated to the saint was rebuilt in the 1850s.

WATERMILLOCK

7 miles SW of Penrith on the A592

Aira Force High Force Gowbarrow Estate

This small village, idyllically situated on the shore of Ullswater, is hidden amongst the woodland that occupies much of the lake's western shores. About four miles southwest of the village, there is a series of waterfalls which tumble down through a wooded gorge and then into Ullswater. The name of the largest fall is **Aira Force** (70 feet high) and the second largest is **High Force**. They can easily be reached on foot through the woodlands of **Gowbarrow Estate**, which is owned by the National Trust.

GLENRIDDING

14 miles SW of Penrith on the A592

Helvellyn

A popular base for walkers about to tackle the daunting challenge of **Helvellyn**, Glenridding is the largest and busiest of Ullswater's

STAINTON

2 miles W of Penrith off the A66 or A592

The Alpaca Centre Just Wood Gallery

The Alpaca Centre was set up in 1997 and has become a focal point for the development and expanding knowledge of the alpaca. The Centre is a working farm, breeding, rearing and selling alpacas and welcomes visits at any time of the year. There's a shop selling an array of garments fashioned from the exceptionally fine alpaca fibre, many handmade in Peru. Upstairs is the **Just Wood Gallery** displaying a superb collection of furniture and ornamental pieces, many crafted in the centre's own workshop by Garry

GREYSTONE HOUSE FARMSHOP & TEAROOM

Stainton, Penrith, Cumbria CA11 0EF
Tel. 01768 866952
website: www.greystonehousefarm.co.uk
Open 10am - 5.30pm daily.

Situated just off the A66, close to junction 40 of the M6, this award-winning **Farmshop and Tearoom** offers a unique opportunity in that you can track your food from the fields, through the shop and onto your dinner plate!

The Dawson family have farmed at Greystone House since 1752. Following the loss of their livestock in the foot and mouth outbreak of 2001, the family readopted the traditional principles of organic farming, as well as converting a barn into a farmshop and tearoom. The traditional butcher's counter offers expert advice and a delicious selection of meats, including home-reared beef and lamb and home recipe Cumberland sausage. The Dawsons have also begun to rear outdoor pigs to meet with demand.

Take your pick from a wide selection of produce in the Farmshop, which specialises in high quality cheeses, preserves, cakes and local produce, to name but a few, as well as a range of gifts and original artworks. If you would rather let someone else do all the hard work, a warm welcome awaits you in the oak-beamed Lofthouse Tearoom, where you can enjoy freshly brewed coffee and a wide range of home cooking, including cakes and light bites all day long, and hot food available from 11.30am onwards.

Recent planting of trees, the development of wildlife strips, ponds and footpaths makes the Dawsons land an attractive place to take a stroll. Open days, in particular during lambing time, allow the public access to the farm so that they can see how the food is produced.

Stevenson and his son Shaun. Also at the centre is G&S Timber Crafts, which supplies hard woods for wood turners, carvers and furniture makers.

GREYSTOKE

5 miles W of Penrith on the B5288

Greystoke Castle · St Andrew's Church

Plague Stone

According to Edgar Rice Burroughs, **Greystoke Castle** was the ancestral home of Tarzan, Lord of the Apes, a fiction that was perpetuated in the 1984 film *Greystoke*. Today, the castle and its 3000-acre estate is an outdoor activity centre. Tarzan's aristocratic credentials would have come as something of a surprise to the dignified Barons of Greystoke whose effigies are preserved in **St Andrew's Church**. As imposing and spacious as a cathedral, St Andrew's boasts a wonderful east window with much 13th-century glass and, in the Lady Chapel, a figure of the Madonna and Child carved by a German prisoner-of-war. About 100 yards from the church stands the **Plague Stone** where, during medieval times, coins were left in vinegar in exchange for food for the plague victims. An ancient Sanctuary Stone, now concealed behind a grille, marks the point beyond which fugitives could claim sanctuary.

Greystoke village itself is a gem, its attractive houses grouped around a trimly maintained village green. Nearby are the stables where Sir Gordon Richards trained his two Grand National winners, Lucius and Hello Dandy.

HUTTON-IN-THE-FOREST

6 miles NW of Penrith on the B5305

Hutton-in-the-Forest

The home of the Inglewood family since 1605, **Hutton-in-the-Forest** was originally a medieval stronghold and the Pele Tower from that period still exists. The house has been added to and altered by successive generations, with the result that an unusual number of architectural and decorative styles can be seen. Among the notable features are the 17th-century Gallery, the Hall dominated by a Cupid staircase, and a room decorated in the Arts and Crafts style. The splendid grounds include a beautiful walled garden built in the 1730s, topiary terraces that were originally laid out in the 17th century, fine specimen trees, and a 17th-century dovecote that forms part of the Woodland Walk.

The Eden Valley and East Cumbria

Eden Benchmarks

Carved through boulder clay and red sandstone, and sandwiched between the Lakeland fells and the northern Pennines, the Eden Valley is green and fertile - in every sense another Eden. This, too, is farming country and many of the ancient towns and villages have a market place. Appleby-in-Westmorland, the old county town of Westmorland, had an important market and also an annual horse fair, the latter of which continues today and has gained a large following.

An attractive man-made feature of the valley is the collection of specially commissioned stone sculptures known as **Eden Benchmarks** dotted along its length. Each created by a different sculptor, they have been located beside public paths and, since they also function as seats, provide the perfect setting in which to enjoy the valley's unspoilt scenery.

Kirkby Stephen

St Stephen's Church Trupp Stone

Loki Stone Croglam Earthworks

Eden Benchmarks

Surrounded by spectacular scenery, the old market town of Kirkby Stephen lies at the head of the beautiful Eden Valley. Although essentially part of the Valley, Kirkby Stephen has a strong Yorkshire Dales feel about it. Indeed, the church, with its long, elegant nave, has been called the Cathedral of the Dales.

Dating from Saxon times, rebuilt in 1220 and with a 16th-century tower, **St Stephen's Church** is one of the finest in the eastern

KATHRYN PEMBERTON SOFT FURNISHINGS

2 Walton's Yard, Market Square, Kirkby Stephen,
Cumbria CA17 4QT
Tel: 01768 372660
e-mail: mail@beautifulcurtains.co.uk
website: www.beautifulcurtains.co.uk

For those in search of a little "something special", **Kathryn Pemberton Soft Furnishings** has just the thing. Kathryn started sewing from home in 1997 and opened her shop in the heart of the attractive market town of Kirkby Stephen in 2005. Within it you'll find a comprehensive and growing range of high quality fabrics with regular additions of new lines. The fabrics are made from predominantly natural fibres sourced from the best fabric houses and mills around the world. Kathryn's pursuit for uncompromising quality in the fabrics and making up service means that customers receive only the very best products. "Customer satisfaction is of the utmost importance," says Kathryn, "and I endeavour to please in any way I can." In her collection, fabrics are manufactured by both machine and hand-woven methods, and made from predominantly natural fibres.

If you are unable to visit the shop, your order can be completed over the internet. But if you do wish to speak to someone, the phone lines are open Monday to Friday from 10am to 5pm. Kathryn works to the highest possible standards and strives to give one hundred percent customer satisfaction. If you require any advice on style, colour or measuring, feel free to contact her.

fells, dominating the northern end of the town from its elevated position. Until the last century the **Trupp Stone** in the churchyard received money from local people every Easter Monday in payment of church tithes. At eight o'clock, the curfew is still sounded by the Taggy Bell, once regarded by local children as a demon. Inside the church are a number of pre-Conquest stones, some of which show Norse influence. The most remarkable is the 10th-century **Loki Stone**, one of only two such carvings in Europe to have survived. Loki was a Norse God and presumably Viking settlers brought their belief in Loki to Kirkby Stephen.

Between the church and the market square stand the cloisters, which served for a long time as a butter market. The Market Square is surrounded by an ancient collar of cobblestones which marked out an area used for bull-baiting - a 'sport' that ceased here in 1820 after a disaster when a bull broke loose. There are many delightful walks from the town, to **Croglam Earthworks** for example, a prehistoric fort, or to nearby Stenkrith Park where the second of the **Eden Benchmarks** can be found. Created by Laura White in Ancaster limestone and titled *Passage*, the sculpture is deceptively simple, suggesting perhaps the course of a river bed. There are also some pleasant strolls along the riverside to a fine waterfall where the River Eden cascades into Coop Karnel Hole. Look out for the unusual shapes of the weathered limestone rock. For more strenuous exercise, walkers could tackle a stretch of the **Coast to Coast** long distance footpath, which passes through the town.

WALK | 4

Kirkby Stephen

Distance: *2.4 miles (3.8 kilometres)*

Typical time: *60 mins*

Height gain: *100 metres*

Map: *Explorer OL19*

Walk: *www.walkingworld.com ID: 2598*

Contributor: *David and Chris Stewart*

ACCESS INFORMATION:

Kirkby Stephen is on the Settle to Carlisle railway line, although the station is a good mile or more away from the village. The village (or small town) is well served with buses from all around. Parking is not usually a problem. If you can't park in the market square by the church, there are usually places along by the shops and there is a free public car park behind the main square.

DESCRIPTION:

Take this peaceful little walk around the back of Kirkby Stephen in the Upper Eden Valley. For the most part it follows the River Eden and, for a while, a disused railway to the bridge at Stenkrith where the river has made extraordinary carvings into the limestone river bed. Talking of interesting carvings - look out along the way for poetry written by Meg Peacocke and carved into large stones by Pip Hall.

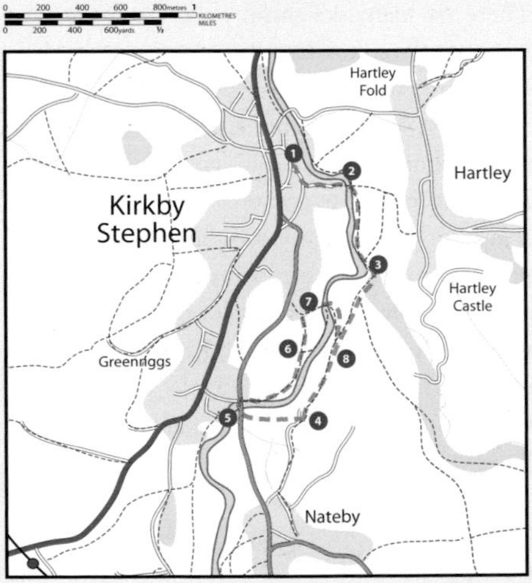

FEATURES:

River, Pub, Toilets, Birds, Flowers, Butterflies, Café, Gift Shop, Food Shop, Public Transport.

WALK DIRECTIONS:

1 | From Kirkby Stephen market place, head down past the toilets, following the signs to Frank's Bridge. Follow a small lane down past some houses and turn left to go over the footbridge. After crossing the bridge turn right to follow the footpath along the river.

2 | As you enter a wide field, bear right to follow the edge of the river. Go past a barn to the edge of the field.

3 | Take the small footbridge over the stream and follow the path through the woods. After a while you come to a bridge over the disused railway line. Continue over the bridge as the path bears to the right.

4 | Go through the gate on the right to drop down onto the track of the old railway. Turn left to follow the gravelled track to Stenkrith bridge.

5 | Bear right over the new blue footbridge over the Eden at Stenkrith bridge. Take time to view the fascinating shapes bored out by the water as it flows through the rocks under the bridge.

6 | Just before reaching the road turn sharp right onto the path following the river. Return this way towards Kirkby Stephen.

7 | At this field keep to the right to continue following the edge of the river. A nice place for a picnic.

8 | Cross the bridge and follow the path up the deep gully on the other side. The path curves round to the right to join the path you originally took on the outward journey. Notice more of Meg Peacocke's poetry carved in stone by the letter-carver Pip Hall near the barn.

9 | Turn left and follow your tracks back to Frank's Bridge.

Pendragon Castle, Outhgill

Around Kirkby Stephen

OUTHGILL

5 miles S of Kirkby Stephen on the B6259

Church of St Mary · Wild Boar Fell

Pendragon Castle · Lammerside Castle

The village **Church of St Mary**, first built in 1311, was repaired by Lady Anne Clifford who has been mentioned earlier on page 124. From 1643, when she finally obtained possession of the Clifford estates, Lady Anne devoted her life to restoring her many properties and lived in each of them for varying periods of time. Her estates included six castles - Skipton and Barden in Yorkshire; Appleby, Brough, Brougham and Pendragon in Westmorland. Lady Anne's zeal for restoration didn't stop at castles: she also repaired the Roman road between Wensleydale and the Eden Valley, a route she often travelled (along with a huge retinue) between her castles and her birthplace at Skipton. The route is now known as Lady Anne's Way, but in times past it was aptly called the High Way since it was a regular place of employment for highwaymen such as Dick Turpin and William 'Swift' Nevison.

The landscape around Outhgill is remote and beautiful. To the south is **Wild Boar Fell**, a brooding, flat-topped peak where the last wild boar in England was reputedly killed, while tucked down in the valley are the romantic ruins of Lammerside and Pendragon Castles.

Pendragon Castle, about a mile north of the village, is shrouded in legend including claims that it was the fortress of Uther Pendragon, father of King Arthur. If so, nothing remains of that 6th-century wooden castle. The present structure dates from the 1100s and was built by Hugh de Morville to guard the narrow pass of Mallerstang, one of the four knights who murdered Thomas à Becket. Twice it was burned by the Scots and twice restored, on the latter occasion by the formidable Lady Anne Clifford in 1660.

Another mile or so downstream, **Lammerside Castle** dates from the 12th century but only the remains of the keep survive. They can be found along a bridle path between Pendragon and Wharton Hall.

RAVENSTONEDALE

5 miles SW of Kirkby Stephen on the A685

Church of St Oswald

Known locally as Rissendale, this pretty village

of stone-built cottages clustered along the banks of Scandal Beck lies on the edge of the Howgill Fells. The parish **Church of St Oswald** is especially interesting: built in 1738, it is one of the few Georgian churches in Cumbria. The window at the east end commemorates the last woman in England to be put to death for her Protestant faith. Elizabeth Gaunt was sentenced in 1685 by the notorious Judge Jeffreys to be burnt at the stake for sheltering a fugitive rebel. She met her end at Tyburn in London.

CROSBY GARRETT

4 miles W of Kirkby Stephen off the A685

Crosby Garrett Church | The Devil

Local legend has it that the **Devil**, seeing all the stones lying ready to build **Crosby Garrett Church**, carried them in his leather apron to the top of a nearby hill. He reasoned that, as people grew old, they would be unable to climb the hill and attend church and thus would come to him rather than go to Heaven. Such tales apart, the church itself is said to be of Anglo-Saxon origin, though the visible fabric is 12th century. Inside there are some superb carvings, particularly near the font. The church is also famous for its hagioscope, cut through the wall to allow people in the north aisle to see the altar. Near the church gates is a tithe barn, built in the 18th century to store farm produce given to the church as a religious tax. To the west of the village runs the Settle - Carlisle Railway whose splendid viaduct dominates Crosby Garrett.

WINTON

3 miles N of Kirkby Stephen off the A685

Winton Hall | Winton Fell

The oldest building in this quiet and picturesque hamlet is **Winton Hall**, built of stone and dated 1665, but looking older with its stone buttresses and mullion windows with iron bars. Those taking a walk on **Winton Fell** are likely to see red grouse lifting off from the large tracts of heather on the fellside. Indeed, the wildlife is much more prolific around this area where the limestone provides more plentiful food than on the fells around the lakes.

Appleby-in-Westmorland

Boroughgate | Moot Hall | Appleby Castle

Rare Breeds Survival Centre

St Lawrence's Church | Gypsy Horse Fair

The old county town of Westmorland, Appleby is one of the most delightful small towns in England. It was originally built by the Norman, Ranulph de Meschines, who set it within a broad loop of the River Eden, which protects it on three sides. The fourth side is guarded by Castle Hill. The town's uniquely attractive main street, **Boroughgate**, has been described as the finest in England. A broad, tree-lined avenue, it slopes down the hillside to the river, its sides lined with a pleasing variety of buildings, some dating back to the 17th century. At its foot stands the 16th-century **Moot Hall** (still used for council meetings and also housing the Tourist Information Centre); at its head rises the great Norman Keep of **Appleby Castle**, which is protected by one of the most impressive curtain walls in northern England. Attractions here include the dramatic view from the top of the five-storey keep and the lovely grounds that are home to a wide variety of animals and include a **Rare Breeds Survival Centre**.

During the mid-1600s, Appleby Castle was

Appleby Horse Fair

the home of Lady Anne Clifford, the remarkable woman who has already been mentioned several times and to whom Appleby has good cause to be grateful. The last of the Clifford line, the diminutive Lady Anne (she was just four feet 10 inches tall) inherited vast wealth and estates, among them no fewer than six northern castles. She lavished her fortune on rebuilding or restoring them all. Churches and chapels in the area also benefited from her munificence and at Appleby, in 1651, she also founded the almshouses known as the Hospital of St Anne, for '12 sisters and a Mother'. Set around a cobbled square, the picturesque cottages and minuscule chapel still serve their original function, maintained by the trust endowed by Lady Anne.

Lady Anne died in 1676 in her 86th year and was buried with her mother, Margaret, Countess of Cumberland, in **St Lawrence's Church**. The church is well worth visiting to see their magnificent tombs and also the historic organ, purchased from Carlisle Cathedral in 1684, which is said to be the oldest still in use in Britain.

Just a few years after Lady Anne's death, James II granted the town the right to hold a Fair during the week leading to the second Wednesday in June. More than 300 years later, the **Gypsy Horse Fair** is still thriving with hundreds of gypsies flooding into the little town (population 1800) with their caravans and horse-drawn carts. The trade, principally in horses, and the trotting races provide a picturesque and colourful spectacle.

Around Appleby-in-Westmorland

BRAMPTON

2 miles N of Appleby-in-Westmorland off the A66

Elizabeth Sleddall

This village, along with the surrounding area, was said to be haunted by the ghost of **Elizabeth Sleddall**, the wife of a 17th-century owner of nearby Crackenthorpe Hall. Elizabeth died believing that she had been cheated out of her share of the estate, so to shame the false inheritors her spirit was seen being driven around the countryside in a coach drawn by four black horses. Her ghost became so troublesome that the local people exhumed her body and reburied the remains under a larger boulder. Her ghost, while no longer upsetting the local people, is said still to visit the hall.

DUFTON

3 miles N of Appleby-in-Westmorland off the A66

Dufton Gill

Behind this delightful hamlet lies **Dufton Gill**, a beautiful, secluded wooded valley through which runs a footpath. Also from Dufton there is a track carrying the Pennine Way up to High Cup Nick, a great horseshoe precipice at the edge of the northern Pennine escarpment that was formed by a glacial lake during the Ice Age.

GREAT ORMSIDE

2 miles SE of Appleby-in-Westmorland off the B6260

Church of St James | General Whitehead

This was once an important fort guarded by a pele tower. Today, the ancient **Church of St James**, which dates from the 11th century, occupies a site on the steep-sided defence mound. Relics of pre-Christian burials have been found in the mound, as well as a Viking sword (now in the Tullie Museum in Carlisle). A silver gilt and enamel bowl from the 7th century has also been found and is regarded as one of the most important pieces of Anglo-

Saxon metalware to survive. A particularly beautiful piece, richly decorated with vine scrolls, birds and animals, it is now on permanent display in the Yorkshire Museum in York. From the village, a path leads across fields to the village of Little Ormside with its large cedar tree said to have been brought back from Lebanon as a sapling by **General Whitehead**. On the voyage home he grew it in his hat and shared with it his daily ration of one pint of water.

WARCOP

5 miles SE of Appleby-in-Westmorland on the B6259

Rush-bearing Ceremony

The largest village in this part of the Eden Valley, Warcop grew up around a crossing point of the river. The bridge, the oldest to cross the river, dates from the 16th century and the red sandstone buildings surrounding the village green, with its central maypole, make this a charming place to visit.

The Church of St Columba is built outside the village on the site of a Roman camp. An interesting building in its own right, it is particularly famous for the **Rush-bearing Ceremony**, which takes place in late June each year.

BROUGH

9 miles SE of Appleby-in-Westmorland on the A66/A685

Brough Castle

This small town, standing at the point where the Stainmore Pass opens into the Vale of Eden, is, in fact, two settlements: Church Brough and Market Brough. Church Brough is a group of neat houses and cottages clustered around a little market square in which a maypole stands on the site of the former market cross. **Brough Castle**, built within the ramparts of the Roman camp of Verterae, was constructed to protect the Roman road over Stainmore Pass. The building of this Norman castle was begun by William Rufus in 1095, but it was largely destroyed in 1174 by William the Lion of Scotland. Another fortification restored by the remarkable Lady Anne Clifford, the castle, with its tall keep 60 feet high, is well worth visiting, if only for the superb panorama of the surrounding fells seen from the battlements.

The distinctive low hills that lie to the west of Brough are drumlins - heaps of material deposited by Ice Age glaciers. In this area many drumlins are marked by broad, grassy ridges, remains of ancient lynchets or ploughing strips.

NORTH STAINMORE

11 miles SE of Appleby-in-Westmorland on the A66

Maiden Castle Rey Stone

The village lies on the Stainmore Pass, which carries the old Roman road, now the A66, through a remote area of the North Pennines and which David Bellamy has described as "England's last wilderness". Near Stainmore summit are the foundations of **Maiden Castle**, a Roman fort built to guard the pass against marauders. A few yards over the Cumbrian border, into County Durham, is the stump of the ancient **Rey Cross**, which was erected before AD946 and which, until 1092, marked the boundary between England and Scotland. It is thought to be the site of the battle at which the last Viking King of York and North England, Eric Bloodaxe, was killed following his expulsion from the city.

GREAT ASBY

4 miles S of Appleby-in-Westmorland off the B6260

This pretty village is set in a wooded hollow, its houses separated by Hoff Beck. Alongside the beck is St Helen's Well, which is said never to run dry or freeze. Nearby, are the splendid almshouses of St Helen's, built between 1811 and 1820. Across a footbridge is Asby Hall (private), built in 1670. It was once the home of the Musgrave family of Edenhall whose crest and coat of arms can still be seen above the door.

TEMPLE SOWERBY

7 miles NW of Appleby-in-Westmorland on the A66

Cross Fell | Acorn Bank

Temple Sowerby prides itself on the title 'Queen of Westmorland villages', an accolade justified by its lovely setting in the Eden valley, but somewhat qualified by its position on the busy A66. A bypass is currently being constructed.

A bonus that comes with living in Temple Sowerby is that the average rainfall here is half that recorded in the Lake District National Park to the west. To the north, the massive bulk of **Cross Fell**, the highest point in the Pennines, swells skywards to provide a spectacular backdrop. The village itself, picturesquely grouped around a sloping green and an 18th-century red sandstone church, takes its name from the medieval Knights Templar who owned the manor of Sowerby until their Order was suppressed in 1308.

From Temple Sowerby there are delightful walks through the Eden Valley or, if you prefer a gentle stroll, it's only a mile to the National Trust gardens at **Acorn Bank** where Crowdundle Beck splashes beneath an elegant 18th-century bridge. The 16th-century manor house is now a Sue Ryder Home and not open to the public, but visitors are welcome to explore the attractive gardens planted with a collection of some 250 medicinal and culinary herbs. There's also a pleasant tearoom that uses fruit and herbs from the gardens. A circular woodland walk runs along the beck to a watermill that was first mentioned on the site as far back as the 14th century. At different times it has been a saw mill, a corn mill and a source of power for the local gypsum mines; now restored, it is open to visitors.

Carlisle

Carlisle Castle | Regimental Museum
Carlisle Cathedral | Prior's Tower | West Walls
St Cuthbert's Church | Old Tullie House
Tullie House Museum & Art Gallery
Linton Visitor Centre | Guildhall Museum
Citadel | Settle-Carlisle Railway
Kingmoor Nature Reserve

Carlisle is the largest settlement in Cumbria, with a population of around 72,500, and is also its county town. The city stands at the junction of three rivers, the Eden, the Caldew and the Petteril, and was already fortified in Celtic times when it was named Caer Lue, the 'hill fort'. It became a major Roman centre as the military base for the Petriana regiment, Luguvallum, guarding the western end of Hadrian's Wall, and also an important civilian settlement with fountains, mosaics, statues and centrally-heated homes.

Today, the squat outline of **Carlisle Castle** (English Heritage) dominates the skyline of this fascinating city. The original Norman castle was built of wood but, during the Scottish occupation in the 12th century, King David I

laid out a new castle with stones taken from Hadrian's Wall. The 12th-century keep can still be seen enclosed by massive inner and outer walls. Entry is through a great 14th-century gatehouse, complete with portcullis, and with a maze of vaulted passages, chambers, staircases, towers, and dismal dungeons. Children, especially, enjoy the legendary 'licking stones' from which parched Jacobite prisoners tried to find enough moisture to stay alive. Archaeologists working outside the castle walls unearthed the remains of three Roman forts, and many of the finds are on display in a special exhibition at the castle. Carlisle Castle is everything a real castle should be, and is still the headquarters of the King's Own Royal Border Regiment, whose **Regimental Museum** is located within the castle walls.

Carlisle Cathedral has many interesting features, including an exquisite 14th-century east window that is considered to be one of the finest in Europe. Below the beautifully painted wooden ceiling of the choir, with its gold stars shimmering against a deep blue background, are the carved, canopied choir-stalls with their medieval misericords. These wonderful carved beasts and birds include two dragons joined by the ears, a fox killing a goose, pelicans feeding their young, and a mermaid with a looking glass. In St Wilfrid's Chapel is the superb 16th-century Flemish Brougham Triptych, which was originally in Cologne Cathedral.

It was at Carlisle Cathedral that Edward I solemnly used bell, book and candle to excommunicate Robert the Bruce, and here, too, the bells were rung to welcome Bonnie Prince Charlie in 1745.

Although an appointment is usually necessary, a visit to the nearby **Prior's Tower** is a must. On the first floor of this 15th-century pele tower is a wonderful panelled ceiling incorporating the popinjay crest and arms of the Prior Senhouse. The 16th-century Prior's gatehouse leads to a narrow lane called Paternoster, named after the monks reciting their offices.

Like many great medieval cities, Carlisle was surrounded by walls. Guided walks and tours are available and the best view is to be found in a little street called **West Walls** at the bottom of Sally Port Steps, near the Tithe Barn. The walls date from around the 11th

Carlisle Cathedral

century and they remained virtually intact until the 1800s.

Close by is **St Cuthbert's Church**, the official city church of Carlisle and where the Lord Mayor's pew can be found. Although the present building dates from 1778, there has been a church on this site since the 7th century and the dedication is obvious, since St Cuthbert was Bishop of Carlisle in AD680. It is a charming Georgian building with several interesting features including a moveable pulpit on rails.

The award-winning **Tullie House Museum & Art Gallery**, in the centre of the city close to the Cathedral, is certainly another place not to be missed. Through skilful and interpretive techniques the fascinating, and often dark, history of the Debatable Lands, as this border region was called, is told. The museum's centrepiece is its story of the Border Reivers who occupied the lands from the 14th to the 17th century. The horrific stories of the Reivers have been passed down through the generations in the Border Ballads, and many of the Reivers family names are still known - the museum even offers a genealogy service, so that visitors can find out if their ancestry goes back to these people. The city of Carlisle dates back far beyond those desperate days and Tullie House also has an extensive collection of Roman remains from both the city and the Cumbrian section of Hadrian's Wall. The Art Gallery features contemporary arts and crafts, and the spectacular underground Millennium Gallery has a stunning collection of local minerals, archaeological finds of wood and leather, artist-made glass and interactive exhibits. **Old Tullie House** showcases paintings and drawings by renowned Pre-Raphaelite artists, as well as other artworks and a selection of fine English porcelain. A short walk from the Museum you'll find the **Linton Visitor Centre** in Shaddongate, which provides an insight into the city's industrial heritage.

The **Guildhall Museum**, housed in an unspoiled medieval building constructed by Richard of Redeness in 1407, provides an ideal setting for illustrating the history of both the

Guilds and the City. Not far from the Guildhall is the **Citadel**, which is often mistaken for the castle. In fact, this intimidating fortress, with its well-preserved circular tower, was built in 1543 on the orders of Henry VIII to strengthen the city's defences. Much of it was demolished in the early 1800s to improve access to the city centre, but what remains is mightily impressive.

Across the road from the Citadel is the railway station. The first railway to Carlisle opened in July 1836 and Citadel Station, which opened in 1850, was built to serve seven different railway companies whose coats of arms are still displayed on the facade. So elegant was its interior - and much of it remains - that Carlisle was known as the 'top hat' station. Today, it is still an important centre of communications; InterCity trains from Glasgow and London now link with lines to Dumfries, Tyneside, West Cumbria and Yorkshire, and it is, of course, the northern terminus of the famous **Settle - Carlisle Railway** line.

One of the last great mainline railways to be built in Britain - it was completed in 1876 - the Settle to Carlisle line takes in some of the most dramatic scenery that the north of England has to offer. Scenic it may be, but the terrain caused the Victorian engineers many problems and it is thanks to their ingenuity and skill that the line was ever finished. During the course of its 72 miles, the line crosses 20 viaducts and passes through 12 tunnels, each of which was constructed by an army of navvies who had little in the way of resources besides their strength and some dynamite to remove the rock.

Located on the northwestern edge of the city, **Kingmoor Nature Reserve** occupies an area of moorland given to the city in 1352 by Edward III. Citizens enjoyed the right to graze sheep on the moors and to cut peat for fuel. Later, Carlisle's first racecourse was established here with annual Guild races being held up until 1850. Then in 1913, Kingmoor became one of the first bird sanctuaries in England and today provides a peaceful retreat away from the bustle of the city. A half-mile circular path wanders through the woodland with gentle gradients of 1 in 20 making it fully accessible to wheelchairs and pushchairs, and with seats every 100 yards or so providing plenty of resting places. Another path links the reserve to Kingmoor Sidings, which since the old railway sheds closed has been colonised by a wide variety of wildlife.

Around Carlisle

WREAY

5 miles S of Carlisle off the A6

Church of St Mary

This little village is known for its extraordinary **Church of St Mary**, designed by a local woman, Sarah Losh, in memory of her sister and her parents. It was built in 1835 and incorporates many Italian Romanesque features. The church is full of beautiful touches, including the carvings, mostly by Sarah herself, on the font.

IVEGILL

8 miles S of Carlisle off the A6 or B5305

High Head Sculpture Valley

The tiny hamlet of Ivegill, hidden away in lovely countryside south of Carlisle, boasts a unique attraction in the shape of **High Head Sculpture Valley** (see panel on page 144). Magnificent life-size sculptures are imaginatively displayed in a natural woodland valley; there are changing exhibitions in the

HIGH HEAD SCULPTURE VALLEY

High Head Farm, Ivegill, Carlisle,
Cumbria CA4 0PJ
Tel/Fax: 01697 473552
e-mail: highheadvalley@aol.com
website: www.highheadsculpturevalley.co.uk

An intoxicating mix of exciting contemporary art, relaxing spa treatments and delicious farmhouse food draw visitors from all over the world to **High Head Sculpture Valley**. Nestling in a tranquil, leafy valley overlooking the Lake District Fells, this unique enterprise rejuvenates mind, body and soul.

Constantly changing exhibitions in the indoor art galleries display high-quality ceramics, glassware, paintings, furniture and sculptures from celebrated artists and craftsmen. Outside, in the dramatic High Head Valley, stunning life-size sculptures emerge from the undergrowth, complementing and reflecting the natural ebb and flow of nature throughout the seasons. On the horizon Cumbria's newest stone circle evokes the area's mysterious ancient history as its shadows trace the time of the day. The stones' ethereal qualities are best appreciated by moonlight.

Find solace in the High Head Spa with a range of health and beauty treatments that relax the mind, invigorate the body and refresh the soul. Combine your visit with a delicious lunch or high tea from the farmhouse kitchen from where you can watch High Head's resident family of inquisitive red squirrels moving through the trees.

On your way out search the *Made in Cumbria* crafts for that perfect gift or call into the High Head Farm Shop, which stocks a large variety of organic produce.

Art Gallery; traditional, freshly prepared Cumbrian food is served in the farmhouse tea room, and the site also contains a farm shop, Dolls' Gallery and a children's play area.

BURGH BY SANDS

5 miles W of Carlisle off the B5307

Church of St Michael

On 7th July 1307, the body of King Edward I was laid out in the village church: he was already a dying man when he left Carlisle to march against his old enemy, Robert the Bruce. A monument to Edward was erected on the marshes and a later monument still marks the spot. At the time of the king's death, the **Church of St Michael** was already well over a century old and is possibly the earliest surviving example of a fortified church. Dating from 1181 and constructed entirely of stones from a fort on the Roman wall, the church was designed for protection against Border raids, which is why its tower has walls seven feet thick.

BOWNESS-ON-SOLWAY

14 miles W of Carlisle off the B5307

Hadrian's Wall

Glasson Moss National Nature Reserve

Hadrian's Wall continues along the Solway coast to Bowness and many of the sandstone cottages around here contain stones from the wall. Some of these stones can easily be identified, such as the small inscribed altar let into a barn near the King's Arms. The Roman fort of Maia once covered a seven-acre site, but today there is only a plaque explaining where it used to be. Bowness is sometimes said to be the end of the Wall, but, in fact, it just turned a corner here and continued south along the coast for another 40 miles.

Two miles south of the village lies **Glasson Moss National Nature Reserve**, a lowland raised mire extending to 93 hectares. Many species of sphagnum moss are to be found here, and the birdlife includes red grouse, curlew, sparrow hawk and snipe.

LONGTOWN

9 miles N of Carlisle on the A7

Arthuret Church

Church of St Michael and All Angels

Situated on the north side of Hadrian's Wall, only a couple of miles from the Scottish border, this is the last town in England. Its position on the River Esk so close to the border has influenced its history from earliest times. The Romans occupied this land and they were followed by other conquerors. The legendary King Arthur attempted to organise the Northern Britons against the pagan hordes who tried to settle and control this territory. In AD573 the mighty battle of Ardderyd was fought here and, according to legend, 80,000 men were slain.

On the outskirts of Longtown is **Arthuret Church**. The earliest records of the church date from 1150 and it was originally served by the monks of Jedburgh. But it is thought that the earliest church here may have been founded by St Kentigern in the 6th century; recent research has led some to believe that King Arthur was actually interred here after his last battle, Camboglanna, was fought a few miles east of Longtown at Gilsland. The present church, dedicated to **St Michael and All Angels**, was built in 1609, financed by a general collection throughout the realm, which James I ordered after a report that the people of Arthuret Church were without faith or religion. The people that he referred to, of course, were the infamous Reivers, ungoverned by either English or Scottish laws. Archie Armstrong, favourite Court Jester to James I and later to Charles I, is buried in the churchyard.

CROSBY-ON-EDEN

4 miles NE of Carlisle off the A689

Solway Aviation Museum

The tiny hamlet of High Crosby stands on the hillside overlooking the River Eden; the small village of Low Crosby sits beside the river, clustered around a Victorian sandstone church. Inside the church there's a modern square pulpit, intricately carved with pomegranates, wheat and vines. It was carved from one half of a tree felled nearby; the other half was used to create a second pulpit, which was installed in the newly-built Liverpool Cathedral.

A couple of miles east of Crosby, The **Solway Aviation Museum** is one of only a few museums located on a 'live' airfield, in this case Carlisle Airport. Opened in 1997, the museum is home to several British jet aircraft of the 1950s and 1960s, among them the mighty Vulcan and the Canberra. Other exhibits include a wartime air raid shelter where a video presentation explains the story behind the museum, displays of the Blue Streak rocket programme, testing for which took place only a few miles from here, and a very impressive engine room, which houses one of Frank Whittle's first development jet engines.

Bewcastle Cross

BEWCASTLE

14 miles NE of Carlisle off the B6318

Castle Bewcastle Cross

Roman legionaries assigned to the fort at what is now Bewcastle must certainly have felt that they had drawn the short straw. The fort stood all on its own, about nine miles north of Hadrian's Wall, guarding a crossing over the Kirk Beck. The site covered around six acres and most of it is now occupied by the ruins of a Norman **Castle**. Most of the south wall is still standing but little else remains and the castle is best admired for its setting rather than its architecture.

A much more impressive survival dominates the village churchyard. Here stands the **Bewcastle Cross**, erected around AD670 and one of the oldest and finest stone crosses in Europe. Standing over 13 feet in height, its intricate Celtic carvings have survived the centuries of weathering and much of the runic inscription can still be made out in the yellow sandstone. One of the carvings, a semicircle with 13 radiating lines, three of which have crossbars, is believed to be a sophisticated sundial, which not only indicated the 12 hours of the Roman clock but also the three 'tides' of the Saxon day - morning, noon and eventide.

WETHERAL

4 miles E of Carlisle off the A69

Parish Church Eden Benchmarks

Constantine's Caves Corby Castle

Wetheral stands above the River Eden, over which runs an impressive railway viaduct, carrying the Tyne Valley Line, which was built by Francis Giles in 1830. Wetheral **Parish Church** lies below the village beside the river and contains a poignant sculpture by Joseph Nollekens of the dying Lady Mary Howard clasping her dead baby. Nearby, occupying a lovely riverside setting, is one of the **Eden Benchmarks**, a sculptured bench in St Bee's sandstone by Tim Shutter, entitled *Flight of Fancy*.

St Constantine was the local patron and the church is dedicated to the Holy Trinity, St Constantine and St Mary. Constantine is said to have lived in caves in what are now National Trust woodlands alongside the river, a location known as **Constantine's Caves**. Constantine died as a martyr in AD657 and a life-sized statue of him can be seen in the grounds of **Corby Castle** to the south of the village. The castle, with its impressive 13th-century keep and terraced gardens overlooking the Eden, is usually open during the summer months.

During the reign of William Rufus, one of his barons, Ranulph Meschin, founded a priory for Benedictine monks at Wetheral above a red-rock gorge of the River Eden. All that remains now is the imposing three-storey gatehouse.

Brampton

Moot Hall Bonnie Prince Charlie

St Martin's Church

Nestling in the heart of the lovely Irthing Valley, Brampton is a delightful little town where the Wednesday market has been held since 1252, authorised by a charter granted by Henry III. Overlooking the Market Place is the town's most striking building, the octagonal **Moot Hall** topped by a handsome clock tower.

Just around the corner, in High Cross Street, is the house (now a shop) which once witnessed one of the high points in **Bonnie Prince Charlie's** rebellion of 1745. It was here that the Prince stayed during the siege of Carlisle and it was here, on November 17th 1745, that the Mayor and Aldermen presented him with the keys to the city. A few months later, following the Prince's defeat, six of his supporters were hanged on the Capon Tree on the south side of the town and in sight of the Scottish hills. The tree survived until the last century and in its place there now stands a monument commemorating the doleful event.

Just off the Market Place is **St Martin's Church**, which was built anew in 1874 and contains one of the best kept secrets of the area - some magnificent stained glass windows designed by one of the founder members of the pre-Raphaelite brotherhood, Edward Burne-Jones. It was his fellow-member of the brotherhood, Philip Webb, William Morris's associate, who designed the church and insisted that contemporary stained glass should be installed.

The area around Brampton had good reason to be grateful to the Dacres of Naworth, who as Wardens of the Northern Marches protected it against marauding Scots. However, the townspeople of Brampton in Victorian times must have had mixed feelings about a later descendant, Rosalind, wife of the 9th Earl of Carlisle. An enthusiastic supporter of total abstinence, she contrived to get most of the small town's 40 public houses and drinking rooms closed.

South of Brampton are Gelt Woods, lying in a deep sandstone ravine carved by the fast-flowing River Gelt. By the river is an inscribed rock called Written Rock, which is thought to have been carved by a Roman standard bearer in AD207.

Around Brampton

TALKIN

2 miles S of Brampton off the B6413

Talkin Tarn

Talkin Tarn, now the focus of a 120-acre country park, has been a popular place for watersports for more than 100 years. Glacial in origin, the Tarn was formed some 10,000 years ago and is continually replenished by underground springs. Modern day visitors can sail, windsurf, canoe or hire one of the original wooden rowing boats. Talkin Tarn Rowing Club has been rowing on the tarn for 130 years and holds its annual regatta in July. Fishing licences are available, and there's a nature trail and an orienteering course, a play area for children under eight, a tea room and a gift shop; guided walks with a warden are also available for organised groups.

Lanercost Priory

LOW ROW

3 miles E of Brampton off the A69

Lanercost Priory   Naworth Castle

Within easy reach of the town is Hadrian's Wall, just three miles to the north. If you've ever wondered where the Wall's missing masonry went to, look no further than the fabric of **Lanercost Priory** (English Heritage). An impressive red sandstone ruin set in secluded woodland, the priory was founded in 1166 by Robert de Vaux. Lanercost is well preserved and its scale is a reminder that it was a grand complex in its heyday. However, the priory suffered greatly in the border raids of the 13th and 14th centuries. One such raid is known to have been led by William Wallace, an early campaigner for Scottish independence from English rule. When the Priory was closed in 1536, the sandstone blocks were recycled once again for houses in the town. But much of the Priory's great north aisle remains intact, set in a romantic and hauntingly beautiful position in the valley of the River Irthing. The Priory is well signposted and lies only three miles off the A69 (leave at Brampton).

Also most impressive is **Naworth Castle**, built around 1335 in its present form by Lord Dacre as an important border stronghold. The castle's supreme glory is the Great Hall, hung with French tapestries and guarded by four unique heraldic beasts holding aloft their family pennants. The Long Gallery extends for 116 feet and was used as a guardroom.

GILSLAND

7 miles E of Brampton on the B6318

Hadrian's Wall · Birdoswald Roman Fort

Popping Stone

Hadrian's Wall was built between AD122 and AD128 as a great military barrier across the narrowest part of Britain, from the mouth of the River Tyne in the east, to Bowness-on-Solway in the west. The wall was finally abandoned in the late 4th century, and in later centuries many of the stones were used for local buildings and field walls. There are many ways of exploring the Wall (including the bus number AD122!), and for those with the energy to walk from end to end the newly-opened Hadrian's Wall National Trail passes some of the country's greatest archaeological monuments.

Located in one of the most picturesque settings along the whole length of Hadrian's Wall, and overlooking the River Irthing, **Birdoswald Roman Fort** is one of the best preserved mile-castles along the Wall and unique in that all the components of the Roman frontier system can be found here. Set high on a plateau with magnificent views over the surrounding countryside, the early turf wall, built in AD122, can be seen along with the fort. Originally, this fort would have covered five acres and it may have been the base for up to 500 cavalry and 1000 foot soldiers.

Birdoswald Roman Fort, Gilsland

Gilsland village is also known for its sulphur spring and there was once a convalescent home for miners and shipyard workers here. It is now owned by the Co-operative Society and people still drink the waters as a cure for arthritis and rheumatism. Near the spring is the **Popping Stone**, traditionally the place where a man 'popped the question' to his lover. It was here that Sir Walter Scott successfully popped the question to Charlotte Carpenter.

LOCATOR MAP

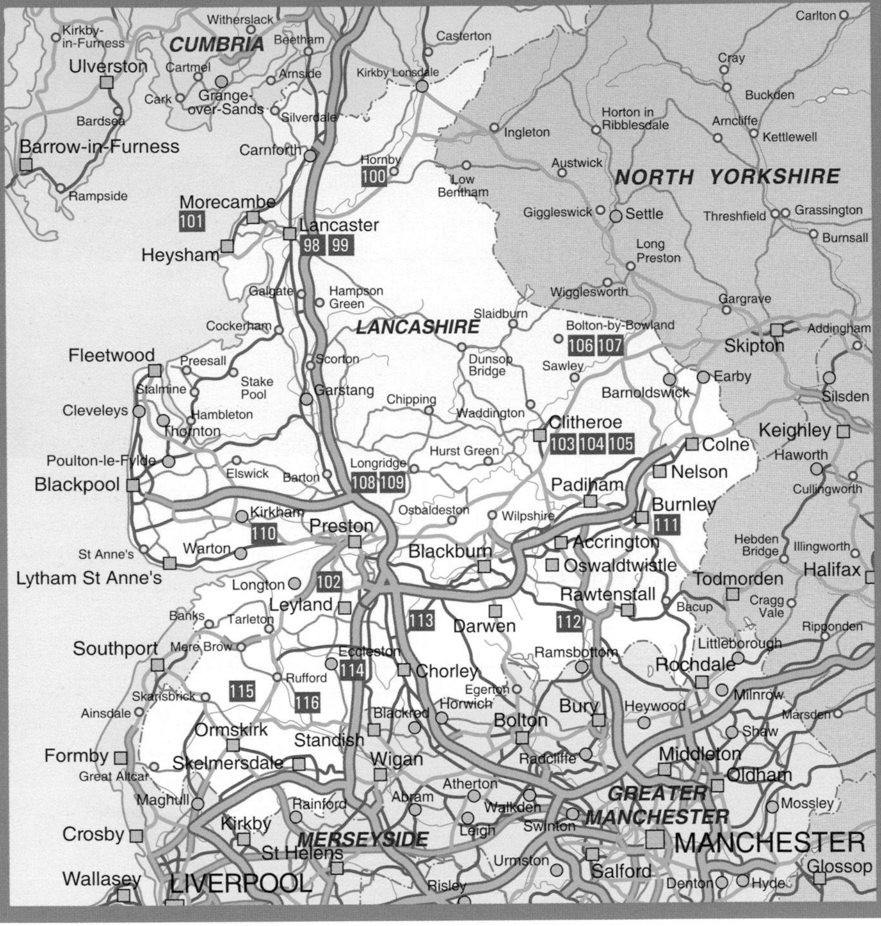

ADVERTISERS AND PLACES OF INTEREST

Accommodation, Food and Drink

102 | Whitestake Farm, Whitestake, nr Preston *pg 174*
105 | Taste@Clitheroe, Clitheroe *pg 178*
106 | Springhead Farm Holiday Cottages, Bolton by Bowland, nr Clitheroe *pg 181*
116 | Art at Cedar Farm, Mawdesley, nr Ormskirk *pg 224*

Activities

102 | Whitestake Farm, Whitestake, nr Preston *pg 174*
109 | Pure Organic Spa, Longridge, nr Preston *pg 186*

Arts and Crafts

101 | Cakes and Cutters, Morecambe *pg 162*
108 | Moss Speciality Gallery Shopkes, Longridge, nr Preston *pg 186*
114 | Hepplestone Fine Art, Eccleston, nr Chorley *pg 217*
116 | Art at Cedar Farm, Mawdesley, nr Ormskirk *pg 224*

Home & Garden

109 | Pure Organic Spa, Longridge, nr Preston *pg 186*
110 | Simply Natural, Kirkham *pg 198*
113 | The Soft Furnisher, Wheelton, nr Chorley *pg 214*
116 | Art at Cedar Farm, Mawdesley, nr Ormskirk *pg 224*

historic building museum and heritage historic site scenic attraction flora and fauna

2 | Lancashire

As the well-known Lancashire comedian, Les Dawson, commented in his book on the county, it is "many things to many people" with "vast smoky grey blocks of heavy industry", but also a countryside of "lakes and woods and rolling hills". It is also a place of great history: the Wars of the Roses; the old Catholic families and their support of Charles I during the Civil War; the trials of the Pendle Witches; and the innovators who started the Industrial Revolution in the textile industry.

The ancient county town of Lancaster is an excellent place to start any journey of discovery. Small and compact, it has the added advantage of having been off the general tourist routes, which can make York, its larger, White Rose equivalent, somewhat hard going in the height of the season.

To the northeast lies Leck Fell, just south of Kirkby Lonsdale and Cumbria. It is easy for the visitor to mistake this for the Yorkshire Dales as there is a typical craggy limestone gorge along the little valley of Leck Beck, as well as one of the most extensive cave systems in the British Isles. A natural route from Kirkby Lonsdale back to the county town is marked by the River Lune. The best way to enjoy this wonderful green and hilly area of Lancashire is to follow the Lune Valley Ramble, which travels the valley's intimate pastoral setting, through woodland, meadows, and along the riverside itself.

To the west lies Morecambe Bay, a treacherous place where, over the centuries, many walkers have lost their lives in an attempt to make the journey to the Furness Peninsula in Cumbria considerably shorter. Walks across the sands should only be undertaken with the aid of one of the highly knowledgeable and experienced guides. Despite its grim history, the bay offers superb views, including glorious sunsets, as well as being an important habitat for a wide variety of birds.

Extending across much of the north of the county is the Forest of Bowland, an ancient royal hunting ground that is dotted with small, isolated villages. With no major roads passing through the area, it has remained little changed and, with so many splendid walks and fine countryside, it is also relatively quiet even during the busiest summer weeks.

ADVERTISERS AND PLACES OF INTEREST

stories and anecdotes | famous people | art and craft | entertainment and sport | walks

Lancaster

Priory Church of St Mary · Priory Tower
Lancaster Castle · Shire Hall · City Museum
Museum of the King's Own Royal Regiment
Maritime Museum · Judge's Lodgings
Cottage Museum · Music Room
Ashton Memorial · Williamson Park
Butterfly House · Lancaster Leisure Park

An architecturally pleasing city, Lancaster is one of the most appealing of English county capitals. Most of the county's administrative offices are now based in Preston, so Lancaster enjoys all the prestige of being the capital without the burden of housing the accompanying bureaucrats. The city also takes pride in the fact that the Duke of Lancaster is the only duke in the kingdom who is a woman – no less a personage than HM the Queen for whom the dukedom is one of many subsidiary titles.

Lancaster's story begins some 2000 years ago when the Romans built a fort on a hill overlooking a sweep of the River Lune, a site now occupied by the unspoiled 15th-century **Priory Church of St Mary.** Right up until the Industrial Revolution, Lancashire was one of the poorest counties in England, lacking the wealth to endow glorious cathedrals or magnificent parish churches. St Mary's is a notable exception, the finest medieval church in the county. It stands on the site of Lancashire's first monastery, which was closed not, like most others, by Henry VIII, but by Henry V in 1413. Henry was at war with France, the monastery's mother abbey was at Sées in Normandy, so the 'alien priory' in Lancaster had to be dissolved. The present church contains treasures rescued from the closed priory such as the sumptuously carved wooden choir stalls from around 1345.

Each stall is covered by a superb canopy, lavishly carved with around a hundred small heads and faces surrounded by abundant foliage. Also of note are the fragments of Anglo-Saxon crosses and some very fine needlework. The **Priory Tower**, also on the hilltop, was rebuilt in 1759 as a landmark for ships navigating their way into the River Lune. Nearby is one of Lancaster's links with its Roman past – the remains of a bath house, which also served soldiers as an inn.

Close by is **Lancaster Castle** (see panel opposite), one of the best-preserved Norman fortresses in the country. Dating back to 1200, and with a massive gatehouse flanked by sturdy twin towers, the castle dominates the centre of the city. For centuries, the castle served as a prison, only relinquishing that function as recently as 1996. At the back of the castle, the **Shire Hall** is still in use as a Crown Court and one of its more macabre attractions is the Drop Room where prisoners were prepared for the gallows. The Court's long history has been blemished by two shocking major miscarriages of justice. The first was in 1612 when the Pendle "witches" (see under Pendle Hill page 204) were convicted of sorcery and executed; the second in 1975 when the "Birmingham Six" were found guilty of an IRA bombing and spent 15 years in prison before their names were cleared.

A short walk from the castle leads into the largely pedestrianised city centre, full of shops, the market, and much besides. The **City Museum** in the Market Place occupies the Old Town Hall, built between 1781-83 by Major Jarrett and Thomas Harrison. As well as the city's art collection and an area of changing exhibitions, there are displays and collections of material illustrating aspects of the city's industrial and social history. Also here is the **Museum of the King's Own Royal Regiment**, a regiment that was based in Lancaster from 1880 onwards.

Lancaster grew up along the banks of the River Lune, which is navigable as far as Skerton Bridge, so there has always been a strong association between the town and its watery highway. Documents from 1297 make reference to the town's small-scale maritime trade, but it was not until the late 1600s and early 1700s that Lancaster's character as a port fully emerged. The splendid buildings of the 18t- century Golden Age were born out of the port wealth, and the layout and appearance of the town was much altered by this building bonanza. Lancaster's importance as a port steadily declined throughout the 19th century so that many buildings originally intended for maritime purposes were taken over for other uses.

Lancaster enjoyed its era of greatest prosperity during the 18th century when its quays were busy servicing a thriving trade with the West Indies in rum, sugar, cotton – and slaves. The city's rich maritime history is celebrated at St George's Quay which, with its great stone warehouses and superb Custom

Lancaster Castle

Shire Hall, Castle Parade, Lancaster, Lancashire LA1 1YJ
Tel: 01524 64998 Fax: 01524 847914
website: www.lancashire.gov.uk/resources/ps/castle/index.htm

Lancaster Castle is owned by Her Majesty the Queen in right of her Duchy of Lancaster. For most of its history the castle has been the centre of law and order for the county, and this magnificent building is still in use as a prison and a crown court.

The castle has dominated the town for almost 1000 years, ever since it was first established in 1093. But the hill on which it stands has a history that goes back a thousand years further, almost to the birth of Christ. The Romans built the first of at least three military forts on the site in AD79.

Little is known about Lancaster until 1093 when the Norman Baron, Roger of Poitou, built a small motte and bailey castle, which was replaced 50 years later by a large stone Keep that still stands today and is the oldest part of the Castle. Throughout its long history it has witnessed many trials, including that of the Lancashire Witches of 1612, which resulted in the execution of 10 people.

Although still a working building, guided tours of the castle include where the witches were condemned to die; the beautiful Gillow furniture in the Grand Jury Room; the dungeons and Drop Room from where the condemned went to their deaths; the Crown Court from where thousands were transported to Australia; Hanging Corner - the site of public hangings, and the magnificent Shire Hall with its display of heraldic shields.

Criminals and convicts, monarchs and majesty, dungeons and death, treason and transportation, witches and martyrs, all have their place in the history of this most fascinating building.

House, is now an award-winning **Maritime Museum** (see panel below). Visitors today are given a vivid insight into the life of the mariners and quayside workers with opportunities for knot-tying and the practising of other maritime skills. Every year, over the four days of the Easter weekend, St George's Quay is home to the Lancaster Maritime Festival with a programme that involves boisterous 'smugglers', sea songs, and shanties.

Fire destroyed most of Tudor and Jacobean Lancaster, but one notable survivor is the **Judge's Lodgings** in Church Street, a charming Jacobean house built in the 1620s and now a museum: two museums in fact. There's the **Museum of Childhood**, which includes the Barry Elder Doll collection, and the **Gillow and Town House Museum** containing many examples of the fine workmanship produced by the famous Lancaster cabinet-makers, Gillows. It was a scion of this family, Richard Gillow, who designed the city's Maritime Museum.

Close by is the **Cottage Museum** in a house, built in 1739, that was divided into two dwellings in 1820. Furnished in the style of an artisan's house of the early to mid-19th century, the museum is open from Easter to the end of September. Just around a corner or two, in Sun Street, is the **Music Room**, an exquisite early Georgian building originally designed as a pavilion in the long vanished garden of Oliver Marton. It is notable for some superb decorative plasterwork.

Lancaster's most prominent landmark, visible for miles around, is the extravagant, temple-like **Ashton Memorial** – "the grandest monument in England" according to Nikolaus Pevsner. Erected in 1907 as a memorial to his wife by the local MP and millionaire lino-manufacturer Lord Ashton, it stands on the highest point in Lancaster, set within a beautifully landscaped park and enjoying sweeping views of the Cumbrian hills and across Morecambe Bay. The building now houses exhibitions and multi-screen presentations about the life and times of Lord Ashton and the Edwardian period.

Williamson Park was Lord Ashton's own personal project as a means of providing work for local people during the cotton famine crisis in the textile industry during the American Civil War in the 1860s. Constructed on the site of old quarries, which gives the park its undulating contours, the park was opened in 1896. As well as the magnificent Ashton Memorial there is

Lancaster Maritime Museum

Custom House, St George's Quay, Lancaster LA1 1RB
Tel: 01524 64637 Fax: 01524 841692

The **Lancaster Maritime Museum** was opened in 1985 and occupies the former Custom House, buit in 1764 by Richard Gillow, and an adjacent warehouse.

Using sound, smells, reconstructions and audio visuals it tells the story of the port of Lancaster, the Lancaster Canal, fishing and the ecology of Morecambe Bay. A number of exhibitions can be seen and there is an education programme for children. Facilities include a shop, café, car parking and disabled access.

also a delightful **Butterfly House** in the now restored Edwardian Palm House, and a Conservation Garden and Wildlife Pool, which opened in 1991.

Another place the whole family can enjoy is **Lancaster Leisure Park** on Wyresdale Road. Set in 42 acres of landscaped parkland, the site includes a mini-marina, a Wild West adventure playground, a miniature railway, a rare breeds unit, a children's farmyard, pony rides, gift shop, tea garden, and pottery shop.

North of Lancaster

NETHER KELLET

4 miles N of Lancaster off the B6254

This farming village has a traditional village green, which features several old wells and pumps. This is appropriate since the Old Norse word *chellet*, now Kellet, means "a spring". Local brewers of home ale still use the spring water because of its purity and absence of chemicals. Quarrying has taken place here for many centuries and lime burning has been an important local industry. Its remains, in the form of lime kilns, can still be seen around the village and the local pub is named the Lime Burners Arms.

The village has its own cave, Dunold Mill, through which flows a large stream that dives underground to appear two miles further north at Carnforth. During the mid-1800s the cave was occupied by a hermit who lived there until his death at the age of 100. His descendants still live in the village.

CARNFORTH

6 miles N of Lancaster on the A6

Carnforth Station Visitor Centre · Lunedale Walk

The town lies around what was once a major crossroads on the A6 that has now been superseded by the M6. It was also a busy railway junction town whose station was used as the setting for the 1940s film classic *Brief Encounter*. The station was later voted one of the most atmospheric film locations in the country. At the award-winning **Carnforth Station Visitor Centre** (free) the refreshment room that featured in the film has been replicated, there are some specialist outlets and guided tours are available. Platform 1 has recently acquired a new use as the venue for a Farmers Market held on the 4th Wednesday of each month.

Bookworms will know Carnforth as home to one of the best second-hand bookshops in the country. The town is also the starting point of the **Lunedale Walk**, a 37-mile circuit of the hills and valleys on the north side of the River Lune.

YEALAND

8 miles N of Lancaster off the A6

Leighton Hall

To the south of the village lies **Leighton Hall** – a fine early 19th-century house that is open to the public. During the Middle Ages the land on which it stands, together with much of the surrounding area, was owned by the d'Avranches family. Over the centuries, the house and the land passed through many hands before becoming the property of the famous furniture-making Gillows family of Lancaster. Now in the hands of the Reynolds family, a branch of the Gillows, the fine furniture seen in the hall reflects the trade that made the family fortune.

As with many estates in Lancashire, Leighton Hall was a Catholic house and one owner, Sir George Middleton, was fined heavily by Cromwell after the Civil War for his loyalty to Charles I and to his religion. Later, another owner of the hall, Albert Hodgson, suffered for his loyalty to Catholicism and the Stuart claim on the throne of England. Taking part in the Jacobite rebellion of 1715, Hodgson was captured at Preston and the Government troops inflicted such damage on the Hall that little remained of the Tudor structure.

The present Hall dates from 1800 when it was built out of pale, local sandstone to the Gothic designs of Harrison, a Chester architect. One of the finest houses in the county, the views from the extensive grounds are magnificent and take in the nearby Leighton Moss Bird Reserve. Guided tours of the Hall are available, there are superb displays from birds of prey, a high quality gift shop, plant conservatory and tea room.

SILVERDALE

10 miles N of Lancaster off the A6

Leighton Moss

The village lies at the northwesternmost corner of the county and has the Lakeland hills as a backdrop as well as superb views over Morecambe Bay. The latter half of the 19th century saw Silverdale develop as a quiet seaside resort where those so inclined could take medicinal baths of fresh sea water in one of the many small villas situated along the coast. One frequent visitor was Elizabeth Gaskell who is said to have written some of her books whilst holidaying here.

However, Silverdale's history goes back well beyond the days of a genteel Victorian resort. Its name comes from a Viking family that settled here and signifies that this was Sigward's or Soevers' valley. Fishing, naturally, was the key provider of local income, but in the 18th century, a copper smelting works was built here. All that remains of the foundry is the chimney near Jenny Brown's Point, said to be named after an old woman who lived here in the 1700s.

Silverdale is well worth visiting for the network of footpaths that pass through the limestone woodlands that are a joy for the botanist, especially in spring when primroses, violets, orchids, bird's eye primroses, rockroses and eglantines abound.

Leighton Moss near Silverdale is a nationally known RSPB bird sanctuary. The reed beds are the most important part of the reserve because they have become a northern stronghold of the rare Bearded Tit and are also the major British breeding centre for the Bittern. Visitors can follow the nature trails, browse in the RSPB shop, or enjoy a meal in the tearoom.

HALTON

3 miles NE of Lancaster off the A683

Castle Hill Church of St Wilfrid

The high mound, **Castle Hill**, which rises above this ancient village on the River Lune was firstly the site of a Roman camp and later a Saxon castle. The village's parish **Church of St Wilfrid** was founded in the 7th century and although nothing survives of that original foundation there are some stone crosses, both inside the building and out, that date from the 9th century. One of them, unusually, bears both pagan and Christian symbols. Roman remains, in the form of a votive altar (where offerings were made before a military operation began), were found on the site in the late 18th century. Around the same time, a labourer tilling his allotment on Halton Moor unearthed more than 1000 coins from the reign of King Cnut (1017-35) and a gold necklace. This treasure trove is now in the British Museum.

The Lune Valley

CATON

4 miles NE of Lancaster on the A683

Littledale

Caton climbs up the hillside from the leafy glades of the Crook o'Lune, subject of one of Turner's paintings, to heather moorlands commanding a panoramic view of Morecambe Bay. A popular commuter town nowadays, in the 19th century Caton was a busy place with no fewer than eight cotton and wood-turning bobbin mills. Just to the south of the village, tucked away among the hills on the northern edges of the Forest of Bowland, is **Littledale**, one of Lancashire's most hidden gems. A walk through the wooded dale alongside Artle Beck to Littledale Hall is well worthwhile and provides a view of Lancashire that is not normally seen.

A mile or so west of Caton is Gray's Seat & Viewpoint where the poet Thomas Gray sat one day in 1769 and described the spectacular view as possessing "Every feature that constitutes a perfect landscape".

CLAUGHTON

6 miles NE of Lancaster on the A683

Old Toll House Garage

The **Old Toll House Garage** on the road into this village (which is pronounced Clafton), is famous for a rather curious reason. In the 1920s the garage owner painted the first white lines in the middle of the road at the nearby corner because of the many accidents that had occurred there. After much debate their value was recognised by the government of the day and from then onwards the use of white lines became accepted as a means of road marking, eventually spreading world-wide.

Claughton has another small claim to fame - the bell in the parish church is believed to be the oldest working bell in the country. It bears the date 1296 and was removed from the original Church of St Chad built in 1100.

HORNBY

8 miles NE of Lancaster on the A683

Loyn Bridge Castle Stede

Church of St Margaret of Antioch

Immortalised in paint by JMW Turner, the ruins of Hornby Castle (private) were incorporated into a picturesque mock-medieval Hall in the 19th century. Perched atop a hill, the castle dominates the attractive village of Hornby. Sadly, it isn't open to the public, but it's visible for miles around and

C.R. AND J. TOWERS HORNBY BUTCHERS

70 Main Street, Hornby, Lancashire LA2 8JT
Tel: 01524 221248

The attractive village of Hornby, set beside the River Lune boasts a mock-medieval castle, a fine medieval church with an unusual and impressive octagonal tower - and an outstanding village shop, **Hornby Butchers.**

A butcher's shop has operated here for more than 100 years, but the Tower's family took over some 20 years ago when it was a third the size it is now. They used to live here but moved out and extended right through the premises with a bakery and larger shop area. Everything sold in the shop is as local as it can be, and if it's not local, it is at least British. The beef and lamb come from a family farm just down the road and the beef is matured for a minimum of three weeks. Also available are their award-winning sausages, home-cured bacon, steak pies and cooked meats, all made on the premises.

The shop sells only free range eggs (which they did before it became trendy) as well as a huge range of jams, chutneys, biscuits, sauces and more. The shop is open from 8am to 5.30pm, Tuesday to Friday, and from 8am to 1pm on Saturday.

there's a particularly photogenic view of it from the bridge over the River Wemming at the southern edge of the village.

The situation of this attractive village, by a bluff overlooking the valley of the River Lune, not only gives Hornby panoramic views of the surrounding countryside, but also makes this a strategic position that has been utilised over the centuries. Just to the north of the village is the attractive stone-built **Loyn Bridge**, which takes the road over the River Lune and on to Gressington. Constructed in 1684, it replaced a ford. Beside the bridge is **Castle Stede**, the best example of a Norman motte and bailey castle in Lancashire.

The graceful **Church of St Margaret of Antioch** dates from around 1300 when it was built as a chapel of ease to the parish church at Melling. Its unusual and impressive octagonal tower was ordered by Sir Edward Stanley, Lord Mounteagle, who made a vow before the Battle of Flodden Field in 1513 that if he returned victorious he would construct the tower in honour of his patron saint, St Margaret.

ARKHOLME

11 miles NE of Lancaster on the B6254

Docker Park Farm · Redwell Fisheries

Children in particular will enjoy a visit to **Docker Park Farm** where they can feed the goats, hens and lambs, or burn off some energy in the play area while their parents browse in the shop or relax in the tea room.

Also in Arkholme, and nestling in a beautiful valley, **Redwell Fisheries** offers five acres of well-stocked lakes abounding in carp, tench, bream and roach.

historic building · museum and heritage · historic site · scenic attraction · flora and fauna

Docker Park Farm, Arkholme

TUNSTALL

12 miles NE of Lancaster on the A683

Church of St John the Baptist

The village is famous for its fine 15th-century **Church of St John the Baptist**, which was known to the Brontë sisters and is referred to in *Jane Eyre* as "Brocklebridge church". When the sisters were attending the Clergy Daughters' School at Cowan Bridge, they walked the six-mile round trip to the church each morning. After attending service, they had their midday meal in the room above the church porch.

WHITTINGTON

12 miles NE of Lancaster on the B6254

This delightful village, in the green and sheltered valley of the River Lune, is well worth a visit. It was Wordsworth, in his *Guide to the Lakes*, who recommended that Kendal be approached via the Vale of Lune and it remains a popular place today.

COWAN BRIDGE

13 miles NE of Lancaster on the A65

The Brontë Family

In 1823, the Rev William Carus Wilson, vicar of neighbouring Tunstall, opened his Clergy Daughters' School at Cowan Bridge. Amongst his early pupils were four daughters of the **Rev Patrick Brontë** of Howarth – Maria, Elizabeth, Charlotte and Emily. Charlotte immortalised the school and its austere regime in *Jane Eyre* where it appears as "Lowood". It can still be seen though it is now part of a row of terraced cottages just north of the bridge on the A65. The school moved to Casterton in 1833.

LECK

13 miles NE of Lancaster off the A65

Green Hill

Over the A65 from Cowan Bridge lies the small village of Leck. To the northeast of this village rises **Green Hill**, surrounded by moorland and the highest point, at 2060 feet, in the county. At just over three feet higher than the top of the neighbouring fell, Gragarth, it was only a recent, more accurate survey, that distinguished Green Hill as the higher. This is the most northerly part of Lancashire and from the summit there are superb views of both Cumbria and North Yorkshire.

West of Lancaster

MORECAMBE

3 miles NW of Lancaster on the A589

Morecambe Bay | Cross Bay Walks

Midland Hotel | Eric Morecambe Statue

Tern Project

Featuring prominently on the Lancashire coastline, Morecambe has long been one of the most successful and popular seaside resorts in the North, and it can truly be said to enjoy one of the finest views from its promenade of any resort in England – a magnificent sweep of coastline and bay,

CAKES AND CUTTERS

60 Queen Street, Morecambe, Lancashire, LA4 5ER
Tel: 01524 420300
e-mail: cakesandcutters@tiscali.co.uk

Cakes and Cutters is a fabulous shop that specialises in designing and creating perfect cakes for weddings and special celebrations. Diane, Barbara and Roy started the business in February 1998 from a small rented shop in Morecambe and since then have put their precious time and effort into making the shop what it is today. Once they realised how successful the cakes were proving to be they decided to expand and opened larger premises in Morecambe in August 2000 where they have been ever since. If you fancy having a go at being creative, sugarcraft equipment and materials for producing your own cakes are also on sale within the shop. Diane has received many awards for her talent in sugarcraft these include a City & Guilds in sugarcraft and Gold and Silver awards from the British Sugarcraft Guild. This goes to show that your that your cake will not only have the personal touch but will also look amazing! If you are looking for a special cake with that 'wow' factor then you must visit Cakes and Cutters.

The shop is open from 9.30am - 4pm Monday, Tuesday, Thursday and Friday, and 9:30am - 2pm on Saturdays. It is closed on Wednesdays and Sundays.

looking across to the Lakeland mountains.

The largest estuary in Britain, **Morecambe Bay** is noted for its rich marine and bird life, for its vast expanse of sands and mudflats – and for their treacherous nature. Over the years, many have lost their lives in the Bay's ever-shifting quicksands while attempting to make the apparently straightforward crossing from Morecambe to Grange-over-Sands on the Cumbrian coast. In medieval times, this perilous track formed part of the main west coast route from Scotland to England and at one time the monks of the Furness peninsula acted as guides to those wishing to make their way to Cumbria without taking the long overland route. Today, you can join one of the **Cross Bay Walks** led by the Queen's Guide to the Sands, Cedric Robinson, who has been guiding walkers across the Bay since 1963. Cedric is the 25th appointed guide to the sands since the original appointment in 1536. More details and times of walks can be obtained from the Tourist Information Centre.

Modern Morecambe is a relatively recent town that grew up as a direct result of the expansion of the railways to the north Lancashire coast. There were originally three villages, Bare, Poulton and Torrisholme that were quiet fishing communities. In 1848 all this changed as the railways brought visitors from the textile towns of Lancashire and, especially, Yorkshire to what was jokingly called Bradford-by-the-Sea. Hotels and boarding houses were built as well as the usual seaside amenities such as parks and promenades and soon the villages were absorbed into one thriving resort.

A lively resort, well-provided with every kind of traditional and modern holiday amusement, Morecambe has always vied with its much larger competitor to the south, Blackpool, in offering varied entertainment for its visitors. During the late 1800s, the town spent lavishly, building two grand piers, an elegant Winter Garden, sumptuous theatres and hotels, but the town's attempt to build a tower to rival Blackpool's was not a success. However, Morecambe did manage to introduce its Autumn Illuminations several years before Blackpool caught on to the idea.

Of the many buildings dating from Morecambe's heyday as a holiday destination, one in particular, the **Midland Hotel**, stands out. Located on the seafront, at the southern end of the promenade, the hotel was built in the early 1930s to designs by Oliver Hill and is concave towards the sea and convex facing inland. The elegant, sweeping balconies of the luxurious rooms remain a superb feature of the hotel. Whilst filming *Brief Encounter* at nearby Carnforth both Celia Johnson and Trevor Howard made their home here along with others working on the film.

Like other resorts, Morecambe has changed with the times and major new attractions include the multi-million pound Bubbles Leisure Park and Superdome, as well as a Wild West Theme Park. WOMAD, Morecambe's annual world music festival, attracts visitors from around the globe. There are also popular seafront illuminations in late summer, together with all the usual lively shops and variety of entertainment associated with a busy seaside resort.

But perhaps the town's most popular attraction is the **Eric Morecambe Statue** near the Stone Jetty. Few can resist the opportunity of posing in suitably one-legged fashion beside sculptor Graham Ibbeson's life-size statue. Lyrics from Eric's best-known song, *Bring Me Sunshine,* are carved into the granite steps leading up to the statue, which is surrounded by flowerbeds and flashing lights that bring this 'stage' to life even after dark.

In 1990 Morecambe was given substantial government funding for programmes of coastal protection and clearance of derelict land. The concept of the **Tern Project** was born. A team of engineers, landscape architects, planners, artists, sculptors and RSPB education officers joined forces to celebrate the bird life of the bay. Among the eye-catching results are steel cormorants and gannets on quarried rock on Central Drive, and flocks of metal birds on the perimeter fencing. At the heart of the project was the rebuilding and extending of the Stone Jetty, all that remains of the 1853 harbour. The designers also created a series of circular pavement features that include a huge stainless steel compass set in granite, a maze and a word search containing the names of more than 70 birds.

HEYSHAM

5 miles W of Lancaster on the A683

St Patrick's Chapel · Church of St Peter

Southwards along the coast, Morecambe merges imperceptibly into Heysham, an

St Patrick's Chapel

ancient settlement with a quaint old main street that winds down to the shore. The town is notable for the tiny **St Patrick's Chapel**, which is reckoned to be the oldest religious building in Lancashire. According to tradition, St Patrick himself built the now-ruined chapel as a thank-you to God after surviving a shipwreck on the rocks below. Historians aren't too sure about the veracity of that legend, but there's no doubting the interest of the chapel graveyard. Hewn out of the rock are six **body-shaped coffins** with an incised space above them in the shape of a cross. These 8th- or 9th-century coffins were originally covered by a similarly shaped slab of stone and would have been created as the final resting-place for Saxon notables.

Body-Shaped Coffins, Heysham

The little **Church of St Peter** on the headland below the chapel is equally interesting. It dates back to Saxon and Norman times, with an Anglo-Saxon cross on which the Madonna and other figures have been crudely carved by 9th-century masons and there is a rare Viking hogback gravestone. It is one of the oldest churches in western Europe to have been in continuous use.

Alongside these antiquities is the modern port of Heysham with regular car-ferry sailings to the Isle of Man and to Northern Ireland and, of course, the two modern nuclear power stations, Heysham A and Heysham B.

SUNDERLAND

6 miles SW of Lancaster off the A683

Sambo

This is an old port and seaside resort, which flourished until larger-berthed ships, silting channels, and the growth in the 19th century of rail-served Morecambe caused it to decline. A little wharf, quiet cottages, some with faded and evocative elegance, a sandy shore where sea thrift flourishes among the pebbles, are all that remains. The River Lune estuary is now a Site of Special Scientific Interest because of its wildlife value – visitors are likely to see such birds as redshank feeding on the rich supplies of worms, shellfish and shrimps on the salt marshes, while a variety of wildfowl such as shell duck, widgeon and mallard, are to be seen in autumn.

A particularly sad story acts as a reminder of Sunderland's time as a port. **Sambo** was a sea captain's servant at the time of the slave trade into Lancaster. Sambo fell ill of a fever just before the captain was setting off to the West Indies and was left in the care of an innkeeper. Sambo, believing himself abandoned, willed himself to die. Because he was not a baptised Christian, Sambo was not allowed to be buried in consecrated ground. In later years, his death and grave, marked by a simple cross and stone, became a potent local symbol of the anti-slavery cause.

His grave can be still seen, in a field at the west side of Sunderland Point. It can be reached by walking along The Lane from the village foreshore, past Upsteps Cottage, where Sambo died, and turning left at the shore then over a stile on the left, which gives access to the simple gravestone. Fresh flowers, which have been anonymously placed, are usually seen on the grave.

GLASSON

4 miles SW of Lancaster on the B5290

Glasson Dock   Lancaster Canal

Cockersand Abbey

A few miles south of Heysham, the river Lune pours into Morecambe Bay. On its south bank is **Glasson Dock**, once an important commercial port for larger boats unable to negotiate the tricky river as far upstream as Lancaster. The dock was built in 1791 and the tiny lighthouse erected at the same time is still in place. The dock could accommodate 25 sea-going ships and traded extensively in slaves, rum, tobacco, sugar and cotton. Glasson Dock today is a busy, colourful marina, serving both sea-going craft and boats arriving at the western terminus of the Lancaster Canal. Constructed in 1797, the **Lancaster Canal** is one of the earliest engineering marvels of the Industrial Age. "The Lanky", as it's known, is a favourite with canal travellers since there's not a single lock in the whole of its 41-mile length, thanks to the ingenuity of the canal's designer, John Rennie. He accomplished his engineering tour de force by linking the level stretches with six elegant aqueducts, the most impressive of them the five-arched Lune Aqueduct near Lancaster, which has attracted a stream of admiring visitors ever since it was first opened in 1797.

The canal was supplemented by the arrival of a railway line in 1883. This railway, long dismantled, is now the footpath and cycle-way to Lancaster's St George's Quay.

From Glasson there is a footpath along the coast to Plover Scar, where a lighthouse guards the River Lune estuary, and further along stand the ruins of **Cockersand Abbey**. The abbey was founded in 1190 by the Premonstratensian Order on the site of a hospital that had been the home of the

Cockersand Abbey, Glasson

hermit, Hugh Garth, before becoming a colony for lepers and the infirm. The 13th-century Chapter House of the abbey remains since it was a burial chapel for the Dalton family of nearby Thurnham who were descendants of Sir Thomas More.

GALGATE

4 miles S of Lancaster on the A6

The village of Galgate was originally located on the banks of the River Conder, which now forms part of the Lancaster Canal for about half a mile at this point. The village still contains some of its original mills, though they have now been put to other uses. One of them, a silk mill, was reputed to be the oldest working mill in the country, dating back to 1760 until it closed down in the 1960s. Galgate has a craft centre, a marina for around 100 boats and there's a well-maintained pathway that leads from the village through locks to Glasson Dock.

DOLPHINHOLME

6 miles S of Lancaster off the A6

This small village of around 600 souls sits in the foothills of the Pennines at the edge of the Forest of Bowland. Dolphinholme was one of the first villages with a main street lit by gas. This was around 1806 and remains of the old gas holder can still be seen. A single street lamp has survived and is now fuelled by bottle gas.

COCKERHAM

6 miles S of Lancaster on the A588

This sleepy little village lies on the shore of Morecambe Bay between the estuaries of the Lune and the Wyre. Cockerham once boasted a windmill but it was in such an exposed position that a gale in 1802 sent the sails spinning and the friction set fire to the mill. Cockerham Hall (private) is a fine and rare example of a medieval timber-framed building that dates from the late 15th century. It is now a farmhouse.

QUERNMORE

3 miles E of Lancaster off the A683

Clougha Pike

Lying at the head of the Conder Valley, this peaceful farming village had a pottery industry as well as slate quarrying in the 17th century. The word 'quern' refers to a particularly ancient form of hand-mill that was hewn from the rocks found on the nearby moorside. Corn milling continued here until World War Two.

To the east of the village lies **Clougha Pike**, on the western edges of the Forest of Bowland, an Area of Outstanding Natural Beauty, and one of the few places in the area that is accessible to walkers. Although it is not the highest peak in the forest – it rises to just over 1300 feet – the walk up Clougha Pike is very pleasant and offers splendid views from the summit, not only of the Lakeland Fells but also of Morecambe Bay and, on a clear day, Blackpool Tower.

LEE

7 miles SE of Lancaster off the A6

Ward's Stone

To the northwest of this typical Bowland village rises the highest summit in the forest, **Ward's Stone**. Dotted with outcrops of gritstone boulders, the top of the fell is marked by two triangulation pillars, one of which is just over three feet higher than the other though, on first inspection, they look the same height. The panoramic views from this point are magnificent - to the north and east, the Three Peaks of Yorkshire can be seen, whilst the Lakeland fells roll away to the northwest.

Forest of Bowland

Designated an Area of Outstanding Natural Beauty in February 1964, this large scenic area is a veritable paradise for walkers and country lovers and is dotted with picturesque villages. The 11th largest of such designated areas, the Forest of Bowland is something of a misnomer. The term 'forest' is derived from the Latin 'foris', which was formerly used to denote a royal hunting ground, an unenclosed tract of land, rather than a distinct wooded area. Throughout the 11th century the area was a 'chase' – a private rather than a royal hunting ground. Before 1066, the broad acres of Bowland were the personal property of Earl Tostig of Northumbria, a brother of King Harold. Banished from his earldom, Tostig, with the help of the King of Norway, attempted to regain his lands and both he and the Norwegian king were killed at Stamford Bridge, just weeks before the fateful Battle of Hastings.

Following the Norman Conquest, Bowland became part of the Honour of Clitheroe and the vast estates that belonged to the de Lacy family. In time, by marriage, they came into the hands of the Earls of Lancaster and in 1399, when the then Duke of Lancaster ascended the throne as Henry IV, Bowland finally became one of nearly 100 royal hunting forests.

Perhaps the most celebrated of the many routes across Bowland is the minor road from Lancaster to Clitheroe, which crosses Abbeydale Moor and the Trough of Bowland before descending into the lovely Hodder Valley around Dunsop Bridge. This is a popular route in the summer months, with most lay-bys and parking places filled as people pause to take in the breathtaking moorland views.

SLAIDBURN

15 miles SE of Lancaster on the B6478

Hark to Bounty

This pretty village of stone cottages and cobbled pavements lies in the heart of the Forest of Bowland. The village's focal point is the 13th-century public house **Hark to Bounty**. The inn was originally named The Dog, but one day in 1875 the local Hunt gathered here. A visiting Squire, listening to the hounds giving voice outside, clearly distinguished the tones of his own favourite hound rising above the others. His exclamation of delight, "Hark to Bounty!" was so wholehearted that the landlord changed the name of his pub on the spot.

The inn also contains an old courtroom, with its original oak furnishings, where from around 1250 the Chief Court of Bowland, or Halmote, was held. The only courtroom between York and Lancaster, it was used by visiting justices from the 14th century onwards. It is said to have also been used by Oliver Cromwell when he was in the area, and continued in use right up until 1937.

From the village, a network of beautiful, little-used lanes radiate westwards up into the fell country with some of the best walking that Lancashire has to offer. One walk in particular that offers solitude as well as excellent views of the Bowland landscape, leads to the lonely valley of the River Whitendale, northwest of the village. To the northeast of Slaidburn lies Stocks Reservoir, another popular walker's destination. Beneath its waters lie the remains of 20-odd dwellings that made up the hamlet of Stocks-in-Bolland. They were submerged in 1925 but in very dry summers the remains of the old Chapel bridge can be seen where it crosses the original Hodder river.

NEWTON

15 miles SE of Lancaster on the B6478

Quaker Meeting House

Little more than a hamlet, Newton lies on the main route between Clitheroe and Lancaster and so, in their time, both John Paslew, the last abbot of Whalley, and the Pendle witches passed through on their way to trial in Lancaster. Here also is a **Quaker Meeting House** that was founded in 1767: the associated Quaker school, where the 19th-century reformer John Bright was a pupil, has long since gone. Regarded with great suspicion by the Church of England, and by other nonconformists, because of their unorthodox views and their informality, the Quakers sought to settle in out-of-the-way villages. Newton is typical of the places where they built their meeting houses and successfully lived according to their beliefs.

DUNSOP BRIDGE

14 miles SE of Lancaster off the B6478

St Hubert's Roman Catholic Church

Often known as the Gateway to the Trough of Bowland, and located in a designated Area of Outstanding Natural Beauty, Dunsop Bridge is, despite its remote location, the centre of the British Isles. The actual centre point, worked out by the Ordnance Survey, lies near Whitendale Hanging Stones. To confirm the claim, the explorer Sir Ranulph Fiennes unveiled a commemorative plaque here. British Telecom also offered the village a unique honour by putting their 100,000th phone box here.

St Hubert's Roman Catholic Church on Lancaster Road has an unusual provenance. It was built by the Towneley family when their racehorse Kettledrum won the 1861 Derby. The family spent a further £1000 on the huge white angel that stands in the graveyard and commemorates Richard Henry Towneley.

WHITEWELL

15 miles SE of Lancaster off the B6478

Little more than a hamlet in the heart of the Forest of Bowland, Whitewell consists of a small church, built in the early 19th century on the site of a medieval chapel, and an inn, built on the site of the old manor house.

Just to the southeast is Browsholme Hall, a Tudor mansion dating from 1507 that has the rare distinction of being occupied by the same family ever since. From the 16th century onwards, the owners, the Parker family, were also bowbearers, or warders, of the Forest of Bowland – the king's agent and upholders of the law in the forest. Though much of the original Tudor house can still be seen, there have been many additions over the centuries but it remains a homely building, perhaps due to the continuous occupation by the same family and as a result of its remote location. The house is not open to the public.

CHIPPING

15 miles SE of Lancaster off the B6243

Post Office | Lizzie Dean | Bowland Boar Park

This picturesque village overlooking the River Loud is now a conservation area and is also home to a **Post Office**, built in 1668, which claims to be Britain's oldest shop. It is also an art gallery with exhibitions of work by local artists, a bookshop and an outlet for HJ Berry furniture. Very much at the heart of the local agricultural communities, Chipping's annual village show is one of the best in Lancashire and its very name comes from the old English word for a market place - *chepyn*.

There are a number of attractive inns here and one of them, the Sun Inn, is associated with a melancholy tale. The story of **Lizzie Dean** whose ghost is said to haunt the inn is poignant, sad – and true. In 1835, Lizzie was 18 years old and a serving wench at the inn. She had fallen in love with a local man and a date had been set for their wedding at the church just across the road from the inn. Lizzie lodged at the inn and on the morning of her wedding she heard the church bells ringing. Looking out of her window she saw her intended bridegroom leaving the church with another maiden on his arm.

Humiliated and distraught, Lizzie crept up into the inn's attic and hanged herself. She left a note requesting that she should be buried beneath the path leading to the church porch so that her faithless lover would have to step across her body every Sunday on his way to divine service.

About three miles south of Chipping, **Bowland Wild Boar Park** is home to wild boar, longhorn cows and other animals. Within the park's mainly wooded 65 acres are a children's playground and a café and shop serving and selling wild boar meat. Pedal tractors are available for young children; tractor, trailer and donkey rides can be enjoyed and there are some attractive walks alongside the River Hodder.

The Ribble Valley

"A dramatic contrast of stark fellsides flecked with woolly sheep, and valleys green with woodland and lush pastures grazed by obviously contented sheep." It's not the conventional image of Lancashire as half-Blackpool, half wall-to-wall grimy chimneys. That's because the Ribble Valley is the county's best-kept secret – 150 square miles of peaceful countryside, almost two-thirds of it designated as Areas of Outstanding Natural Beauty.

The best overview of this beautiful area can be enjoyed by walking or driving along Longridge Fell. Within the space of a few miles, huge vistas unfold, not just of the Ribble Valley from Pendle Hill to Preston, but also of the Fylde Plain, the Loud and Hodder valleys, and the Forest of Bowland. This is captivating countryside so it's no wonder that, according to one of her biographers, the Queen herself has divulged that she would like to retire to this region of rural Lancashire.

Flowing between the Forest of Bowland to the north and the hill country of Pendle to the south, the River Ribble cuts a pleasant and green course along a narrow valley. The Ribble Way middle-distance footpath follows the full 70 miles of the river, from its source at Ribblehead in North Yorkshire to the flat, tidal marshes of its estuary west of Preston.

The central point of the valley is Clitheroe, a typical ancient Lancashire market town that clusters around one of the smallest Norman castles in the country. The valley is also home to two great houses. The first, Stonyhurst, was originally the home of the Shireburn family and is now the world-famous Roman Catholic public school. The second, on the outskirts of Preston, is Salmesbury Hall, a wonderful 14th century house that is also a major attraction for antiques collectors.

Finally, at the mouth of the river lies Preston, the county's administrative centre and

Chipping

Distance: *5.0 miles (8.0 kilometres)*

Typical time: *180 mins*

Height gain: *200 metres*

Map: *Explorer OL41*

Walk: *www.walkingworld.com ID: 3336*

Contributor: *Jim Grindle*

ACCESS INFORMATION:

Chipping can be reached by buses from Clitheroe and Preston. It is on a minor road and is signposted from Longridge, on the B6342, or from Whalley, just off the A59. There is a large free car park near the church.

DESCRIPTION:

Despite its short length this walk will take you quite high and to the very fringe of Bowland - at Waymark 12 there is a sign for the new access land next to the footpath. Consequently for most of the time there are good views of Bowland, Pendle, Longridge Fell, even a glimpse of Beacon Fell) with a very gradual climb and no steep descents. Chipping with its pubs and tearoom makes a very pleasant base for the day.

ADDITIONAL INFORMATION:

The chair factory, which is passed at the start of the walk, will almost certainly have the raw material in the shape of huge tree trunks stacked outside. The factory makes much more than just chairs and produces the well-known Priory range of furniture.

FEATURES:

Hills or Fells, Toilets, Play Area, Church, Wildlife, Birds, Flowers, Great Views, Good for Wheelchairs, Butterflies, Café, Food Shop, Public Transport, Tea Shop, Woodland.

WALK DIRECTIONS:

1 | From the car park take the path leading past the toilets. Turn left on the road by the wall around the church and pass the red telephone box. Just after the last houses the road forks.

2 | Take the right fork, going downhill and past the chair factory. Continue until you come to the lodge (the pond feeding the mill). On the right you will find a stile next to a house.

3 | Cross it, go uphill to a fence, turn left and follow it to the second stile. Now cross the field, roughly in the direction of the telegraph pole. The route stays high above a stream on an embankment and passes to the right of a deep hollow before you come to a stile at the end of a stone wall. From here, aim for the left of the group of buildings. The path crosses two muddy patches over streams and brings you to a gate with a stile to its right.

4 | Turn left on a farm track that leads to Windy Hill farm and a barn just before it on the right.

5 | Turn right on a path uphill following the field boundary on your right until a gate and stile lead to an open area. Keep ahead until just before the low hill in front; then go left, making for a plank footbridge and a stile on the far side of the field. Now go half right to a stile in the field corner.

6 | Turn right on the track that leads uphill to Burnslack where the footpath is well signposted by a ladder stile before you reach the farm. There is a diversion here which may not be on your map, but it is very well marked and an enclosed path now takes you around to the back of the buildings.

7 | Just in front of you is a signpost for the new access area. Turn left and follow the wall that makes a sharp turn left just before a group of derelict barns. On the bend is a stile, which you cross to continue by the wall so passing the barns. The wall is intermittent after this, sometimes full height, sometimes low, and sometimes replaced with fencing, but the way is clear enough and after 1km brings you to Saddle End. Turn left in front of a gate and notice board to pass between the farm buildings.

8 | After you have gone through the farm, watch out for a power line post on the right - there is a stile up on an embankment here which is not too obvious from the direction in which you are walking. When you have crossed the stile, turn left and go to the end of a small wood, which contains a flock of geese. Leave by the stile at the far end and then drop to a gate, which you will see just below you on the left.

9 | This field is very big and there is no obvious path. Just walk at right angles to the fence and soon you will see a small barn ahead of you. Make for the left of this.

10 | To the right of the telegraph pole is a gate and a lane. Turn right on the lane and in 150 metres you will find the entrance to Peacock Hey Farm on the left.

11 | Don't take the footpath signposted up the farm track but cross the stile, behind which the path is now enclosed at first and brings you to the back of Nan King's Farm. Turn left to go around the building and then ahead looking out for a signpost beneath a tree. Go straight across the field to the far side where you will find a stile on the left of a small copse. Cross it, turn right and go through the copse to a stile on the other side. Go to the far right corner of the field, crossing a gravelled drive, to a stile. Go over this and follow the right hand edge of the field to a ladder stile under a tree.

12 | An enclosed path between newly planted trees brings you to a lane.

13 | A left turn here will bring you back to Waymark 3 should you wish to cut the walk short. To continue, though, cross the lane and the stile on the other side and then go over a footbridge. A little spur here leads up to the left-hand telegraph pole where an arrow directs you left to follow a fence. You will find yourself at the back of the cottages at Old Hive.

14 | Cross the stile in front and follow the path between the houses to a lane where you turn left. 100 metres down the lane you will find a stone track going up to the right. Turn up here and where the track turns left to enter a garden you will find a stile on the right. Turn left and follow the field edge to a lane.

15 | Turn left to a T-junction.

16 | Turn left once more on this lane, which leads back into Chipping.

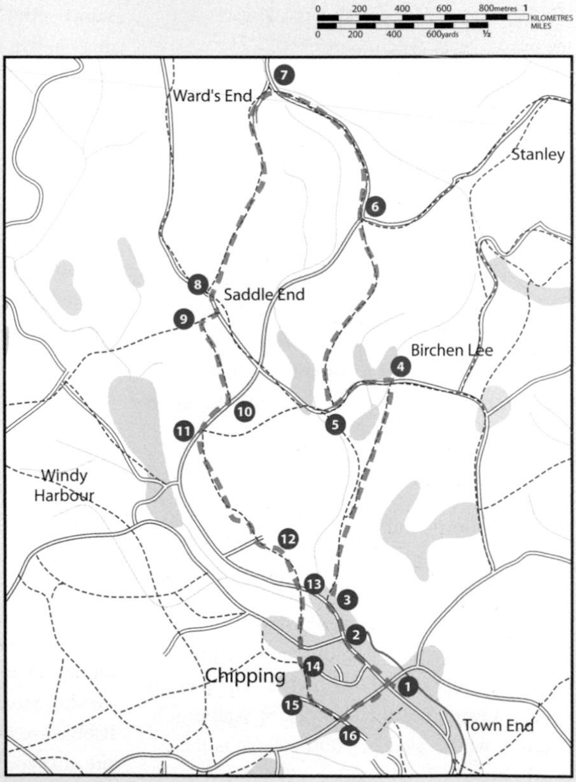

a town with more to offer than first appearances would suggest. Our exploration of the Ribble Valley begins at its estuary near Preston and travels upstream through a fertile and versatile valley to the river's remote source in the bleak Pennine Hills.

Preston

- Millennium Ribble Link
- Ribble Steam Railway
- Easter Egg rolling
- Miller Park
- Guilds Celebrations
- Richard Arkwright
- John Horrocks
- Harris Museum & Art Gallery
- Museum of Lancashire
- Queen's Lancashire Regiment Museum
- Penwortham Old Bridge
- Ribble Viaduct
- National Football Museum

'Proud Preston' is the largest town in the county and its administrative centre. It's 'Proud' because it was the first town in the county to receive a borough charter (in 1179), the first borough in which every male over 21 had a vote in parliamentary elections (1798), the first town outside London to light its streets with gas lamps (1816), and in 1958, the Preston bypass was the first stretch of motorway to be built in Britain. Civic pride was fostered even more by Preston's elevation in 2002 to the status of a city, one of only six in the UK so honoured to mark the Queen's Diamond Jubilee. Around the same time, multi-million pound plans were announced to redevelop the City Centre.

During the 19th century, Preston became a 'town of spires' as the evenly-split Protestant and Roman Catholic communities vied to build the most splendid churches. The palm is usually awarded to the Catholic St Walburge's Church, whose slender 300ft steeple is the third tallest in England.

In Victorian times, Preston was a major cotton-weaving centre. The mill-owners' ruthless exploitation of the cotton workers provoked a major strike in 1854 and the bitter confrontation attracted the attention of Charles Dickens. He had already started to write a novel highlighting the degrading conditions and pitiful wages imposed on industrial workers by outrageously wealthy mill-owners. He came to Preston, staying at the Bull and Royal Hotel in Church Street, and his first-hand observations of the unacceptable face of Victorian capitalism displayed in that conflict were embodied in the grimmest novel he ever wrote, *Hard Times.* Many of Preston's old red-brick mills still stand, although now converted to a variety of imaginative uses.

Lancaster may enjoy the distinction of being the elegant county town, but Preston revels in its macho role as Lancashire's administrative centre – always busy, enterprising, forward-looking, but still proud of a historical legacy that stretches back to Roman times. The port activity may have declined but the dockland area, now called Riversway, has become an area of regeneration with a marina catering for pleasure craft, yachts and windsurfers. The complex is part of the **Millennium Ribble Link**, which forms a three-mile-long linear waterpark providing opportunities for walking, angling, cycling and boating as well as a newly commissioned sculpture trail. Also in Riversway is the new **Ribble Steam Railway**, opened in 2005, which boasts the largest single collection of standard gauge industrial locomotives in the country with more than 40 on site. Steam train rides alongside the River Ribble are available on open weekends and the site also contains a museum, shop and buffet.

Though the town has both a Roman and a medieval past, nothing of this is visible today. However, the lasting legacy of those days is reflected in the famous **Guilds Celebrations**, which have been taking place every 20 years since 1500. The last Guild Celebration was in 1992 and, already, preparations are being made for the next one in 2012.

A popular annual event is the **Easter Egg Rolling** event held in Avenham Park, one of the city's two splendid Victorian parks: the other is the adjacent **Miller Park,** noted for its impressive floral displays and an elaborately designed fountain.

Preston featured in the *Domesday Book* although at that time it was known as Priest-town and, in the 1260s, the Greyfriars settled here. The Catholic traditions of Preston continued, as they did elsewhere in the county, and this has, along with the associated loyalty to the crown, had a great part to play in the town's history. During the Civil War it was the Battle of Preston in 1648 that confirmed the eventual defeat of the supporters of Charles I. Later, at the time of the 1745 Jacobite rebellion, Preston played host to Prince Charles Edward, Bonnie Prince Charlie.

The many public buildings of Preston all reflect the prosperity of the town during the Victorian age. This wealth was built upon the textile industry, helped by the general location of the town - midway between London and Glasgow, on a major railway route, and with extensive docks. Though the town's prosperity was built on cotton, textiles were not new to Preston, as linen had been produced here from as far back as Tudor times. Preston was also the place where, in 1768, the single most important machine of the textile industry was invented, **Richard Arkwright's** water-frame cotton spinning machine. Almost overnight, the cottage industries of spinning and handloom weaving were moved from the workers' homes into factories, and the entrepreneurs of Preston were quicker than most to catch on. One gentleman in particular, **John Horrocks**, saw the potential of combining the spinning and weaving operations under the same roof, and so he was able to take in raw cotton and produce the finished article. His firm became the largest of its kind in the world, further adding to the town's prosperity, but it did not do Horrocks himself much good as, by the age of 36, he was dead.

Although the great days of the textile industry are long gone in Preston, as elsewhere in Britain, the cotton workers of the town are remembered in a statue that stands outside the old Corn Exchange.

One of the best places to start any exploration of the town is the **Harris Museum and Art Gallery**. Housed in a magnificent neoclassical building that dominates the Market Square, the museum and art gallery were opened in 1893. As well as the fine collection of paintings and watercolours by major 19th-century British artists, there is an excellent exhibition detailing the story of Preston. A varied programme of events and exhibitions continues throughout the year.

There are two other major museums in the town. Housed in the former county court building, and with limited opening times, the **Museum of Lancashire** helps visitors experience aspects of the county's fascinating past. The Fulwood Barracks, which were built in 1848 of Longridge stone, are home to the **Queen's Lancashire Regiment Museum** (free). With a rich history that covers many campaigns, the exhibits here are numerous and include the famous silver mounted Maida Tortoise, items connected with General Wolfe, souvenirs from the Crimea War, and artefacts from the Defence of Kimberley, the diamond town in South Africa which the 1st Battalion the Loyals defended without assistance from any other troops.

Preston's **Guild Hall**, built in 1972 to celebrate that year's Guild, has a comprehensive diary of shows and performances throughout the year ranging from ballet, opera and concerts to pop music, musical theatre and comedy tours.

As might be expected for a town on the banks of a river, there are many bridges but two crossings are particularly worthy of note. **Penwortham Old Bridge** is perhaps the most attractive in Lancashire; slightly hump-backed and built of a mixture of stone. Constructed chiefly of buff gritstone and pink sandstone in 1756, it replaced a bridge that had collapsed. By 1912, traffic had increased to such an extent that its use by motor cars and heavy carts was prohibited. For over 150 years, the bridge was the lowest crossing of the River Ribble. By contrast, the **Ribble Viaduct** is a completely different structure. One of the oldest works of railway engineering in the area and a construction of great elegance and dignity, it was built in 1838 and brought the railway from Wigan to the centre of Preston.

Located on the northern outskirts of the city is one of Preston's most popular visitor attractions, the **National Football Museum**. Containing the world's most significant football collections, including the official FIFA collection, the museum offers more than 1000 objects, photographs, more than 90 minutes of film and a number of lively interactive displays, including one that gives the visitor access to every League ground in England.

Salmesbury Hall

Around Preston

SALMESBURY

4 miles E of Preston on the A59

Salmesbury Hall

To the east of the village, close to the busy A59, stands **Salmesbury Hall**, built by the Southworth family. The hall seen today, an attractive black and white timbered manor house, is actually the second house they built since their original hall was burned to the ground by Robert the Bruce in the early 1300s. Thinking that the original position, close to a crossing of the River Ribble, was too vulnerable to attack, the family built their subsequent home in what was then an isolated location.

More peaceful times followed and the hall, surrounded by a moat and with a drawbridge, was a reflection of the family's wealth. A staunchly Catholic family, their 15th-century chapel contains a mullioned Gothic window that was rescued from Whalley Abbey after the Dissolution in the 1530s. However, it was the loyalty to their faith that finally brought about the demise of the Southworth family. Their continued practice of Catholicism saw Sir John Southworth imprisoned in Manchester in the late 16th century and, by the time of his death a few years later, the family, having kept their faith, had seen their fortune dwindle away.

The hall was sold to the Braddyll family who, having a house near Ulverston, simply stripped Salmesbury Hall of its assets. Somehow the hall survived, but by the 1870s it was in a shocking state of repair. First, Joseph Harrison stepped in and began a successful restoration programme, to the point where he was able to entertain the likes of Charles Dickens. However, the building work took all his money and, facing ruin, Harrison committed suicide. By 1925, the hall was once again in a dilapidated condition and was only saved from demolition by a timber merchant by the efforts of the Salmesbury Hall Trust, a group that is still managing the property today. Any profits made by the Hall go towards its upkeep. On Sundays, Henry VIII is in residence at the Hall and provides an entertaining free tour, which explores life in medieval and Tudor times. The Hall stands in three acres of beautifully maintained grounds that includes the Quatrefoil rose garden and a herb garden that supplies the Hall's restaurant.

Clitheroe

- Platform Gallery · Sculpture Trail
- Clitheroe Castle · Clitheroe Castle Museum
- Church of St Mary Magdalen
- Royal Grammar School · Grand Cinema
- Edisford Picnic Site · Stepping Stones
- Browsholme Hall

Perhaps the most appealing little market town in Lancashire, Clitheroe nestles around its miniature Norman castle. The town has a reputation for high quality specialist shops acclaimed for their individuality, some of which have gained international recognition: establishments such as Cowman's Sausage Shop in Castle Street, which offers 75 different varieties of sausage, amongst them Welsh pork and leek, venison and wild boar. Seventy-six varieties if you count the special Christmas sausage, only available during the festive season and containing exotic ingredients such as port, juniper berries and ground almonds. As with the French, traditional Lancashire meat cuisine wastes no part of the animal. Black pudding, tripe and onions, chitterlings, lamb's fry and sweetbreads are still popular dishes here, although rarely seen in southern England.

In King Street there's Byrne's Wine Merchants, which stocks more than 1550 wines and 100 malt whiskies. *Which? Wine Guide* judged the shop to be the best wine merchant in the country. Also well worth visiting is the **Platform Gallery**, housed in a refurbished railway station of 1870. The gallery presents a regularly-changing programme of visual art exhibitions – paintings and prints, textiles, glassware, ceramics, jewellery, papier maché and baskets, with the majority of the work on show produced by regionally based artists.

Clitheroe also has a **sculpture trail** leading from Brungerley Bridge to Crosshill Quarry. The trail was started in 1993 by Thompson Dagnall who worked on this commission in the Ribble Valley for seven months. His main sculpture, *Saving Sheep*, portrays a shepherd rescuing a sheep from the swelling river's current. It stands on the site of Victorian bathing huts. New sculptures by different artists are added from time to time.

Clitheroe is Lancashire's second oldest borough, after Wigan, receiving its first charter in 1147 and since then the town has served the surrounding villages of the Ribble Valley as their market town. Like Lancaster, it too is dominated by an 800-year-old **Castle** standing on a 100ft high limestone crag high above the town. Today only the keep remains, the second smallest in England and one of the oldest stone structures in Lancashire.

According to local legend, the large hole in the keep's east wall was the work of the Devil who threw a large boulder from the summit of nearby Pendle Hill. Historians say it was Oliver Cromwell's troops who inflicted the damage. Modern day visitors can stand within the keep as hidden voices recount the castle's history, complete with appropriate sound effects.

Standing on another prominent limestone mound close to the castle is **Clitheroe Castle**

Museum. Currently, the museum, along with the North West Sound Archive building, is undergoing major restoration and is scheduled to re-open at Easter, 2009. Still open to the public though are the 16 acres of beautiful formal gardens featuring a skate park and playground for kids, a bandstand, landscaped gardens and the first Labyrinth in Lancashire.

A short walk from the Castle Museum stands the parish **Church of St Mary Magdalen** which, though it was rebuilt by the Victorians, was founded in the 13th century. At that time the town also had a school; however, the present **Royal Grammar School** was not established until 1554. The school's official charter, granted by Mary Tudor but lost for many years, was eventually found in the vaults of a local solicitor's office in 1990.

The town's narrow, winding streets are full of character and charm and amidst the ancient buildings is the rather incongruous **Grand Cinema**. Built in 1874 as a public hall, and converted to a cinema in the 1920s, this unspoilt monument to the golden days of the silver screen is still lined with plush velvet, has retained its grand piano that was used to accompany the silent films, and remains the town's cinema today.

Just outside the town can be found **Edisford Picnic Area**, a popular place for family outings that stands on the site of a battleground where the Scots fought the Normans. Also near Clitheroe, at Brungerley, are a set of **stepping stones** across the river that are said to be haunted. Apparently the evil spirit living in the water drags a traveller to his watery death every seven years.

There are few grand houses in the Ribble Valley open to the public, but **Browsholme Hall** near Clitheroe is open at certain times in the summer. Dating back to the early 1500s, the Hall has been the family home of the Parkers for 500 years and there's a special pleasure in being shown around the house by a member of the family. The Parkers took their name from the family's hereditary role in medieval times as keepers of the deer park in the royal hunting ground of the Forest of Bowland.

Around Clitheroe

WEST BRADFORD

1 mile N of Clitheroe off the B6478

This tucked away village, just south of the Forest of Bowland, was mentioned in the Domesday Book and there are records of some villagers paying the first poll tax levied by Richard II in 1379. The old part of the village is set around a green bordering the River Ribble. It's a pleasant spot with a stream running alongside the road through the bottom half of the village and access to the houses bordering the beck is made by crossing a quaint stone bridge.

WORSTON

1 mile NE of Clitheroe off the A59

Hidden away down a lane off the main road, Worston has remained unchanged over the years and can certainly be described as unspoilt. Keen-eyed film fans may even recognize the surrounding countryside, since this was one of the locations used during the filming of *Whistle Down the Wind*. Behind the village inn, where the amusing and bizarre ritual of the village's Mock Corporation was revived in 1989, can still be seen the bull ring. Set into a stone, this was where the beast was tethered and baited with specially trained dogs in the belief that the 'sport' tenderised the meat.

DOWNHAM

3 miles NE of Clitheroe off the A59

Some 40-odd villages are sprinkled along the banks of the Ribble Valley, all of them built in the appealing local stone. One of the prettiest is Downham, set at the foot of Pendle Hill and renowned as the setting for the cinema classic *Whistle Down the Wind*. The village also provides location scenes for BBC TV's period drama series *Born & Bred*. Thanks for Downham's unspoilt appearance must go to the Clitheroe family, which has owned the whole village since 1558 – the same year in which they acquired Whalley Abbey. It was the present Lord Clitheroe's grandfather who paid for the electricity supply cables to be laid underground back in the 1930s and the

Old Well House, Downham

present squire, Lord Clitheroe of Downham, still refuses to permit the skyline to be spoilt by TV aerials, satellite dishes, and even dormer windows. The village phone box has also come under the influence of the family and is not painted a distinctive pillar box red, but grey, to tone in with the surroundings.

SAWLEY

4 miles N of Clitheroe off the A59

Sawley Abbey

At the centre of this historic village, easily missed as the main road by-passes it, are the slight remains of **Sawley Abbey**, founded in the 13th century by the Cistercian monks of Fountains Abbey. Although during the reigns of Edward I and II the abbots of Sawley were called to the House of Lords, none of the abbots were men of note except, perhaps, William Trafford, the last head of the community. With his colleague and neighbour, the last Abbot of Whalley (see Whalley page 207), Trafford took part in the Pilgrimage of Grace in 1536 and, for his part in the failed uprising, was taken prisoner. Tried for treason at Lancaster in 1537, Trafford, with others like him, was found guilty and executed. Although little of the abbey remains – much of the stone was cannibalised for village buildings – the site is wonderfully quiet and peaceful.

River Ribble, Sawley

RIMINGTON

5 miles NE of Clitheroe off the A59

This small hillside village has twice won Lancashire's Best Kept Village competition. Its name means "farmstead on the boundary" and as the Lancashire/Yorkshire boundary has changed over the years the village has been transferred from one county to the other. The most recent transfer was in 1974 when people who had been Yorkshire born and bred suddenly found themselves Lancastrians.

This pleasant rural village was the home of Francis Duckworth, the famous composer of hymn tunes. These included one he named *Rimington*. His parents ran the village post office and shop next door to the Methodist chapel and a plaque on the chapel, now a private house, commemorates him.

GISBURN

7 miles NE of Clitheroe on the A59

Like Rimington, this village was also once in Yorkshire - and, as many locals would like to believe, it still is! One of the Ribble Valley's most pleasant and picturesque villages, Gisburn's history is dominated by the Lister family who, from humble beginnings, rose to become the Lords of Ribblesdale. Their house, built in the early 17th century in Gisburne Park, is still standing though it is now a private hospital.

BOLTON BY BOWLAND

7 miles NE of Clitheroe off the A59

Pudsey Tomb

Lying alongside a 'bow', or bend, in the River Ribble, this tranquil village with its two ancient greens, stone cross and old stocks, lies on the southern edge of the forest area. Part of the Bolton Hall estate, the village has been protected from insensitive development – the most recent dwelling to be built is already more than 100 years old. The 15th-century village Church of St Peter & St Paul is home to the famous **Pudsey Tomb** with its engraved figure of Sir Ralph Pudsey in full armour alongside figures of his three wives and their 25 children. In the folds of each lady's gown an inscription with a Roman numeral indicates how many children she bore – respectively six, two and 17.

HOLDEN CLOUGH NURSERY

Holden, Bolton-by-Bowland, nr Clitheroe,
Lancashire BB7 4PF
Tel: 01200 447615 Fax: 01200 447197
e-mail: enquiries@holdencloughnursery.com
website: www.holdencloughnursery.co.uk

In the scenic Forest of Bowland, with distant views of majestic Pendle Hill, you will find **Holden Clough Nursery** nestling in the small village of Holden. Established as a working nursery in 1927, it is owned and run by Peter Foley, a plantsman all his working life and a well-known lecturer and broadcaster. In addition to an ever-growing range of Alpine plants including auriculas, saxifrages and sempervivums, the nursery grows many herbaceous perennials, choice shrubs and climbers, dwarf conifers, heathers and hardy ferns, as well as ornamental grasses. Peter is ably assisted by his son John who has an impressive collection of South African crocosmia (*montbretia*) that was featured on BBC2's *Gardener's World* and in *The Garden* magazine of the Royal Horticultural Society.

Much of the stock is propagated on site in this Pennine location, thus ensuring hardiness. Throughout the year, popular RHS Nursery Event days are held in collaboration with local businesses. In addition to a presentation and question time session, there is a demonstration, nursery walk and a chance to view other areas of the nursery not generally open to the public. Booking for these events is essential. The nursery is open from 9am to 5pm, Monday to Friday (March to October), and on Saturdays throughout the year, with other times and group visits by appointment. A worldwide mail-order service is available.

PAYTHORNE

10 miles NE of Clitheroe off the A682

Although the source of the River Ribble lies to the north in Yorkshire, near the famous Three Peaks of Whernside, Ingleborough and Pen-y-ghent, this village is the first on its banks on this side of the county boundary. It also marks the end of the river's journey through the rugged limestone scenery of moorlands and the start of its picturesque course through a lush green valley.

BARNOLDSWICK

10 miles NE of Clitheroe on the B6251

- Bancroft Mill Engine Museum
- Town Criers Contest

If you approach this former cotton town from the south, off the A56, you may wonder why the road is so straight. The answer is that it was specially constructed in the 1930s to service the new Rolls-Royce factory in the town. The 'B' in the names of jet engines such as the RB211 stands for Barnoldswick which, incidentally, is known locally as 'Barlick'.

At the western end of the town is **Bancroft Mill Engine Museum**. The mill was the last weaving shed to be built in Lancashire, in 1922. The mill closed in 1978 but the grand 600hp cross-compound steam engine was preserved and there are regular demonstrations of it in action. It was originally used to drive 1250 looms weaving cotton. The museum also displays tools and documents connected with the weaving industry.

Barnoldswick is one of the few towns in the country to have a woman as its Town Crier. Liz Woolnough took the post in 2005 and each year has been a prominent figure in the annual **Town Criers Contest** when there's an explosion of colourful costumes

WADDINGTON

2 miles NW of Clitheroe on the B6478

This is one of the area's best-known villages – its attractive Coronation Gardens have appeared on many postcards and even on biscuit tin lids. King Henry VI spent a whole year here in 1464/5, not because he particularly appreciated its charms, but because he was hiding at Waddington Hall from the Yorkists who had defeated him at the Battle of Hexham. When his hiding place was discovered he escaped by a secret tunnel that led from the Hall's dining room. He was quickly captured at Brungerley Bridge, down river near Clitheroe, then imprisoned in the Tower of London where he died in 1471.

Waddington has several times won first prize in Lancashire's Best Kept Village competition and it's easy to see why. Waddington Brook splashes the length of the village and 18th-century almshouses cluster around the green.

About 12 years ago, Waddington's villagers enjoyed a certain amount of fame when, for the sake of a TV series, they agreed to renounce their TVs for a whole month. This cold turkey treatment proved too much for some and they had to be resuscitated by having their sets returned.

GREAT MITTON

3 miles SW of Clitheroe on the B6246

All Hallows' Church · Shireburn Chapel

Standing opposite the Three Fishes Hotel, which takes its name from the three fishes on the Whalley Abbey coat of arms, is the attractive **All Hallows' Church.** Housing some of the finest relics to be seen in any British church, this is most certainly worth a visit. It was built around 1270 and little has been done to the building since, although a tower was added in 1438 and the pews are Jacobean. However, it is the **Shireburn Chapel** that draws most visitors to the church. It was added in 1440 by the Shireburn family of Stonyhurst who

Waddington Village

claimed to be the direct descendants of the first rector, Ralph the Red of Mytton. The family tombs here are regarded as the best in the county. One of the earliest is the fine alabaster tomb of Sir Richard Shireburn (who died in 1594) and his wife Maude, who is dressed in capacious petticoats. The latest is of another Richard who died in 1702 at the age of nine after eating poisonous berries. Following the fashion of the time, the monument displays copious macabre items – a skull, hour glass, sickle, more bones than seem necessary and, emerging from the ground, two skeletal hands.

Confirmation that a settlement existed here before the days of the land ownership by the abbey comes with the name of the village itself. Mitton is derived from the Saxon word 'mythe', which means a farm at the junction of two rivers – perfectly describing the location as, close by, the River Hodder feeds into the River Ribble.

HURST GREEN

5 miles SW of Clitheroe on the B6243

Stonyhurst College · Sir Richard Shireburn

St Peter's Church · Sir Arthur Conan Doyle

This pretty village of stone-built cottages nestling in the Ribble Valley is best known for its nearby public school. **Stonyhurst College**, the world-famous Roman Catholic school, began life as the residence of the local lords of the manor. The present building, begun around 1523, was the work of Hugh Shireburn, although additions were made in 1592 by Sir Richard Shireburn. The core of this imposing building set beside a lake is late-Elizabethan, but there have been major additions almost every century, all of them blending remarkably well with their predecessors.

Sir Richard Shireburn was an ambitious man who served the Tudor monarchy well. As well as being the Chief Forester of Bowland, he was also one of Henry VIII's commissioners studying the state of the monasteries. He was an eager participant in the suppression of Whalley Abbey. Though the family publicly adopted the new Protestant religion under Elizabeth I, it was with little enthusiasm, and in a short time the Shireburn family, like many other Lancashire families, returned to their Catholic faith. It seems strange then that Cromwell, on his way to and from the Battle of Preston, should take shelter at Stonyhurst, although rumour has it that the ardent Puritan slept with a pistol at his side and his guards around him.

In 1794, after the house had been left empty for some considerable time and had fallen into a state of disrepair, the owner, Thomas Weld, offered the property to the Jesuits who had set up an English Catholic School in Flanders. Unwelcome in France following the revolution, the Jesuits gladly accepted, and after restoring the original building, they extended it during the 19th century. Their finest addition must be the replica of King's College in Cambridge: **St Peter's Church** was built in 1835 and contains many treasures including a 7th-century copy of St John's Gospel and a cape of Henry II that was used by Henry VIII at the battle of the Field of the Cloth of Gold.

One of Stonyhurst College's most famous sons was **Sir Arthur Conan Doyle**, the creator of Sherlock Holmes. The Conan Doyle desk (into which he carved his name) is one of the many artefacts on show when the college is occasionally open to the public during the summer holidays. The exterior of the college can always be seen from the minor road that runs through its grounds.

STYDD

7 miles SW of Clitheroe off the B6245

Norman Chapel

Bremetannacum, Ribchester

Just to the north of Ribchester is the small hamlet of Stydd. All that remains of the monastery founded here by the Knights Hospitallers of St John of Jerusalem is the **Norman Chapel**, standing alone surrounded by meadows. It contains effigies of some of the knights. A crusading and military order established in 1113, the Knights Hospitallers provided help and assistance to pilgrims travelling to the Holy Land. Their religious houses were known as commanderies and at one time there were more than 50 of their small monasteries in the country.

RIBCHESTER

8 miles SW of Clitheroe on the B5269

Bremetannacum Roman Museum

St Wilfrid's Church

Situated on the banks of the River Ribble, the village is famous for its Roman Fort, **Bremetannacum**, on the northern bank. It was the Roman governor Gnaeus Julius Agricola who in 79AD first established a fort here at the crossroads of two important roads, one linking Manchester and Carlisle; the other running from York to the west coast. It also guarded a ford over the River Ribble. Although little of the fort's walls remain, the granary or storehouse with its hypocaust (underfloor heating) has been excavated and has revealed some interesting coins, pottery, sculptures and inscriptions.

The fort's **Roman Museum** is designed to transport visitors back to the days of the Roman occupation and offers an excellent insight into those times. Amongst the dramatic displays are life-size figures of a splendidly attired Roman Legionary and a cavalryman. Sadly, the finest artefact unearthed here, an ornate bronze parade helmet recovered in 1795, is not on display, although they do have a replica. The original can be seen at the British Museum in London.

In the village itself, the discovery of some pre-Norman crosses in and around **St Wilfrid's Church** suggests that this 13th-century building occupies the site of a Saxon church. The church is named after the first Bishop of Ripon who, in the 7th century, played a prominent part in the Synod of Whitby.

LONGRIDGE

10 miles SW of Clitheroe on the B6243

Longridge Fell Club Row

After Clitheroe, bustling Longridge is the only other town of any size in the area. Like

MOSS SPECIALITY GALLERY SHOP

1 Lower Lane, Longridge, Preston PR3 3SL
Tel: 01772 786576
website: www.mossinteriors.co.uk

Occupying purpose-built premises in the bustling town of Longridge, **Moss Speciality Gallery Shop** is a unique shop opened by Julie Rainford in the autumn of 2005. Julie is a self-taught textile and watercolour artist who has exhibited her work in the Mall Galleries, London, and in Tuscany. Everything on display at Moss has been made by hand using only the finest authentic materials, sourced locally, to produce unique pieces of art and home furnishings. The stunning textures and forms, vibrant colours and creative composition work in unison to provide a strong sense of space and serenity. Julie is always happy to discuss ideas for your own personal interior décor and commissions are always welcome.

The striking design of the Moss premises, with its green oak beams, solid oak doors and featured staircase, is to be credited to Julie's husband, David, who is both a farmer and a joiner. David and his brother Richard have also built 18 state-of-the-art timber holiday lodges nearby, which can be rented through the shop. David and Julie's daughter, Laura, runs the Pure Organic Spa, which shares the same premises (see below).

PURE ORGANIC SPA

1 Lower Lane, Longridge, Preston PR3 3SL
Tel: 01772 786576

Occupying the same premises as Moss Speciality Gallery Shop (see above), **Pure Organic Spa** specialises in organic skin and body care treatment. It was opened in November 2006 by Laura Rainford, daughter of Julie who owns and runs Moss. Laura trained as a beautician specialising in organic treatments and natural make-up using I.d. bare minerals.

The Spa offers the Eselle and Spiezia 100% organic range of treatments. Spiezia is the only beauty company to have Soil Association approval across its whole range. These products are suitable for even the most sensitive of skins. The treatments range from a 1-hour organic facial, through a 2-hour Hot Rock Massage, to a 30-minute Back Massage. Other treatments include hands and feet therapy, and a 45-minute Make-up Session providing personal instruction on how to correctly apply make-up suitable for your skin tone and colouring. Waxing, eyelash and eyebrow tinting, Pre-Holiday pampering and Wedding Hair - an experienced stylist visits your home for your wedding day - are also part of the extensive range on offer. As Laura puts it, "We have created a pure organic spa, which is dedicated to relaxation, rejuvenation and good health, in a peaceful and tranquil environment"

Clitheroe it offers a good selection of independently owned shops along with a range of antiques galleries. It is widely known for its Lancashire Cheese Dairies.

The village lies at the foot of **Longridge Fell** from whose 1150ft elevation there are superb views northwards over the Loud Valley to Chipping: to the south the land drops away towards the River Ribble. For many years this area was an important source of building stone and several of Preston's civic buildings, including the Harris Library and Museum, and the docks at Liverpool were constructed with Longridge stone.

In the 1790s the stone was also used to build a row of 20 terraced cottages in Longridge – numbers 4 to 44 Higher Road, which now have listed building status. They were erected by a group of quarrymen who formed a club into which each member paid a fixed weekly sum. The money was used to pay the cost of materials, £138.3s.6d (£138.17p), for building each cottage. When a cottage was completed, the members drew lots as to who should occupy it. Known as **Club Row**, these mutually-funded cottages are the earliest known example of properties built on the principles of a Building Society and have earned themselves an entry in the *Guinness Book of Records*.

GOOSNARGH

12 miles SW of Clitheroe on the B5269

Chingle Hall

Just to the west of the village stands **Chingle Hall**, a small moated manor house that was built in 1260 by Adam de Singleton. A Catholic family, the Singletons are said to have a chapel with three priest hides. As well as being the birthplace of St John Wall, one of the last priests to die for his faith, in 1620, it enjoys the reputation of being one of the most haunted houses in Britain and has featured in countless TV and radio programmes.

BASHALL TOWN

2 miles W of Clitheroe off the B6243

Bowland Brewery

Idyllically located on the edge of the Forest of Bowland, the **Bowland Brewery** produces award-winning real ales using traditional methods with the finest malts and hops. In the free Visitor Centre there are viewing windows into the brew house itself, and a shop - the only retail outlet for the Brewery's bottled beers. Alternatively, you can enjoy a brew with a meal at the neighbouring Bashall Barn farm shop and café. Tours of the brewery can be arranged by appointment for groups of 10 or more.

GRIMSARGH

11 miles W of Clitheroe on the B6243

Tun Brook Wood

As well as having one of the largest village greens in Lancashire, covering some 12 acres, Grimsargh is also home to **Tun Brook Wood**. Following the line of the brook until it meets the River Ribble, this is one of the largest areas of deciduous woodland in the country.

The Fylde

The Fylde derives its name from the Anglo-Saxon word *gefilde* meaning level, green fields, an apt description of this low-lying area that extends from Fleetwood in the north to Lytham St Anne's in the south. It was once known as Windmill Land but nowadays windmills are few and far between. A notable exception is the striking example on the waterfront at Lytham. It was built in 1805, worked until 1929, and now houses a small museum.

This historic area of coastal Lancashire is known to most because of Blackpool: the brash, seaside resort that has been entertaining holidaymakers for generations. To the south lies another resort, Lytham St Anne's, which is not only somewhat more genteel, but also the home of one of the country's best known golf courses and host to the British Open Championships. Both places grew up as a result of the expansion of the railway system in the Victorian age when they were popular destinations for the mill workers of Lancashire and Yorkshire.

However, the Fylde is also an ancient region that was known to both the Saxons and the Romans. To the north of this region, around the Wyre estuary, the salt marshes have been exploited for more than 2000 years and the process continues at the large ICI plant. Fishing and shipping too have been important sources of revenue here.

Inland, the fertile, flat plain has been farmed for many centuries and, with few major roads, the quiet rural communities lie undisturbed and little changed by the 21st century. A haven for wildlife, and particularly birds and plants, the two estuaries of the Ribble and the Wyre provide habitats that abound with rare and endangered species of plants and birds. A relatively undiscovered region, the Fylde has much more to offer than a white-knuckle ride and candy floss and is well worth taking the time to explore.

Blackpool

Blackpool Tower · Tower Ballroom
Pleasure Beach · Sandcastle Waterpark
Sea Life Centre · North Pier
Grundy Art Gallery · Blackpool Tramways
Dr Who Monster Museum · Martin Mere
Stanley Park · Blackpool Zoo · Norman arch

Blackpool is as unique to England as Las Vegas is to the United States. Everyone is familiar with Blackpool's brash, warm-hearted attractions, but did you know that this single town has more beds available for the 16 million people who visit each year than the whole of Portugal has for its visitors?

Stanley Park, Blackpool

Today, Blackpool is the largest town in the present county of Lancashire. Little more than a fishing village among the sand dunes of the Fylde coast 150 years ago, Blackpool's huge expansion followed the arrival of the railway. Up until then, travel to and from the village involved considerable discomfort, taking a day from Manchester and two days from York. The great Victorian railway companies put Blackpool well and truly on the map by laying the railway lines right to the coast and building the grand stations – the town once had three. Local developers enthusiastically began creating new attractions for their visitors. The first pier was constructed in 1863, followed by two more over the next 20 years. A glass-domed Winter Gardens opened in 1875, and 10 years later the town's electric tram system began operating, the first in Britain and today the only one. The **Pleasure Beach** with its permanent fairground rides and amusements arrived in 1890 with the aim of providing "an American-style amusement park where adults could feel like children again".

But the developers' real masterstroke was the construction of the world-famous **Blackpool Tower**. Modelled on the Eiffel Tower and completed in 1894, the tower stands some 518 feet high and incorporates a Ballroom and Grand Theatre, both of which are decorated in a wonderfully over-the-top rococo style. There's also an aquarium, 3D cinema, circus workshop and the famous **Tower Ballroom**, a much loved institution where tea dances are still a regular feature. It was, for many years from the 1960s to the 1980s, the venue for BBC TV's enormously popular *Come Dancing* series.

The introduction of the Blackpool Illuminations helped extend the summer season into autumn, and the late 20th century saw yet more visitor attractions added to the mix. The Pleasure Beach now boasts the tallest, fastest and, it is claimed, the most thrilling rollercoaster ride in the world; **Sandcastle Waterpark** is an all-weather indoor complex where visitors can enjoy waterslides, wave pools and water flumes in sub-tropical temperatures; and **The Sea Life Centre** provides close-up views of a wide range of marine creatures, including deadly sea snakes, and boasts one of the largest collections of tropical sharks in Europe.

The **North Pier**, designed by Eugenius Birch, was opened at the beginning of the 1863 season. It soon became the place to promenade and is now a listed building. Eugenius Birch (1818-1884) was the most famous of all the pier engineers; he was also a talented artist and mechanic. His Blackpool pier was one of many – others included Margate, Aberystwyth, Brighton West, Eastbourne, Hastings, Lytham and Plymouth – the last opened in the year of his death. Currently, the Promenade between the North Pier and Sandcastle Waterpark is being extended and improved to provide a stylish new seafront and to bolster coastal defences.

One of the town's less well known attractions is the **Grundy Art Gallery** in Queen Street, which has an interesting collection of Victorian oils and watercolours, contemporary prints, modern British paintings and a fascinating exhibit on Old Blackpool.

Despite its reputation as a brash and lively resort, Blackpool also has its quiet, secluded corners where visitors can escape the hustle of the crowds. There are seven miles of sea front, from the North Shore down as far as Squire's Gate and Lytham, where the pace of life is gentler and the beaches are quieter. **Blackpool Tramways** have provided a most enjoyable way of exploring these less busy sides of the town and its environs for many years. Opened in 1885, it was the world's first electric street tram system. The route was extended along the Lytham road in 1895 and later connected with other routes in nearby Lytham St Anne's. Still a popular means of transport here today, many of the tramcars

Martin Mere, nr Blackpool

date from the 1930s or 1950s and the managing company has a special selection of vintage cars, which they run on special occasions such as the ceremonial lighting of the Illuminations.

A fairly recent addition to the town's attractions is the **Dr Who Monster Museum** where visitors come face to face with monsters, props and costumes from more than 40 years of the cult programme. The Tardis is there along with Daleks and Davros that you can even get inside.

A couple of miles inland from The Pleasure Beach, **Martin Mere** is a Wildlife and Wetlands Trust bird reserve where more than 160 species have been recorded (see panel on page 222). The 10-acre lake is the year-round home for hundreds of geese, swans, ducks and even flamingos, and a temporary resting place for thousands more. Nearby, **Stanley Park** is spacious, well-maintained and peaceful, and noted for its Italian garden and pleasure lake. Within the park is Blackpool Model Village, 2½ acres of gardens, entertaining model displays and a couple of ponds stocked with koi carp. Adjacent to the park, **Blackpool Zoo** is home to more than 400 animals from all around the world, including lions, tigers, elephants, gorillas, lemurs, exotic birds and creepy-crawlies. A popular attraction is the Dinosaur Safari, which takes visitors back through time to the world of dinosaurs, experiencing erupting volcanoes, spouting geysers and terrifying reptiles along the way. The latest addition is Amazonia, a walk-round exhibit that houses five species of monkey, along with South American wildfowl, parrots and agouti.

In a town that places such emphasis on novelty, it's something of a surprise to find a magnificent **Norman arch** in one of its churches. All Hallows Church itself is 19th century, but the arch was retained from an earlier building. It is carved with the signs of the zodiac and is remarkably well-preserved.

Around Blackpool

CLEVELEYS

5 miles N of Blackpool on the A584

This popular seaside resort is less boisterous than its neighbour, Blackpool, to the south and it is altogether more attractive architecturally. This is hardly surprising as the town began to grow after an architectural competition, organised in 1906, in which Sir Edwin Lutyens, the designer of modern Whitehall in London, was involved.

FLEETWOOD

8 miles N of Blackpool on the A587

Fleetwood Museum Fisherman's Friend

Cleveleys in turn links up with Fleetwood, which until 1836 was just a small fishing village. Local landowner Sir Peter Hesketh-Fleetwood decided to develop the area as a seaside resort and employed the leading architect, Decimus Burton, who had designed large parts of St Leonards-on-Sea and Hove.

The opening of the railway extension from Preston to Fleetwood was a key factor in the town's development and the impressive North Euston Hotel, which opened in 1842, reflects those railway links. Queen Victoria used Fleetwood as she travelled to Scotland for her annual holiday. However, this was all before the railway companies managed to lay a railway over Shap Fell in Cumbria in 1847 and thus provide a direct rail link to Scotland. Sir Peter was bankrupted but the town itself continued to flourish as a port and seaside resort.

The town's **Museum**, overlooking the River Wyre, illustrates the town's links with the fishing industry, which suffered greatly from the Icelandic cod wars of the 1970s.

The town's most famous product is known around the world. In 1865, a local chemist named James Lofthouse created a compound of liquorice, capsicum, eucalyptus and methanol designed to relieve the sore throats and bronchial troubles endured by fishermen at sea. He called the mixture **Fisherman's Friend** and it was remarkably successful. The only problem was that the bottles in which it was sold frequently shattered in the rough Atlantic seas. So Lofthouse transformed the liquid into a lozenge which is still produced by his descendants and has enormous sales world-wide.

ROSSALL POINT

9 miles N of Blackpool off the A587

Situated at the northern tip of the Fylde coast, Rossall Point is where the Hesketh-Fleetwood family, the force behind the creation of Fleetwood, had their home. Their impressive mansion is still standing and is now part of Rossall School.

POULTON-LE-FYLDE

3 miles NE of Blackpool on the A586

Danes Pad · Church of St Chad

Teanlay Night · Skippool Creek

This is one of the oldest towns in the ancient area known as Amounderness. The Romans were known to have been in the area and it was probably their handiwork that constructed the **Danes Pad**, an ancient trackway. The town developed as a commercial centre for the surrounding agricultural communities and its Market Place remains its focal point. In 1732, a great fire, started by sparks from the torches of a funeral procession, destroyed most of the thatched cottages that surrounded the market square in those days. Consequently, little of old Poulton can be seen in the centre of the town.

The present **Church of St Chad** dates from the early 17th century, though the majority of the building is Georgian. It stands on the site of the original Norman church. Inside there's a splendid Georgian nave from which a magnificent staircase leads to typically Georgian galleries running around three sides. As Poulton was a key town in the area for centuries, it is not surprising that there are several magnificent memorials to the local Fleetwood-Hesketh family to be found here.

Fire seems to have played an important role in the life of the town and one ancient custom still kept is **Teanlay Night**, which involves the lighting of bonfires on Hallowe'en. Each bonfire is encircled with white-coloured stones, which are then thrown into the flames by the onlookers and

left until the next day. The successful retrieval of one's own stone is considered a good omen for future prosperity.

Strolling around Poulton-le-Fylde now, it is hard to imagine that the town was once a seaport. But, until relatively recently, ships sailed up the River Wyre to **Skippool Creek**. Today, the creek is home to the Blackpool and Fleetwood Yacht Club and from here the ocean-going yachts compete in major races around Britain.

The town had a rail link long before Blackpool and it was here that the early holidaymakers alighted from their trains to take a horse and trap the remaining few miles. Fortunately for Poulton, in 1846, the railway reached Blackpool and the town could once again return to a more peaceful existence. It is this quiet and charm, as well as sensitive approaches to planning, that have led it to become, in recent years, a much sought after residential area for businessmen now able to travel the M55 to Manchester and Liverpool.

Incidentally, Poulton's "le-Fylde" tag was added to distinguish the town from Poulton-le-Sands – nowadays better known as Morecambe.

THORNTON

5 miles NE of Blackpool on the B5268

Marsh Mill · Wyre Estuary Country Park

Wyreside Ecology Centre

Situated in the west bank of the Wyre estuary, this small town is dominated by **Marsh Mill**, which stands over 100 feet high and was constructed in 1794. The grinding of corn ceased here soon after World War One but the building has been restored and it is now a tourist attraction.

At this point the Wyre estuary is wide and provides shelter for shipping, an advantage that was utilised by both the Romans and the Scandinavians. They both took advantage of the salt deposits here and, today, the large ICI plant is still extracting salt. The **Wyre Estuary Country Park**, taking in the whole estuary from Fleetwood up river as far as Shard Bridge, is an excellent place from which to discover the area. An initial stop at the **Wyreside Ecology Centre**, which provides all manner of information about the estuary, is a sensible starting point. From here a number of footpaths take in many of the places along the river, as well as leading visitors through important areas of salt marsh that contain a wide range of plants, insects, and birds.

HAMBLETON

6 miles NE of Blackpool on the A588

Shard Bridge

A centre for ship building in medieval times, Hambleton is now a quiet village set around a bend of the River Wyre. A network of narrow lanes radiate from the village and wind through the charming north Fylde countryside.

The village stands on one of the narrowest parts of the river and relics have been found to indicate there was certainly a ford here in Roman time. It is probable that the ford goes back even further, to the Iron Age around 500BC. On the site of the ford stands the 325-yard **Shard Bridge**, built in 1864 and still operating as a toll bridge.

GREAT ECCLESTON

8 miles NE of Blackpool off the A586

This quiet traditional agricultural community on the banks of the River Wyre was, during the 17th and 18th centuries, known locally as Little London because it was the social centre for the surrounding area. This was probably directly linked to the generous number of public houses and inns in the village at that time.

Every Wednesday, a bustling open air market is held in the charming village square. However, unlike most local markets, Great Eccleston's first took place in 1974 following a campaign started by the parish council a few years previously. The wide variety of stalls attract visitors from not only the immediate surroundings but also coaches from outside the area.

PREESALL

9 miles NE of Blackpool on the B5270

The village's original name, Pressoude, mentioned in the *Domesday Book*, is thought to mean a salt farm near the sea. In 1872 rock salt deposits were discovered beneath the village. From then on, for around 30 years, Preesall became a centre for salt mining. The bulk of the salt was extracted in the form of brine, and by the end of 1891 there was a reliable pipeline pumping the salt under the River Wyre to Fleetwood. However, as much of the salt was extracted from underneath the expanding village, subsidence soon became a problem. In 1923 this led to the opening up of a huge pit, known locally as "Bottomless", to the west of the village.

ST MICHAEL'S ON WYRE

9 miles NE of Blackpool on the A586

The River Wyre at this point is still tidal and for centuries the inhabitants of St Michael's and other villages in the area have suffered the threat of flooding. An old flood bank has been constructed from the village bridge and below, beyond the overgrown banks, are the fertile fields of the flood plain.

Mentioned in the *Domesday Book* as Michelscherche, it is likely that the first church in the village was founded in the 7th century. As well as many memorials to the Butler family, the church also contains a splendid 14th-century mural that was only discovered in 1956 when repair work was being undertaken in the sanctuary.

The Butler family, whose home – Rawcliffe Hall – lies a few miles down river, are known to have been in this area for 800 years and their house is built on the site of a Saxon dwelling. Another of the staunchly Catholic Lancashire families, the Butlers finally lost their house and the influence that they had in the area. The house is now part of a private country club.

KNOTT END-ON-SEA

10 miles NE of Blackpool on the B5270

This small coastal resort on the River Wyre estuary grew into a substantial fishing settlement in the 17th and 18th centuries. It was also a pilot base for the upstream ports of Wardleys and Skippool, and later developed into a ferry port. Today its broad flat sands and bracing sea air, along with the decline in the fishing industry, have turned the town into a small, quiet holiday resort that is also favoured by those who have retired.

Looking out to sea, at low tide, a rocky outcrop can be seen which, some historians have suggested, is the remains of the masonry of a Roman harbour. Whether this is the port that in the 2nd century Ptolemy marked on a map as Portus Setantiorum is certainly in doubt, but it is undeniable that such a building existed as the Romans were planning an invasion of Ireland from this stretch of coast.

CHURCHTOWN

12 miles NE of Blackpool on the A586

Church of St Helen

This delightful village has many buildings of both architectural and historic interest and none more so than the **Church of St Helen**, which dates back to the days of the Norman Conquest. Featuring architectural styles from almost every period since the 11th century, this church is well worth exploring. The oldest parts of the building are the circular pillars near the nave, which date from around 1200. The roof is the original Tudor structure. Built on the site of a Saxon church, St Helen's is dedicated to the mother of Emperor Constantine and the circular churchyard is typical of the Saxon period.

Known as the "Cathedral of the Fylde", the church has been subjected to flooding by the River Wyre. In 1746, such was the damage caused by the rising waters that the rebuilding of the church looked necessary. However, the builder brought in to survey the scene, suggested that moving the river would be a cheaper option and this method of preserving the church was undertaken. The original course of the river can be seen by taking the footpath from the churchyard in the direction of the new river course.

PILLING

11 miles NE of Blackpool off the A588

Old St John's   Olde Ship Inn

This quiet scattered village, on the edge of rich, fertile marshland, was for many years linked to the market town of Garstang by a little, winding, single-track railway known affectionately as the "Pilling Pig", because the train's whistle sounded like a pig having its throat cut. The last passengers were carried in 1930; the last goods train ran in 1950.

Said to be the second largest village in Britain, Pilling boasts no fewer than five churches. One of them, **Old St John's**, is notable as a 'time-warp' church, virtually unchanged since its completion in 1717. Flagged floors, pews and box-pews of unvarnished oak, and a three-decker pulpit have all survived unscathed thanks to the building of a new church in the village in 1887.

There has been a watermill at Pilling since 1242. The present windmill dates back to 1808 and was built on a raft of brushwood. It is now a private residence.

Another building of interest is the **Olde Ship Inn**, built in 1782 by George Dickson, a slave trader. Now a listed building, the inn is reputed to be haunted by a lady dressed in

Georgian attire wandering around with a worried look on her pale face.

GARSTANG

12 miles NE of Blackpool on the A6

Discovery Centre | Greenhalgh Castle

Gubberford Bridge | Toll House

Turnpike Milestones

This is an ancient, picturesque town whose market dates back to the time of Edward II and is still held every Thursday in the central square with its handsome former Town Hall of 1755. A bell is rung at 10am to signify the opening of trading. Another long-standing institution is the Garstang Agricultural Show, which was founded in 1809 and is held on the first Saturday in August.

The town is also home to an excellent **Discovery Centre**, which deals with a variety of aspects of the region, including the history of the nearby Forest of Bowland and the natural history of the surrounding countryside.

Greenhalgh Castle, Garstang

Just to the east of the town, on the top of a grassy knoll, are the remains of **Greenhalgh Castle**, built in 1490 by Thomas Stanley, the first Earl of Derby. Severely damaged during a siege by Cromwell's troops in 1645-46, the castle was one of the last strongholds in Lancashire to have held out and only surrendered when its Governor died.

Nearby **Gubberford Bridge** is reputedly haunted. It was during the Civil War siege that a Roundhead soldier named Peter Broughton was standing on the bridge one winter evening when he was approached by a beautiful woman dressed all in white. To his amazement, he recognised the wife who had left him for another man some five years earlier.

She was advancing towards him, smiling and with her arms outstretched, when a Royalist captain, Robert Rowton, burst onto the bridge. In the altercation that followed it emerged that she had bigamously married the captain. Enraged, Rowton stabbed her in the breast and she died within minutes. The two soldiers from opposing sides then joined forces to bury beside the bridge the body of the woman they had both known as wife. It was only a death-bed confession by Peter Broughton many years later that brought the deed to light. By then Rowton was dead, but the unquiet soul of the White Lady has found no rest and on misty winter evenings she paces silently up and down the bridge.

A little to the north of Garstang, on the B6430, are the remains of a stone-built **Toll House**, which probably dates from the 1820s when parts of the turnpike from Garstang to Lancaster were realigned. Although a ruin, the toll house is more than usually interesting as the posts for the toll gates can still be seen on either side of the road. This stretch of road also features some of the finest **Turnpike Milestones** in the county. To the south of Garstang they are round-faced stones with cursive lettering dating from the 1750s, but to the north the stones are triangular, with Roman lettering, and date from the time of the turnpike's realignment in the early 19th century.

SINGLETON

5 miles E of Blackpool on the B5260

Robert Gillow · St Anne's Church

Singleton Maize Maze

Singleton's most famous son is **Robert Gillow** who lived here in the first half of the 18th century. He left to become an apprentice joiner at Lancaster and later founded the cabinet-making business that became Waring & Gillow of Lancaster.

The village Gillow knew was completely demolished in 1853 after it was bought for £70,000 by Alderman Thomas Miller, a cotton manufacturer from Preston. He then rebuilt it as a model village complete with a church, school, public house - The Millers Arms, naturally - and an ornate black-and-white shed for the village fire engine, which still stands although it is now an electricity sub-station.

The parish church of this quiet little Fylde village, **St Anne's Church**, was built as part of Miller's model village in 1860. In the sanctuary is a black oak chair that bears the inscription "John Milton, author of *Paradise Lost* and *Paradise Regained* 1671" but no one seems to know where the chair came from and whether the great author did indeed use it.

Just outside the village, at Mount Farm, is the **Singleton Maize Maze**, constructed within a growing crop of corn. There are large indoor and outdoor play areas, picnic tables and refreshments are available.

WOODPLUMPTON

11 miles E of Blackpool off the B5269

St Anne's Church · Margaret Hilton

This charming little village, centred around its church, still has its well-preserved village stocks behind which is a mounting block that is now designated as a historic monument. **St Anne's Church** is also a building of historic note and the keen-eyed will be quick to spot the octagonal cupola shape of tower that is reminiscent of the architecture of Christopher Wren. Completed in 1748, the tower was built to house a new timepiece, a clock, which replaced the sundial that for many years adorned the old tower. Bearing the date 1637, this can now be found in the churchyard.

Many small towns and villages in Lancashire have their own tale of witches to tell and Woodplumpton is no exception. In St Anne's churchyard a huge boulder marks the grave of **Margaret Hilton**, better known in her day as "Meg the Witch". It's said that one day the local squire made a wager with her that she could not turn herself into a hare and outrun his pack of dogs. (This transformation into a hare was apparently a standard feature of any self-respecting witch's repertoire.) Meg accepted the bet, stipulating only that one particular black dog should be excluded.

The race duly took place but the squire cheated, letting slip the black dog, which managed to nip the hare's back legs just before it vanished into thin air. From that day, Meg suffered from a severe limp – and a nasty temper. Every kind of rural mishap was attributed to her black arts. She was eventually found dead in her cottage, crushed between a water barrel and a well. Her body was buried in the churchyard by torchlight on May 2nd 1705. But her body kept rising to the surface, so a massive boulder was rolled over her grave. (Similar measures were taken at Samlesbury, to the east of Preston. In the churchyard there's a witch's grave through which iron spikes have been driven to prevent her from returning to plague her neighbours.)

CLOUGHTON-ON-BROCK

12 miles E of Blackpool off the A6

Cobble Hey Farm & Gardens

An award-winning visitor attraction with something for the whole family, **Cobble Hey Farm & Gardens** enjoys spectacular views over the Forest of Bowland. It has a lapwing conservation area, some excellent walks, a collection of rare breed animals, a café serving refreshments made from local produce, a children's play area and a large garden stocked with unusual plants, including a national collection from Catforth Gardens.

PEEL

4 miles SE of Blackpool off the A583

Penny Farm

A short drive out of Blackpool, at Peel just off the A583, is **Penny Farm**, a recovery and rehabilitation centre run by the International League for the Protection of Horses. The site has stabling for around 55 horses, open-fronted barns where visitors can make friends with the horses, an exercise area and a visitor centre with a coffee shop and gift shop.

FRECKLETON

9 miles SE of Blackpool on the A584

American Liberator

This is the largest village in the Fylde with a population of more than 7000. The name is derived from the Anglo-Saxon *Frecheltun* meaning 'an enclosed area' and this is how it featured in the Domesday Book. Situated on the northern banks of the River Ribble, the long straggling village was, until the river was canalised, surrounded by marshland.

During World War Two, the village suffered an appalling tragedy. On a sweltering, thundery day in August 1944 an **American Liberator** plane took off from nearby Warton aerodrome but because of the adverse weather, the pilot decided to turn back. As it descended over Freckleton, the plane clipped some trees and crashed into the village school. Thirty-six children and 36 adults perished. A disaster fund was set up but villagers bitterly disagreed about how it should be spent. It wasn't until 33 years later that the money was used to build the village's Memorial Hall.

KIRKHAM

7 miles SE of Blackpool off the A583

Mentioned in the *Domesday Book*, there was a settlement here in Saxon times, known as Ciric-ham, and before that the Romans had a fort though it is now lost under a modern housing estate. Kirkham was first granted a charter to hold a weekly market in 1287 and since then it has been serving the needs of the surrounding farming communities. Some fine Georgian inns and houses reflect the town's importance in stagecoach days, and the steep main street contains a number of old-

SIMPLY NATURAL

26 Poulton Street, Kirkham,
Lancashire PR4 2AB
Tel: 01772 671489
website: www.simplynatural.org.uk

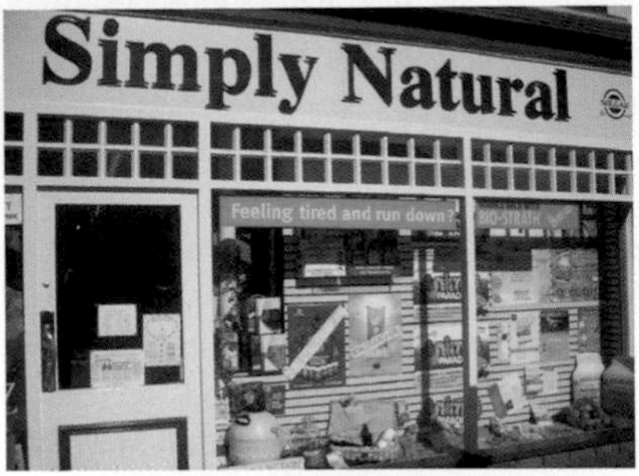

Simply Natural was established in 1996 by husband and wife team Shaun and Susan Fisher in the market town of Kirkham in Lancashire.

The original shop was half the size it is now and crammed full of pills, lotions and foods, some you will be familiar with and others not. In 2004 they moved into the present shop - all that extra space was just what they needed to expand their enthusiasm and business. The shop has friendly and polite staff with a very good knowledge of herbal remedies and available to give advice and help should it be required. The shop sells a vast array of items that they cannot always put on the website because of the sheer volume, but feel free to contact them should you have problems locating something; they will most likely have it somewhere.

The homebrew section is a recent addition that came about because the customers wanted it. There is the added bonus that Shaun is a very keen homebrew enthusiast, so questions to him please!

fashioned family-run shops. In the cobbled market square, used for markets and fairs since 1296, The Fishstones are still to be seen – flat stone slabs set on stone uprights to form a broken circle. These were the counters from which fish was sold.

LYTHAM ST ANNE'S

4 miles S of Blackpool on the A584

- St Anne's Pier Lytham Hall
- Lytham Hall Country Park Lytham Windmill
- Lifeboat Museum
- Lytham Motive Power Museum
- Lytham St Anne's Nature Reserve
- Royal Lytham & St Anne's Golf Course

Located on the northern bank of the Ribble Estuary, Lytham St Anne's is based on a much older community, already well-established by the time of the Norman Conquest. It has a beautifully restored Victorian pier, a gracious Victorian Promenade, and an attractive grassy expanse called the Beach. Here stands a handsome whitewashed windmill, one of very few to have survived from the days when the flat plain of the Fylde was dotted with hundreds of them. The spacious sandy beach was recently awarded a national Quality Coast Award by ENCAMS for being exceptionally clean and safe.

There are actually two towns here: Lytham, which is mentioned in the *Domesday Book*, and St Anne's, which was largely developed in the 1870s as a rather upmarket resort. Before the development of the resort in the Victorian age, Lytham was an important port on the Ribble estuary and was home to the first fishing company on this stretch of the northwest coast. Shipbuilding also continued here until the 1950s, when the last vessel constructed in the shipyards was the Windermere Car Ferry. During the 1940s, parts of the famous Mulberry harbour were built in secret here in preparation for the invasion of Normandy in 1944.

The arrival of the railway linking Lytham with Preston prompted a group of Lancashire businessmen to plan the construction of a health resort between the old established port and the rapidly expanding town of Blackpool to the north. There was scarcely a cottage on their chosen site when the work began in 1875, but the growth of the carefully planned town was spectacular. In just 30 years the population increased from 1000 to 17,000 inhabitants.

The Promenade, running the full length of the seafront from St Anne's to Lytham, was constructed in 1875, and on the landward side there are several fine examples of Victorian and Edwardian seaside villas. Beyond the attractive Promenade Gardens, laid out by a local character, Henry Gregson, is **St Anne's Pier**. Opened in 1885, the elegant pier was built in a mock-Tudor style and up until 1897 fishing smacks and pleasure boats were able to tie up at the end of the jetty. Lytham also had a pier, built in 1865, but during a gale in 1903 two sand barges dragged their anchors and sliced the structure in two. Undeterred, and with the Pavilion still standing at the far end, the pier was rebuilt only to be almost entirely destroyed by fire in 1928.

The town has had its fair share of disasters associated with the sea. By far the worst of these occurred in 1886 and it is still Britain's greatest lifeboat disaster. The crew of the St Anne's lifeboat, with the help of the Southport lifeboat, set out to answer a distress signal put up by a German ship, the *Mexico*. The sea was so rough that 15 members of the lifeboat crew were lost. The tragedy led to the improvement of lifeboat design. In the Alpine Garden on the Promenade is a monument that pays tribute to the men who lost their lives. The statue features the stone figure of a coxswain looking out to sea with a rope in one hand and a lifebelt in the other.

As well as being an elegant place full of fine Victorian and Edwardian architecture, Lytham St Anne's also contains some reminders to the more distant past. **Lytham Hall**, now privately owned by a large insurance company, started life as a farming cell of Durham cathedral in 1190. After the Reformation, the estate changed hands several times until in 1606 it became the property of Sir Cuthbert Clifton, the first squire of Lytham. The fine Georgian hall standing today was the building that John Carr of York built for Thomas Clifton between 1757 and 1764. The extensive grounds, once part of the estate, are now **Lytham Hall Country Park**, where visitors can follow several nature trails to discover the birds and wildlife living here, which includes three species of woodpecker, the Lesser Whitethroat and the Hawfinch.

There has been a **Windmill** at Lytham for more than 800 years though the present structure dates from 1805. A well-known landmark along the coast, the building has a solid white tower with a cap that looks rather like an upturned boat. In 1929, the wind set the four sails turning the wrong way, ruining the machinery and firing the mill, which has never worked since. Now renovated, the windmill is home to a permanent exhibition on the building's history and on the process of breadmaking. Adjacent to the windmill, and the original home of the Lytham lifeboat, Old Lifeboat House is home to the **Lifeboat Museum** which is due to re-open in 2008. Both buildings have limited opening times. Another museum worthy of a visit is the **Lytham Motive Power Museum**, with its large model railway layout and an outdoor display of rolling stock.

For those interested in discovering more about the abundant wildlife of the dune system here, a visit to **Lytham St Anne's Nature Reserve** is a must. Established in 1968, the reserve is an important scientific site as well as being just a small part of what was once a very extensive sand dune system. As well as the rich plant life, the dunes are home to several rare species of migrating birds including osprey, black redstart and Lapland buntings.

No description of Lytham St Anne's is complete without a mention of the **Royal Lytham and St Anne's Golf Course**. The club originated after a meeting held in 1886 when a group of 19 keen golfers sought to furnish themselves with suitable facilities. The course opened in 1898 and it is still considered by many to be one of the finest golf links in the country and is a regular host of the British Open.

The Forests of Pendle and Rossendale

The Pennine Hills, the 'backbone of England', are such a well-known geographical feature that it comes as something of a surprise to find that the name was created as recently as 1750 by a fraudulent professor. Charles Bertram claimed to have discovered a medieval chronicle describing Britain as it was in Roman times. In this non-existent tome, he said, the Romans had named this range of hills 'Alps Penina' because they resembled the Apennine Hills of central Italy. The professor's fake chronicle was soon discredited, but his spurious name, the 'Pennines', has been universally adopted.

In the 1720s, Daniel Defoe jogged on horse-back through the area and wrote it off as "a howling wilderness.... the English Andes". A century later the wild, poverty-stricken area Defoe had travelled through was throbbing with the sound of churning mill wheels, its sky murky with the smoke of thousands of coal-fuelled factories. That sooty, industrial image lingers on despite the fact that this area of Lancashire has re-invented itself in the past few decades. The waste from coal-pits has been transformed into smoothly-landscaped country parks and energetic local councils are also striving to make the most of the region's natural attractions: swooping hills, stark moorlands and contrasting wooded valleys.

But the area still takes pride in its industrial past, now recognised by its designation as an official Heritage Area. Bacup, for example, as well as being the highest town in Lancashire at 827ft above sea level, is also acknowledged by English Heritage as the best-preserved cotton town in Britain. And the Queen Street Mill at Haile Syke near Burnley is the only surviving steam-powered cotton mill in the country. Here, more than 300 deafening Lancashire looms clatter away in the imposing weaving shed where hundreds of metres of cotton cloth are produced weekly. In Burnley itself, the Weaver's Triangle is one of the finest examples of a Victorian industrial townscape still in existence.

South-east Lancashire also possesses some grand buildings from an earlier era. Gawthorpe Hall at Padiham is a Jacobean gem; Towneley Hall, dating back to the 1400s, houses Burnley's excellent Museum & Art Gallery; and Turton Tower, north of Bolton, is a lovely old building which began life as a medieval pele.

Despite its industrial history, the southern border of Lancashire boasts some attractive villages. Withnell Fold, five miles southwest of Blackburn, is an idyllic model village entirely built by the Parke family in the mid-1800s to house the workforce employed at their paper mill. Rivington, near Chorley, is a captivating small village set around a village green and alongside a huge reservoir beneath whose waters half of the old village lies submerged.

Burnley

Town Hall · Weaver's Triangle
Oak Mount Mill · Queen Street Mill
Towneley Hall Art Gallery & Museum
Museum of Local Crafts & Industries
Burnley Heritage Centre · The Stables Museum
Rosehill Hotel · Moorhouses
Forest of Burnley · Singing-Ringing Tree

This cotton town is rich in history as well as being the largest town in this area of East Lancashire. Incorporating some 50 square miles, the town offers visitors a wealth of contrasts, from some of the best-preserved industrial landscapes in Britain to the magnificent, untouched moorlands just to the east. First established at the beginning of the 9th century, the town nestles in a basin between the River Calder and the River Brun, from which it takes its name.

With the Industrial Revolution and the building of the Leeds and Liverpool Canal, Burnley not only expanded but grew in stature until, by the end of the 19th century, it was the world's leading producer of cotton cloth. Burnley's fine Victorian **Town Hall** of 1888, is one of many monumental public buildings in the area erected during that period of unparalleled English prosperity.

A walk along the towpath of the Leeds and Liverpool Canal, through an area known as the **Weavers' Triangle** is like taking a step back in time. This is an area of spinning mills and weaving sheds; foundries where steam engines and looms were made; canal-side warehouses; domestic buildings, including a unique row of workers' cottages; and a Victorian school house. The Weavers' Triangle Visitors Centre is housed in the former wharfmaster's house and canal toll office. The centre is open to the public on several afternoons a week during the summer months and on most bank holidays.

A short walk from the Visitors' Centre is **Oak Mount Mill** engine house. The splendid old steam engine, originally installed in 1887, has recently been restored and is now operated by electric motor. Opening times are variable.

Even more impressive is the **Queen Street Mill** in Briercliffe which is the only surviving steam-powered cotton mill in Britain. A visit here provides a unique insight into Victorian factory life as the 300 deafening looms are powered by the magnificent steam engine, Peace. The mill was recently designated by the government as a museum with an outstanding collection – one of only 53 in the country to receive the award. It has also featured in BBC TV's productions of *Life on Mars* and Elizabeth Gaskell's *North and South*.

The history of Burnley can also be explored by boat along the Leeds and Liverpool Canal. This famous waterway leaves the Weaver's Triangle via a huge embankment which carries the canal across the town. Known as the 'straight mile', it is in fact less than that but no less exciting and, at 60 feet above the ground, is one of the most impressive features of the canal's length.

Situated on the Todmorden Road on the outskirts of Burnley, is the **Towneley Hall Art Gallery and Museum** (see panel on page 202). The home of the Towneley family from

14th century right up until 1902, parts of the present building date from the 15th century. Visitors can view the art collections, the Whalley Abbey Vestments, the museum of local crafts and industries, and also take in a tour of the house. The kitchens, with their open fires, the servants' hall, a priest's hole and the fascinating family rooms are all on display. The grounds too are open to visitors and contain a traditional Victorian flower garden, woodland nature trails, and a fascinating series of sculptures hewn from the trees. Subjects include a giant magpie, a crocodile emerging from the water, and a huge cricket. The grounds also include a natural history centre, a **Museum of Local Crafts and Industries** and facilities for golf, tennis, bowls, and other outdoor pursuits.

Two other interesting places to visit whilst in Burnley are the **Burnley Heritage Centre**, where memorabilia on display from the town's past include old photographs, a Lancashire loom, and a replica 1930s kitchen and living room. **The Stables Museum**, at Shores Hey Farm in Briercliffe, is run by the Horses and Ponies Protection Association, which takes

Towneley Hall Art Gallery & Museum

Burnley, Lancashire BB11 3RQ
Tel: 01282 424213
website: www.towneleyhall.org.uk

Towneley Hall offers the perfect day out for all the family - a country house, a museum and an art gallery all in one. Towneley Hall was the home of the Towneley family from the 14th century until 1902. Charles (1737-1805) was one of the 18th-century's best-known collectors of antique sculpture and gems. His portrait can be seen in the gallery. Today, visitors can still catch a glimpse of how the family lived. Original period rooms include the Elizabthan long gallery and the Regency rooms. See how they compare with life below stairs in the Victorian kitchen and the servants' dining room.

The museum's collections surround you - glass, ceramics and 17th-century Lancashire oak furniture. Pictures by many favourite Victorian artists can be seen in the art galleries, including works by Sir Edward Coley Burne-Jones, John William Waterhouse and Sir Edwin Landseer. The Whalley Abbey vestments are another highlight. Embroidered in silk and silver thread on cloth of gold, they were brought to Towneley in the 16th century and are now extremely rare. A programme of temporary exhibitions ensures something new to see on every visit. Open daily except Fridays - check for opening times.

care of neglected horses, ponies and donkeys at the farm. A must for horse lovers, the exhibitions include information about the rescue and care of neglected horses, ponies and donkeys as well as a display of the life of the canal horse. Some of the Association's animals are available for adoption.

Lovers of ghost stories will want to visit the **Rosehill Hotel**, which has a resident ghost. She's called Rose and she was an employee at the hotel. In 1860, Rose had an affair with a relative of the hotel proprietor and became pregnant. This was an era when Victorian sexual morality was at its most rigid (and hypocritical). If Rose's illicit pregnancy became known, the hotel's reputation would suffer disastrously. Rose disappeared, completely. The hotel owner said she had been dismissed and left the town, but those who knew of her condition suspected murder. Beneath the hotel there were cellars that were later filled with tons of rubble and it's believed that poor Rose was buried there, emerging from time to time when her successors as chambermaids were cleaning the rooms. She has been heard talking to herself about the daily chores to be done but otherwise has never troubled either the maids or the guests.

Burnley town centre has more than 30 pubs and bars and even its own award-winning brewery, **Moorhouses**, which offers evening tours for groups. Visitors can follow the brewing process from selecting the finest ingredients to tasting the finished product. The tour is followed by a pie & peas supper in the brewery's own pub where you can sample their real ales such as Pendle Witch or Black Cat.

Shedding its perceived image as a grimy industrial wasteland, Burnley has asserted its green credentials by establishing the **Forest of Burnley**. Since 1997, this project has seen the planting of more than one million trees, including a 3000-tree urban arboretum throughout the town.

High above the town, at Crown Point, stands Burnley's equivalent to Gateshead's Angel of the North. The **Singing-Ringing Tree** is an inspired sculpture in the form of a tree bending in the wind. As the wind blows, the sculpture produces a low, musical hum through pipes that are tuned so that they do not disturb the wildlife.

North of Burnley

NELSON

4 miles N of Burnley on the A56

British in India Museum

A modern textile town, Nelson is now inseparable from its neighbours Colne and Burnley and shares the same valley running along the length of Colne Water. It was originally two settlements, Great Marsden and Little Marsden. However, when the railway was being built, the company did not want to name the new station Marsden as there was already a Marsden on the line. As the station was built close to the Nelson Inn, they named it Nelson Inn, Marsden. Over the years, only the 'Nelson' has been retained.

Nelson is also the rather unlikely home of the **British in India Museum**, where exhibits covering many aspects of British rule over the subcontinent from the 17th century until 1947 can be seen. The collection includes coins, medals, uniforms, swords, kukris, model soldiers and a working model of the railway from Kalka to Simla.

PENDLE HILL

5 miles N of Burnley off the A6068

Pendle Witches   Pendle Heritage Centre

Apronfull Hill

Dominating the landscape here is the great whale-backed mass of Pendle Hill, rising to 1920 feet above sea-level. The hill became notorious in the early 1600s as the location where the **Pendle Witches** supposedly practised their black arts. It also has a more uplifting association, though, since it was from the summit of Pendle Hill in 1625 that George Fox saw a vision that inspired him to found the Society of Friends, or Quakers.

Pendle Hill lies at the heart of Lancashire's 'Witch Country', so-called because of the events of 1612. On the 18th March of that year, a Halifax pedlar named John Law refused to give some pins to a beggar, Alison Device. She spat out the usual beggar's curse on him. He died almost immediately of a heart attack. The effect of a curse or just a coincidence? The early 1600s were the years of the great witch-hunts so the authorities had little difficulty in attributing John Law's sudden death to Alison Device's supernatural powers.

Alison was arrested. Under torture, she incriminated eight other 'witches'. All of them were then charged with communing with the Devil and committing a total of 16 murders. They were tried, found guilty and hanged at Lancaster Castle on August 20th 1612. All except one: Old Mother Demdike, 80 years old and half-blind, escaped the gallows by dying in gaol. During their trial, the 'Pendle Witches' seem to have taken pride in implicating each other. In effect, they hanged themselves by their fanciful tales of spells, potions and the coven's naked caperings, fuelling the popular imagination that there really were witches who could affect the lives of other people. The infamous witches were, in the main, old women who dabbled with plants and herbs, knowing which could heal and which, when ingested, would spell certain death.

The Victorian novelist WH Ainsworth was inspired to write a colourful melodrama based on the trial, *The Lancashire Witches – A Romance of Pendle Forest*, and although it's doubtful that 'witchcraft' was any more prevalent around Pendle Hill than anywhere else in the country at that time, the legend has proved very durable. Every year now, on the evening of October 31st, *Halloween*, Pendle Hill is flecked with the dark figures of masked, black-cloaked figures making their way to its summit.

The story of the Pendle Witches is known to everyone with an interest in the occult, but there has always been something of a mystery about why one of them, Alice Nutter, was involved. Unlike the others who were either very poor or even beggars, Alice was a lady of substance. She lived at Roughlee Old Hall, a captivating Elizabethan manor house of 1576, which still stands (but is not open to the public). A recent theory is that she was a Roman Catholic and on her way to a clandestine service when she was caught up with the witches. To avoid betraying her co-religionists, she kept silent about her real motives for being on Pendle Hill on the crucial night.

Something of this old, dark tragedy still broods over Pendle and many memories and places which hark back to those grim days remain. Those interested in finding out more about the trials should visit the **Pendle Heritage Centre** in Barrowford, about three miles southeast of the Hill. The centre is housed in a sturdy 17th-century farmhouse built by the Bannister family, one of whose descendants was Roger Bannister, the first man to run a mile in less than four minutes. The centre also houses an art gallery, a cruck frame barn with animals, an 18th-century walled garden and a pleasant woodland walk. There's also a shop and tearoom/restaurant.

To the west of the hill's summit rises **Apronfull Hill**, a Bronze Age burial site that is said to be the place from which the Devil threw stones at Clitheroe Castle, creating what is known as the Devil's Window.

COLNE

6 miles NE of Burnley on the A56

St Bartholomew's Church · Town Museum

Before the Industrial Revolution turned this area into a valley devoted to the production of cotton cloth, Colne was a small market town that specialised in wool. There are few reminders of the days before industrialisation, but **St Batholomew's Church**, founded in 1122, is still here and contains some interesting interior decorations and furnishings. In the centre of the town, next to the War Memorial, is another memorial. The statue is of Lawrence Hartley, the bandmaster on the ill-fated *Titanic* who, heroically, stayed at his post with his musicians and played *Nearer my God to Thee* as the liner sank beneath the waves of the icy Atlantic in 1912.

Collectors of curiosities will enjoy the unique form of punishment devised for minor malefactors in Colne and preserved in the **Town Museum.** Stocks and pillories enjoyed a long history as a way of humiliating offenders and providing amusement for bystanders. But many of Colne's busy citizens could not spare the time to leave their work and make their way to wherever the stocks were fixed. So a movable cart was constructed, capable of seating three offenders side by side, and the Town Beadle would wheel it around the town so that everyone could join in the fun.

WYCOLLER

9 miles NE of Burnley off the B6250

Wycoller Country Park · Clam Bridge

Wycoller Hall · The Atom

Wycoller Craft Centre

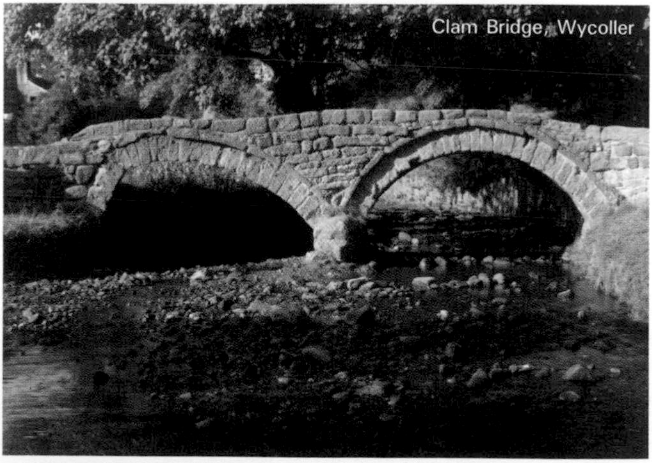
Clam Bridge, Wycoller

This hamlet lies amidst the moorlands that rise to the east of the textile towns of the Colne valley and up to the bleak summits of the Pennines. Now almost deserted, this was once a thriving place as an important centre for the wool trade and as a handloom weavers' settlement, but it lost most of its inhabitants to the new factories in the west.

Fortunately, the place has been saved by the creation of **Wycoller Country Park**, surrounding the village, and many of the buildings have been restored. There is also a delightful old hump-backed packhorse bridge crossing a stream and, above the village, a single slab gritstone bridge, **Clam Bridge**, that is thought to date from the Iron Age.

Now a ruin, **Wycoller Hall** was the inspiration for Ferndean Manor in Charlotte Brontë's *Jane Eyre*: Wycoller was one of the villages to which the sisters walked from their house at Haworth. Atop a hill within the Park is **The Atom**, part of a visionary scheme to create a unique series of 21st-century landmarks across East Lancashire as symbols of the renaissance of the area. The unique, egg-shaped and bronze-coated Atom provides both a striking contemporary viewing point and a shelter from which to enjoy the stunning surrounding landscape.

Located in the centre of the village, **Wycoller Craft Centre** has paintings and crafts by local artists, cards, gifts and collectable tin plate toys. It also has a tea-room with a flower-filled courtyard.

EARBY

10 miles NE of Burnley on the A56

Yorkshire Dales Mining Museum

The town lies almost on the county border with Yorkshire and here can be found the **Yorkshire Dales Mining Museum** housed in the Grade II-listed former Grammar School building. Re-opened in 2006 after total refurbishment, the museum boasts what is probably the largest collection of lead mining artefacts in the UK, including examples of the minerals extracted, a lead crushing mill, and other working models. Also on site are a tearoom and gift shop.

NEWCHURCH

4 miles N of Burnley off the A6068

Annual Rushbearing

This charming Pendle village was named following the consecration of a new church in 1544 by John Bird, Bishop of Chester. Earlier, during the Middle Ages, Newchurch was a cow and deer rearing centre, as well as part of the old hunting forest of Pendle, but by the reign of Elizabeth I the area was becoming deforested and farming was beginning to take over as the primary source of income.

An old tradition continues here – the **Annual Rushbearing** when dry rushes are scattered on the church floor and in the pews. Originally this was to keep parishioners warm, and although the advent of central heating makes it no longer necessary, the villagers still process through the village carrying rushes and singing hymns accompanied by a brass band. A Rushbearing Queen is crowned and, after a short service in the church, everyone repairs to the school for a grand tea.

PADIHAM

3 miles W of Burnley on the A646

Gawthorpe Hall Brontë Way

This charming small town of narrow winding lanes and cobbled alleyways still retains characteristics typical of the early days of the Industrial Revolution. However, there was a settlement here long before the Norman Conquest, and Padiham was also the market town for the western slopes of Pendle. A market is still held here every Wednesday and Friday.

One of Lancashire's most impressive stately homes is **Gawthorpe Hall** (National Trust), which stands on the bank of the River Calder, surrounded by gardens and woodland. The

Shuttleworth family lived at Gawthorpe from the early 1400s, but the present house is a gracious 17th-century mansion, restored and extended in the 1850s by Sir Charles Barry. This was the era of High Victorian extravagance and no expense was spared on the opulent decorations and furnishings. The Hall has many pictures on loan from the National Portrait Gallery, which add extra lustre to the already notable collection. Open to the public between Easter and October, the house has beautiful period furnishings, ornately decorated ceilings and the original wood-panelled walls, and is also home to the nationally important Kay-Shuttleworth collection of fine needlework and lace.

Whalley Abbey

The novelist Charlotte Brontë was a close friend of the Kay-Shuttleworth family and the Hall is now the starting point of the **Brontë Way**, a linear walk from Burnley via Wycoller and Haworth to Oakworth, near Bradford.

WHALLEY

6 miles NW of Burnley on the B6246

Whalley Viaduct   Whalley Abbey

Parish Church

One of Lancashire's most attractive villages, Whalley grew up around a crossing of the River Calder. There are old cottages and Tudor houses, Georgian houses in the main street and three out of the four inns at the crossroads date from the 1700s. Soaring above the village is the **Whalley Viaduct**, an impressive 48-arched structure built in 1850 to carry the Blackburn to Clitheroe railway line across the broad valley of the Calder. Rather touchingly, where the viaduct crosses the lane leading to **Whalley Abbey**, the arches have added Gothic details that harmonise with the nearby 14th-century gatehouse to the abbey.

The abbey was the last to be built in Lancashire, started in the early 1300s, but for the Cistercian monks whose work it was, Whalley was not their first choice. In 1172 they had established a religious house at Stanlow, on the banks of the River Mersey. That site now lies beneath a huge oil refinery.

Seeking somewhere less harsh and more fertile land, the monks moved to Whalley in 1296, but their attempts to build were hampered as Sawley Abbey felt threatened by the competition for the donations of land and goods expected from the local population. Building finally began in 1310 and by 1400 the imposing and impressive abbey had taken shape. The demise of the

Stone Crosses, Whalley Church

abbey came, as it did to all religious houses, under Henry VIII but Whalley's abbot, joining forces with the abbot of Sawley, took part in the Pilgrimage of Grace in an attempt to save their houses. This failed and the abbots were both executed.

Now owned and cared for by the Diocese of Blackburn, Whalley Abbey is one of the best-preserved such places in the country and its future is secure as it also acts as a conference centre.

Whalley's **Parish Church** is almost a century older than the abbey, its oldest parts dating back to 1206. Built on the site of an even older place of worship, the churchyard is home to three ancient crosses and the church itself contains a set of some of the finest choir stalls anywhere. They were brought here from the abbey after the Dissolution and though they are not elaborate there are some intriguing carvings on the lower portions. Even more intriguing though are the puzzling tombstones in the churchyard, each one inscribed with impossible dates such as April 31st 1752 and February 30th 1839.

PENDLETON

6 miles NW of Burnley off the A59

Nick of Pendle

Recorded in the *Domesday Book* when the village was part of the vast parish of Whalley, this small settlement of cottages and working farms has retained much of its traditional air – only seven new houses have been built here in the past 100 years. A beck runs through the middle of the village which was designated a Conservation Area in 1968. The discovery of a Bronze Age burial urn in the village in 1969 would indicate that there were settlers here as long ago as 1600BC.

From the village there is a steep road to the southeast that climbs up to the **Nick of Pendle** from where there are magnificent views.

RISHTON

7 miles W of Burnley on the A678

Originally a Saxon settlement, the name means the fortified village or dwelling place amid the rushes. During the Middle Ages, the village grew in importance as an early textile centre with the operation of its fulling mill. By the 17th century, Rishton had gained a name for the manufacture of linen cloth and in 1766 it became the first village to weave calico. As the Industrial Revolution advanced, the industry moved from the weavers' homes into newly-built mills.

OSWALDTWISTLE

7 miles W of Burnley on the A679

Oswaldtwistle Mills

This typical Lancashire textile town has produced many miles of cotton cloth over the years. You can still hear the deafening clatter of looms at **Oswaldtwistle Mills** in Collier Street, one of the last working cotton mills in the country. Cotton has been woven here for more than 200 years under the watchful eyes of just two owners – the Walmsleys and the Tattersall/Hargreaves family. The town can justifiably be considered the heart of the industry since it was whilst staying here, at what is now Stanhill Post Office, that James Hargreaves invented his famous Spinning Jenny in 1764. Although he was forced to leave the area after sometimes violent opposition to his machine from local hand-spinners, the town's prosperity is largely due to textiles and, in particular, calico printing. However, Oswaldtwistle is a much older settlement than its rows of Victorian terraced houses would suggest, as the name means the boundary of the kingdom of Oswald, who was a 7th-century Northumbrian king.

GREAT HARWOOD

6 miles W of Burnley on the B6535

John Mercer

Before the Industrial Revolution, this was a quiet village of farms and cottages nestling between two streams. At the beginning of the 19th century, the village was famous for its fine woollen cloth, but by the 1850s, the introduction of the factory system and the cotton mills took over. Today only one mill remains, but at the industry's height the town supported 22 mills. Not surprisingly, Great Harwood's most famous son was very much linked with cotton. In 1850, **John Mercer**, an industrial chemist, developed the technique of processing cotton to give it a sheen and the technique, mercerisation, is still used today. The free-standing clock tower in the Town Square was erected in 1903 to commemorate Mercer's contribution to the life of his home town.

ACCRINGTON

5 miles SW of Burnley on the A680

Market Hall · Lancashire Food Festival

Clog Dancing Festival · Haworth Art Gallery

Joseph Briggs · Accrington Railway Viaduct

This attractive Victorian market town, as is typical in this area, expanded as a result of the boom in the textile industry of the 18th and 19th centuries. Of all Lancashire's indoor markets, Accrington enjoys the grandest surroundings, housed in a magnificent **Market Hall** built in 1868. Accrington is also the place to visit for a real flavour of the old Lancashire: In April it hosts the **Lancashire Food Festival,** followed in May by the annual **Clog Dancing Festival**.

Haworth Art Gallery is one of the most appealing galleries in the country – a charming Jacobean-style house built in 1909 and set in beautiful parkland. The gallery owns the largest collection of Tiffany glass in Europe – there are 130 pieces in all. The collection was presented to the town by **Joseph Briggs**, an Accrington man who emigrated to New York and worked with Louis Tiffany for nearly 40 years. Briggs joined the studio in 1890 and rose through the company ranks to become the manager of the Mosaic department before finally becoming Tiffany's personal assistant.

After the World War One, the fashion for Tiffany glassware waned, and during the economic depression of the 1920s Briggs was given the sad job of selling off the remainder of the Tiffany stock. Returning to his native Accrington in 1933 with his collection of glass, Briggs gave half to the town and distributed the remainder amongst his family.

To the west of the town centre, the **Accrington Railway Viaduct** is another magnificent monument to Victorian builders. Erected for the former East Lancashire Railway it sweeps across the River Hyndburn in a graceful curve of 19 arches 60 feet high. Also worth a visit are the imposing Town Hall with its Corinthian portico, and the elegant glass-roofed Arcade of 1880.

BACUP

7 miles S of Burnley on the A671

Coconut Dancers

At 827 feet the highest town in Lancashire, Bacup was built in the 19th century for the sole purpose of cotton manufacture. It remains one of the best examples of a textile town in England even though the town suffered more than most when the mills began to close. A stroll through the town centre will reveal carefully restored shops and houses, with the grander homes of the mill owners and the elegant civic buildings acting as a reminder of the town's more prosperous times. Also, look out for what is claimed to be the shortest street in the world – Elgin Street off the Market Place which is just 17 feet long.

An excellent time to visit the town is during the Easter weekend when the town's famous troop of Morris dancers take to the streets. Known as the **Coconut Dancers**, their costume is unique and involves wearing halved coconut husks strapped to their knees and blackening their faces. The dancers maintain that the correct name is Moorish, not Morris, dancers, and that the tradition goes back to the times of the Crusades.

RAWTENSTALL

7 miles S of Burnley on the A682

Weaver's Cottage | Rossendale Museum

East Lancashire Railway | Irwell Sculpture Trail

The town first developed as a centre of the woollen cloth trade with the work being undertaken by hand-workers in their own homes before steam-powered mills were introduced in the early 19th century. The introduction of the cotton industry to the town happened at around the same time. Lower Mill, now a ruin, was opened in 1840 by the Whitehead brothers who were some of the area's first manufacturing pioneers. The **Weaver's Cottage**, purpose-built for a home weaver, is one of the last buildings remaining of its kind and is open to visitors at weekends during the summer.

Housed in a former Victorian mill owner's house called Oakhill is the **Rossendale Museum**. Naturally, the area's industrial heritage is given a prominent position, but collections of the region's natural history, fine art and furniture, and ceramics are on display, too.

At one end of the town stands a new railway station that marks the end of a very old railway line – the **East Lancashire Railway**. Opened in 1846 and run commercially until 1980, when the last coal train drew into Rawtenstall, the line is now in the hands of the East Lancashire Railway Preservation Society. Running a passenger service (at weekends with additional summer services), the steam trains offer an enthralling 17-mile round trip along the River

Irwell between Rawtenstall and Bury, via Ramsbottom. The railway also operates regular Red Rose Diner trains with Pullman-style dining cars offering travellers a gourmet meal and an evening of pure nostalgia.

Rawtenstall itself is noted for having the only remaining temperance bar in Britain – Herbal Health on Bank Street, which serves traditional non-alcoholic drinks such as sarsaparilla or dandelion and burdock.

At Rawtenstall, you can join the **Irwell Sculpture Trail**, the largest public art scheme in the United Kingdom. New sculptures are appearing all the time and more than 50 regional, national and international artists are being commissioned to produce sculptures with an environmental theme. The Trail follows a well-established 30-mile footpath stretching from Salford Quays through Bury into Rossendale and on up to the Pennine Moors.

HASLINGDEN

7 miles S of Burnley on the A56

Haslingden Miser

The market in this town, which serves much of the Rossendale Valley, dates back to 1676, when the charter was granted by Charles II. Tuesdays and Fridays, market days, still bring the town alive as people flock to the numerous stalls. In Victorian times a familiar figure at the market was Miles Lonsdale, better known as the **Haslingden Miser**. To avoid spending money on food he would gather up discarded fish-heads from the fishmonger's and fry them up for an unpalatable, if inexpensive, meal. After his death in 1889 it was discovered that Miles owned stocks and shares worth more than £16,000 - about £1.2m in today's money.

HELMSHORE

8 miles S of Burnley on the B6214

Helmshore Mills Textile Museum

This small town still retains much evidence of the early Lancashire cotton industry. Housed in an 18th-century water-powered fulling mill and a Victorian cotton spinning mill, is the **Helmshore Mills Textile Museum** (see panel below) which is scheduled to re-open in February 2008. The older building dates from 1789 and was one of the first fulling mills to be built in the Rossendale area. The two

Helmshore Mills Textile Museum

Holcombe Road, Rossendale, Lancashire BB4 4NP
Tel: 01706 226459

An 18th-century water powered fulling mill and a Victorian cotton spinning mill, both in working order on one site. Newly designated as a museum with a collection of outstanding national importance, the **Helmshore Mills Textile Museum** has recently developed an interactive gallery for families on the history of the Lancashire cotton industry. Spinning mules, a water wheel, an original Arkwright's Water Frame and other machinery dating from the Industrial Revolution can also be seen. Easily reached from Junction 5 of M65 (Haslingden) or from the end of the M66. Open from Easter to October every afternoon, closed Saturdays.

working mills are packed with national textile treasures and in the 'Revolution' gallery visitors can have fun with fibres and fabrics, follow the lives of the Weaver family, trace the history of Lancashire's textile industry and meet the great Lancashire inventors - Arkwright, Kay, Hargreaves and Crompton.

GOODSHAW

5 miles S of Burnley on the A682

- Goodshaw Chapel

Just to the north of Crawshawbooth in the small village of Goodshaw, and set high above the main road, stands **Goodshaw Chapel**, a recently restored Baptist house of worship that dates from 1760.

Blackburn

- Lewis Textile Museum
- Museum & Art Gallery
- St John's Church
- St Mary's Cathedral
- Witton Country Park
- Corporation Park

The largest town in East Lancashire, Blackburn is notable for its modern shopping malls, its celebrated three-day market, its modern cathedral, and Thwaites Brewery, one of the biggest independent brewers of real ale in the north of England. At the height of the textile industry's prosperity, Blackburn was the biggest weaving town in the world. At that time there were 120 mills in operation, their multiple chimneys belching out soot and smoke.

In 1931, the town received arguably its most influential visitor when Mahatma Gandhi toured the area on a study trip of Lancashire's textile manufacture. Examples of the early machines, including James Hargreaves' Spinning Jenny and his carding machine, invented in 1760, can be seen at the **Lewis Textile Museum**, which is dedicated to the industry. The town's **Museum and Art Gallery** has amongst its treasures several paintings by Turner, the Hart collection of medieval manuscripts, and the finest collection of Eastern European icons in Britain.

Mentioned in the *Domesday Book*, the town was originally an agricultural community before the production of first woollen and

Blackburn Cathedral

then cotton cloth took over. Much of the town seen today was built on the prosperity brought by the cotton trade, a fact symbolized on the dome of **St John's Church** (1789) where there's a weathervane in the shape of a weaving shuttle.

Blackburn's importance as a centre for the surrounding community was recognised in 1926 when the Diocese of Blackburn was created and the Gothic-style St Mary's Church, built in 1826, became the **Cathedral** of the See of Blackburn. The church was expanded to the east but the advent of World War Two curtailed the original grand design. Inside there are two notable modern features – a spiky metalwork crown over the high altar and, above the west door, a modern metalwork sculpture of the figure of Christ, his hands raised in benediction.

The town's old manor house, Witton House, has long since been demolished but the grounds have been turned into an excellent local amenity. The 480 acres of **Witton Country Park** contain nature trails through woodlands up on to heather-covered hilltops. Closer to the town centre, the 60-acre **Corporation Park** is one of the county's most attractive urban parks.

Around Blackburn

HOGHTON

4 miles W of Blackburn on the A675

Hoghton Tower

Originally a collection of hamlets with handloom weavers' cottages, the village was, during the 17th century, a place where Roman Catholics still practised their faith in defiance of the law. It was at Arrowsmith House that Edmund Arrowsmith said his last mass before being captured and sentenced to death for being a Catholic priest and a Jesuit.

Today, the village is best known as the home of Lancashire's only true baronial residence, **Hoghton Tower**, which dates from 1565. The de Hoghton family have owned the land in this area since the time of the Norman Conquest and the house was built in a style in keeping with their social position and importance. The famous banqueting hall, on the ground floor, is where James I is said to have knighted the Sir Loin of Beef in 1617. The name of the house is today rather misleading since the tower was blown up by Cromwell's troops in 1643 when they overran the Royalist garrison stationed

Hoghton Tower

here. Another famous visitor, who caused less disruption, was William Shakespeare who came to perform with William Hoghton's troupe of players. As well as the famous banqueting hall, other rooms open to the public include the beautifully preserved ballroom, the King's bedchamber, and the audience chamber. The grounds, too, are well worth a visit and are as perfectly preserved as the house.

BRINDLE

5 miles SW of Blackburn on the B6256

St James' Church

Brindle's **St James' Church** celebrated its 800-year anniversary in 1990. The church was originally dedicated to St Helen, the patron saint of wells. 'Bryn' is the old English word for a spring and there are still numerous springs in the village.

WITHNELL FOLD

5 miles SW of Blackburn off the A674

A short walk from Brindle, which crosses the Leeds and Liverpool Canal, leads to the village of Withnell Fold whose name comes from 'withy knool' – a wooded hill. It was developed as a model village in the 1840s with 35 terraced cottages each with its own garden. The whole village was owned by the Parke family who also owned the cotton mills and paper mill for whose workers the houses were provided. The mills have long since closed but the old mill chimney still towers above the village. Withnell Fold does have a small claim to fame. The paper mill, built in 1844 overlooking the canal, was once the world's biggest exporter of high-quality bank note paper.

TOCKHOLES

3 miles SW of Blackburn off the A666

United Reformed Chapel | Parish Church

Roddlesworth Nature Trail | Hollinshead Hall

Wishing Well

This interesting textile village was once an isolated centre of nonconformism. Standing next to a row of cottages is the **United Reformed Chapel**, founded in 1662, though it has been rebuilt twice, in 1710 and in 1880. The **Parish Church** also has some unusual features. As well as the unique lance-shaped windows, there is an outdoor pulpit dating from the days when the whole congregation could not fit inside the building. Close to the pulpit is the grave of John Osbaldeston, the inventor of the weft fork, a gadget that allowed power looms to weave intricate patterns.

Just to the south of the village runs the **Roddlesworth Nature Trail**, a path that follows the line of an old coach drive. Along the trail, for which details can be obtained at the information centre, can be found the ruins of **Hollinshead Hall**. Built in the 18th century and once very grand, the ruins were tidied up in the early 1990s but, fortunately, the **wishing well** has withstood the ravages of time and neglect. Reminiscent of a small Georgian chapel, the well inside dates back to medieval times when its waters were thought to cure eye complaints.

DARWEN

3 miles S of Blackburn on the A666

Darwen Tower · India Mill · Sunnyhurst Wood

Visitors to the town may be forgiven for thinking they have been here before as Darwen will be familiar to all viewers of the BBC series *Hetty Wainthropp Investigates,* which stars Patricia Routledge. Dominating the town from the west and situated high on Darwen Moor, is **Darwen Tower**, built to commemorate the Diamond Jubilee of Queen Victoria in 1897. The view from the top of the tower, which is always open, is enhanced by the height of the hill on which it stands (1225 feet), and with the help of the plaques at the top much of the Lancashire landscape, and beyond, can be identified.

A striking landmark, very visible from the tower, and standing in the heart of Darwen is the chimney of the **India Mill**. Constructed out of handmade bricks, it was built to resemble the campanile in St Mark's Square, Venice.

To the west of Darwen lies **Sunnyhurst Wood** and visitor centre in the valley of a gentle brook that originates on Darwen Moor to the south. Acquired by public subscription in 1902 to commemorate the coronation of Edward VII, this area of woodland, covering some 85 acres, is rich in both bird and plant life. The visitor centre, housed in an old keeper's cottage, has an ever-changing exhibition and there is also the Olde England Kiosk, built in 1912, which serves all manner of refreshments.

West Lancashire

This area of Lancashire, with its sandy coastline and flat fertile farmland, is home to some elegant seaside resorts and ancient market towns. Following the reorganisation of the county boundaries in the 1970s and the creation of Merseyside, much of the coast and the southwestern area of Lancashire became part of the new county, and the towns of Southport, Crosby and Formby and their neighbours and hinterlands will be considered in the Merseyside chapter.

Behind the coast, the flat lands of the West Lancashire plain were once under water. Now with an extensive network of ditches, drainage has provided the old towns and quaint villages with rich fertile land that produces a wealth of produce all year round. Roadside farm shops are very much a feature of the area.

Although there are several rivers flowing across the land, the chief waterway, which is hard to miss, is the Leeds to Liverpool Canal. Linking the port of Liverpool with industrial Leeds and the many textile villages and towns in between, this major navigation changed the lives of many of the people living along its length. The section through West Lancashire, passing rural villages, is perhaps one of the more pleasant stretches. There are plenty of charming canal-side pubs in the area and walks along the towpath, through the unspoilt countryside, have been popular for many years.

Chorley

Church of St Lawrence · Henry Tate

Astley Hall

A bustling and friendly place, Chorley is a charming town that is locally famous for its market that dates back to 1498. Today, there are two markets – the covered market and the open, 'flat iron' market. This peculiar and intriguing name stems from the ancient practice of trading by displaying goods on the grounds without the use of stalls.

Dating back to 1360 and standing on the site of a Saxon chapel, the **Church of St Lawrence** is the town's oldest building. The church is said to contain the remains of St Lawrence, brought back from Normandy by Sir Richard Standish. Whether they are his relics or not, during the Middle Ages the saint's shrine certainly brought pilgrims to the parish.

The Civil War also brought visitors to the town, albeit less welcome ones. Following defeat at the nearby Battle of Preston, Royalist troops were twice engaged in battle here by Cromwell's victorious forces.

Chorley was the birthplace, in 1819, of **Henry Tate.** The son of a Unitarian minister, Henry was apprenticed in 1832 to the grocery trade in Liverpool and by 1855 he had set up his own business and opened a chain of six shops. Selling the shops, Henry entered into the world of the competitive sugar trade and founded the world famous business of Tate and Lyle. Opening a new sugar refinery equipped with the latest machinery from France, Henry cornered the refining business in Britain and amassed a huge fortune. A great benefactor, Henry not only gave away vast sums of money to worthy causes but also to the London art gallery, which now bears his name.

The jewel in Chorley's crown is undoubtedly **Astley Hall**. Built in the late 16th century and set within some beautiful parkland, the hall is a fine example of an Elizabethan mansion. A notable feature is its south wing – described as "more glass than wall". Inside, the moulded ceilings of the main hall and the drawing room are quite remarkable, as are the painted panels dating from the 1620s and representing a range of heroes that include Elizabeth I, Philip II of Spain and the Islamic warrior, Tamerlane.

Extended in 1666, and again in 1825, this is truly a house of history. The rooms, which reflect the passing of the centuries, contain superb items of furniture from 1600 to the Edwardian period. Whether or not Cromwell stayed at the hall following the Battle of Preston is open to debate but his boots are here on display.

The hall was given to the borough in 1922 by Reginald Tatton and it was he who insisted that the building should incorporate a memorial to those who had died in World War I. As a result, a small room has been devoted to the local men who fought and died for their country. Along with the display of photographs, there is a Book of Remembrance.

Around Chorley

LEYLAND

4 miles NW of Chorley on the B5253

British Commercial Vehicle Museum

St Andrew's Church

The town is probably best known for its associations with the manufacture of cars and lorries. The **British Commercial Vehicle Museum**, the largest such museum in Europe, stands on the site of the former Leyland South Works, where commercial vehicles were produced for many years. On display are many restored vans, buses, fire engines and lorries, along with exhibits ranging from the horse-drawn era, through steam-powered wagons right up to present-day vans and lorries. Perhaps the most famous vehicle here is the one used by the Pope and popularly known as the Popemobile. Also on site are a gift shop and café.

Leyland is, however, an ancient settlement. Documentary evidence has been found that suggests that the town was a Crown possession in Saxon times, owned by Edward the Confessor. The village cross marks the centre of the old settlement around which the town expanded and it is in this area of Leyland that the older buildings can be seen. Founded in the 11th century, much of the present **St Andrew's Church** dates from 1220, although there was some restoration work undertaken in the 1400s. The Eagle and

Child Inn is almost as old, said to date from around 1230, and it served the needs of travellers journeying along the ancient highway that passed through the town.

CHARNOCK RICHARD

2 miles SW of Chorley off the A49

Magical Kingdom of Camelot

The **Magical Kingdom of Camelot** is a popular theme park where visitors can see the magical sorcery of a wizard one minute and knights battling it out in spectacular jousting tournaments the next. A place where you can learn the art of wizardry, meet the animals on a real working farm, be gripped by the full force of the Whirlwind spinning rollercoaster, and enjoy exciting water rides.

CROSTON

6 miles W of Chorley on the A581

Coffee Day Bastille Day/Twinning Fair

This historic village in the heart of rural West Lancashire has been a centre for local farmers since it was granted a weekly market charter in 1283. Set beside the banks of the River Yarrow, a tributary of the River Douglas, much of the village, including the 17th-century almshouses and the lovely 15th-century church, is a designated conservation area. Church Street is a fine example of an 18th-century Lancashire street, some of the houses bearing the date 1704. Even older is the charming packhorse bridge dated 1682. The strong links with agriculture are still apparent in this area and the open farmland actually extends right into the village centre.

On **Coffee Day** the village turns out with decorated farm horses and carts to take part in a procession led by a band and morris dancers. The name is derived from the former 'Feoffing Day' when tenants paid their fees, or rents, to the squire. The following weekend, the village celebrates its **Bastille Day/ Twinning Fair** when visitors from its twin town, Azay-le-Rideau in the Loire, share in sporting and musical events.

Ormskirk

Church of St Peter & St Paul

Farmer Ted's Farm Park

In the days when Liverpool was just a small fishing village, the main town in this area was Ormskirk, founded around 840AD by a Viking leader called Orme. Surrounded by rich agricultural land, the town has always been an important market centre with the locally-grown potatoes, Ormskirks, a firm favourite right across the northwest. The market is still flourishing, held every day except Wednesday and Sunday. In late Victorian times, one of the traders in Ormskirk market was a certain Joseph Beecham who did a roaring trade selling his medicinal Little Liver Pills. Joseph became a millionaire through the sales of his little pills; his son, the conductor Sir Thomas, went on to become the most popular and flamboyant figure of English musical life during the first half of the 20th century.

The town received its first market charter from Edward I in 1286, and today the market is still a key event in the region. The partial drainage of Martin Mere in the late 18th century, to provide more rich, fertile agricultural land, as well as the growth of nearby Liverpool, increased the prosperity of the town. Ormskirk was also touched by the Industrial Revolution and, while the traditional farming activities continued, cotton spinning and silk weaving also became important sources of local income. Today, the town has reverted to its traditional past.

The **Church of St Peter and St Paul**, in the centre of the town, unusually has both a steeple and a tower. The tower, added in the 16th century, was constructed to take the bells of Burscough Priory after that religious community had been disbanded by Henry VIII. However, the oldest feature found in the church is a stone carving on the outer face of the chancel's east wall that was probably the work of Saxon craftsmen.

A couple of miles southwest of Ormskirk, the recently opened **Farmer Ted's Farm Park** is designed for families with children up to 12 years old. Resident animals include llamas, pigs, sheep and goats; tractor rides and pedal tractors are available, and other facilities include a large fun barn, sand pit, farm shop and refreshment area.

Around Ormskirk

MERE BROW

7 miles N of Ormskirk on the B5246

Martin Mere

Just to the south of the village lies the Wildfowl and Wetlands Trust at **Martin Mere** (see panel on page 222), more than 350 acres of reclaimed marshland, which was established in 1976 as a refuge for thousands of wintering wildfowl. Until Martin Mere was drained in the 1600s to provide rich, fertile farmland, the lake was one of the largest in England. Many devotees of the Arthurian legends believe that the pool into which the dying king's sword Excalibur was thrown (to be received by a woman's arm rising from the water *clothed in white samite, mystic, wonderful)*, was actually Martin Mere.

Today, the stretches of water, mudbanks and grassland provide homes for many species of birds and, with a network of hides, visitors can observe shy birds such as the Ruff, Black-tailed Godwit and Little Ringed Plover in their natural habitats. There are also a series of pens, near to the visitor centre, where many other birds can be seen all year round at closer quarters. The mere is particularly famous for the vast numbers of pink-footed geese that winter here, their number often approaching 20,000. Although winter is a busy time at Martin Mere, a visit in any season is sure to be rewarded. The visitor centre caters for everyone and, as well as the shop and café, there is a theatre and a wealth of information regarding the birds found here as well as the work of the Trust.

BURSCOUGH

2 miles NE of Ormskirk on the A59

Burscough Priory · Windmill Animal Farm

Situated on the banks of the Leeds and Liverpool Canal, the village's Parish Church was one of the Million, or Waterloo, churches built as a thanks to God after the final defeat of Napoleon in 1815. A later addition to the church is the Memorial Window to those of the parish who died for their country during World War One.

Little remains of **Burscough Priory**, founded in the early 1100s by the Black Canons. Receiving lavish endowments from the local inhabitants, the priory was at one time one of the most influential religious houses in Lancashire.

To the north of the village, **Windmill Animal Farm** offers visitors the opportunity to experience the everyday running of an actual working farm and the

Mere Sands

Distance: *4.3 miles (6.9 kilometres)*

Typical time: *120 mins*

Height gain: *0 metres*

Map: *Explorer 285*

Walk: *www.walkingworld.com ID: 1305*

Contributor: *Jim Grindle*

ACCESS INFORMATION:

The Reserve is signposted off the A59 near Rufford Old Hall, itself signposted for miles around. The walk may be started from Rufford Station, which is near Waymark 10 (trains on the Preston/Liverpool line). There is also a birdwatchers' bus service at weekends, which does the rounds of the many superb sites in this area. It begins from Ormskirk Station. (For details ring Ormskirk County Information Centre on 01695 579062.)

DESCRIPTION:

The route is centred on Mere Sands Wood Nature Reserve and follows a stream and a canal towpath near Rufford Old Hall, before taking to a bridleway around the edge of Rufford New Hall (still marked on OS maps as a hospital but now very exclusive apartments).

ADDITIONAL INFORMATION:

Mere Sands Wood was originally planted by Lord Hesketh who lived in the New Hall. The name indicates both that it stood on the edge of a lake (Martin Mere, formerly one of the largest in England, although shallow) and of course that the soil was sandy. This valuable mineral was extracted between 1974 and 1982 with a planning agreement that it would become a reserve when the sand was exhausted. The belt of trees on the edge of the site was left untouched during the sand-winning, while the quarried areas were landscaped to create lagoons with shallow edges. When you have finished your walk it would be worthwhile taking the path on the left of the car park and visiting the many hides. The Trust asks for a donation for parking and you will find toilets inside the visitor centre.

Rufford Old Hall belongs to the National Trust and when it is open (Easter to October roughly) the walk may be started there by following the canal along the towpath away from the hall, until the swing bridge between Waymarks 10 and 11 is reached. The hall is amongst Lancashire's finest Tudor buildings and was in the hands of the Hesketh family in Shakespeare's time. There is strong evidence that Shakespeare spent some of his so-called missing years as an actor here, before turning up in London. The Great Hall with its wooden screen and hammerbeam roof are superb and in contrast to the Victorian life portrayed in the rest of the house. (The café, shop and toilets at the hall are accessible without paying for entry to the hall, if you come on foot from the towpath.)

FEATURES:

Pub, Toilets, Church, Stately Home, National Trust/NTS, Wildlife, Birds, Food Shop, Woodland.

WALK DIRECTIONS:

1 | With your back to the visitor centre return across the car park, towards the entrance to the reserve. On the right several nature trails are signposted. Turn right along this gravel track around the edge of the reserve. Pass the entrance to a hide and continue until you come to a drainage ditch, on the far side of which are some houses. On the left is a gate.

2 | Go through the gate with the stream on your right and pass along the edge of the village cricket-field. You reach a gate and a lane. Cross to the signpost on the far side and walk with the stream now on your left. You come to another lane, with a chapel on the far side.

3 | Cross the bridge and continue by the stream, which is again on your right. You come to yet another lane. Cross the bridge and again walk by the stream, this time on your left. You will pass an industrial site with lots of JCBs and scrap vehicles . The path goes into a field where there is a large road bridge over the A59.

4 | The OS maps are not quite right here. The path turns right when you reach the bridge and about 50 metres along, a few steps lead up to the main road. You need to cross this but you will have a better view of the traffic if you turn right and walk about 100 metres along the road, until you are opposite a swing bridge over the canal.

5 | The white metal gates are usually open. Cross the A59 and then the canal to the towpath on the far side.

6 | Turn left and follow the towpath (the OS maps suggest that there is no towpath a little further on, but there is). You come to a bridge when Rufford Church is in sight, just past some locks.

7 | As you approach the bridge it seems as if you will have to cross the road, but at the last moment the towpath dips and goes under the bridge. There is a pub just along the road to the right at this point. Continue past Rufford Old Hall on the opposite side of the canal and past a swing bridge. If you wish to visit the hall halfway round the walk, this bridge gives access to the grounds. Otherwise stay on the towpath until you reach the next road bridge.

8 | Go under the bridge to find the steps up, for this is where you leave the towpath. Turn right and when you have crossed the canal you will see a lane on the far side of the road. Go along this short lane to its junction with the A59 by the Rufford Arms Hotel.

9 | A nice spot for a drink. Cross to the newly surfaced lane opposite. This leads up to the gates of the renovated Home Farm where a gravelled track has been laid on the right to go round the gardens. Follow the track and rejoin the tarmac at gates on the opposite side of the house. This leads to a road.

10 | Turn right - there is a pavement. In a few moments you will see the entrance to the Reserve on the far side of the road, although the Cattery sign is perhaps more obvious.

11 | Go down the entrance drive past Waymark 2 to the car park and the visitor centre.

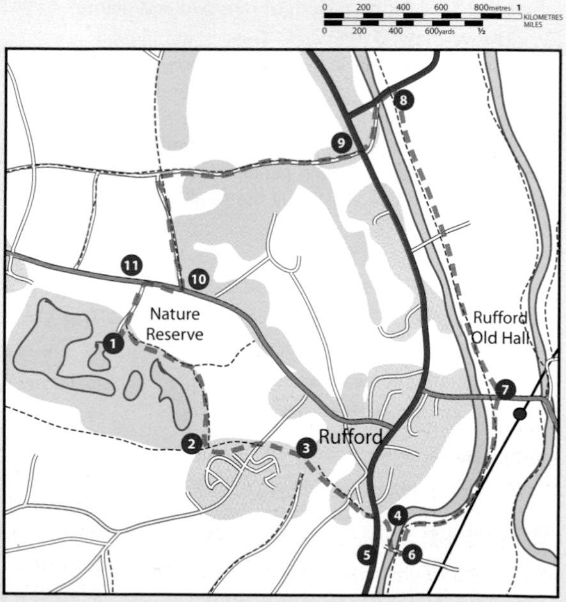

WWT Martin Mere

Burscough, Ormskirk, Lancashire L40 0TA

WWT Martin Mere is one of nine Wildfowl & Wetlands Centres run by the Wildfowl & Wetlands Trust (WWT), a UK registered charity. Visit WWT Martin Mere and come in close contact with wetlands and their wildlife. You can feed some of the birds straight from your hand. Special events and exhibitions help to give an insight into the wonder of wetlands and the vital need for their conservation.

People of all ages and abilities will enjoy exploring the carefully planned pathways. You can go on a journey around the world, from the Australian Riverway, through the South American Lake, to the Oriental Pen with its Japanese gateway, observing a multitude of exotic ducks, geese, swans and flamingos along the way. In winter, WWT Martin Mere plays host to thousands of pink-footed geese, whooper and Bewick's swans and much more. Visitors can see swans under floodlight most winter evenings.

Covering 150 hectares, the reserve (one of Britain's most important wetland sites) is designated a Ramsar Site and SSSI for its wealth of rare wetland plants.

The Wildfowl & Wetlands Trust is the largest international wetland conservation charity in the UK. WWT's mission is to conserve wetlands and their biodiversity. These are vitally important for the quality and maintenance of all life. WWT operates nine visitor centres in the UK, bringing people closer to wildlife and providing a fun day out for all the family.

chance to watch, feed, touch and play with the animals. There are various indoor and outdoor play areas, pedal tractors, train rides to the lake and picnic areas, also a coffee shop and an attractive craft and gift shop.

LATHOM

3 miles NE of Ormskirk off the A5209

Top Locks · Chapel of St John the Divine

The stretch of the famous Leeds and Liverpool Canal that passes through this village is well worth a visit as it includes the **Top Locks** area, a particularly interesting part of this major canal route.

To the south of the village, in Lathom Park, is Lathom House (private), formerly home of Lord Stanley, Earl of Derby, a Royalist who was executed during the Civil War. Only one wing of the original house remains, but within the grounds are the ancient **Chapel of St John the Divine**, consecrated in 1509, and 10 adjoining almshouses built for the chapel bedesmen. It's a charming cluster of buildings in an attractive setting and visitors are welcome at the services held in the chapel every Sunday.

RUFFORD

5 miles NE of Ormskirk on the B5246

Rufford Old Hall

Philip Ashcroft Museum of Rural Life

This attractive village of pretty houses is notable for its church and its beautiful old hall. Built in 1869, the church is a splendid example of the Gothic revival period and its tall spire dominates the skyline.

Rufford Old Hall (National Trust) is an enchanting building. Its medieval part is constructed of richly decorated black-and-white timbering enclosing a glorious Great Hall where angels bearing colourful heraldic shields float from massive hammer-beam trusses. The Hall's 17th-century additions are less spectacular, but still very attractive, and contain displays of historic costumes as well as an interesting local folk museum.

Generally regarded as one of the finest timber-framed halls in the country, the hall was the ancestral home of the Hesketh family, who lived at this site from the 1200s until Baron Hesketh gave the hall to the National Trust in 1936. From the superb, intricately carved movable wooden screen, to the solid oak chests and long refectory table, the atmosphere here is definitely one of wealth and position.

Later additions to the house were made in the 1660s and again in 1821. Parts of these are now devoted to the **Philip Ashcroft Museum of Rural Life** with its unique collection of items illustrating village life in pre-industrial Lancashire. Another attraction here is the spacious garden alongside the canal.

PARBOLD

5 miles NE of Ormskirk off the A5209

Parbold Hill   Ashurst Beacon

This is a charming village of pretty stone cottages as well as grand, late-Victorian houses built by wealthy Manchester cotton brokers. The village houses extend up the slopes of **Parbold Hill**, one of the highest points for miles around and from which there are superb views of the West Lancashire plain. At the summit stands a rough hewn monument, erected to commemorate the Reform Act of 1832, that is known locally, due to its shape, as Parbold Bottle.

Ashurst Beacon, another local landmark, was re-erected on Ashurst Hill by Lord Skelmersdale in 1798 when the threat of a French invasion was thought to be imminent.

MAWDESLEY

6 miles NE of Ormskirk off the B5246

Cedar Farm Galleries

A past winner of the Best Kept Village of Lancashire award, Mawdesley lies in rich farming country and was once associated with a thriving basket-making industry. The village has a surprising number of old buildings. Mawdesley Hall (private), originally built in the 1500s and altered in the late 18th century, was for many generations the home of the Mawdesley family.

At the other end of the village is Lane Ends House, built in 1590, which was occupied by a Catholic family and has a chapel in one of its attics. Other venerable buildings include Ambrose House (1577), Barret House Farm (1695), Back House Farm (1690) and Jay Bank Cottage (1692). By contrast, the oldest of the village's three churches dates back only to 1840.

ART AT CEDAR FARM

Mawdesley, Ormskirk, Lancashire L40 3SY
Tel: 01704 822358
e-mail: info@cedarfarmcrafts.co.uk
website: www.cedarfarmcrafts.co.uk

art@cedarfarm is at the heart of Cedar Farm Galleries, an art and specialist shopping complex. It is home to nine creative art, craft and design businesses, along with an espresso bar, roastery and a gallery area. The studios provide space for some of the best professional British designers, artists and makers to design and create their beautiful hand-made products on the premises. Many are then sold nationally and internationally. You will find paintings, ceramics, textiles, glass, cards, photography, jewellery and baskets. There are also changing and varied exhibitions in the foyer - and freshly roasted coffee!

Surrounded by beautiful countryside, **Cedar Farm Galleries** is a small complex of craft studios and shops where the emphasis is definitely on the quirky and unusual. There's also a café serving homemade food and a children's playground.

STANDISH

9 miles E of Ormskirk on the A49

St Wilfrid's Church

This historic old market town has several reminders of its past, not the least of which is the splendid **St Wilfrid's Church.** Built in a size and style that befitted the importance of the town in the late 1500s, the building stands on the site of a church that was certainly here at the beginning of the 13th century. A look around the interior of the church will provide a potted history of the area: there are tombs and memorials to all the important local families including the Wrightingtons, Shevingtons, and the Standish family.

RIVINGTON

13 miles E of Ormskirk off the A673

Rivington Pike Lever Park

One of the county's prettiest villages, Rivington is surrounded by moorland of outstanding natural beauty that forms the western border of the Forest of Rossendale. Overlooking the village and with splendid views over West Lancashire, **Rivington Pike**, at 1191 feet, is one of the area's high spots. It was once a site of one of the country's chain of signal beacons.

Just to the south of the village, on the lower slopes of Rivington Moor, lies **Lever Park**, which was made over to the public in 1902 by William Hesketh Lever, who later became Lord Leverhulme. The park comprises an awe-inspiring pot pourri of ornamental, landscaped gardens, tree-lined avenues, ancient cruck-framed barns, a Georgian hall, and a treasure trove of natural history within its 400 acres. The park's moorland setting, elevated position, and adjoining reservoirs provide scenery on a memorably grand scale.

AUGHTON

3 miles SW of Ormskirk off the A59

This picturesque village, surrounded by agricultural land, is dominated by the spire of St Michael's Church. An ancient place, it was mentioned in the *Domesday Book*; the register of church rectors goes back to 1246 and much of the building's medieval framework remains though it was restored in 1914.

HALSALL

4 miles W of Ormskirk on the A5147

St Cuthbert's Church

This is a charming unspoilt village lying in the heart of fertile West Lancashire and close to the Leeds and Liverpool Canal – the longest canal in Britain, extending for 127.25 miles and with 92 locks. **St Cuthbert's Church**, which dates from the middle of the 13th century, is one of the oldest churches in the diocese of Liverpool and it remains one of the prettiest in the county. The distinctive spire, which was added around 1400, rises from a tower that has octagonal upper stages.

SCARISBRICK

3 miles NW of Ormskirk on the A570

Scarisbrick Hall

Scarisbrick, which is part of the largest parish in Lancashire, lies in the heart of rich agricultural land that is intensively cultivated for vegetables, including carrots, Brussels sprouts, cabbages and early potatoes. A feature of this area is the large number of farm shops by the side of the road selling the produce fresh from the fields.

The first **Scarisbrick Hall** was built in the reign of King Stephen, but in the middle of the 19th century the hall, which is screened from the road by thick woodland, was extensively remodelled in 1867 by the Victorian architect Augustus Welby Pugin and is regarded as one of the finest examples of Victorian Gothic architecture in the country. The building is now occupied by a private co-educational school but there are occasional guided tours.

3 The Isle of Man

Although only 33 miles long and 13 miles wide, the Isle of Man contains a rich diversity of scenery and heritage and, perhaps best of all, exudes a sense of peacefulness epitomised by the Manx Gaelic saying: *traa-dy-liooar* – "Time enough".

Many British mainlanders are surprised to discover that the island is not part of the United Kingdom, but a Crown Protectorate with the Queen as Lord of Mann represented on the island by the Lieutenant Governor. Its Parliament, the Tynwald, dates back more than 1000 years to 979AD - the oldest continuous parliament in the world. It does not exact capital gains or inheritance tax, and personal tax allowances and reliefs are much more generous than in the UK itself. The island issues its own stamps, coins and notes with the currency having an equivalent value to that of the UK. Recently issued coins include Harry Potter crowns (2001), another crown marking the Chinese Year of the Horse, 2002, and, each year, a limited number of 50p coins featuring the Tourist Trophy (TT) races.

This island is perhaps best known for these annual TT motorcycle races, its tailless cat, Manx kippers, and as a tax haven for the wealthy. However, there is much more to this beautiful island. With around 100 miles of coastline and several resorts, each with its own individual style and character, there is plenty to interest the visitor.

This magical place became an island around 10,000 years ago when the melt water of the Ice Age raised the sea level. Soon afterwards, the first settlers arrived, working and developing the island into the landscape seen today. The distinctive influences of the various cultures who have lived here still remain, leaving a land with a unique and colourful heritage.

Among the first arrivals were the Vikings. Evidence of their era, from the early chieftains to the last Norse King, abounds throughout the island. Against the skyline on the seaward side of the road between Ballaugh and Bride are some ancient hilltop Viking burial mounds and, at the ancient castle in Peel, an archaeological dig revealed many hidden Viking treasures, which are now on display at the Manx Museum in Douglas.

Despite their reputation for plunder, rape and pillage, the Vikings also made some positive contributions to life on the island, not least of which was the establishment of the Manx governmental system, known as Tynwald. The Manx name for Tynwald Hill is 'Cronk Keeill Eoin', the hill of St John's Church. Although there is no evidence to confirm the story that it contains earth from all of the 17 parish churches here, it is not unlikely that token portions of soil were added to the mound in accordance with Norse tradition.

The Tynwald ceremony continues still with an annual meeting of the island's governors on Midsummer's Day at the ancient parliament field at St John's, where Manx citizens can also petition parliament.

The island's famous three-legged symbol seems to have been adopted in the 13th century as the armorial bearings of the native kings of the Isle of Man, whose dominion also included the Hebrides. After 1266, when the native dynasty ended and control of the island passed briefly to the Crown of Scotland and then permanently to the Crown of England, the emblem was retained. Among the earliest surviving representations are those on the Manx Sword of State, thought to have been made in 1300. The Three Legs also appeared on Manx coinage from the 17th to the 19th century, and are still seen in everyday use in the form of the official Manx flag.

LOCATOR MAP

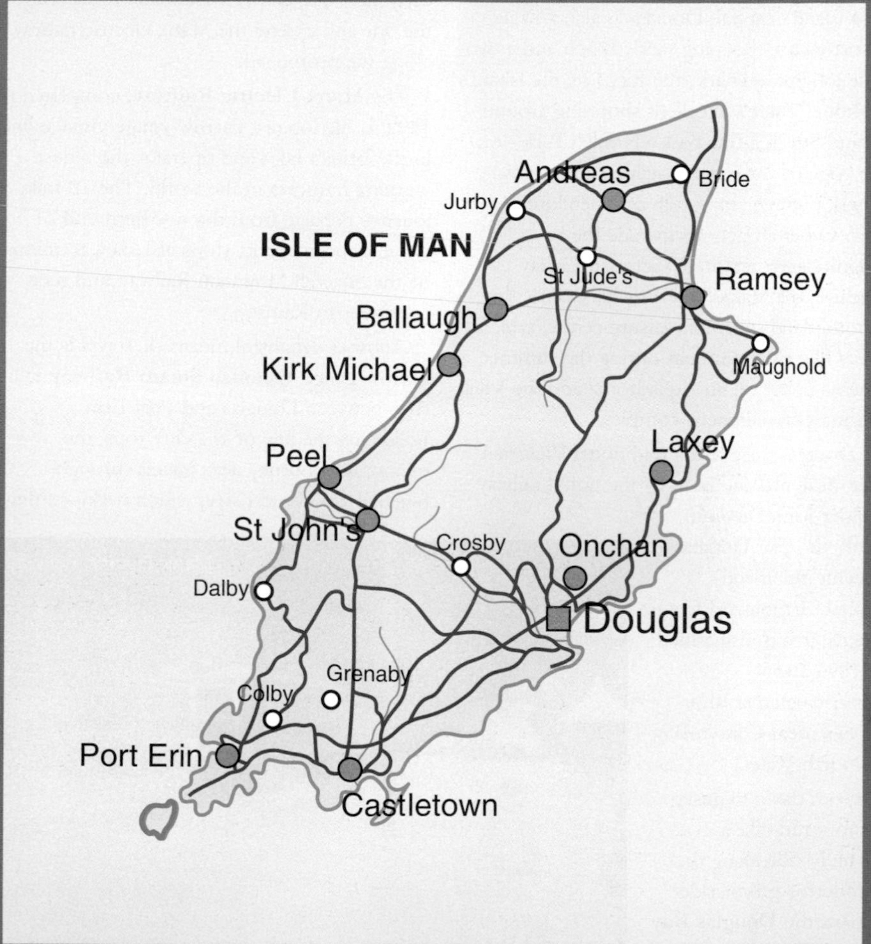

Douglas

- Douglas Bay Horse Tramway
- Manx Electric Railway Steam Railway
- The Heritage Trail Manx cat Manx Museum
- Tower of Refuge TT races
- Great Union Camera Obscura
- Home of Rest for Old Horses

The island's capital, Douglas is also a lively resort with a sweeping sandy beach and a two-mile long promenade, the focus of the island's nightlife. There's excellent shopping around Strand Street, a fine park - Noble's Park - on the edge of town with facilities for tennis, bowls, putting, crazy golf and a children's play area. Other attractions include the magnificently restored Victorian Gaiety Theatre, the Manx Superbowl, a casino, the Summerland sport and leisure centre, which hosts live entertainment during the summer, a cinema complex, an Aquadrome and the Villa Marina entertainment complex.

(Douglas once had a traditional Victorian pier, designed and built by the noted railway builder John Dixon in 1869, the year Douglas became the island's capital. A thousand feet in length, it was dismantled in 1896 and reconstructed at Rhos-on-Sea, near Colwyn Bay in North Wales.)

From dawn to dusk, visitors can take a leisurely ride along the wonderful promenade aboard the **Douglas Bay Horse Tramway**, a remarkable and beautiful reminder of a bygone era and the only surviving horse tramway in Britain. It was the brainchild of a civil engineer, Thomas Lightfoot, who retired to the island and, seeing the need for a public transport system along this elegant promenade, designed in 1876 the system still in use today. That the Douglas Tramway has survived into the 21st century is remarkable especially since, in the early 1900s, attempts were made to electrify the line and extend the Manx electric railway along the promenade.

The **Manx Electric Railway**, completed in 1899, is the longest narrow-gauge vintage line in the British Isles and operates the oldest working tramcars in the world. The 18-mile journey departs from the northern end of Douglas promenade, stops at Laxey, terminus of the Snaefell Mountain Railway, and then continues to Ramsey.

Another delightful means of travel is the narrow-gauge Victorian **Steam Railway** that runs between Douglas and Port Erin. Following the line of the cliff tops, the memorable journey also travels through bluebell woods and steep-sided rocky cuttings.

Manx Electric Railway

This section of line is all that remains of a railway that once served the whole of the island. Many miles of the old railway network have been developed as footpaths. From Quarterbridge in Douglas **The Heritage Trail** is a 10.5-mile former railway route that cuts across the island to Peel on the west coast. It's a scenic but undemanding trail that passes close to historic Tynwald Hill. Picnic sites and useful information boards are sited along the way.

The Isle of Man's most famous export is probably the **Manx cat**, notable for having no tail. There are several stories of how the cat lost its tail but one, in particular, is delightful. At the time that Noah was building the Ark there were two Manx cats, complete with tails. Noah sent for all the animals to come to the Ark, two by two, but the Manx cats replied that there was plenty of time and continued to play outside. Finally, when the cats did decide to board the Ark, Noah was just slamming the door and the cats lost their tails. A variation on this tale is that one of the cats reached the Ark safely, the other had its tail chopped off by the closing doors. The tailless cat went on to become the Manx cat and the one who managed to keep its tail became the ever grinning Cheshire cat.

No trip to the island is complete without a visit to the **Manx Museum** where the award-winning *Story of Mann* audio-visual presentation uncovers 10,000 years of the island's history. The Manx Museum complex also contains the superb National Art Gallery, the National Library & Archives, and a Natural History Gallery, as well as exhibits portraying many other aspects of life on the island, including the famous TT races. A recent addition to the displays is the Viking and Medieval Gallery.

One of the Isle of Man's most famous landmarks, the **Tower of Refuge**, stands on a rock in Douglas Bay. Sir William Hilary, founder of the Royal National Lifeboat Institution, lived in a mansion overlooking the bay and, following a near disaster in 1830 when the Royal Mail Steam Packet *St George* was driven on to rocks in high seas, Hilary launched the Douglas lifeboat. Miraculously, all the crew of the *St George* were saved without the loss of one lifeboat man despite the extremely treacherous conditions. It was following this incident that Hilary decided that a form of refuge should be built for shipwrecked mariners to shelter in and so, with Hilary laying the foundation stone in 1832, the Tower of Refuge was built on Conister Rock out in the bay. The tower was kept well stocked with fresh water and bread, ready to provide shelter from the weather and sea.

Noble's Park leads to the Grandstand that is the control centre for the **TT races**, rightly billed as the greatest motorcycle show on earth in the road racing capital of the world. Road racing started on the island as a practice for a race to be run in France for the Gordon Bennett Cup, presented by James Gordon Bennett, owner of the *New York Herald*. An Act of Parliament outlawed racing on public highways in Britain, but at a special session of the Tynwald in 1904, a bill entitled The Highways (Light Locomotive) Act gave permission for limited racing on the roads of the island on a few days a year. Interest in racing, both cars and motorcycles, swiftly grew, and in 1907 the first TT race was run over a short course based around St John's. Twenty five machines started, 10 finished, and the winner was CR (Charlie) Collier, who achieved an average speed of 38mph on his single-cylinder Matchless. In 1911, the mountain course was adopted and has remained more or less unchanged since. The course covers 37.7 miles, has 220 corners to negotiate and rises to 1400 feet near Snaefell. Drivers can reach up to 190mph and the record average lap speed is an astonishing 130mph.

Perched on a headland overlooking Douglas Bay is a camera obscura known as the **Great Union Camera Obscura**. The camera was originally situated on the old iron pier, but when this was demolished in the 1870s the camera was resited on Douglas Head. In the camera, the natural daylight is focused on to a white panel through a simple system of lenses and angled mirrors and so provides a living image of the scene outside. At first apparently still, as with a photograph, viewers soon become fascinated as the 'picture' begins to move.

The Isle of Man was ruled for several centuries by the Stanley family, one of whom became Earl Derby. This notable gentleman organised the first Derby horserace, predating the Epsom Derby by many years. The main point of starting horse-racing on the island was to encourage the breeding of good horses. Fifty horses and donkeys who have retired or fallen on hard times are kept at the **Home of Rest for Old Horses**, set in 92 acres of open countryside just outside Douglas, on the A5 Castletown road.

North of Douglas

ONCHAN

2 miles NE of Douglas on the A2

Captain Bligh Peter Heywood

Virtually a suburb of Douglas, Onchan is the location of the Lieutenant Governor's residence. An entry in the Onchan parish register records the marriage in 1781 of William Bligh RN to Miss Elizabeth (Betty) Betham, the daughter of the island's customs officer. In 1787, **Captain Bligh** took command of HMS *Bounty*, later the scene of the famous mutiny. The island has another connection with the *Bounty*. **Peter Heywood,** son of a deemster (member of the Tynwald parliament), was born on the island in 1773, joined the Navy at the age of 13 and was 14 at the time of the mutiny. Though he was confined to his quarters when the mutiny took place, he was arrested in Tahiti and brought back to England in the frigate *Pandora*. On the way home, the *Pandora* was wrecked in a storm and several of the crew and prisoners drowned. Heywood survived and eventually arrived in England in June 1792. He was immediately put on trial, convicted of not endeavouring to suppress the mutiny and condemned to death. He appealed successfully and resumed his career in the Navy, eventually rising to the rank of captain.

PORT GROUDLE

3 miles NE of Douglas on the A11

Groudle Glen Groudle Glen Railway

Close to Port Groudle lies **Groudle Glen**, a deep and, in places rocky, valley with a bubbling stream running through its length. Excellent specimens of beech grow in the upper sections of the glen whilst, lower down, pines and larches are abundant. There is also a small waterwheel in the lower half of the glen. Railway enthusiasts will be delighted to learn that on certain days in the summer the **Groudle Glen Railway** operates. Running on a track just 2ft wide for three-quarters of a mile along the cliffs, the railway's lovingly restored carriages are pulled by *Sea Lion* and *Annie*, the original 1896 steam engines.

LAXEY

5 miles N of Douglas on the A2

Laxey Glen · Great Laxey Wheel

Great Laxey Mine Railway · Laxey Woollen Mills

Ballalheanagh Gardens · Snaefell

Snaefell Mountain Railway

Murray's Motorcycle Museum

Set in a deep, wooded valley, this village is one of interesting contrasts. Tracing the river up from its mouth at the small tidal harbour leads the walker into **Laxey Glen**, one of the island's 17 National Glens that are preserved and maintained by the Government's Forestry Department.

Further up the glen is one of the island's most famous sights, the **Great Laxey Wheel** that marks the site of a once thriving mine where huge quantities of lead, zinc and copper ore were extracted. Known as the Lady Isabella Wheel, with a circumference of 228 feet, a diameter of 72 feet, and a top platform some 72 feet off the ground, it is the largest working waterwheel in the world.

It was Robert Casement, an engineer at the mines, who constructed this mechanical wonder in 1854 and designed it to pump 250 gallons of water a minute from a depth of 200 fathoms. Officially opened in 1854, it was named the *Lady Isabella* after the wife of the then Lieutenant Governor of the Isle of Man. After considerable repair and reconstruction work, the wheel now operates just as it did when it first opened and it stands as a monument to Victorian engineering as well as the island's industrial heritage.

Since 2004, visitors have been able to travel in a tiny carriage on the original tramway used to transport the ores from the mine. Complete with working replicas of the 19-inch gauge steam locomotives built in 1877, the **Great**

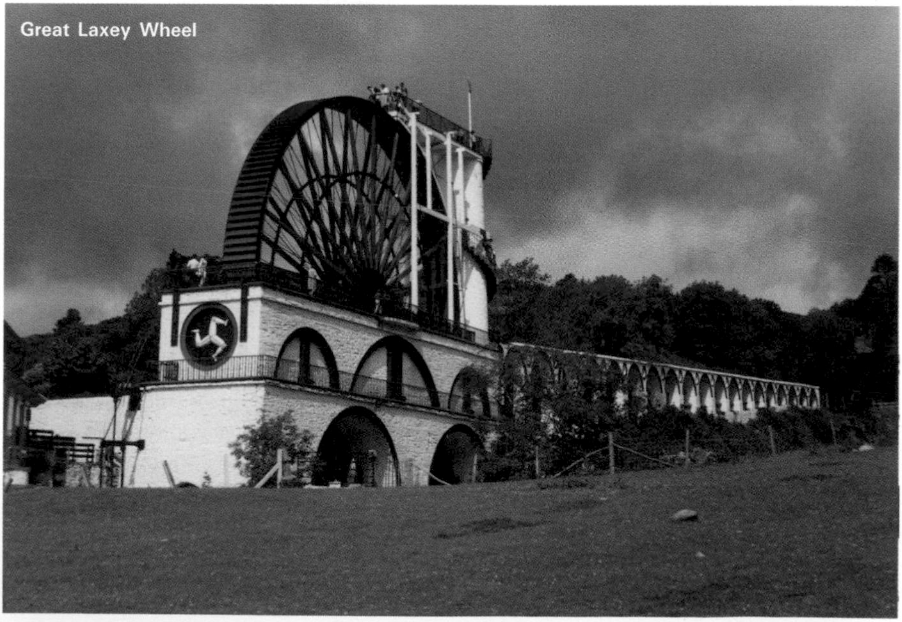

Great Laxey Wheel

Laxey Mine Railway travels through the island's longest railway tunnel to a picnic site and footpath just a five minute walk from the Great Wheel.

Also working in traditional style are the machines at **Laxey Woollen Mills** where genuine Manx tweed is woven on double-width and power looms: the finished products are on sale in the shop.

Situated above Laxey, in a beautiful natural glen, are the magnificent **Ballalheanagh Gardens**. The steep-sided valley with winding paths and a crystal clear stream running through the bottom, is packed with rhododendrons, shrubs, bulbs and ferns, and is certainly a gardeners' delight.

From Laxey station, the **Snaefell Mountain Railway** carries visitors to the top of the island's only mountain. Built in 1895, the six original tram cars still climb the steep gradients to **Snaefell's** 2036 feet summit. Those reaching the top are rewarded with outstanding views of the whole island and out across the sea to Ireland, Scotland and England. There is also a café at the summit offering welcome refreshments.

Near the top of the mountain is **Murray's Motorcycle Museum**, where more than 120 machines are on display, including Mike Hailwood's 1961 TT-winning Honda. Some date back to the late 1800s.

Ramsey

Mooragh Park · Yn Chruinnaght

The Grove · Manx Electric Railway Museum

Millennium Way

The second largest town in the island, Ramsey occupies a scenic location at the foot of North Barrule. This northernmost resort on the island has a busy working harbour, a long stretch of beach and a wide promenade. A popular amenity is **Mooragh Park**, a 40-acre expanse of gardens and recreational facilities with a 12-acre boating lake and lakeside café. During the summer months there's live musical entertainment in the park and around the third week of July each year the park is one of several venues hosting events during **Yn Chruinnaght,** an inter-Celtic festival of music, dance and literature.

Other major crowd-pullers are the Round the Island Yacht Race, held each summer and starting and finishing in Ramsey, and the Ramsey Motorcycle Sprint, part of the TT festival, when bikers show off their skills along Mooragh Promenade.

In the mid-1800s the town assumed the title of Royal Ramsey following an unscheduled visit by Queen Victoria and Prince Albert in 1847. The royal yacht anchored in Ramsey Bay following a stormy crossing from Scotland so that the seasick Queen could recover. While Her Majesty recuperated on board, Prince Albert walked to the top of Lhergy Frissel and was much impressed by the view. A few years later the Albert Tower was erected to commemorate the Prince Consort's visit.

Just to the north of the town is **The Grove**, a pleasantly proportioned Victorian house that was built as a summer retreat for Duncan Gibb, a wealthy Victorian shipping merchant from Liverpool, and his family. The rooms have all been restored to their Victorian splendour with sumptuous original furnishings, costumes and a wealth of accumulated possessions. The outbuildings have not been neglected and they contain an interesting collection of vehicles and agricultural instruments that were seen on Manx farms in the late 19th century.

Ramsey is the northern terminus of the Manx Electric Railway, built in 1899. The **Manx Electric Railway Museum** tells the fascinating story of this world-famous Victorian transport system. From Ramsey the railway follows a scenic route southwards to Douglas, accompanied most of the way by the equally delightful coastal road, the A15/A2.

For serious walkers, there's the **Millennium Way**, which starts about a mile from Parliament Square in Ramsey. Established in 1979 to mark the millennium year of the Tynwald parliament, the 26-mile long path passes through some magnificent countryside, picturesque towns and villages, before ending at the island's former capital, Castletown.

Around Ramsey

ANDREAS

5 miles NW of Ramsey on the A17

Andreas was originally a Viking settlement and the village church contains intricately carved crosses dating back to the days of those early residents. The church tower's mutilated spire goes back to the 1940s when part of it was removed in case it proved to be dangerous to aircraft from the nearby wartime airfields.

POINT OF AYRE

7 miles N of Ramsey on the A16

The Ayres

This is the northernmost tip of the island and, not surprisingly, there is a lighthouse situated here. The area around the point is known as **The Ayres** and, at the Ayres Visitor Centre, a whole wealth of information can be found about this fascinating part of the island. Amongst the inland heath moorland, a variety of species of birds can be found nesting whilst, on the pebbled beaches, can be seen terns. The offshore sandbanks provide a plentiful supply of food for both the diving gannets and the basking grey seals.

Carved Crosses, Andreas Church

SULBY

5 miles W of Ramsey on the A3

Sulby Glen Tholt-y-Will Glen

Situated in the heart of the island, the village lies on the famous TT course, a circular route on the island's roads that takes in Douglas, Ramsey, Kirk Michael and St John's. There are several scenic and picturesque walks from the village, which take in **Sulby Glen** and **Tholt-**

y-Will Glen, both of which are renowned beauty spots. Bird watchers particularly will enjoy the walks over the higher ground as it provides the opportunity to see hen harriers, kestrels, peregrines and curlews.

BALLAUGH

7 miles W of Ramsey on the A3

Curraghs Wildlife Park

The village, which also lies on the TT race course, is close to the island's most extensive area of marshland, the perfect habitat for a range of birds, including woodcock and grasshopper warbler, as well as being the largest roost for hen harriers in Western Europe.

Situated on the edge of the Ballaugh Curraghs, **Curraghs Wildlife Park** is home to a wide variety of wetland wildlife that come from all over the world. Curraghs is the Manx word for the wet, boggy, willow woodland that is typical of this part of the island and the site, which was opened in 1965, gives visitors the opportunity to see the animals in their natural environments. This world-renowned wildlife park has been divided into several different habitats, including The Pampas, The Swamp, The Marsh and the Flooded Forest, and here endangered animals from around the world, such as Canadian otters, spider monkeys, rhea and muntjac deer, live as they would in the wild.

The Curraghs Wildlife Park also has an enviable breeding record and, as many of the species are becoming rare in the wild, this is a very important aspect of the Park's work. Not only have they successfully bred bald ibis, one of the most endangered birds in the world, but tapirs, lechwe antelope and many others also flourish in this environment. Not all the animals and birds are exotic – there are a great number of native species to be seen here, too.

Visitors to the park are able to wander around the various habitats, following a well laid out path and, aided by the illustrated brochure, the whole family will find this an interesting and informative trail. There is also an adventure play area for young children and, during the summer, a miniature railway runs around the park. The lakeside café is open during the day for refreshments and, during the main summer season when the park is open until 9pm, barbecues are held here.

The Park was responsible for a rather unusual addition to the Isle of Man's wildlife. A few years ago some wallabies managed to escape from the park and now frequent the northern plain around Ballaugh.

Peel

Peel Castle   Moore's Kipper House

The House of Mananan   Leece Museum

Three-wheel 'Peel' car

Located on the western side of the island, Peel is renowned for its stunning sunsets and the town is generally regarded as best typifying the unique character and atmosphere of the Isle of Man. Traditionally the centre of the Manx fishing industry, including delicious oak-smoked kippers and fresh shellfish, Peel has managed to avoid any large-scale developments. Its narrow winding streets exude history and draw the visitor unfailingly down to the busy harbour, sweeping sandy beach, and magnificent castle of local red sandstone.

Peel Castle, one of the Isle of Man's principal historic monuments, occupies the important site of St Patrick's Isle. The imposing curtain wall encircles many ruined

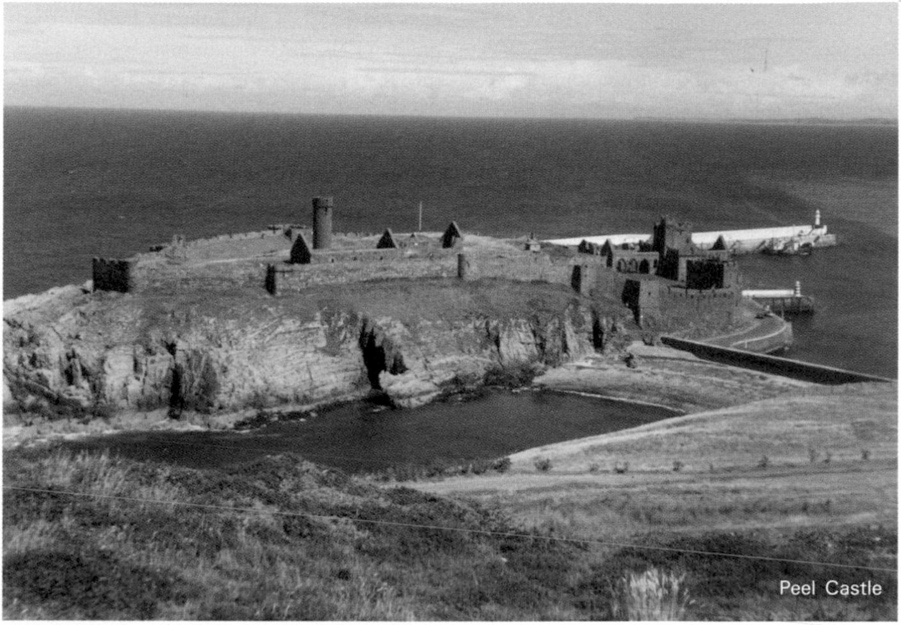

Peel Castle

buildings, including St Patrick's Church, the 11th-century Round Tower and the 13th century Cathedral of St Germans – the cathedral of Sodor and Mann, which was the very first diocese established in the British Isles, pre-dating even Canterbury. The great curtain wall also encloses the later apartments of the Lords of Mann. In the 11th century the castle became the ruling seat of the Norse Kingdom of Man and the Isles, first united by Godred Crovan – the King Orry of Manx folklore. Today, the castle provides a dramatic backdrop for a variety of plays and musical events during the summer.

Recent archaeological excavations have discovered exciting new evidence relating to the long history of the site. One of the most dramatic finds was the Norse grave of a lady of high social status buried in pagan splendour. The jewellery and effects buried with her can be seen on display, with other excavation finds, at the Manx Museum. The castle is also said to be haunted by the Black Dog, or Mauthe Dhoo. On dark windy nights, it can be heard howling in the castle's dungeons.

Connoisseurs of kippers speak highly of the tasty Manx oak-smoked kipper. At **Moore's Kipper House** you can watch a kipper-curing process that has remained unchanged since the late 1700s. This is the only place kippers are cured in traditional Manx style.

The House of Manannan, a state-of-the-art heritage attraction. Manannan is the mythological sea god and he is graciously present to guide visitors through the island's rich Celtic, Viking and maritime past. There are full-size reconstructions of a Manx Celtic roundhouse and a Viking longhouse.

The specially built Odin's Raven Viking longship was actually sailed from Norway to Mann as part of the Millennium of Tynwald celebrations.

For those researching their family history, The **Leece Museum** on the Quay of Peel's harbour has an archive of documents and photographs of the town along with a varied display of artefacts connected with the life of a busy fishing port.

Peel gave its name to the only production car ever made on the island. The **three-wheel 'Peel'**, produced between 1962 and 1966, was one of the tiniest cars ever made – the first model was only 4½ feet long and was powered by a 49cc DKW engine. The claim that it could carry a driver and a shopping bag was disputed by some who thought that it was a question of one or the other!

Around Peel

KIRK MICHAEL

6 miles N of Peel on the A3

Glen Wyllin | Raad ny Foillan

Close to the village lies **Glen Wyllin**, another of the island's 17 National Glens, and one that certainly deserves exploration. The varied woodland contains elm, ash, sycamore, alder, beech, lime, holm oak and chestnut, and in spring the woodland floor is carpeted with bluebell, primrose, wood anemone and wild garlic. Kirk Michael also lies on a 16-mile footpath that follows the route of an old railway line from Peel to Ramsey. After following the coast, and part of the **Raad ny Foillan** (road of the Gull), the footpath branches off through pastoral countryside before reaching the port of Ramsey on the other side of the island.

ST JOHN'S

3 miles E of Peel on the A1

Tynwald Day Ceremony | Tynwald Arboretum

Tynwald Mills | Sayle Art Gallery

Roads from all over the island converge at the village of St John's because this is the site of the ancient **Tynwald Day Ceremony**, held on July 5th, which is a public holiday throughout the island. This grand open-air event takes place on Tynwald Hill just north of the village. Here the Tynwald Court – a parliament that can trace its origins to the 10th

Tynwald Hill, St John's

century – assembles and the new laws of the land are proclaimed in both Manx and English. The serious business over, the rest of the day is devoted to various celebrations and activities culminating in a firework display.

Thatched Cottages, Niarbyl Bay

Adjoining Tynwald Hill, the 25-acre **Tynwald Arboretum** was established in 1979 to mark the millennium of the island's parliament.

Just outside the town is the island's largest shopping mall, **Tynwald Mills**, with more than 20 shops, two cafés, a children's playground and the **Sayle Art Gallery**, named after the popular Manx artist Norman Sayle, and specialising in the work of Manx artists and craftspeople.

GLENMAYE

3 miles S of Peel on the A27

A spectacular bridged gorge and waterfall dominate this glen, which is one of the most picturesque on the island. Comprising over 11 acres, its beautiful sheltered woodland includes some relics of the ancient forests that once covered much of the Isle of Man. Another feature of this glen is the Mona Erin, one of the many waterwheels that once produced power for the Manx lead mines.

DALBY

4 miles S of Peel on the A27

Niarbyl Bay

Just southwest of Dalby village, **Niarbyl Bay** takes its name from the Manx Gaelic, Yn Arbyl, meaning "the tail", so named because of the long reef that curves out from the shoreline. There are stunning views to the north and south, and the grandeur of the southwestern coast is seen at its best from this typically Manx setting. The beach here is an ideal place for picnics, relaxing and enjoying the tranquillity of the setting.

Castletown

World Tin Bath Championship | Castle Rushen

Old House of the Keys | Nautical Museum

Old Grammar School

Manx Aviation and Military Museum

Museum of the Manx Regiment

The original capital of the island, Castletown is full of character and charm, especially around the harbour area. Here, in August, is held the **World Tin Bath Championship**, one of the sporting world's more unusual contests, as well as snake racing and many other aquatic events.

The harbour lies beneath the imposing

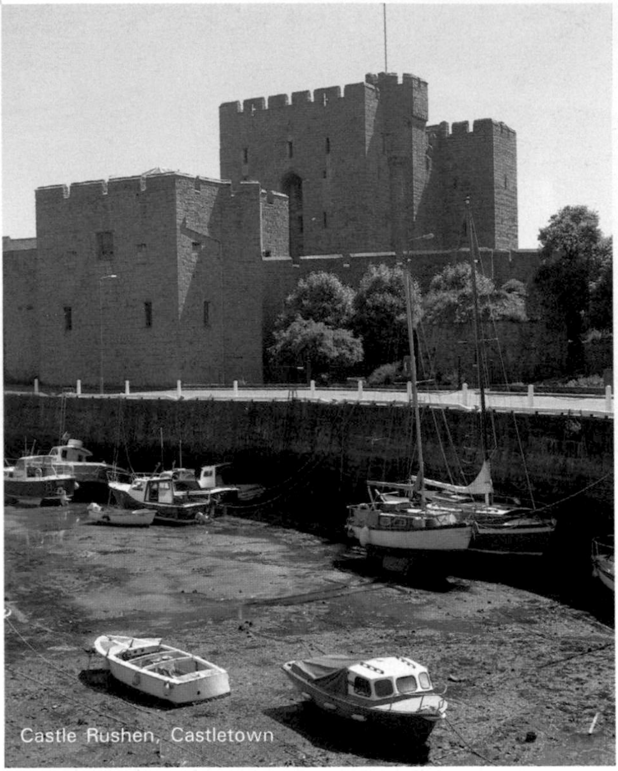
Castle Rushen, Castletown

battlements of **Castle Rushen**, once home to the Kings and Lords of Mann. One of Europe's best preserved medieval castles, the present building was mostly constructed between 1340 and 1350. It has been restored to provide today's visitors with a vivid impression of what life was like in the fortress many years ago by presenting in authentic detail the sights, sounds and smells of its heyday. Among the many points of interest is a unique one-fingered clock that was presented to the castle by Elizabeth I in 1597 and which still keeps perfect time.

The castle is also still used as a courthouse for the swearing-in of new governors, and for registry-office weddings. During the summer months there are regular spectacular displays re-enacting scenes from the castle's history, especially the events of 1651 when Royalists were forced to surrender Castle Rushen to Cromwell's parliamentary troops.

Like Peel Castle, Rushen too is said to the haunted The ghost, known as the White Lady, is believed to be of Lady Jane Gray who travelled to the island from Scotland with her family. The spectre has been seen walking the battlements at night and occasionally passing straight through the castle's closed main gate during the day.

Recently restored to its 19th-century state of grace, the **Old House of the Keys** was the seat of the Manx parliament until it removed to Douglas in 1874. In the rather cosy former debating chamber, visitors become members of the House and can vote on various issues that the parliament faced in the past, and some they may face in the future.

Castletown is also home to the island's **Nautical Museum** where the displays centre around the 1791 armed yacht *Peggy,* which sits in her own contemporary boathouse. Part of the original building is constructed as a cabin room from the time of the Battle of Trafalgar and there are many other artefacts on display, all with a maritime theme.

Rushen Abbey, Ballasalla

The **Old Grammar School** was originally built as the first town church around 1200. It changed in role in 1570 to become the Grammar School and continued to educate the children of the town for more than 350 years, finally closing in 1930. Inside, rows of bench desks with ink wells are reminders of early Victorian school days.

A mile or so northeast of Castletown is Ronaldsay, the island's principal airport. Adjacent to the airport and open weekends, race weeks and bank holidays only, the **Manx Aviation and Military Museum** (free) presents the story of the island's wartime and civil aviation history in the 20th century. On the same site, the **Museum of the Manx Regiment** celebrates the history of the 15th (Isle of Man) Light Anti-Aircraft Regiment, which saw active service throughout World War Two. More than 100 of the Regiment's men were captured on the island of Crete in 1941. A special display recounts the four years they spent in German prisoner-of-war camps and exhibits a secret radio they built and kept hidden in a hollow log.

Around Castletown

BALLASALLA

2 miles N of Castletown on the A5

Rushen Abbey   Fairy Bridge

Rushen Abbey is the most substantial medieval religious site in the Isle of Man. This ancient Cistercian monastery now has an interpretive centre that explains the abbey's past importance and illustrates the daily life of the monks. There is an interactive viewing room where visitors can follow live archaeological digs; a Heritage Shop, Garden walkways and picnic area.

A couple of miles further along the A5 road towards Douglas, look out for the **Fairy Bridge**. For centuries, Manx people have taken no chances when it comes to the little people and it is still customary to wish the fairies who live under the bridge a "Good Morning" when crossing.

PORT ERIN

4 miles W of Castletown on the A5

Isle of Man Steam Railway

Mananan International Festival of Music & the Arts

Situated between magnificent headlands, Port Erin's beach is certainly a safe haven. It is also a place of soft sands cleaned daily by the tide with rock pools to one side and a quay to the other. A long promenade above the sheltered sandy beach has a number of cafés, and other amenities include bowls, tennis, putting, nearby Rowany golf course and some superb walks along coastal paths out to Bradda Head. Port Erin is also the southern terminus of the **Isle of Man Steam Railway**, which runs from here to Douglas, a 15-mile journey through unspoilt countryside.

The town has its own Erin Arts Centre, which since 1975 has hosted the annual **Mananan International Festival of Music and the Arts**, now recognised as one the island's most prestigious cultural events. The two-week long festival takes place from mid- to late-June and the eclectic programme ranges through classical music, opera and ballet, jazz and theatre, to films, Indian music and art exhibitions, as well as special events for children.

Port Erin is one of several coastal towns on the island offering boat trips with the hope of seeing basking sharks - the world's second longest fish - whales, and dolphins. If you're very lucky you might even see a leatherback turtle. They swim to these waters from the Caribbean just to feed on large white jellyfish.

PORT ST MARY

4 miles W of Castletown off the A31

Raad ny Foillan The Chasms

This delightful little working port has both an inner and outer harbour, two piers, and excellent anchorage for visiting yachts. The beach, reached by a scenic walkway from the harbour, is no more than two miles from the beach at Port Erin, but it faces in almost the opposite direction and lies in the most sheltered part of the island.

One of the finest walks on the Isle of Man is the cliff-top route from Port St Mary to Port Erin along the **Raad ny Foillan** - the road of the gull - a long-distance footpath that follows the coastline right around the island. From Port St Mary, the first part of the walk takes in **The Chasms**, gigantic vertical rifts that, in some places, descend the full 400 feet of the cliffs.

CREGNEASH

6 miles SW of Castletown on the A31

National Folk Museum Harry Kelly's Cottage

Perched close to the southwestern tip of the island this village is now a living museum, **National Folk Museum at Cregneash.** It offers a unique insight into Manx traditional life within a 19th-century crofting community. Its isolated position led the village to become one of the last strongholds of the island's ancient skills and customs and all this is beautifully preserved today. Visitors can watch fields being worked with horse-drawn equipment, the processing of Manx loghtan wool, and wood-turning in the Turner's Shed.

By combining small scale farming with other occupations, a small settlement of Manx men and women have successfully prospered here since the mid-1600s. In the carefully restored buildings, visitors can see the conditions in which they lived and managed to sustain life in this rugged landscape.

The centrepiece of Cregneash is without doubt **Harry Kelly's Cottage**. Henry, who died in 1934, was a renowned Cregneash crofter and the last known speaker of the Manx language only. Opened to the public in 1938, his cottage, still filled with his furniture, is an excellent starting point to any tour of the village. There are various other buildings of interest, including a smithy and the Karran Farm.

The village is also one of the few remaining places where visitors get a chance to view the unusual Manx Loghtan four-horned sheep, a breed which, thanks to Manx National Heritage and other interest groups, now has a secure future.

CALF OF MAN

7 miles SW of Castletown

Calf Sound

This small island, situated just off the southwestern tip of the island, is now a bird sanctuary owned by the National Trust. The puffins should be grateful – one of the previous owners, the Dukes of Athol, requested that his tenants living on the Calf pickled the nesting puffins! In 1777, a stone was found on the isle in the garden of Jane's Cottage, though in those days it was called The Mansion. Known as the Calf Crucifixion Cross, the stone is believed to date from the 8th century and it is one of the earliest Christian finds in Europe. The cross can be seen in the Manx Museum in Douglas.

In 2002, a new **Visitor Centre** was opened at the southernmost tip of the island. The scenic four-acre site also has a shop, café and car park, and provides grand views of Spanish Head, the Calf of Man and the Irish Mountains of Mourne.

Calf Sound, the stretch of water between the island and the Isle of Man has seen many ships pass through and it was here that the largest armada of Viking longships ever assembled in the British Isles congregated before setting off to invade Ireland. Centuries later, men from nearby Port St Mary were awarded a gallantry medal by Napoleon when they came to the rescue of the crew of the *St Charles* schooner from France, which had foundered in the sound. It is thought to be the only such medal he presented to British subjects.

LOCATOR MAP

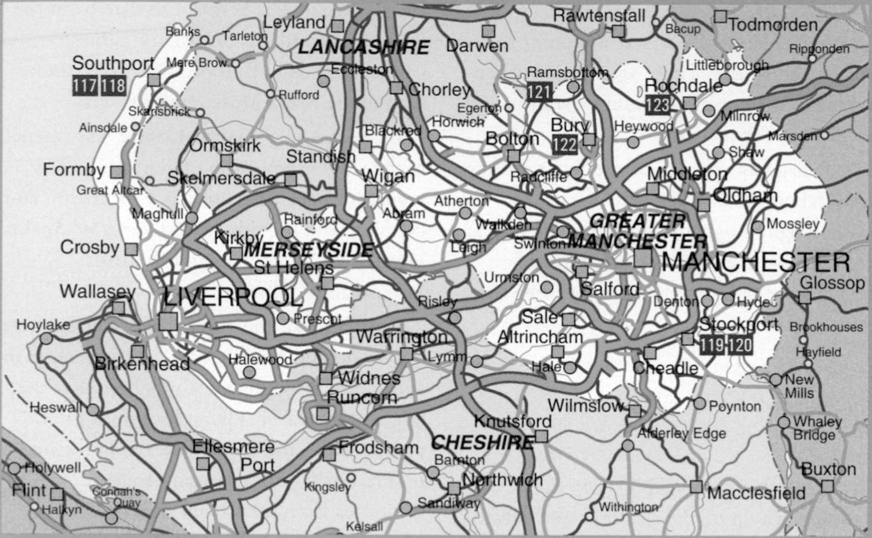

ADVERTISERS AND PLACES OF INTEREST

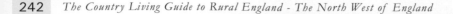

Accommodation, Food and Drink

119 | Bramall Hall, Stockport *pg 261*
121 | Ramsons, Ramsbottom *pg 267*

Activities

122 | East Lancashire Railway, Bury *pg 268*

Arts and Crafts

117 | The Patched Pumpkin, Southport *pg 253*

Home & Garden

117 | The Patched Pumpkin, Southport *pg 253*

Place of Interest

118 | British Lawnmower Museum, Southport *pg 254*
119 | Bramall Hall, Stockport *pg 261*
120 | Stockport Air Raid Shelters, Stockport *pg 262*
122 | East Lancashire Railway, Bury *pg 268*
123 | Rochdale Pioneers Museum, Rochdale *pg 271*
149 | Grantham's, Alderley Edge *pg 337*
125 | The Boat Museum, Ellesmere Port *pg 285*
134 | Jodrell Bank Science Centre and Arboretum, Lower Withington, nr Macclesfield *pg 302*
136 | Stapeley Water Gardens, Stapeley, nr Nantwich *pg 306*
146 | Tatton Park, Knutsford *pg 326*

4 | Merseyside and Greater Manchester

The metropolitan county of Merseyside comprises the districts of Liverpool, Knowsley, St Helens, Sefton and The Wirral (places of interest in The Wirral will be found in the Cheshire chapter). Merseyside is centred round Liverpool, one of the country's leading cities and currently enjoying its role as the European City of Culture for 2008. After decades of neglect and under-investment the city has been transformed and has become one of the most vibrant and exciting in the land. Liverpool first began to show a different face to the world at the time of the Merseybeat Era in the 1960s.

Liverpool has two magnificent cathedrals, both of which should be on the itinerary of any visitor to the city. Football fans will be sure to visit the grounds of Liverpool or Everton. There are many organised walks and tours covering all aspects of city life, and the Mersey ferry is a favourite way of admiring the city's transformed waterfront. Aintree is the home of the world's most famous steeplechase, the Grand National, and Merseyside has another major racecourse in Haydock Park at Newton-le-Willows.

Liverpool Cathedral

Outside the city, Merseyside has its share of grand houses and rural attractions. Notable among these are Croxteth Hall and Country Park, Knowsley Safari Park and the National Trust's Speke Hall. The Trust also has the care of a stretch of coast at Formby, an internationally important site for wildlife and home of the famous Formby red squirrels. The whole stretch of coastline from the Mersey Estuary to north of Southport, is a haven for birdwatchers. Southport itself is a delightful spot that combines Victorian elegance with all the amenities of a popular seaside resort and a generous supply of culture.

The metropolitan county of Greater Manchester comprises the

districts of Bolton, Bury, Manchester, Oldham, Rochdale, Salford, Stockport, Tameside, Trafford and Wigan. Manchester, like Liverpool, has been transformed over the past few years, and is notable for many fine buildings; some, like the Town Hall and the Cathedral, have long been city landmarks, while the new generation of buildings include Trinity Bridge and the City of Manchester Stadium. Manchester's museums and galleries are the most numerous and diverse outside the capital, ranging from the Museum of Science & Industry to the John Rylands Library and the Whitworth Gallery. In Salford, the Lowry is a stunning cultural complex overlooking the Manchester Ship Canal.

Albert Memorial, Manchester

Visitors to Manchester do not have to travel far to be in the country: Tameside, for example, offers country parks, woodland, moorland and reservoirs. It was the 3rd Duke of Bridgewater who commissioned the first canal in the country, linking his coal mines with Manchester and Liverpool. By 1850, 4000 miles of canals transported 30 million tonnes of freight throughout the country each year. They have long since ceased to fulfil their original role, but many stretches have been restored to become a splendid leisure amenity.

The main towns of Greater Manchester - Bolton, Bury, Oldham, Rochdale, Stockport, Wigan - have all retained a great sense of history with restored old industrial buildings and a variety of museums, and careful, public-spirited planning has ensured that they all offer plenty of green spaces for walking and leisure activities. Among the finest of the attractions outside the towns are Bramall Hall, a wonderful old 'magpie' house near Cheadle Hulme, Haigh Hall and Country Park near Wigan, and Hall I' th' Wood near Bolton.

River Bollion, nr Altrincham

Liverpool

Albert Dock · ACC Liverpool · The Beatles Story
Mendips · 20 Forthlin Road
Casbah Coffee Club · Tate Liverpool
Merseyside Maritime Museum
Walker Art Gallery · Liverpool Town Hall
St George's Hall · Chinese Arch · FACT
Liverpool Cathedral · Cathedral of Christ the King
Liverpool Football Club Museum
Everton Football Club

Liverpool has been completely transformed in recent years and is currently glorying in its role as the European City of Culture for 2008. The title is awarded by the European Union to celebrate the cultural identity of Europe's greatest cities and alternates annually among the member states. Liverpool's profuse programme of events include the only European showing of Art in the Age of Steam, celebrating the work of Turner, Monet, Van Gogh and Hopper; a concert performed by the Berliner Philharmoniker Orchestra conducted by Liverpool-born Sir Simon Rattle; and the start of the Tall Ships Race in July.

Major projects being completed for this momentous year include **ACC Liverpool**, a multi-purpose arena for sports as diverse as motocross and darts, and a complete redevelopment of the Paradise Street area in the city centre.

The most striking example of Liverpool's transformation is **Albert Dock**, a painstakingly restored masterpiece of Victorian architecture. Designed by Jesse Hartley and built to hold the biggest sailing ships of the day, it was opened by Prince Albert in 1846. By the end of the 19th century steam had largely replaced sail and the Dock was in decline. It finally closed in 1972 and stood derelict for some years. 1984 saw the start of its rebirth, and now the Dock is among the country's most popular heritage attractions, with some four million visitors a year. Behind the giant cast-iron columns and huge brick facades are dozens of visitor attractions, shops and retail outlets, restaurants, cafés, offices, TV studios and luxury apartments. The whole docklands area has been accorded World Heritage Site status by UNESCO.

A curiosity to look out for in Albert Dock is a vintage Post Office pillar letter box. Dating back to 1863, this unique example is topped by a full size gold and royal blue crown.

In modern times, it was the Beatles who really put the city on the map worldwide, and the Fab Four are still responsible for a large proportion of the millions of tourists who now flock here each year. The annual Beatle Week is by far the busiest time to visit Liverpool, and 2008 sees its 25th anniversary. **The Beatles Story** is the city's major tribute to its four most famous sons, a walk-through experience that re-creates the sights and sounds of the Merseybeat era. The National Trust is responsible for two of the Beatles' homes. **Mendips** was the childhood home of John Lennon, where he lived with his Aunt Mimi and Uncle George, while **20 Forthlin Road** was the terraced home of Paul McCartney during the early years of the Beatles. Here they composed and rehearsed their earliest songs. Visits to these houses start from Albert Dock or Speke Hall. The only venue where the Beatles played that is still in place is the **Casbah Coffee Club**. It is unchanged and complete with rooms painted by the famous four. Tours are by pre-arranged bookings only.

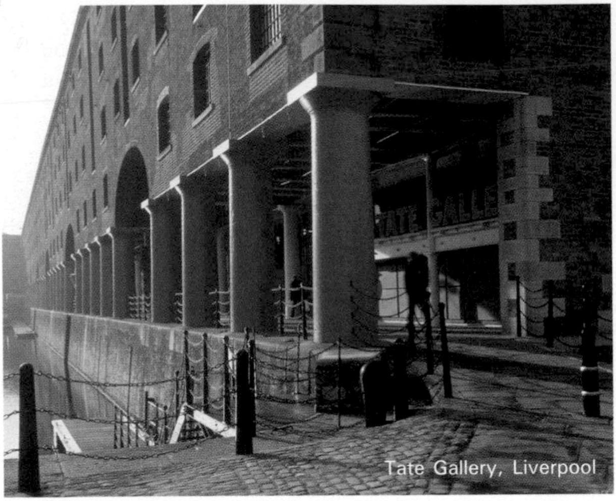

Tate Gallery, Liverpool

Albert Dock's many other visitor attractions include **Tate Liverpool**, which occupies a beautiful converted warehouse and is the largest gallery of modern and contemporary art outside London and specialises in works from 1900 to the present day. Spread over four floors, it is one of four Tates, the others being Tate Britain and Tate Modern in London and Tate St Ives in Cornwall. Tate Liverpool hosts regular special exhibitions and has a year-round programme of tours, informal gallery talks, study days and Sunday family events.

Merseyside Maritime Museum is three museums in one - the Maritime Museum with its Transatlantic Slavery Gallery, the Museum of Liverpool Life and HM Customs & Excise National Museum, which tells the exciting story of smuggling and contraband from 1700 to the present day.

Liverpool has many other notable architectural gems away from the Albert Dock area. Among these are the **Walker Art Gallery**, presenting 600 years of art including masterpieces by Rubens, Rembrandt, Poussin, Gainsborough and Hogarth; **Liverpool Town Hall**, a superb 18th-century Grade I listed building with a dome topped by a statue of Minerva, Goddess of Wisdom; and **St George's Hall**, one of the finest neo-classical buildings in the world. In a completely different genre of architecture, the **Chinese Arch** in Chinatown rises 50 feet and spans Nelson Street. Brilliantly decorated, it is the largest such arch outside China. A short walk from the Chinese Arch brings you to **FACT** (Foundation for Art and Creative Technology), a cinema, café, bar and gallery with a strong leaning towards the moving image.

Liverpool boasts two spectacular cathedrals, one Anglican, the other Roman Catholic. The Anglican **Liverpool Cathedral** is an amazing 20th-century Gothic-style masterpiece, begun in 1904 when the foundation stone was laid by King Edward VII, and completed in 1978, when Queen Elizabeth II attended the celebrations. Even through two world wars, work never ceased, and, though the city was assailed repeatedly by enemy bombs, the cathedral escaped serious damage. Designed by Giles Gilbert Scott, and built mainly of locally quarried sandstone, the cathedral abounds in superlatives; the largest Anglican cathedral in Europe; the largest church organ in the world, with 9,765 pipes; the highest and heaviest ringing peal of bells in the world.

The Metropolitan Cathedral of Christ the King is a dramatic modern masterpiece, its focal point being a circular nave of glass

Speke Hall, Speke

and concrete, the work of Sir Frederick Gibberd. The Lantern Tower of the nave contains the world's largest stained-glass window, designed by John Piper and Patrick Reyntiens. This cathedral was completed in 1967, but in the previous century there was a scheme to build a cathedral second only in size to St Peter's. Only the crypt was built, and that can be visited on a guided tour.

The Liverpool Football Club Museum & Tour Centre celebrates all things Liverpool, past, present and future, including a re-creation of the standing Kop. The tour takes in the dressing room, the team dug-out and the tunnel, and displays in the museum cover the whole history of the club. Fans of The Toffees will make for Goodison Park for a tour of **Everton Football Club**.

Around Liverpool

SEFTON PARK

3 miles SE of Liverpool City Centre

Palm House

The beautifully restored centrepiece of the park is the **Palm House**, opened in 1896 and rescued from a dilapidated state in the early 1990s. Re-opened in 2002, The Grade II* listed octagonal three-tiered structure houses plants from around the world in the Liverpool Botanical Collection and stages a year-round programme of events and concerts.

SPEKE

8 miles SE of Liverpool City Centre off the A561

Speke Hall

Dating from 1490, **Speke Hall** is one of the greatest half-timbered houses in the country, set in splendid gardens and woodland that belie its location in the Liverpool suburbs close to the airport. The interior spans the centuries, from the Tudor Great Hall to Jacobean plasterwork and the Victorian oak parlour and kitchens. Other attractions include the restored Home Farm building, a children's play area and a giant maize maze. The Hall also hosts a programme of events from Easter onwards.

KNOWSLEY

5 miles E of Liverpool City Centre off the A580

Knowsley Safari Park

National Wildflower Centre

Easily reached from the city, via the A580 and the M57 (Junction 2), **Knowsley Safari Park** brings visitors face to face with the great outdoors and creatures of the wild. A five-mile safari drive gets close to baboons, lions, tigers, zebras, elephants, rhinos, bison, ostriches, camels, wildebeest and many other creatures. In the walkabout area are a reptile house, children's lake farm, otter pools, giraffes and meerkats, performing sea lions and parrots, as well as a restaurant and snack bar and over 20 rides, including dodgems, a rope course, a pirate ship and a mini railway.

The only one of its kind in the UK, the **National Wildflower Centre** in Court Hey Park is a peaceful place where visitors can learn about the huge variety of colourful wildflowers native to this country.

ST HELENS

12 miles E of Liverpool City Centre

World of Glass

St Helens was once a centre of the glass industry, a heritage that is illustrated in the fascinating displays in the **World of Glass**. Here, visitors can learn about the history and the techniques, both through interactive displays and regular demonstrations by the resident glass artists. The complex also includes a café, children's play area and gift shop.

NEWTON-LE-WILLOWS

15 miles E of Liverpool on the A580

Haydock Park · William Huskisson

One mile from Junction 23 of the M6, **Haydock Park** is the region's premier year-round racecourse, with 30 days racing on the flat and over the jumps. Highlights of the year include the Peter Marsh Chase and Swinton Hurdle under National Hunt rules, and the Stanley Leisure Sprint Cup on the flat.

Newton-le-Willows was the site of the first fatal railway accident. **William Huskisson**, MP for Liverpool, alighted from a carriage on the opening day of the Manchester & Liverpool Railway and was struck by a train hauled by George Stephenson's *Rocket*.

WEST DERBY

4 miles NE of Liverpool City Centre close to the M57/A580 junction

Croxteth Hall and Country Park

Croxteth Hall and Country Park is the Edwardian country estate of the Earl of Sefton, a place with many attractions for all ages. The Hall itself - elegant, opulent and beautifully maintained - stands in a 500-acre estate that includes a working farm, a lovely walled garden and a country park with woodland, wildlife, an adventure playground and a riding centre. Special events staged throughout the year include flower shows, family-fun days and murder mystery nights.

AINTREE

3 miles N of Liverpool City Centre on the A59

Grand National Experience

One of the most popular sporting attractions around Liverpool is the **Grand National Experience** at Aintree racecourse. The tours, which take place at 11am and 2pm on Tuesday and Friday, take in the museum and picture gallery, the weighing room, parade ring, stables, stewards room, a simulated race of champions, a virtual reality ride, Red Rum's statue, Red Rum's grave, a tour of the actual racecourse, souvenir shop, coffee shop and picnic area. Red Rum's record in the world's greatest steeplechase is one that will probably never be equalled: three times a winner (1973, 1974 and 1977) and twice runner-up (1975 and 1976).

Year by year, the facilities for spectators at the Grand National are improving, and there are other meetings apart from the three-day

Grand National fixture: Ladies Night May evening meeting, Family Day meeting in October, and Becher Chase Day in November. The visitor centre at the course is open Tuesday to Friday late May to late October, and at other times by appointment.

SEFTON

5 miles N of Liverpool off the A59

St Helen's Church

This quiet old village stands at the edge of a rich and fertile plain of farmland that lies just behind the West Lancashire coast. It formed part of the estate of the Earls of Sefton (descendants of the Molyneux family) right up until 1972. The village has a pub, a 16th-century corn mill and a delightful church, **St Helen's**, with a 14th-century spire. Inside, there's a beautifully restored ceiling with bosses and moulded beams, 16th-century screens, well-preserved box pews, two medieval effigies of knights, and an elaborately carved pulpit of 1635. A series of brasses recounts the history of the Molyneux family from their arrival in Britain with William the Conqueror. Though this is a small village, its name has also been given to the large metropolitan district of north Merseyside, which stretches from Bootle to Southport.

INCE BLUNDELL

6 miles N of Liverpool off the A565

Church of the Holy Family

The village takes part of its name from the Blundell family who have for centuries exerted much influence on the village and surrounding area. Ince comes from the Celtic word 'Ynes', which means an island within a watery meadow and it would have perfectly described the village's situation before the surrounding land was drained.

The annual candlelight service at the village **Church of the Holy Family** is an ancient custom that appears to be unique to this county. The people of the parish decorate the graves in the cemetery with flowers and candles before holding a service there. Common in Belgium, this custom was brought to the village at the beginning of the 20th century.

LYDIATE

7 miles N of Liverpool on the A5147

St Katherine's Chapel The Scotch Piper

This is another pleasant old village bordering the flat open farmland created from the West Lancashire swamps. Lydiate itself means an enclosure with a gate to stop cattle roaming. Though the age of the settlement here is uncertain, the now ruined **St Katharine's Chapel** dates from the 15th century. However, the most frequented building in the

St Katharine's Chapel, Lydiate

Freshfield

Distance: *3.7 miles (5.9 kilometres)*

Typical time: *120 mins*

Height gain: *0 metres*

Map: *Explorer 285*

Walk: *www.walkingworld.com ID: 257*

Contributor: *Jim Grindle*

ACCESS INFORMATION:

The walk starts at Freshfield station on the Southport/Liverpool line. Access by road is from the A565. Follow the tourist signs to Formby Point (National Trust). The route crosses the railway line where there is parking. Alternatively, park in the National Trust reserve and start the walk from Waymark 10.

DESCRIPTION:

The walk follows the railway line to a crossing and then goes through a golf course. An extensive plantation of Corsican Pine is entered on a track leading to the beach. You turn into the National Trust property and through the woods again before a short road walk to the station.

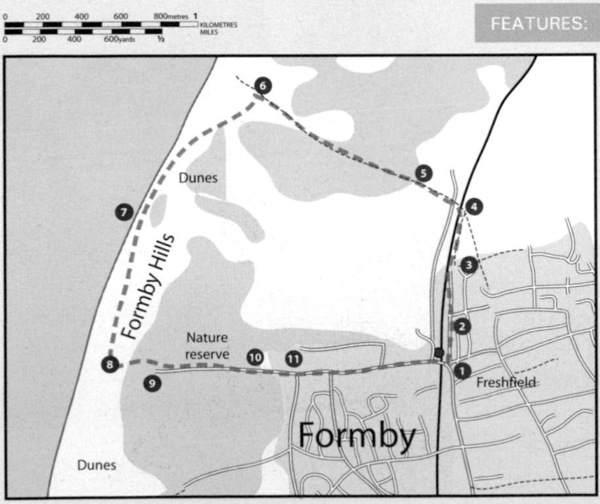

ADDITIONAL INFORMATION:

There are several shops by the station where you can buy food and drink. The Freshfield Hotel can be found by turning left at the crossroads 200 metres inland from the level crossing. There are toilets suitably concealed inside a man-made sand dune in the National Trust reserve. There are usually ice-cream vans here also.

The reserve is one of the remaining strongholds of the red squirrel in England and they can be seen throughout the woods. The place where you would be unlucky not to see one would be in the area near the Warden's hut shown at Waymark 10. These woods are also the first place recorded in Britain where the collared dove nested after it spread from its traditional habitat in central Europe in the 1950s. On the beach, but more particularly in winter, are thousands of waders and sea birds.

Overhead you may see some of the huge flocks of pink-footed geese that winter here from Iceland. From the beach you can usually see the North Wales coast with the Clwydian hills (highest point Moel Famau) to the left and the Carneddau to the right. In the other direction, the Lake district can also be seen but usually needs colder air; Blackpool Tower is often visible, however.

FEATURES:

Sea, Pub, Toilets, National Trust/NTS, Wildlife, Birds, Flowers, Great Views, Good for Wheelchairs.

WALK DIRECTIONS:

1 | On leaving the platform turn left and left again at the telephone box. Walk past this row of shops and then the station car park.

2 | At the end of the car park you can continue on the road or branch left onto the bridleway - they join up again further on. The tarmac ends at the last house and becomes a gravelled track.

3 | Take the fork left on the wider track, following the railway line as far as a level crossing.

4 | Go over the railway line and follow the track through a golf course, until you reach a metal gate at the entrance to the National Nature Reserve.

5 | Take the left fork, which takes you for 1km between the golf course on the left and the reserve on the right. White-topped posts indicate the right way, but you have only to keep to the broad, gravelled track. Go through a more open area where the pines give way to birch, willows and sea-buckthorn with orange berries. There is a last stand of pine and you reach a junction by the sand dunes. This is as far as you can go in a wheelchair, but it is very pleasant - reverse your outward route.

6 | Take the left fork, which winds between buckthorn, with the woods to the left and the sea behind the dunes to the right. After 1km the path leads to the beach. Again there are white-topped posts. Ahead of you is the Welsh coast.

7 | Keeping in the same direction, ie the sea on your right, walk along the beach. Paths off the beach are marked by 2 metre-high posts with yellow tops and a name. Go as far as the fourth of these, marked 'Victoria Road'.

8 | Turn left and climb by the fence to the top of the dunes.

9 | A board walk leads down into the car park. Keep going right through and onto a concrete road leading to the Wardens' hut and the exit from the National Trust property. Just before this hut you will find the toilets and also drinking water for dogs. Look on the right for 'Squirrel Walk' - this is the best place to see them. The wardens sell food that will tempt the squirrels to eat out of your hand.

10 | Keep straight on and the concrete road gives way to tarmac - Victoria Road.

11 | You can check that you are on Victoria Road at the postbox. It is less than 1km back to the station, directly down this road.

village is **The Scotch Piper**, a lovely cruck-framed building with a thatched roof that is believed to be the oldest pub in the region. It was originally built around a massive tree, which still holds up part of the roof.

FORMBY

12 miles N of Liverpool off the A565

Formby Point · Freshfield Nature Reserve

Like Ormskirk, Formby has a connection with potatoes. It's said that sailors who had travelled with Sir Walter Raleigh to Virginia brought back potatoes with them and grew them in the fields around what was then a small village. There are still many acres of potato fields being cultivated in the area. To the west of the town, **Formby Point** and Ainsdale National Nature Reserve form the most extensive dune system in Britain, 450 acres of wood and duneland. Formby Point was the site of Britain's first lifeboat station, built in 1776 and still to be seen.

The origins of this small coastal town lie in the time of the Vikings. The name Formby comes from the Norse Fornebei meaning Forni's town. Between the Norman Conquest and the time of the Dissolution in 1536, there were a succession of landowners but, by the mid-16th century, the Formby and Blundell families emerged as the chief owners. Formby Hall (private), built for William Formby in 1523, occupies a site that was first developed in the 1100s.

Today, Formby is perhaps better known as a quiet and desirable residential area and also the home of an important red squirrel sanctuary at the National Trust **Freshfield Nature Reserve** and pine forest. From the shoreline there are magnificent views over the Mersey estuary and, on a clear day, the hills of Wales and of Lakeland are also visible. The whole stretch of this coastline is filled with birding sites, from Seaforth Nature Reserve on the Mersey Estuary to Marshside RSPB Reserve north of Southport.

AINSDALE

17 miles N of Liverpool on the A565

Ainsdale National Nature Reserve

Towards the sea, from the centre of the village, lies what was Ainsdale-on-Sea with its old Lido and the more modern Pontin's holiday village. Between here and Formby, further down the coast, the sand dunes form part of the **Ainsdale National Nature Reserve**, one of the most extensive dune systems in the country. It's also one of the few remaining habitats of the endangered natterjack toad, which breeds in the shallow pools that form in the sand dunes. This quirky creature is the only species of toad that walks rather than hops. As well as supporting the toads, the salt pools are the natural habitat for a variety of rare dune plants, including Dune Helleborine, Grass of Parnassus and Round-Leaved Wintergreen.

CROSBY

9 miles NW of Liverpool on the A565

Another Place

Crosby's two-mile long beach recently gained national attention with the installation of sculptor Antony Gormley's figures of 100 identical iron life-size men. Called **Another Place**, the sculptures were originally intended to be a temporary installation but will now remain permanently in place. They are placed at varying distances from the high water mark so that at any one time some may appear to be paddling while others have only their heads appearing above the water. The beach itself has only really been stabilised in the last half a century or so with the planting of old Christmas trees amongst the dunes and the building of a sea wall. Before this was done, at high tides the sea could come in as far as the first row of houses.

For a comparatively small town, Crosby, has an extraordinary roll call of well-known residents. Amongst them are the Right Reverend Lord Robert Runcie, 102nd Archbishop of Canterbury; George Melly, the jazz performer and writer; novelist Dame Beryl Bainbridge; Lord Birt, former Director-General of the BBC; comedians Kenny Everett and Nigel Rees; Cherie Blair, the QC and wife of ex-Prime Minister, Tony Blair; writer Lynda La Plante, screenwriter and actress; and Anne Robinson, journalist and television presenter. Even more remarkable is that three of the leading figures in the *Titanic* disaster were from Crosby: Bruce Ismay, Managing Director of the White Star Line and creator of *RMS Titanic*; Edward J Smith, the captain of the doomed ship; and Arthur Henry Rostron, the captain of the *RMS Carpathia* which famously rescued *Titanic* survivors.

Southport

'Duke' Sutton · Wayfarers Arcade · Town Hall

Atkinson Art Gallery

British Lawnmower Museum · The Monument

Model Railway Village · Marine Lake

Pier · New Pleasureland

Flower Show · Red Rum

Besides offering a step back in time, the broad promenades of Southport, its elegant tree-lined streets, and its superb shopping still makes this one of the most visited towns in this region.

The fashion for sea-bathing is usually reckoned to have originated with George III's regular dips at Weymouth in the late 1700s, but at Southport they'd already been doing it for generations. Only once a year though, on St Cuthbert's Eve, the Sunday following August 20th. The holiday became known as "Bathing Sunday, when folk travelled some distance to throw off their clothes and frolick naked in the sea". The tradition was associated with the legend, or fact, that St Cuthbert had once been shipwrecked but had miraculously been able to swim to the shore and safety.

Southport's history as an all-year, rather than a one-day-a-year resort began in 1792 when its first hotel was built. A local man, **'Duke' Sutton**, went to the beach, gathered all the driftwood he could find, nailed it together, put in the minimum of furniture, and opened for business.

Within a few years other houses and hotels had sprung up among the dunes and by 1802 'Duke' Sutton felt confident enough to rebuild his makeshift, if environmentally-friendly hotel, in stone. Over-confident as it turned out. The following year he was thrown into Lancaster gaol for debt and later died a pauper.

Southport though continued to thrive and by the 1860s was by far the most popular seaside resort in Lancashire. The town's only problem was that its main attraction, the sea, was getting further and further away as silt from the Ribble estuary clogged the beach. The town council's response was to build the second-longest pier in the country, complete with a miniature railway, which is still operating. They also created numerous parks and gardens, and constructed elegant boulevards such as Lord Street. All that activity in Victorian times imbued the town with an appealingly genteel atmosphere, which, happily, it still retains.

The town's central, main boulevard, Lord Street, is a mile-long road that was built along the boundary bordering the lands of the two neighbouring lords of the manor. A superb shopping street today, the exceptionally wide pavements, with gardens along one side and an elegant glass-topped canopy along most of the other side, make this one of the most pleasant places to shop in the country. Many of the town's classical style buildings are found along its length and it has been

British Lawnmower Museum

106-114 Shakespeare Street, Southport PR8 5AJ
Tel: 01704 501336 Fax: 01704 500564

The **British Lawnmower Museum** located in the picturesque Victorian seaside holiday resort of Southport, Lancashire, houses a private collection of over 200 pristine exhibits of special interest (part of 400) built up over a period of 50 years. It is a tribute to the garden machinery industry which has developed over the past 170 years from the Industrial Revolution to the present day, and all the benfits of modern technology. Many of the machines have been rescued from the scrap yard and restored to their present very high standard. In addition to early grass cutting and garden machines dating from the 1830s, the exhibition houses the largest collection of vintage toy lawnmowers and games in the world.

The lawnmower was invented in 1830 by Edwin Budding of Gloucester, thought of as a madman testing the strange contraption at night. Originally designed to trim the nap from cloth, the cylinder machine he devised has not changed in principle since that date. It has been the only traditional lawnmower for formal lawns used throughout Great Britain, although somewhat unique in so far as every other country in the world use the more recently introduced (circa 1930) rotary grass cutter.

The museum has now become one of the world's leading authorities on vintage lawnmowers and is the largest specialist in antique garden machinery, supplying parts, archive conservation of manuscript materials, including 500 original patents from 1799, and valuing machines from all over the world. The museum retains a character not often seen in these modern times.

Included in this unique national collection are manufacturers not normally associated with the garden industry, names such as Rolls-Royce, Royal Enfield, Daimler, Hawker Sidley, Perkins Diesel, British Leyland and many more. A lot of the memorabilia and industrial artifacts are from the Victorian and Edwardian era, restored in order to keep a small part of British engineering heritage alive.

designated a conservation area. Off Lord Street, there is one of the town's several covered arcades – **Wayfarers Arcade**, built in 1898 and a fine example of these popular shopping malls. The modest entrance opens out into a beautiful cast-iron and glass conservatory with a first floor gallery and splendid central dome. Originally named the Leyland Arcade after the town's Member of Parliament, it took its present name in 1976 after the arcade's most successful leaseholder.

Morris Dancers, Lord Street, Southport

In a central position along Lord Street stands Southport's rather modest **Town Hall**. Built in 1852 of a classical design, its facade includes a beautiful carving in bold relief of the figures of Justice, Mercy and Truth picked out in white against a Wedgwood blue background. Further along, the Atkinson Central Library was built in 1879 as the premises of the Southport and West Lancashire Bank. The original ceiling of the banking hall can still be seen as can its fireplace. On the first floor is the **Atkinson Art Gallery**, which contains collections of British art and Chinese porcelain. In Shakespeare Street, the **British Lawnmower Museum** (see panel opposite) is a tribute to the gardening machinery industry, with an unrivalled collection of machines, many from the Victorian and Edwardian eras, as well as lawnmowers once owned by such celebrities as Princess Diana and Vanessa Feltz.

Not all the notable buildings in Southport are Victorian, and the Mecca Bingo Club, originally called the Garrick Theatre, was held to be the finest theatre when it was opened in 1932. With much of its exterior as it would have appeared when it first opened, it is a wonderful example of the Art Deco style. Finally, Lord Street is also home to the town's war memorial, **The Monument**. Opened on Remembrance Day 1923 by the Earl of Derby, this is a large and grand memorial that remains the town's focal point. Its design was the subject of a competition and the winning entry was submitted by Garyson and Barnish, designers of the famous Royal Liver Building in Liverpool. The central obelisk is flanked by twin colonnades on which the names of the town's more than 1000 dead are inscribed.

Every self-respecting Victorian resort had a Promenade and Southport's is a typical example, flanked by grand hotels on the land side and a series of formal gardens on the other. Here you'll also find the **Model Railway Village** set in beautifully landscaped and sheltered gardens. Based upon typical southwest Lancashire architecture, the layout consists of a country scene, village and town. Movement is generated in the Model Village by one of the largest 45mm garden railway systems in the UK with five LGB trains continuously running on 500 metres of track.

As the silting up of the Ribble estuary progressed unchecked, the **Marine Lake** was constructed at the northern end of the promenade. At over 86 acres, this man-made lake is the largest in Britain and as well as being an attractive site and a place for the pursuit of all manner of watersports, it is also host to an annual 24-hour yacht race.

From the centre of the promenade extends Southport's **Pier** which, at 1460 yards long, was the longest pier in the country until 1897. Following a fire in 1933 it was shortened, but it remains the second longest in the country. Looking at the pier today it is hard to imagine that at the end of the last century pleasure steamers were able to depart from here to Barrow in Cumbria, Bangor, Wales, and the Isle of Man. Along the shore line, and opened in the spring of 1998, the new sea wall and Marine Drive is a wonderful modern construction, the length of Southport's sea front, that blends well with the town's Victorian heritage.

The normal attractions of a seaside resort have not been forgotten and **New Pleasureland,** re-opened in July 2007, is the obvious choice for those seeking thrills and hair-raising rides; the 100+ rides and attractions include the country's tallest, fastest looping coaster, go-karts, kids' quad bikes and bumper boats. Keen gardeners will know Southport for its splendid annual **Flower Show**, second only to Chelsea, and golfers will be familiar with the name of Royal Birkdale Golf Course, just south of the town centre. Southport has one more sporting association of which it is justly proud. From behind a car showroom in the 1970s, Ginger McCain trained **Red Rum** on the sands of Southport to a record-breaking three magnificent wins in the Grand National run at Aintree. A statue of the great horse can be seen in Wayfarers Arcade.

Around Southport

CHURCHTOWN

1 mile NE of Southport on the A5267

Meols Hall · Botanic Gardens

This charming village, complete with thatched cottages, has retained much of its village feel and is certainly worthy of exploration in its own right. Considerably predating the seaside resort, Churchtown is, as its name suggests, centred around its church. Since it is dedicated to St Cuthbert, it is possible that while fleeing from the Danes, the monks of Lindisfarne rested here with the remains of their famous saint.

There was certainly a thriving fishing village here in the early 1100s. In 1224, Robert de Coudrey granted the village the right to hold a market, the likely location for which is the cross standing opposite the church in the heart of the village.

As the settlement lay on a crossroads and at the start of a route over the sands of the Ribble estuary, it was a place of considerable importance. It was also here that the tradition of sea bathing in this area began, when, in 1219 St Cuthbert's Eve was declared a fair day, which later became known as Bathing Sunday.

There is still plenty to see in this small village. The present **Meols Hall** dates from the 17th century but its appearance today is largely thanks to the work carried out by the late Colonel Roger Fleetwood Hesketh in the

1960s. When the colonel took over the house in the late 1930s, the older and larger part of the hall had been demolished back in 1733 and the remaining building was rather nondescript. Taking the gabled bay of the late 17th century as a start, extensions were added to give the house a varied roofline and a three dimensional frontage.

Meols Hall, Churchtown

The hall is the last home of the Hesketh family who at one time had owned most of the coastal area between Southport and Heysham. Originally, the manor had been granted to Robert de Coudrey but came into the Hesketh family by marriage in the late 16th century. There has been a house on this site since the 13th century. Occasionally open to visitors, the hall has a fine art collection and, in the entrance hall, three carved chairs that were used in Westminster Abbey during the coronation of Charles II. During World War One, Moels Hall was used as a military hospital.

Planned on the site of the old Churchtown Strawberry Gardens in 1874, the **Botanic Gardens**, restored in 1937, are beautifully maintained and present a superb example of classic Victorian garden design. With magnificent floral displays, a boating lake, wide, twisting paths, and a fernery, little has changed here since the day the gardens were first opened by the Rev Charles Hesketh. Also within the gardens are a café, gift shop and pottery shop.

Manchester

- Town Hall
- Museum of Science & Industry
- Jewish Museum
- Manchester Museum
- Urbis
- Manchester United Museum
- Manchester Art Gallery
- Whitworth Gallery
- John Rylands Library
- Trafford Centre
- Barton Swing Aqueduct
- Heaton Park
- Tameside

Like Liverpool, Manchester has seen an urban renaissance as new buildings and open spaces have been developed, transforming the face of the city. The Beetham Tower, Santiago Calatrava's Trinity Bridge, Bridgewater Hall, home of the Hallé Orchestra, and the City of Manchester Stadium take their places as landmarks alongside the splendid Town Hall, the Cathedral, and the Baroque Church of St Ann with its rare glass by William Peckitt of York. The Victorian **Town Hall**, perhaps the finest in the country, is the work of Alfred Waterhouse; its many treasures include a wealth of stained glass and mosaic, and Ford Madox Brown's murals in the Great Hall.

Museum of Science & industry, Manchester

Manchester's museums and art galleries are the most impressive and diverse outside London. All repay lengthy visits, and in particular the world-class **Museum of Science & Industry**, telling the story of the world's first major industrial city; the **Jewish Museum** housed in the city's oldest purpose-built synagogue; **Manchester Museum** in the University, famed for its Egyptian collections; the ultra-modern **Urbis** with interactive displays exploring life in different cities of the world; the **Manchester United Museum** in Trafford; the **Manchester Art Gallery**; the **Whitworth Gallery**, home to some of the UK's finest collections of art and design, including modern and historic fine art, prints, textiles and a rare collection of wallpapers; and the impressive Gothic-style **John Rylands Library**, designed by Basil Champneys to display the library of the cotton magnate. Housed in one of Manchester's most beautiful buildings, the library was re-opened in the spring of 2007 following a £16.8 million transformation.

Another essential venue, and not just for shoppers, is the breathtaking **Trafford Centre**. Beneath a stunning arched steel and glass roof, are some 230 stores, 55 restaurants, cafés and bars, a 20-screen cinema and lots of other entertainment.

Just a 15-minute walk from the Trafford Centre is the astonishing **Barton Swing Aqueduct** (free), a 235ft-long engineering marvel built to carry the Bridgewater Canal over the Manchester Ship Canal. The aqueduct swings while full of water - 800 tons of it - a spectacle that attracts visitors from around the world.

Four miles to the north of the city centre, **Heaton Park** is the largest of Manchester's open spaces. Its 640 acres nestle in the foothills of the Pennines, and over the past few years its rolling landscape has been

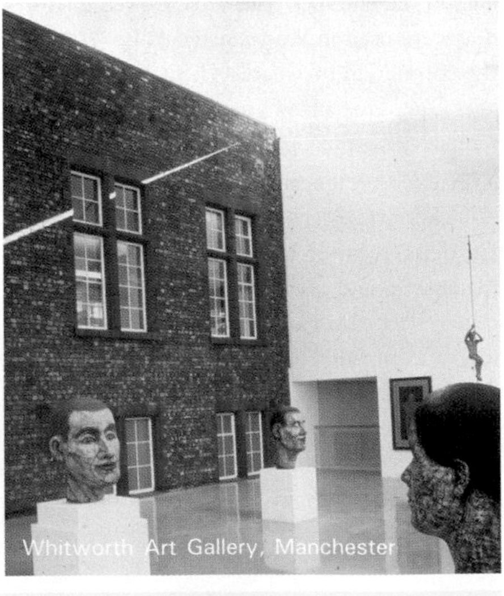

Whitworth Art Gallery, Manchester

restored to its original character when it was part of the estate surrounding Heaton Hall, home of the Earls of Wilton. The hall itself was rebuilt from 1772 onwards by the architect James Wyatt and is a striking example of neo-classical decoration. The newly restored Orangery is also open to the public and a popular venue for wedding celebrations and receptions. The park also contains a championship golf course and an Animal Centre.

Seven miles to the east of Manchester is the district of **Tameside**, much of which is open land comprising moorland, country parks, reservoirs and woodland. At Portland Basin, where three canals meet, is a new heritage centre that hosts special events throughout the year, including the Tameside Canals Festival.

Salford Quays

Around Manchester

SALFORD

4 miles W of Manchester city centre off the M602

The Lowry · Imperial War Museum North

Salford Museum & Art Gallery · Ordsall Hall

Blackleach Country Park · Clifton Country Park

Salford's major attraction is undoubtedly **The Lowry**, located in the fashionable Salford Quays. A stunning modern complex overlooking the Manchester Ship Canal, The Lowry houses two theatres and an exciting children's activity gallery as well as the eponymous Lowry collection. L S (Laurence Stephen) Lowry, noted for his distinctive paintings of Northern urban landscapes, spent some time as a rent collector. He was granted the freedom of Salford in 1965 and is buried in Manchester Southern Cemetery, which is also the final resting place of Sir Matt Busby, for 50 years intimately associated with Manchester United. A footbridge to the Trafford side of the canal leads from The Lowry to the **Imperial War Museum North**, a fantastic aluminium-clad building whose three metal 'shards' represent conflict on air, sea and land. Its exhibits are dedicated to ordinary people and their stories, whether far from home in a battle zone, or growing up in the midst of war.

Also within the Quays complex is the **Salford Museum & Art Gallery**, which houses art from the 19th century to the

Charter in 1290 and is still very active, although the old houses that de Quincey also noted have sadly gone. The market is now centred on a Victorian hall opened in 1880, and the range of stalls is splendidly diverse (though the goods for sale do not now run to wives - it is recorded that in 1823 a man sold his wife by auction for the equivalent of 7½p!). A modern bustling town, Altrincham nevertheless has a long history, with clear evidence that there was a settlement beside the River Bollin some 6000 years ago. Even older than that is the prehistoric body preserved in peat discovered on Lindow Common nearby. From Victorian times, Altrincham has been a favoured retreat for Manchester businessmen and the town is well supplied with inns, restaurants and shops - notably the £30 million redevelopment of the Stamford Shopping Centre. The town has also seen a major investment in the building of a new Ice Dome, which was opened in the spring of 2007, and a new six-screen cinema opened a few months earlier. Other cultural venues include the Garrick Playhouse, opened in 1932, the Club Theatre, a small but thriving intimate theatre established in 1896, and the **Waterside Arts Centre**, comprising a 350-seat theatre, exhibition gallery, creative learning spaces and a unique outdoor events plaza.

present day; a fine collection of statuary; a unique reconstruction of a Victorian cobbled street and hands-on displays of local history. Another museum, **Ordsall Hall**, occupies Salford's oldest building, a superb black and white timbered structure dating from Elizabethan times. Within this Grade I listed building, exhibits cover more than 600 years of the town's history.

Just minutes from the town centre are two great lungs: **Blackleach Country Park**, reclaimed from former industrial land to become a scenic oasis; and **Clifton Country Park**, which has been imaginatively developed from what was the Wet Earth Colliery, one of the first deep mines to be sunk in the Irwell Valley and established around 1740.

ALTRINCHAM

8 miles SW of Manchester on the A560

Waterside Arts Centre

The writer Thomas de Quincey visited Altrincham in the early 1800s and thought its bustling market "the gayest scene he ever saw". The market was established by Royal

CHEADLE HULME

7 miles S of Manchester on the A34

Bramall Hall

Developed in Victorian times as a commuter town for better-off workers in Manchester,

Bramall Hall

Stockport, Cheshire SK7 3NX
Tel: 0161 485 3708

Bramall Hall is known as one of England's treasures. It is a magnificent black and white Tudor manor house with Victorian additions set in 70 acres of beautiful parkland, which is landscaped in the style of 'Capability' Brown. Take a tour of this beautiful house and you'll discover the spectacular Tudor plaster pendant ceiling, a 16th-century embroidered table carpet and the wonderful wall paintings discovered by the Victorian owner.

The new costumed interpretation will give you a feel of the household at Bramall in 1890, with glimpses of the family from upstairs and the staff from downstairs. After a tour around this beautiful house, relax in the tearoom or restaurant and be tempted by delicious cakes, scrumptious light refreshments or a three-course lunch. Bramall Hall provides a pleasurable learning experience with a fascinating day out.

Cheadle Hulme is a busy place with a fine park on its eastern edge in which stands one of the grandest old 'magpie' houses in Cheshire, **Bramall Hall** (see panel above). This eye-catching, rambling perfection of black and white timbered buildings overlooks some 62 acres of exquisitely landscaped woods, lakes and formal gardens. The oldest parts of the Hall date from the 14th century: for five of the next six centuries it was owned by the same family, the Davenports. Over the years, the Davenport family continually altered and extended the originally quite modest manor house. But whenever they added a new Banqueting Hall, Withdrawing Room, or even a Chapel, they took pains to ensure that its design harmonised happily with its more ancient neighbours. Along with Little Moreton Hall and Gawsworth Hall, Bramall represents the fullest flowering of a lovely architectural style whose most distinctive examples are all to be found in Cheshire.

STOCKPORT

6 miles SE of Manchester on the A6

- Hat Works
- Stockport Museum
- Air Raid Shelters
- Stockport Art Gallery
- Staircase House
- Stockport Viaduct
- Chadkirk Chapel

Nearly 50 per cent of the borough is green space, so visitors will find plenty of opportunities for walking and enjoying the countryside. One of the town's most fascinating attractions is the **Hat Works**, located in the restored Wellington Mill. It is the country's first and only museum dedicated to hats and hat-making. Visitors can learn about Stockport's historic links with hatting (more than 4500 people were employed in the industry here at the end of the 19th century), see the original machinery and enjoy an amazing display of some 400 hats of all shapes and sizes, from miniature hats made by

Stockport Air Raid Shelters

Stockport, Cheshire SK1 1NP
Tel: 0161 474 1940

Stockport's unique **Air Raid Shelters** have been carved into the natural sandstone cliffs in Stockport Town Centre and are the largest purpose built Second World War civilian underground air raid shelters. They were boarded up after the war and rediscovered a few years ago, since when they have been imaginatively restored to give visitors the feel of wartime Britain.

Visitors can explore the labyrinth of underground passages and wander through the reconstructed warden's post, toilets, first aid room, canteen, tool stores, benches and bunkers that once housed over five thousand people a night during the Blitz.

apprentices to the world's tallest topper. Close by are the **Stockport Museum** – one of the first purpose-built museums in the UK and located in the Market Place - and the **Air Raid Shelters** (see panel above), near the Merseyside Shopping Centre, which provide a trip back in time to World War Two when tunnels were built into the red sandstone rock to accommodate thousands of people seeking refuge from air raids.

One of the town's most imposing buildings is the **Stockport Art Gallery** with its grand portico of four Corinthian columns. Opened in 1925, the gallery has a magnificent marble hall with inspirational exhibition spaces. The gallery offers a changing programme of contemporary art and craft exhibitions and artist-led workshops.

Only recently opened to the public, **Staircase House** in the Market Place is a beautifully restored medieval town house famous for its rare cage newell staircase, a Jacobean masterpiece that is one of only three surviving in the UK. Visitors journey through time from the building's humble beginnings as a cruck-framed structure to the splendour of the 17th-century town house.

The town's most dominating architectural feature is the **Stockport Viaduct**, which is 500 metres long and has 27 arches. When it was completed in 1839 it was one of the largest free-standing brick-built structures in the world.

A few miles east of Stockport is another fascinating building, the **Chadkirk Chapel**. Set in the heart of Chadkirk Country Estate, this immaculately restored 14th-century chapel has associations with the 7th-century missionary St Chad. Visitors can relax in the peace of the chapel, then take a walk through woodlands and along the scenic Peak Forest Canal to Etherow Park.

OLDHAM

7 miles NE of Manchester on the A627

Gallery Oldham

Set high in the Pennine Hills and dominated by St Mary's Church on its summit, Oldham in its industrial heyday had 250 working cotton mills, which between them kept 18 million spindles busy. Today the town is energetically striving to regenerate itself in the post-industrial era. The striking **Gallery Oldham**, which opened in 2002, was the first phase in the creation of the town's Cultural Quarter. The gallery's changing exhibition programme features items from Oldham's extensive collections of fine and decorative art, social history and natural history, alongside touring exhibitions and newly commissioned work. Adjoining the Gallery is the second phase of the programme, the Oldham Library and Lifelong Learning Centre. Designed by the same award-winning architects who built the Gallery, the Centre is open seven days a week and offers extensive free computer facilities.

The Panhandle

The narrow finger of land pointing up to West Yorkshire was chopped off from Cheshire in the 1974 Local Government redrawing of boundaries and put into Greater Manchester, but more than 30 years on most of its population still consider themselves Cheshire folk. At its northern end lie Longdendale and Featherbed Moss, Pennine scenery quite unlike anywhere else in the region.

MARPLE

10 miles SE of Manchester on the A626

Christopher Isherwood

Marple's most famous son is probably the poet and novelist **Christopher Isherwood**, who was born at Marple Hall in 1904 and could have inherited it from his grandfather had he so wished. Instead, the author of *Mr Norris Changes Trains* and *Sally Bowles* (the source material for the musical *Cabaret*) renounced the life of a country squire for the more sybaritic attractions of California. But Marple made a great impression on him as is evident in his book *Kathleen and Frank,* based on the letters and diaries of his parents. Isherwood revels in the wildness of the Goyt Valley, not just its scenery but also its weather - "it never really dries out," he wrote.

Marple is also famous for its flight of 16 locks on the Peak Forest Canal and the mighty three-arched aqueduct that carries the canal over the River Goyt. At Marple, the Peak Forest Canal is joined by the Macclesfield Canal and there are some attractive towpath walks in both directions.

STALYBRIDGE

6 miles E of Manchester on the A57

Rev Joseph Rayner Stephens

Set beside the River Tame and with the North Pennine moors stretching for miles to the east, Stalybridge was one of the earliest cotton towns and its mill workers among the most radical and militant during the Chartist troubles of the 1840s. Oddly, one of their leaders was a former Methodist minister, the **Rev Joseph Rayner Stephens**, who had broken away from the Wesleyan ministry and established his own 'Stephensite' chapels – one in King Street, Stalybridge, the other in its sister town across the Tame, Ashton-under-Lyme. He campaigned tirelessly against the long hours worked in the factories and the policy, introduced in 1834, of refusing poor relief outside the workhouse.

When in 1842 the mill-owners tried to impose reductions in pay, the workers' embryonic trade union closed all the mills in north Cheshire and south Lancashire. Stephens was tried and sentenced to 18 months in Chester gaol. On his release, he continued his efforts to improve the workers' pay and conditions for another 38 years. His funeral was attended by thousands and the workers erected a granite obelisk to his memory in Stalybridge's attractive Stamford Park. On it is inscribed a quotation from the speech he delivered at his trial: "The only true foundation of Society is the safety, the security and the happiness of the poor, from whom all other orders of Society arise".

Merseyside and Greater Manchester

Before the Industrial Revolution this was a sparsely populated region of remote hill farms and cottages that relied, chiefly, on sheep farming and the wool trade. Many of the settlements date back to before the Norman Conquest, and although little may have survived the rapid building of the 19th century, there are three surprisingly wonderful ancient houses to be seen here: Smithills Hall and Hall-i'-th'-Wood at Bolton, and Turton Tower, just to the north.

However, there is no escaping the textile industry. Lancashire's ideal climate for cotton spinning and weaving – damp so that the yarn does not break – made it the obvious choice for the building of the mills. There are numerous valleys with fast-flowing rivers and streams, and the development of the extensive coalfields around Wigan supplied the fuel to feed the power-hungry machinery. Finally, there was a plentiful supply of labour as families moved from the hill-top sheep farms into the expanding towns and villages to work the looms and turn the wheels of industry.

In a very short time, smoke and soot filled the air and the once clear streams and rivers became lifeless valleys of polluted squalor. There are many illustrations in the region of the harsh working conditions the labourers had to endure and the dirt and filth that covered most of the area. Now that much of this has been cleaned up, the rivers running once again fast, clear, and supporting wildlife, the lasting legacy of those days is the splendid Victorian architecture of which every town has at least one example.

Bolton

Earl of Derby · Town Hall · Octagon Theatre

Museum, Art Gallery & Aquarium

Reebok Stadium · Hall-i'-th'-Wood

Smithills Hall · Animal World & Butterfly House

Barrow Bridge Village · Bolton Steam Museum

Synonymous with the Lancashire textile industry, Bolton is also an ancient town that predates its expansion due to cotton by many centuries. First settled during the Bronze Age, by the time of the Civil War, this was a market town supporting the surrounding villages. The town saw one of the bloodiest episodes of the war when James Stanley, **Earl of Derby**, was brought back here by Cromwell's troops after the Royalists had been defeated. In a savage act of revenge for the massacre his army had brought on the town early in the troubles, Stanley was executed and his severed head and body, in separate caskets, were taken back to the family burial place at Ormskirk. Whilst in captivity in the town, Stanley was kept prisoner at Ye Olde Man and Scythe Inn, which, dating from 1251, is still standing in Churchgate today and is the town's oldest building.

The centre of Bolton is a lasting tribute to the wealth and prosperity generated by the spinning of high quality yarn for which the town was famous. The monumental **Town Hall**, opened in 1873, is typical of the classical style of buildings that the Victorian

Pigeon Tower, Lever Park, Bolton

town fathers favoured – tours are available. The hall is still the town's central point and it is now surrounded by the recently refurbished pedestrianised shopping malls, market hall, and the celebrated **Octagon Theatre**. The town's excellent **Museum, Art Gallery & Aquarium** is one of the largest regional galleries in the northwest with excellent collections of fine and decorative art, including examples of British sculpture and contemporary ceramics. There are collections of natural history, geology, and Egyptian antiques here, as well as some fine 18th- and 19th-century English watercolours and some contemporary British paintings and graphics.

Bolton's most recent major attraction is the state-of-the-art **Reebok Stadium**, home of Bolton Wanderers, one of the world's oldest football clubs. Visitors can take a look behind the scenes at one of Europe's finest stadiums, seeing everything from the players' changing-rooms to the bird's-eye vantage point of the Press Box.

Bolton is fortunate in having two particularly fine old mansions, both on the northern edge of the town. **Hall-i'-th'-Wood**, is a delightful part-timbered medieval merchant's house dating from 1530 to 1648. A fine example of a wealthy merchant's house, Hall-i'-th'-Wood was saved from dereliction by Lord Leverhulme in 1900 and has been restored and furnished with displays of fine 17th- and 18th-century furniture along with interesting items of local importance. The hall has a second claim to fame since, for a number of years, one of several tenants here was Samuel Crompton, the inventor in 1799 of the spinning mule. Naturally, the hall has a replica of Crompton's mule on display.

Bolton's second grand house, **Smithills Hall**, stands on an easily defended hill and was built in the 1300s as a pele, or fortified dwelling. It was extended over the years and this superb Grade I listed building now displays some of the best examples of medieval, Tudor and Victorian Arts & Crafts architecture in the region. The hall was bought by Bolton Corporation in the late 1930s and has been beautifully restored. In addition to the impressive collection of furniture and artifacts on display, the hall also hosts changing exhibitions throughout the year. As well as seeing one of the oldest and best-preserved fortified manor houses in the county, visitors can also wander along the hall's wooded nature trail.

Close to Smithills Hall, in Moss Bank Park, is **Animal World & Butterfly House** which provides a safe habitat for a variety of animals and birds ranging from farm animals to chipmunks, from wildfowl to tropical birds. In the tropical atmosphere of the Butterfly House, are free-flying butterflies and moths as well as insects, spiders, reptiles and tropical plants.

On the northwestern edge of the town is **Barrow Bridge Village**, a small model village built in the 1820s to house workers at the two six-storey mills that used to operate here. Small bridges cross a picturesque stream and a flight of 63 steps leads up the hillside to the moors. Barrow Bridge village was the inspiration for Benjamin Disraeli's famous novel *Coningsby*.

Also to the northwest of the town is the **Bolton Steam Museum**, which is located in a former cotton store on the old Atlas Mills site off Chorley Old Road. On display here is a superb and extensive collection of fully restored textile mill steam engines. These were in common use throughout the North of England from the early 1800s until the 1960s when textile production declined dramatically and many mills closed.

There is a notable and rare 1840 twin beam engine and a unique 1893 'non-dead-centre' machine. Although no steam supply is yet available, most engines are in running order and can be seen in motion, under electric drive, on Open Days.

Around Bolton

TURTON BOTTOMS

4 miles N of Bolton off the B6391

Turton Tower

Turton Tower near Bolton was built both for defensive purposes and as a residence. In 1400, William Orrell erected his sturdy, four-square pele (fortified dwelling) in search of safety during those lawless and dangerous years. Some 200 years later, in more settled times, a lovely, half-timbered Elizabethan mansion was added. Successive owners made further additions in a charming motley of architectural styles. Quite apart from its enchanting appearance, Turton is well worth visiting to see its display of old weapons and a superb collection of vintage furniture, outstanding amongst which is the sumptuously carved Courtenay Bed of 1593.

TOTTINGTON

4 miles N of Bolton on the B6213

Tottington's pub is named after a dog. The Hark to Towler, in the centre of the town, is very much a locals' pub that happily welcomes visitors. Dating back to the 1800s, this imposing red brick pub's unusual name means call - hark - to the lead dog of the hunt - Towler.

An unspoilt farming town on the edge of moorland, Tottington escaped the industrialisation of many of its neighbours due to its then isolated position and it is still an attractive place to visit.

WALMERSLEY

2 miles NE of Bolton on the A56

Hidden away in the village of Walmersley, just north of Bury, is Hark to Dandler, an attractive pub dating from the mid-19th century that is thought to have originally been a vicarage. During a recent refurbishment, a very old child's coffin was found, full of early 19th-century artefacts, behind the cellar walls. Along with the two resident ghosts, this certainly adds an air of mystery to the pub. The name is more easily explained as it is named after a lead dog of the local hunt.

RAMSBOTTOM

6 miles NE of Bolton on the A676

Peel Tower · Charles Dickens
Irwell Sculpture Trail

Ramsbottom is a no-nonsense stone-built Pennine hill town with steep roads leading out of town to the east and west. One of these leads to the **Peel Tower**, which dominates the surrounding countryside. Erected in 1852 to commemorate the life of the area's most famous son, Sir Robert Peel, the tower is some 128 feet high. Now restored, the tower itself is occasionally open to the public and provides some spectacular views.

In the Market Place is the Grant Arms, which commemorates two chief bigwigs of the town in the early 1800s. The Grant brothers were immortalised by **Charles Dickens** as the Cheeryble brothers in *Nicholas Nickleby*. These generally philanthropic mill owners made sure of the profits of their pub by paying their workforce in tokens that could only be redeemed in the Grant Arms.

Ramsbottom is placed on the **Irwell Sculpture Trail** and in the Market Place is the wonderful *Tilted Vase* by Edward Allington. This two-ton sculpture is classical in shape to reflect the surrounding buildings, but also bolted together to reflect the old industries.

BURY

6 miles E of Bolton on the A58

Robert Peel · John Kay · The Met
Art Gallery & Museum · East Lancashire Railway
Bury Transport Museum · Burrs Country Park
Lancashire Fusiliers Museum

There was a settlement at Bury in Bronze Age times, but as late as 1770 it was still just a small market town, surrounded by green fields. That was the year a man named **Robert Peel** established his Ground Calico Printing Works, the first of many mills that would follow. The opening of the works along with the subsequent mills, print and bleach works so dominated this part of the Irwell Valley that not only did they transform the landscape but also heavily polluted the river. At the height of the valley's production it was said that anyone falling into the river would dissolve before they had a chance to drown.

East Lancashire Railway

Bury - Ramsbottom - Rawtenstall
Tel: 0161 764 7790

The **East Lancashire Railway** offers visitors an opportunity to step back in time to the age of steam as they travel along this delightful stretch of track. Your journey can be broken at Ramsbottom or Irwell Vale stations where you could enjoy a lineside picnic.

On Platform 2 at Bury Bolton Street Station, the period tearooms offer views of the locomotives arriving or departing from the station, while you enjoy a snack or meal in the pleasant surroundings. The rooms can be pre-booked for special occasions.

A wide variety of events take place throughout the year, including Santa Specials, a Day Out with Thomas and Friends, 1940s Wartime weekend and Steam Enthusiasts Weekend - ring for current details. Adults can actually drive a steam or deisel locomotive on the 'Footplate Experience', or an entire train can be hired for a special occasion or event. Facilities for the disabled are extremely good with access at all the stations, toilets at the main stations and a specially adapted carriage with wide doors and hydraulic lift.

Today, thankfully, the valley towns are once again clean, the river clear and fast-flowing, and a massive regeneration project is transforming the town centre. An indication of this greener Bury is the fact that in 2007 it was awarded a silver medal in the Royal Horticultural Society's Britain in Bloom national competition.

With the family fortune gleaned from those prosperous mills, Robert Peel junior, born in the town in 1788, was able to fund his illustrious career in politics, rising to become Prime Minister in 1841. Famous for the repeal of the Corn Laws, Robert Peel was also at the forefront of the setting up of the modern police force – hence their nickname 'Bobbies'. A statue of Bury's most distinguished son stands in the Market Square and there's an even grander memorial near the village of Holcombe, a few miles to the north.

Another of Bury's famous sons was **John Kay**, inventor of the Flying Shuttle. Sadly, Kay neglected to patent his invention. He moved to France where he died a pauper and is buried in an unmarked grave. The people of Bury, however, remembered him. In his memory, they created the delightful Kay Gardens in the town centre and erected a splendidly ornate clock-house tower.

A short walk from Kay Gardens, **The Met** is a lively arts centre, which puts on performances to suit all tastes, from theatre and children's shows to rock nights and world music. The Met also organises Bury's Streets Ahead Festival each May, a colourful street carnival that attracts artistes from around the world.

This part of town has become known as the 'Culture Quarter', since Bury's **Art Gallery & Museum** is also located here. Re-opened in 2005 after extensive refurbishment, the gallery has a fine collection of paintings, including works by Turner, Constable and Landseer, and the outstanding Thomas Wrigley collection of Victorian oil paintings. The building also houses the Bury Archives Service which makes available local records dating from 1675 to the present day.

The town has a real treat for those who thrill to the sight, sound and smell of steam locomotives. Bolton Street Station is the southern terminus of the **East Lancashire Railway** (see panel opposite) which operates regular services along a nine-mile scenic route through the lovely Irwell Valley to Rawtenstall. For the really smitten, there's the opportunity to actually drive one of the steam or diesel locomotives. Serious devotees of transport history will also want to explore the **Bury Transport Museum**, just across the road from the station. The museum houses a wonderful collection of vintage road and rail vehicles, ranging from a 19th century steam road-roller to a "Stop Me and Buy One" ice-cream vendor's tricycle. The museum is only open on Sundays from Easter to the end of September.

Another museum of interest is the **Lancashire Fusiliers Museum** which tells the story of Lancashire's famous regiment from its foundation in 1688 and has an outstanding collection of medals and period uniforms. It is currently undergoing refurbishment but is scheduled to re-open in 2008.

A major shopping centre for the northwest, Bury is also proud of its ancient Market which has been operating since 1440. Held on Wednesdays, Fridays and Saturdays, the market is now the largest in the north with more than 370 stalls offering a huge choice of some 50,000 different product lines. Don't leave without purchasing one of Bury's famous black puddings.

Looking at Bury today it seems hard to imagine that at one time this typical Lancashire mill town had a castle. A settlement probably existed here in the Bronze Age and there is certainly evidence that the Romans passed through this area. By the 12th century, the town was the manor of the Norman de Bury family and, in the mid-14th century, the land came under the ownership of the Pilkingtons. It was dismantled following the Battle of Bosworth in 1485 at which Henry VII defeated Richard III. Unlucky Thomas Pilkington had backed the wrong side. The foundations of the castle have recently been excavated and form the centrepiece of Castle Square.

On the outskirts of the town lies **Burrs Country Park**, which, as well as offering a wide range of activities, also has an interesting industrial trail around the historic mill site.

WIGAN

7 miles SW of Bolton on the A49/A577

Trencherfield Mill Steam Engine

Leeds & Liverpool Canal Viaduct

Pennington Flash · Haigh Country Park

Wigan International Jazz Festival

Haigh Music Festival · Drumcroon Centre

Wickham Gallery · Wigan Town Centre Art Trail

Wigan's reputation took a long while to recover from George Orwell's devastating description of its dark industrial townscapes in his 1936 novel, *Road to Wigan Pier*. But over the past few years imaginative planning has transformed the town built on coal and cotton into a lively self-confident community. The Wigan Pier Quarter itself has recently undergone a multi-million pound development that will include an arts and heritage learning centre with the majestic

Trenchefield Mill Steam Engine as its centrepiece. Built and installed in a specially designed engine house in 1907 by John and Edward Wood of Bolton, the four-cylinder engine is the world's largest working steam engine, originally designed to power the cotton looms inside Trencherfield Mill.

An attractive feature of Wigan is the stretch of the **Leeds and Liverpool Canal Viaduct** that passes high above the town. Originally designed for transporting coal to the cotton mills of Lancashire, the canal now provides a haven for a variety of wildlife. Abram Flashes (lakes) and Ince Moss, which adjoin the Leigh Branch of the canal, have been designated Sites of Special Scientific Interest. There is more fine countryside surrounding the town, including the Douglas Valley Trail, **Pennington Flash**, a large lake formed by mining subsidence that is now a country park and nature reserve, and **Haigh Country Park**, one of the first to be designated in England.

Culturally, too, Wigan has blossomed. The **Wigan International Jazz Festival** held each year in July is now well-established, while the Georgian Haigh Hall provides a contrasting backdrop to a one-day contemporary **Haigh Music Festival**. The **Drumcroon Centre** is dedicated to quality modern art exhibitions; traditionalists on the other hand will be more at home in the **Wickham Gallery**. A fairly recent addition to the town's cultural attractions is the **Wigan Town Centre Art Trail** - 13 installations scattered across the town centre and including the Market Cross Mosaic in New Market Square and some massive moving metal heads adorning the fascia of Trencherfield Mill.

Rochdale

Town Hall · Rochdale Pioneers Museum

Touchstones

St John the Baptist Catholic Church

Greater Manchester Fire Service Museum

Rochdale Canal

Lying in a shallow valley formed by the little River Roch, the town is surrounded to the north and east by the slopes of the Pennines, which are often snow-covered in winter. With its origins in medieval times, the town, like so many others in Lancashire, expanded with the booming cotton industry. Its magnificent Victorian **Town Hall** (1871) rivals that of Manchester in style if not in size. There are tours of this impressive building that include its spectacular Grand Staircase, hammer-beamed Great Hall, stained glass, statuary, ceramics and paintings. There's a scheduled tour every Friday afternoon; at other times by arrangement.

However, it is not textiles for which Rochdale is most famous, but for its role as the birthplace of the Co-operative Movement in 1844. In carefully restored Toad Lane, to the north of the town centre, is the world's first Co-op shop, now the **Rochdale Pioneers Museum** (see panel opposite). Today, the Co-op movement represents a staggering 700 million members in 90 countries around the world, and the celebration of its 150th anniversary in 1994 focused attention on Rochdale. The story of the Rochdale Pioneers and other aspects of the town's heritage are vividly displayed in the Arts and Heritage Centre, **Touchstones**. The restored Grade II listed building of 1889 was originally a library, but now contains interactive high-tech exhibitions, five art galleries, the Tourist Information Centre, a

Rochdale Pioneers Museum

31 Toad Lane, Rochdale OL12 ONU
Tel: 01706 524920
e-mail: museum@co-op.ac.uk website: www.co-op.ac.uk/toad lane

The **Rochdale Pioneers Museum** is regarded as the home of the world wide co-operative movement. It's the perfect place to come and see how your ancestors did their shopping.

In Toad Lane on December 21st 1844 the Rochdale Equitable Pioneers Society opened their store selling pure food at fair prices and honest weights and measures, starting a revolution in retailing.

See the re-creation of the original shop with its rudimentary furniture and scales. Here, the basic needs of daily life such as butter, sugar, flour and oatmeal first went on sale over 150 years ago.

Journey back in time with early advertising, packaging and retailing artifacts, Co-operative postage stamps, commemorative china, and rare dividend coins and commodity tokens. See the development of 'dividend' and the Co-op's success.

local studies centre, with free internet access, café/bar, bookshop and performance studio.

As well as the Pioneers, Rochdale was home to several other famous sons and daughters, amongst them the 19th-century political thinker, John Bright, the celebrated singer Gracie Fields (who now has a theatre here named after her), and Cyril Smith, Rochdale's former Liberal Member of Parliament.

The town's most distinctive church is **St John the Baptist Catholic Church**, which has a beautiful dome modelled on the Byzantine Santa Sofya in Istanbul. The church is unique in England because of its huge mosaic of Italian marble depicting the Resurrection of Christ.

Rochdale's multi-cultural diversity is reflected in the area known as the Curry Quarter with its numerous restaurants offering what has been characterised as England's national dish.

The **Greater Manchester Fire Service Museum** (free) in Maclure Road features several full-size fire appliances, along with equipment, uniforms, models, photographs, medals and insignia, as well as some interesting memorabilia. Visitors can also enjoy a stroll down a replica Victorian street – complete with fire station, insurance office and fire equipment suppliers. There is also a chance to take a trip back to the World War Two and look around a scene from the Blitz.

Running from the southeast corner of the town, the **Rochdale Canal** is a brave piece of early-19th-century civil engineering that traversed the Pennines to link the River Mersey with the Calder and Hebble Navigation. Some 32 miles in length and with 91 locks, it must be one of the toughest canals ever built and, though the towpath can still be walked, the last commercial boat passed through the locks in 1937. The canal was officially abandoned in 1952, but exactly half a century later the entire 32-mile long waterway was re-opened to full navigation. Together with the newly restored Huddersfield Narrow Canal it allows a complete circuit of the South Pennine Ring.

North of Rochdale

HEALEY

1 mile N of Rochdale on the A671

Healey Dell Nature Reserve

Lying in the valley of the River Spodden, this old village, now almost engulfed by the outer reaches of Rochdale, is an area rich in wildlife as well as folklore. Opened in 1972, **Healey Dell Nature Reserve** has a wealth of wildlife to be discovered along the nature trails. This is an ancient area, which has only been invaded by the construction of the commercially non-viable Rochdale to Bacup railway in the late 19th century. The oak and birch woodland on the northern river bank is all that remains of a prehistoric forest and, whilst the owners of Healey Hall made some impact, little has changed here for centuries.

WHITWORTH

4 miles N of Rochdale on the A671

This pleasant town of cottages and farms lies on Pennine moorland above Rochdale. Between here and Bacup, a distance of only seven miles, the railway line, in another feat of Victorian engineering, climbs more than 500 feet. Not surprisingly, there were many problems during its construction, such as frequent landslides, but once finished this was a picturesque line with attractive station houses with neat well-tended gardens along the route. The line, like so many, fell to the extensive railway cuts of the 1960s.

LITTLEBOROUGH

3 miles NE of Rochdale on the A58

Littleborough Coach House & Heritage Centre

Roman Causey   Aigin Stone

Hollingworth Lake Activity Centre

Hollingworth Lake Country Park

Occupying a Grade I listed building dating from the late 1700s, the **Littleborough Coach House and Heritage Centre** hosts regular exhibitions by local artists and has arts and crafts for sale.

Roman Causey, Littleborough

This small town lies beside the River Roch and on the main route between Lancashire and Yorkshire first laid down by the Romans. Known as the **Roman Causey**, it was an impressive structure 16 feet 6 inches wide, cambered and with gutters at each side. In the middle of the road is a shallow groove, which has been the subject of endless controversy – no one has yet come up with a satisfactory explanation of its purpose. The road cuts across the bleak Pennine moors by way of Blackstone Edge where some of the best-preserved parts of the Roman structure can still be seen. At the summit is a medieval cross, the **Aigin Stone**, from which there are spectacular views over Lancashire right to the coast.

Between Rochdale and Littleborough lies Hollingworth Lake, originally built as a supply reservoir for the canal, but for many years a popular area for recreation known colloquially as the 'Weavers' Seaport', as cotton workers unable to afford a trip to the seaside came here. Now part of the **Hollingworth Lake Country Park** and with a fine visitor centre, there are a number of pleasant walks around its shores.

Hollingworth Lake Activity Centre offers sailing, canoeing, windsurfing, rowing and, during the summer months, lake trips on the *Lady Alice.*

SUMMIT

5 miles NE of Rochdale off the A6033

At Summit, the Rochdale to Halifax railway line dives into a tunnel that runs for a mile and a half under the Summit Ridge of the Pennines before emerging in Yorkshire. This extraordinary feat of engineering, the longest tunnel in the world when it was completed in 1844, is as remarkable in its way as the Roman Causey, which follows a similar route on top of the hills.

South of Rochdale

MILNROW

2 miles E of Rochdale on the A640

Ellenroad Engine House · John Collier

One of the finest examples of a giant steam Mill Engine in the country can be seen at the **Ellenroad Engine House** next to Junction 21 of the M62. The 3000-horsepower twin engines *Alexandra* and *Victoria,* both built in 1892, were once used to power the Ellenroad Cotton Spinning Mill, which closed long ago, but the Engine House with its steam-raising plant and 220ft chimney have been carefully preserved. The

Hollingworth Lake Country Park

engines are in steam on the first Sunday of every month except January.

It was to this small industrial town in the foothills of the Pennines that **John Collier** came as the schoolmaster in 1729. Collier is perhaps better known as Tim Bobbin, the first of the Lancashire dialect poets. Collier remained in Milnrow for the rest of his life and, drinking rather more than he should, earned extra money by selling his verse and by painting pub signs. The local pub, which dates back to the early 1800s is, appropriately, named after him.

SHAW

3 miles SE of Rochdale on the A633

Jubilee Colliery

A typical mill town, founded on the wealth of the cotton trade, Shaw was also a market town for the surrounding area. Closed since 1932, **Jubilee Colliery**, to the northeast of the town centre, has been reclaimed as a nature reserve and it is now an attractive haven for wildlife in the Beal Valley.

DENSHAW

5 miles SE of Rochdale on the A640

Cricketers Row

In the moorland above the village is the source of the River Tame, which flows through the Saddleworth area and eventually joins the River Goyt at Stockport. A charming 18th-century village, Denshaw's Scandinavian name would suggest that there has been a settlement here for many centuries.

Until 1974, the Saddleworth area was part of the West Riding of Yorkshire and residents of the parish are still eligible to play for the Yorkshire cricket team. Cricket has always been a passion here. One 19th-century mill owner built **'Cricketers Row'** near Denshaw to house his team and the terrace even includes a residence for the 12th man.

DELPH

7 miles SE of Rochdale on the A6052

Castleshaw

Taking its name from the old English for quarry, this is probably a reference to the bakestone quarries found to the north of the village. Also close by, high on a hill above the village, lies **Castleshaw**, one of a series of forts the Romans built on their military road between Chester and York. The banks and ditches give visitors an excellent indication of the scale of the fort and many of the items found during recent excavations are on show in Saddleworth Museum in Uppermill.

DOBCROSS

7 miles SE of Rochdale off the A6052

This attractive Pennine village, once the commercial heart of the district of Saddleworth, retains many of its original weavers' cottages, clothiers, and merchants' houses, and little has changed around the village square in the past 200 years. Used as the location for the film *Yanks*, Dobcross is also notable as the birthplace of the giant Platt Brothers Textile Machinery business which was, in the latter part of the 19th century, the largest such machine manufacturing firm in the world.

UPPERMILL

8 miles SE of Rochdale on the A62

Saddleworth Parish Church

Saddleworth Museum Brownhill Visitor Centre

Of the 14 villages that make up Saddleworth parish, Uppermill is the most central. It is home to the area's oldest building, **Saddleworth Parish Church**, which was originally built in the 12th century by the Stapletons as their family chapel. Extended over the years, it has several interesting features including a gravestone to commemorate the Bill's o'Jack's murders. In 1832, the people of Saddleworth were stunned to learn that the landlord of the Bill's o'Jack's Inn and his son had been bludgeoned to death. Several thousand people turned out for the funeral but the case was never solved. The tombstone relates the whole story.

Almost a century-and-a-half later, the whole country was horrified by the Moors Murderers, Ian Brady and Myra Hindley, who buried four of their victims on Saddleworth Moor.

The story of this once isolated area is illustrated at the **Saddleworth Museum**, housed in an old mill building on the banks of the Huddersfield Canal. There is a reconstruction of an 18th-century weaver's cottage, as well as a collection of textile machinery, a local history gallery and local art exhibitions.

Also in Uppermill is the **Brownhill Visitor Centre**, which has information on the northern section of the Tame Valley and exhibitions on local wildlife and the area's history.

DIGGLE

8 miles SE of Rochdale off the A62

Oldham Way Standedge Canal Tunnel

Above the village, on Diggle Moor, lies Brun Clough Farm where, it is said, the cries of child slaves who were ill-treated in the early days of the textile mills can still be heard coming from the outhouses. Part of the **Oldham Way** footpath, a 30-mile scenic walk through the countryside on the edge of the Peak District National Park, crosses the moorland.

Much of the village itself is a conservation area, where the pre-industrial weaving community has been preserved along with some of the traditional skills. However, Diggle Mill, which used to operate the second largest waterwheel in the country, no longer exists.

The Huddersfield Narrow Canal, completed in 1811, is one of the three canals that crossed the difficult terrain of the Pennines and linked Lancashire with Yorkshire. The entrance to the **Standedge Canal Tunnel**, the longest and highest canal tunnel in Britain, can be seen in the village.

LOCATOR MAP

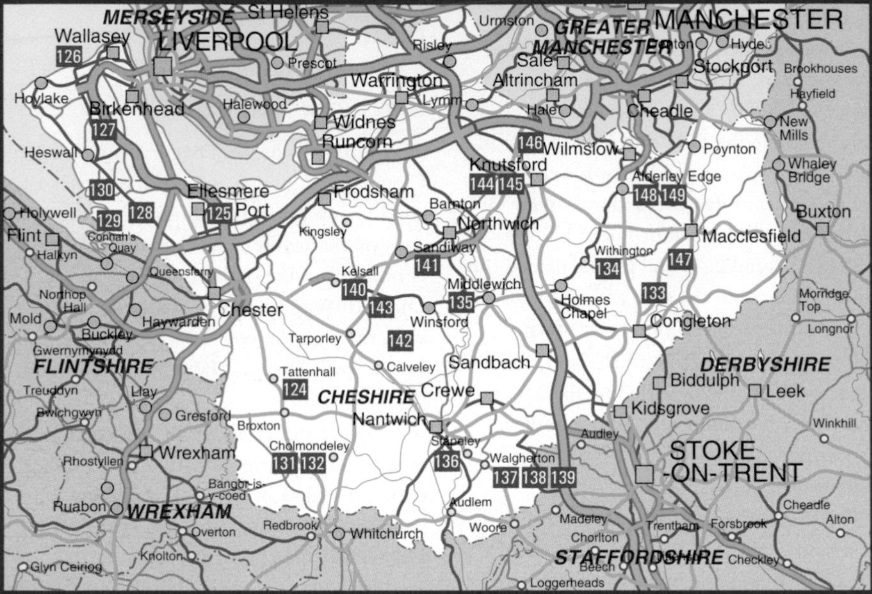

ADVERTISERS AND PLACES OF INTEREST

historic building · museum and heritage · historic site · scenic attraction · flora and fauna

5 | Cheshire

Recently, Cheshire has received a bad press from writers such as Jeremy Clarkson and AA Gill who have portrayed the county as a kind of *Footballer's Wives* territory, packed with Porsches, bloated with bling and mindlessly devoted to conspicuous consumption. It's certainly true that more millionaires live in this captivating corner of the country than anywhere else in England. Britain's richest peer, the Duke of Westminster, with an estimated wealth of £5600 million, lives on a large estate just south of Chester. And more champagne is quaffed here than anywhere else in the UK.

But that's only a tiny part of the county's 2000-year-long story, which effectively begins with the arrival of the Romans. But even before the 20th Legion established the garrison of Deva in 70AD, Cheshire was famous for its salt mines. By the time of the *Domesday Book*, the salt towns, or 'wiches' - Nantwich, Northwich and Middlewich - were firmly established. The process at that time involved pumping the salt brine to the surface and boiling it to produce granular salt. In 1670, huge deposits of rock salt were discovered and these are still being mined, mostly for use in keeping Britain's roads free from ice.

In the early 1700s, in the course of his *Tour through the Whole Island of Great Britain*, Daniel Defoe came to Chester by the ferry over the River Dee. He liked the city streets, "very broad and fair"; admired the "very pleasant walk round the city, upon the walls", disliked its cathedral, "built of red, sandy, ill-looking stone", but had nothing except praise for its "excellent cheese". Cheshire cheese has been famous for generations. John Speed, the well-known Elizabethan map-maker and a Cheshire man himself, noted: "The soil is fat fruitful and rich....the Pastures make the Kine's udders to strout to the pail, from whom the best Cheese of all Europe is made". Later, some enthusiasts even promoted the idea that the name Cheshire was actually short for cheese-shire.

One thing that visitors don't get to see is the county's best known character, the grinning Cheshire Cat. The expression 'to grin like a Cheshire cat' was in use long before Lewis Carroll adopted it in *Alice in Wonderland.* Carroll spent his childhood in the Cheshire village of Daresbury and would have regularly seen the local cheeses moulded into various animal shapes, one of which was a grinning cat.

ADVERTISERS AND PLACES OF INTEREST

stories and anecdotes famous people art and craft entertainment and sport walks

Chester

King Charles Tower · Chester Cathedral
Dewa Roman Experience · Grosvenor Museum
On The Air · Chester Toy and Doll Museum
Chester Military Museum · The Rows
Eastgate Clock · Amphitheatre · Chester Zoo

Chester occupies a strategic site on the River Dee close to the Welsh border and was important even before the Romans arrived in 70AD. They based a large camp here and called it Deva after the Celtic name for the river. It was during this period that the splendid city walls were originally built – two miles round, and the most complete in the country.

In Saxon times 'Ceastre' became the administrative centre of a shire, and was the last major town in England to fall to William the Conqueror during his dreadful Harrowing of the North. William pulled down half of Chester's houses and reinforced the message of Norman domination by building a castle overlooking the Dee.

Subsequent Earls of Chester (the present Prince of Wales is the current one) were given a free, firm hand in dealing with the local Saxons and with the still rebellious Welsh, who continued to make a nuisance of themselves right through the Middle Ages. In return for its no-nonsense dealing with these problems Chester received a number of royal privileges: borough status, a licence for a market and, around 1120, the first commission in England for a Sheriff, long before his more famous colleague in Nottingham received his.

The problem with the Welsh was finally resolved in 1485 when a Welsh-based family, the Tudors, defeated Richard III at Bosworth Field and Owen Tudor claimed the throne as Henry VII. For more than 150 years Chester enjoyed an unprecedented period of peace and prosperity. Then came the Civil War. Chester supported the King, but Charles I had the galling experience of watching from the city walls as his troops were defeated at nearby Rowton Moor. For two long years after that rout, the city was under siege until starvation finally forced its capitulation. The **King Charles Tower** on the wall is now a small museum with displays telling the story of the siege.

James Boswell, Dr Johnson's biographer, visited Chester in the 1770s and wrote, "I was quite enchanted at Chester, so that I could with difficulty quit it." He was to return again, declaring that, "Chester pleases my fancy more than any town I ever saw." Modern visitors will almost certainly share his enthusiasm.

Pavement Artists, Eastgate, Chester

Probably the best introduction to this compact little city is to join one of the frequent sightseeing tours conducted by a Blue Badge guide. These take place every day, even

Christmas Day, and leave from the Chester Visitor Centre. The Centre can also provide a wealth of information about the city, including a full calendar of events that range from the Chester Regatta, the oldest rowing races in the world, and Chester Races, the oldest horse races in Britain, to the Lord Mayor's Show in May and the Festival of Transport, featuring an amazing parade of vintage cars, in August.

King Charles Tower, Chester

Towering above the city centre is **Chester Cathedral**, a majestic building of weathered pink stone, which, in 1992, celebrated its 900th birthday. It was originally an abbey and is one of very few to survive Henry VIII's closure of the monasteries in the 1540s. The cloisters are regarded as the finest in England and the monks' refectory is still serving food - although nowadays it is refreshments and lunches for visitors. There's a fine 14th-century shrine to St Werbergh, the princess/abbess who founded the first church on this site in Saxon times, and some intricately carved quire stalls almost 800 years old, which are reckoned to be the finest in Britain. It was at Chester Cathedral, in 1742, that George Frederick Handel personally conducted rehearsals of his oratorio *The Messiah* before its first performance in Dublin: a copy of the score with annotations in his own hand is on display.

Chester is famous for its outstanding range of museums. At the **Dewa Roman Experience** visitors can re-live the sights, sounds, and even the smells, of daily life in Roman Chester. A superb array of artefacts from Chester and elsewhere in the Roman Empire is on display and kids love dressing up in replica suits of Roman armour. In the **Grosvenor Museum** are furnished period rooms, the Timeline Gallery travelling back through the city's history, the Natural History Gallery, the Silver Gallery featuring the Chester race cups, a gallery of paintings by local contemporary artists, and many more attractions, events and activities that make this a great place for all the family to visit. **On The Air** broadcasting museum chronicles the world of radio and television from the pioneering days of BBC radio, to satellite and digital TV, while the **Chester Toy and Doll Museum** is a nostalgic treasure-house of antique playthings. The **Cheshire Military Museum** recounts the story of the county's military history using computers, tableaux and hands-on exhibits to present the soldier's life through the past 300 years.

Quite apart from its historical attractions, Chester is also one of the major shopping centres for the northwest and north Wales. All the familiar High Street names are here - often housed in much more appealing buildings than they usually inhabit - along with a great number of specialist and antique shops. A unique shopping experience is provided by the world-famous, two-tiered galleries of shops under covered walkways known as **The Rows**, which line both sides of Bridge Street. The Rows are an architectural one-off: no other medieval town has anything like them. Many of the black and white, half-timbered frontages of The Rows, so typical of Chester and Cheshire, are actually Victorian restorations, but crafted so beautifully and faithfully that even experts can have difficulty distinguishing them from their 13th-century originals.

Close by is the **Eastgate Clock**. It was erected in 1897 to celebrate Queen Victoria's Diamond Jubilee, a beautifully ornate construction which is one of the most photographed timepieces in the world.

Chester's famous City Walls were originally built by the Romans to protect the fortress of Deva from attacks by Celtic tribes. Nowadays, the two-mile long circuit – an easy, level promenade - provides thousands of visitors with splendid views of the River Dee, of the city's many glorious buildings and of the distant Welsh mountains. Here, during the summer months, Caius Julius Quartus, a Roman Legionary Officer in shining armour, conducts a patrol around the fortress walls and helps to re-create the life and times of a front-line defender of the Empire. At one point, the wall runs alongside St John Street, which has a curious history. In Roman times it was the main thoroughfare between the fortress and the **Amphitheatre**, the largest ever uncovered in Britain, capable of seating 7000 spectators. During the Middle Ages, however, this highway was excavated and turned into a defensive ditch. Over the years, the ditch gradually filled up and by Elizabethan times St John Street was a proper street once again.

No visit to Chester would be complete without a trip to **Chester Zoo** on the northern edge of the city. Set in 110 acres of landscaped

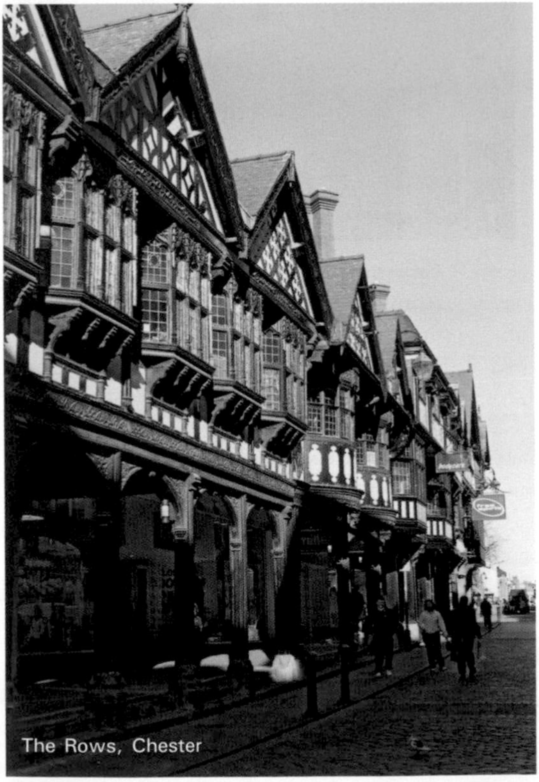

The Rows, Chester

gardens, and the brainchild of George Mottershead, it's the largest zoo in Britain, caring for more than 7000 animals from some 400 different species. The zoo also provides a refuge for many rare and endangered animals, which breed freely in near-natural enclosures. What's more, it has the UK's largest elephant facility and is the only successful breeder of Asiatic elephants in this country. The zoo has more than a mile of overhead railway providing a splendid bird's-eye view of the animals and the Roman Garden. Other attractions include the Rare Penguin Breeding Centre with windows enabling visitors to see the birds 'flying' underwater; a Forest Zone with spacious homes for buffy-headed capuchin monkeys; and special enclosures for the black rhinos and red pandas (Lushui and Lushan are great favourites with visitors). And in the award-winning Spirit of the Jaguar enclosure are the spotted jaguars Sofia, Carlos, Salvador and Ebony. Offering more than enough interest for a full day out, the zoo is open every day of the year except Christmas Day. Children can romp happily in the Fun Ark, and recently added attractions include A Dragons in Danger exhibit.

Around Chester

TARVIN

5 miles E of Chester off the A54 or A51

Baker Way

In the *Domesday Book* Tarvin is recorded as one of the larger manors in Cheshire, and by the 1300s was the centre of an extensive parish. The present church was begun at this time and boasts the oldest surviving timber roof in Cheshire. The village came to prominence in the Civil War when General Sir William Brereton made it his headquarters during the siege of Chester. In August 1644 there was fighting around the church and bullet marks can still be seen around its west door. One of them even penetrated a brass by the chancel in memory of a former Mayor of Chester and remained there for many years until a Victorian vandal prised it out and made off with it.

Tarvin is about halfway along the **Baker Way**, which runs from Chester Station to Delamere Station at the edge of Delamere Forest Park. The trail follows the Shropshire Union Canal from Chester to Rowton Bridge, thence to Hockenhull Platts, Tarvin, Ashton, Brines Brow and Delamere Forest.

GATESHEATH

8 miles SE of Chester off the A41

Country Centre

Occupying a Victorian farmhouse in Gatesheath, the **Country Centre** at New Russia Hall is a unique attraction. To begin with, there's the Orchard Paddock, a magnet for children with its appealing collection of farm animals and pets, swings and crazy golf. Anyone interested in flower arranging can watch the staff of the Dried Flower Workshop creating unique arrangements - for sale, or you can buy all the materials to make your own - and painted plant pots, boxes and small pieces of furniture. There is a comprehensive display of greeting cards and gifts, a tearoom, and Uncle Peter's Fudge Kitchen where you can try the superbly tasty fudge. The name New Russia Hall has nothing to do with Russia but comes from a corruption of 'rushes', which once grew abundantly in the marshy ground nearby and provided the basic materials for local basket-makers.

THE MANOR FARM SHOP

Manor Farm, Newton Lane, Gatesheath, Tattenhall, Cheshire CH3 9AY
Tel: 01829 771438
e-mail: brian@rydersfarmshop.co.uk
website: www.rydersfarmshop.co.uk

The Manor Farm Shop is very much a family business, owned and run by the Ryder family who have been in beef farming for three generations. Brian, who has spent a lifetime in farming, has three daughters and four grandchildren. The eldest grandchild, aged seven, has already expressed an interest in following his grandfather's footsteps into farming. The three daughters are all connected with agriculture in some way or another: Heather is into dairy farming; Lesley, into beef and sheep; whilst Liz concentrates on beef and is the director of Manor Farm.

The Ryders' idea in opening a family shop was to sell top-of-the-range beef and traditional farm produce, including pork, lamb, poultry, fresh fruit and vegetables, dairy produce, pies and cakes, to the local community for a fair price. The Ryders believe that food miles should be kept to a minimum wherever possible - all the food on sale in the shop is locally sourced and, where possible, locally grown. They also endeavour to stock a range of organic produce in the store.

The Ryders have been suppliers of traditional GM-free beef to Sainsbury's for more than 10 years, and they now also supply the Jamie Oliver Taste the Difference range of traditional meats. All animals have traceability from the day they are born to the day they are slaughtered. The Ryders are firm believers that the health and welfare of the animals is paramount - people are welcome to go and see the animals at the farm, all year round. They keep 500 feeders and 90 suckler cows, with a mixture of Limousins and Belgian Blues.

In addition to the traditional fresh beef, raised on Manor Farm and not pre-packed, the shop stocks home-cured dry bacon (cured on the premises), spit-roast chicken, a selection of sausages and black puddings, a range of marinated meats and stir-fries, and a selection of cooked meats. Also available is a wide selection of fresh fruit and vegetables, as well as a variety of soft drinks and fruit juices.

A new addition is the café, selling food based on local produce and scheduled to open early in 2008.

TATTENHALL

8 miles SE of Chester off the A41

Cheshire Ice Cream Farm

Tattenhall is a fine old village within sight of the twin castles of Beeston and Peckforton perched atop the Peckforton Hills. It has some attractive old houses and a Victorian church with a graveyard, which gained notoriety during the 19th century because of the activities of a gang of grave-robbers. They lived in caves in the hills nearby and, once they had disposed of the bodies to medical gentlemen, used the empty coffins to store their booty from more conventional thieving. At that time Tattenhall was a busy little place. The Shropshire Union Canal passes close by and the village was served by two railway stations on different lines. Today, only one railway line survives (and no stations), the canal is used solely by pleasure craft, but the village is enjoying a new lease of life as a desirable community for people commuting to Chester, a short drive away.

Brown tourist signs on the A41 point the way to **Cheshire Ice Cream Farm**, where real dairy ice cream is made in more than 30 different flavours, including rhubarb and custard, Cointreau and orange, and a seasonal sherry trifle. Visitors can watch the cows being milked, and a video shows the whole process of making ice cream 'from cow to cone'. Young visitors can romp in the Playbarn, and the farm is home to many rare breed animals (alpacas, miniature donkeys, pygmy goats, Jacob sheep), rescued birds of prey and hedgehogs.

BELGRAVE

4 miles S of Chester on the B5445

The Grosvenors

Belgrave is hardly large enough to qualify as a hamlet but it has given its name to the London area known as Belgravia. Both are owned by the Duke of Westminster, Britain's richest landowner, whose family home, Eaton Hall, stands beside the River Dee a couple of miles west of the village. The duke's family, the **Grosvenors**, were well established in Cheshire by the 1300s, but it was acquisition by marriage of a large estate to the west of London that brought them huge riches. As London expanded westwards during the 18th and 19th centuries, their once rural estate was developed into elegant squares and broad boulevards, many with names reflecting the Duke's Cheshire connections – Eaton Square, Eccleston Square, Grosvenor Place and Chester Row.

The Grosvenor's vast Victorian mansion suffered badly when it was occupied by the military during the World War Two. In the 1970s it was demolished and replaced by a more modest concrete structure, which has divided architectural opinion as to its merits – one writer described it "as modern as a 1970s airline terminal". The house is not open to the public but its gardens occasionally are.

The Wirral (partly in Merseyside)

Ness Gardens

Two Old English words meaning heathland covered with bog myrtle gave The Wirral its name, and well into modern times it was a byword for a desolate place. The 14th-century author of *Sir Gawayne and the Green Knight* writes of

The wilderness of Wirral:
few lived there
Who loved with a good heart
either God or man.

The Wirral's inhabitants were infamous for preying on the ships tossed on to its marshy coastline by gales sweeping off the Irish Sea. It was the 19th century development of shipbuilding at Birkenhead that brought industry on a large scale to the Mersey shore and also an influx of prosperous Liverpool commuters who colonised the villages of the Caldy and Grange Hills and transformed the former wilderness into leafy suburbia. The 1974 Local Government changes handed two thirds of The Wirral to Merseyside, leaving Cheshire with by far the most attractive third, the southern and western parts alongside the River Dee. Tourism officials now refer to The Wirral as the Leisure Peninsula, a fair description of this appealing and comparatively little-known area. One of its major attractions is **Ness Gardens**, a 62-acre tract of superbly landscaped gardens on the banks of the River Dee. Founded in 1898 by Arthur Kilpin Buley, a Liverpool cotton broker, the gardens have been developed into one of the country's leading botanic gardens. Ness is now run by the University of Liverpool as an Environmental and Horticultural Research Station and provides magnificent displays all year round. There are children's play and picnic areas, well-marked interest trails, a visitor centre with weekly summer exhibitions, a gift shop and licensed refreshment rooms.

ELLESMERE PORT

8 miles N of Chester on the A5032

Stephen Hitchin | Boat Museum

Blue Planet

An interesting 8½-mile trail for walkers and cyclists runs along the Shropshire Union Canal between Chester and Ellesmere Port. It passes through communities and countryside, and along its route are 10 sculptures that mark important gateways to the canal. Local artist **Stephen Hitchin** designed each sculpture to reflect the character of its location and to provide directions along the route. Among the places of interest on the trail are the Backford Gap, marking the southern end of the Wirral Peninsula, and Caughall Bridge, constructed by Thomas Telford. The northern end of the canal lies within the Mersey Community Forest, a network of small woodlands with public access. Railways gradually replaced the canals in the 19th century, and the Shropshire Union had more or less ceased its working life by the 1920s. Since the 1960s, this and many other canals have found a new role supporting the leisure industry. The history of the canal can be explored at the **Boat Museum** (see panel opposite) set in Ellesmere Port's historic dock complex. The museum has the world's largest floating collection of canal craft, along with working exhibitions of restored steam, diesel and gas engines in the Power Hall and Pump House. Porters Row re-creates the dockworkers' cottages of 1840, 1900, 1930 and 1950. Boat trips run most days throughout the summer.

Ellesmere Port's other major attraction is **Blue Planet**, billed as Britain's biggest and best aquarium adventure. On the moving walkway that runs through the underwater safari tunnel visitors can see rays, sharks and more than 1000 other fish and marine life at close quarters. The piranha exhibit is one of the largest in Europe, and among the many other attractions are a display of amphibians, shark feeding and regular special events.

EASTHAM

10 miles NW of Chester off the A41

Eastham Woods Country Park is a 76-acre oasis of countryside amidst industrial Merseyside, and enjoys considerable status among birdwatchers as one of the few northern woodlands with all three species of native woodpecker in residence. Just a mile or so from the Park is Eastham village, another little oasis with a church and old houses grouped around the village green. The yew tree in the churchyard is reputed to be the oldest in England.

BEBINGTON

12 miles NW of Chester off the A41

Port Sunlight · Sunlight Vision Museum

Lady Lever Art Gallery

Much of the Wirral's Merseyside is heavily industrialised, but a dramatic exception is **Port Sunlight** near Bebington. This model village was created in 1888 by William Hesketh Lever, later 1st Viscount Leverhulme, to house the workers in his soap factory and was named after his most famous product, Sunlight Soap. Leverhulme wanted to provide "a new Arcadia, ventilated and drained on the most scientific principles". Some 30 architects were employed to create the individually designed rows of rustic cottages and the village is now a Conservation Area. The history of the village and its community is explored at the **Sunlight Vision Museum** where there are scale models of the village, a Victorian port and Sunlight House, original plans for the building and displays of period advertising and soap packaging. The jewel in the crown of Port Sunlight is the **Lady Lever Art Gallery** (free), which houses a magnificent collection of pre-Raphaelite

KRUGER JEWELLERS

34 Seaview Road, Wallasey, Wirral,
Cheshire CH45 4LA
Tel: 0151 639 4431
e-mail: kruger.jewellery@btconnect.com
website: www.krugerjewellers.co.uk

A family business established in England in 1988, **Kruger Jewellery** is noted for designing and making fine jewellery. Mr Kruger served a seven-year apprenticeship from the age of 16 and now has 35 years of expertise to devote to his profession. Each and every piece of jewellery he makes is individually designed and meticulously crafted, based on photographs and drawings. Each piece has its own unique hallmark and also the designer's 'signature' mark. Customers' commissions are welcome. The team of designers at Kruger Jewellery have all been trained in-house and all designs are carried out on the premises in the open.

In addition to its own in-house creations, Kruger Jewellery also carries branded designer pieces such as those from Pandora - the full range can be seen on their website. The company also carries out quality repairs and undertakes valuations.

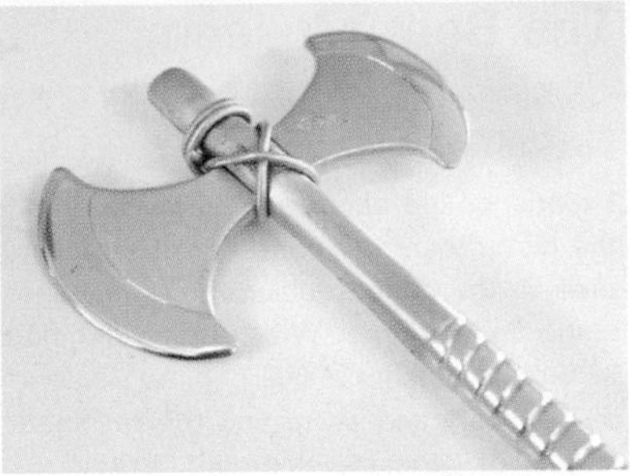

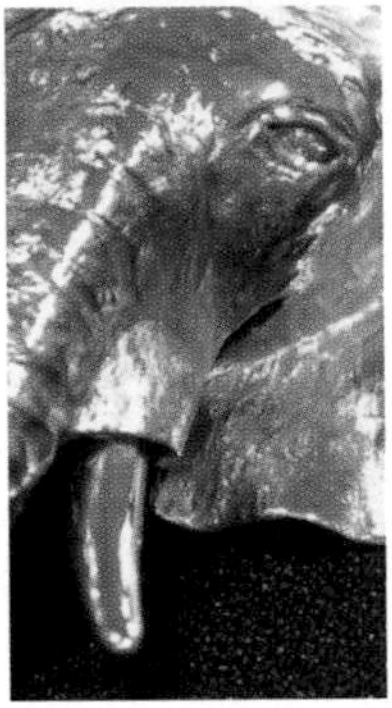

paintings by Millais, Ford Madox Brown and Rosetti, portraits by Gainsborough and Reynolds, dramatic landscapes by Turner and Constable, an impressive Wedgwood collection, and some superb pieces of 18th-century furniture. The gallery also has a gift shop and a popular tearoom, the Lady Lever Café. Lord and Lady Leverhulme are buried in the graveyard of Christ Church.

BIRKENHEAD

20 miles NW of Chester off the M53

Wirral Museum — Birkenhead Heritage Trail
Shore Road Pumping Station — Birkenhead Priory
Birkenhead Park — Tam O'Shanter Urban Farm
Williamson Art Gallery & Museum

If you were asked, "Where is the largest group of Grade I listed buildings in England?", Birkenhead would probably not be your first guess. But you can find these buildings in Hamilton Square where also stands the Town Hall, now the **Wirral Museum**, although that only merits a Grade II rating. Opened in 1887 by John Laird, this grand building houses an exhibition telling the story of the famous Cammell Laird shipyard, a model of the Woodside area in 1934 when King George V opened the Queensway road tunnel under the Mersey, a collection of delightful Della Robbia pottery and mayoral and civic silver. Also within the Town Hall are an art gallery, theatre, cinema and concert hall.

The **Birkenhead Heritage Trail** guides visitors around the town's various attractions and includes trips on a genuine Hong Kong tram and a beautifully restored Birkenhead tram of 1901. The trail takes in the **Shore Road**

THE DRAWING ROOM

50 Christchurch Road, Oxton, Birkenhead,
Merseyside CH43 5SF
Tel/Fax: 0151 652 8452
e-mail: jane@drawingroom-oxton.co.uk
website: www.drawingroom-oxton.co.uk

The Drawing Room is located in Oxton, a village of historical beauty, unique character and stylish shops. Sisters Jane and Sara had both bought period properties and enthused about renovating them. They particularly enjoyed sourcing furniture and accessories and decided to share their love of interiors by launching The Drawing Room in May 2002. The top floor (The Drawing Room) is filled with all manner of delightful accessories for your home and garden, eg lamps, cushions, bedding, art, frames, bistro sets, candles, gifts for all occasions...

Downstairs (The Dressing Room) has a slightly boudoir feel bursting with jewellery, handbags, scarves, hats and a small selection of exclusive clothing for women. There are, of course, plenty of gifts for men, too, from scarves to soap and from silk ties to sentimental keepsakes. The whole shop is essentially vintage but don't be fooled into equating that with old-fashioned, The Drawing Room is anything but. It upholds the tradition of good customer service and a purchase from this magical shop would enhance any home built in this or any other century. The Drawing Room also offers a wedding list service and a gift wrapping service.

Opening Hours: 10am – 5.30pm Tuesday to Saturday.

Directions: 10 minutes from Liverpool City Centre through the Queensway Tunnel. 5 minutes from junction 3 of the M53.

Pumping Station with its 'Giant Grasshopper' steam pump. It was one of several used to extract water from the Mersey railway tunnel – Europe's very first underwater rail tunnel. Other attractions along the trail include an Edwardian Street scene display, a unique historic transport collection, and the Pacific Road Arts and Exhibition Centre. Just along from Pacific Road is Egerton Bridge, which offers a bird's-eye view over the docklands and has models and information about the Birkenhead Dock system.

Moored alongside East Float Dock Road are two historic warships, now museums. Both the frigate *HMS Plymouth* and the submarine *HMS Onyx* served during the Falklands War and are now preserved as they were in the 1980s. *HMS Plymouth* saw action throughout the campaign and while carrying out a lone daylight bombardment was hit by four bombs. *HMS Onyx* was the only non-nuclear submarine to take part in the conflict. She carried 20 men from the SAS and SBS in addition to her own full crew, and was so crowded that she fully deserved her nickname 'The Sardine's Revenge'. Also on display is a German U-boat, *U534*, whose sinking marked the end of the Battle of the Atlantic in May 1945. The submarine was recovered after lying on the seabed for 50 years. The latest addition to the Birkenhead fleet is *HMS Bronington*, a 'Ton' class minesweeper launched in 1953. The 'Tons', the last wooden warships built for the Royal Navy, were all named after towns

Birkenhead Priory

and villages listed in the *Domesday Book* whose names ended with 'ton'. HRH Prince Charles commanded *HMS Bronington* from February 1976 until December 15th of that year, the final day of his active service in the Royal Navy.

Birkenhead Priory, a Benedictine monastery established around 1150, is the oldest standing building on south Merseyside. The site contains museum displays, concert space and a chapel dedicated to *HMS Conway*. A climb up St Mary's is rewarded with magnificent views across Birkenhead to the Welsh Hills, and across the Mersey to Liverpool.

Birkenhead Park, to the east of the town centre, is a remarkable example of an early Victorian urban park with two lakes, a rockery, a Swiss bridge and formal gardens. This vast parkland was designed by Sir Joseph Paxton, architect of London's Crystal Palace, who also designed the spectacular main entrance, which is modelled on the Temple of Illysus in Athens. Interestingly, it became the model for an even more famous park – Central Park in New York.

Just out of town is the purpose-built **Williamson Art Gallery and Museum** which exhibits a wealth of local and maritime history, a permanent display of Victorian oil paintings, tapestries by Lee and English watercolours. It also hosts a full programme of temporary exhibitions.

On the outskirts of the town, **Tam O'Shanter Urban Farm** is centred around a thatched cottage and has a collection of farm animals, a nature trail, play equipment and an activity room, as well as a café.

WEST KIRBY

18 miles NW of Chester on the A540

Kirby Marine Lake · Hilbre Islands

Wirral Way · Hadlow Road Station

Set beside the Dee estuary and looking across to the Welsh mountains, West Kirby was just a small fishing village until the railway link with Liverpool was established in the 1880s. Today, it's a bustling seaside town with some 28,000 inhabitants. A big attraction here is the **West Kirby Marine Lake**, a 52-acre man-made saltwater lake. With a maximum depth of five feet it offers a degree of safety unobtainable on the open sea. Courses in sailing, windsurfing and canoeing are available at the Wirral Sailing Centre.

West Kirby is well known to birdwatchers and naturalists because of the **Hilbre Islands** (see walk on page 290), 'part-time' islands that can be reached at low tide across Dee Sands. Permits (free) from the Wirral

Borough Council are required to visit the main island, where there is a resident warden. Two smaller islands, Middle Eye and the tiny Little Eye, do not require permits. The latter is notable for its impressive number of wader roosts.

West Kirby is also the starting point for the **Wirral Way**, a 12-mile-long linear nature reserve and country park created mostly from the track bed of the old West Kirby to Hooton railway. When it was opened in 1973 it was one of the first Country Parks in Britain. The local council has also produced a series of circular walks based around the former stations along the line. One of these, **Hadlow Road Station**, a short distance from the centre of Willaston, is especially interesting. The station hasn't seen a train since 1962, but everything here is spick-and-span, the signal box and ticket office apparently ready for action, a trolley laden with milk churns waiting on the platform. Restored to appear as it would have been on a typical day in 1952, the station's booking office still has a pile of pre-decimal change at the ready, including sixpences, half-crowns and eight-sided threepenny pieces.

HESWALL

14 miles NW of Chester on the A540

Set on a steep hillside, Heswall was an important port before the silting up of the River Dee. After decades of decline, the town flourished again as a choice retreat for Liverpool commuters following the opening of the railway tunnel under the Mersey in 1888. If you take the road down to the beach from the town centre, there are outstanding views across the Dee estuary to the hills of Wales. Heswall's most famous son is the cricketer Ian Botham.

BRIMSTAGE

14 miles NW of Chester via M53 and A5137

Brimstage Hall

The most striking building in this tiny hamlet is **Brimstage Hall**, a medieval pele, or fortified tower. It's not known why such a tower, more appropriate to the lawless border regions, should have been built in peaceful Cheshire, nor when – estimates range from 1175 to 1350. A pile of human bones found at the bottom of a long-forgotten well in 1957 failed to resolve any of these questions. There is another puzzle too: could the stone carving of a smirking domestic cat in the old chapel be the original of Lewis Carroll's Cheshire Cat, which was wont to disappear leaving only its grin behind? Today, the old courtyard is home to a cluster of craft and speciality shops, and an excellent tearoom and restaurant.

THORNTON HOUGH

14 miles NW of Chester via the A540 & B5136

The huge village green at Thornton Hough, covering some 14 acres and surrounded by half-timbered black and white houses, was one of the most picturesque spots in Cheshire until it was relocated to Merseyside in 1974. The village boasts two churches, one of which has no fewer than five clocks – the fifth was installed by Joseph Hirst, a Yorkshire mill owner who also built houses here and wished to see a church clock from his bedroom window.

PARKGATE

12 miles NW of Chester via the A540 & B5134

John Wesley · George Frederick Handel

JMW Turner · Emma Hamilton

Mrs Fitzherbert

After Neston port became unusable, maritime traffic moved along the Dee Estuary to

Hilbre Islands

Distance: *5.0 miles (8.0 kilometres)*

Typical time: *120 mins*

Height gain: *25 metres*

Map: *Explorer 266*

Walk: *www.walkingworld.com ID: 1738*

Contributor: *Jim Grindle*

ACCESS INFORMATION:

Merseyrail to West Kirby Station. There is a large car park at the rear of the leisure centre next to the station.

DESCRIPTION:

The walk from West Kirby to Hilbre is not exacting, but can be done only if there is sufficient time between tides. It is also quite a bracing place to visit, so you need to wrap up warm on most occasions. The rewards are an open vista of the estuary and the nearby Welsh hills, seabirds and waders and grey Atlantic seals; highly recommended.

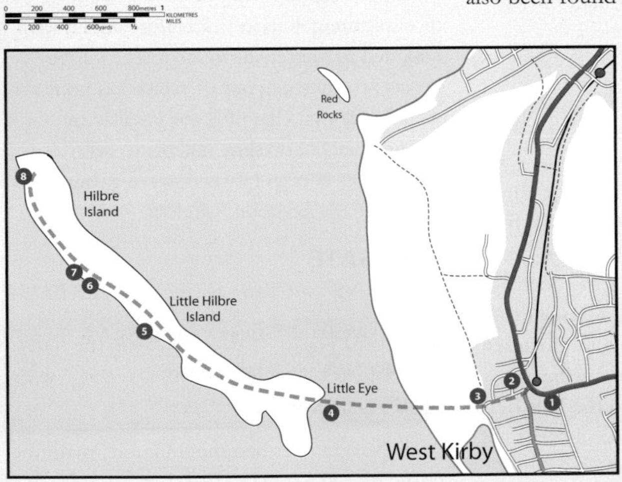

ADDITIONAL INFORMATION:

All the facilities are on the mainland; there are no toilets or café and very little shelter on the islands apart from a visitor centre. You can ring the Ranger Service for information about the tides on 0151 648 4371.

It is advised that you leave the islands three hours before high water. The three islands form part of the Dee Estuary SSSI which is one of the 10 most important estuaries in Europe for the overwintering of wildfowl and waders and as a resting place for other birds on migration. The bright red rock is Bunter sandstone, which also forms Thurstaston Hill on the mainland.

Many flint arrowheads and other artefacts from Neolithic times have been found on the islands, while a bronze axe-head and a burial urn show occupation during the Bronze Age. The Romans had a signal station here and there is written evidence of the Normans' presence. In 1864, a burial slab with four skeletons beneath was discovered, while a cross head dating from about 1000AD has also been found (you will find what looks like a grave carved out of the stone as you approach Waymark 8).

The Dean and Chapter of Chester Cathedral owned and leased out the islands for many years in a period when they were visited by passengers waiting to embark for Ireland. At that time there was a public house on Hilbre. Later still, there was a telegraph signal station and a lifeboat station.

FEATURES:

River, Sea, Pub, Toilets, Play Area, Church, Wildlife, Birds, Flowers, Great Views, Café, Gift Shop, Food Shop, Good for Kids, Mostly Flat, Public Transport, Nature Trail, Restaurant, Tea Shop.

WALK DIRECTIONS:

1 | Turn to the right outside the station and in a few moments you will see the ornate Barclays Bank building on the other side of the road. If unsure, ask anybody to direct you to Morrisons.

2 | Turn left here, pass Morrisons and you will come to the shore.

3 | Just to the left there are toilets and, more important, a notice board with good advice for anybody about to make the crossing. It is important that you follow the instructions. Do not attempt to go half-right directly to Hilbre, but go out at right angles towards the first, smaller island.

4 | This is Little Eye. Here you turn right and make for the next island.

5 | It isn't Hilbre though, but Middle Eye (or Little Hilbre). You can go around it on either side but it is much easier to climb onto it. There are some steps towards the left-hand side. Go the whole length of the island, climb down the easy rocks on the far side and make for Hilbre itself.

6 | Head for the left where you will find a ramp.

7 | Go up the ramp onto the island and walk the whole length, passing a number of buildings, including a visitor centre. At the far end are the remains of a lifeboat station, which is as far as you can go.

8 | The buildings ahead are the old lifeboat station. From here, retrace your steps back to West Kirby.

Parkgate, which, as the new gateway to Ireland, saw some notable visitors. **John Wesley,** who made regular trips to Ireland, preached here while waiting for a favourable wind, and **George Frederick Handel** returned via Parkgate after conducting the first public performance of *The Messiah* in Dublin. The great artist **JMW Turner** came to sketch the lovely view across to the Flintshire hills. A little later, Parkgate enjoyed a brief spell as a fashionable spa. Lord Nelson's mistress, **Emma Hamilton** (who was born about 1761 at nearby Ness where you can still see the family home, Swan Cottage), took the waters here in an effort to cure an unfortunate skin disease. The daughter of a poor labourer, and baptised Amy, she worked as a nurse girl in Hawarden and then in London, where her beauty captivated many famous men. In 1791 she married Sir William Hamilton, British Ambassador in Naples. She met Lord Nelson in 1793 and again in 1798, and bore him a child in 1801. Another visitor was **Mrs Fitzherbert**, already secretly married to the Prince Regent, later George IV. When Holyhead developed into the main gateway to Ireland, Parkgate's days as a port and watering-place were numbered. But with fine Georgian houses lining the promenade, this attractive little place still retains the atmosphere of a gracious spa town.

NESTON

11 miles NW of Chester off the A540

Right up until the early 19th century, Neston was the most significant town in the Wirral, one of a string of small ports along the River Dee. In Tudor times, Neston had been one of the main embarkation points for travellers to Ireland, but the silting up of the river was so swift and inexorable that by the time the New

GORDALE NURSERY AND GARDEN CENTRE

Chester High Road, Burton, South Wirral, Cheshire CH64 8TF
Tel: 0151 336 2116 Fax: 0151 336 8152
e-mail:admin@gardale.co.uk
website: www.gardale.co.uk

For more than 60 years, **Gordale Nursery and Garden Centre** has been a leader in its field. Attention to detail has put it head and shoulders above the rest, and owners Jill and Peter Nicholson never stop looking for ways to make a top-notch business even better. Superbly laid out in extensive purpose-built premises that cover 12 acres, the centre stocks everything connected with gardens - and a great deal more besides. Each department is run by a highly trained manager, some of whom have more than 20 years of service.

The range of plants for sale is second to none, with plants sourced from leading nurseries across Europe. Traditional roses, rhododendrons, azaleas, alpines, heathers, climbers, perennials, fruit and conifers stand alongside the increasingly fashionable tree ferns, bamboos, ferns, palms, citrus and grasses. Bedding and house plants are kept in climatically controlled greenhouses ensuring the best quality whatever the season. Staff are always at hand to provide advice. Birdbaths, sundials, traditional and modern sculptures from the stoneware department and wonderful pots all provide talking points for a garden.

The range of garden furniture and accessories is as wide as you'll find anywhere, with tables and chairs in wood, resin, metal and glass, indoor cane furniture for conservatories, sun loungers, side tables and footstools, parasols and cushions, garden lighting, gas and charcoal barbecues, and picnic ware in all styles. Other departments display books, clothes, speciality foods, ceramics, fresh and silk flowers, along with a huge selection of gifts for birthdays, weddings and other special occasions. Naturally, you'll also find the departments you would expect in a traditional garden centre - bulbs, seeds, composts, tools, garden care and watering equipment. There's also a 180-seat coffee shop, which is open throughout the day for coffee, tea, homemade cakes and light meals.

The children's play area, combined with the extensive landscaped grounds, wild fowl, ducks and peacocks make the centre a worthwhile day trip for the entire family, while its regular programme of promotional events, including an Orchid Weekend and the annual Fun Day, provide interest throughout the seasons. But it is at Christmas time that the centre takes on a magical quality. With regular demonstrations by leading florists, late-night shopping, Santa's Grotto and one of the best Christmas displays in the North West, Gordale has everything you need to complete your Christmas shopping, all under one roof.

Gordale Garden Centre's recent awards include Retail Outlet of the Year from the Horticultural Trades Association, Britain's Best Garden Centre from Pan Britannic Industries and Highly Commended in Britain's Best Retailer.

DOVECOTE NURSERIES

Station Road, Burton, Neston, South Wirral CH64 5SB
Tel: 0151 336 5748
e-mail: dovecote_nurseries@hotmail.com
website: www.dovecotenurseries.com

Dovecote Nurseries is a small, family-run plant nursery offering a wide range of plants, most of which are grown on site, as well as some sourced from elsewhere. Owners Neville and Linda Jones are especially proud of their perennials, grown entirely at the nursery, and providing probably the largest selection on offer on the Wirral. As it is a retail nursery, selling home-grown plants directly to the public, they are usually able to sell at prices below those of the larger garden centres.

It was back in the 1920s that Neville's grandfather bought the seven-acre plot when much of the Burton Manor Estate was sold off. Neville himself studied Botany at University, graduating with an honours degree in 1976. He later became a Glasshouse Supervisor at the famous Ness Gardens, leaving in 1982 to become self-employed. Initially he and Linda grew mainly bedding plants, they now grow and stock a large range of basket and patio plants, many of which are offered as plug plants. They still grow an extensive range of bedding plants, including all the popular lines such as impatiens, begonias and petunias, and also grow some of the more unusual varieties such as cosmos, coleus, cornflowers, cerinthe, rudbeckia and zinnia.

TRACEY'S FOOD HALL

10 Brook Street, Neston,
Cheshire CH64 9XL
Tel: 0151 353 1465

Tracey's Food Hall has had experience in farming since 1951 and are Master Butchers offering an extremely high standard of quality local meats and delicatessen products. The Hall has its own farm in Burton, which provides the meat for its butchers. They will prepare a cut as you wish, and take time to discuss everything from the making of their sausages to the finer points of roasting a joint of beef. Owner Tracey makes sure that they have both the knowledge of their products that you would expect and the personality - "No long faces behind the counter at Tracey's!" she says. "And we all act as an informal tasting panel for the meats and pies that we offer". If you order a hot or cold sandwich, it will be prepared in front of you - the bread itself comes from a local baker. In addition to sandwiches, the deli offers salad or pasta boxes, jacket potatoes, quiches, sausage rolls, cooked chickens, Scotch eggs, savoury ducks and much more. Also available is a selection of homemade cheeses from a local Shropshire farm. The Food Hall is open from 8am to 5pm, Monday to Friday, and from 8am to 2pm on Saturday.

CHOLMONDELEY CASTLE FARM SHOP

Cholmondeley, Malpas, Cheshire SY14 8AQ
Tel: 01829 720201
Fax: 01829 720891

Owned by the Cholmondeley Estate whose magnificent gardens are world-famous, the **Cholmondeley Castle Farm Shop** stocks many products from the estate's own farm. There's beef from the long-horned cattle, pork from the Gloucester Old Spot pigs, as well as seasonal fresh vegetables grown in the Cholmondeley walled garden. "My customers shop here as they can buy quality local products that aren't available in the supermarkets," says manageress Terina Bailey. "They recognise that here all our products are really fresh and the flavour of the meat and vegetables farmed on the estate is worth the shopping trip." The farm shop also has a vital role to play in helping to sustain the local rural economy by stocking locally produced specialities, ranging from sausages to bread, and from fudge to wines. The farm shop also fulfils another important role in rural life by having a Post Office counter. The shop and Post Office are open from 8am to 6pm, Monday to Friday, from 8am to 12.30pm on Saturday; and the farm shop only is also open on Sunday from 9am to 4pm.

THE CHOLMONDELEY ARMS

Cholmondeley, Malpas, Cheshire, SY14 8HN
Tel: 01829 720300 Fax: 01829 720123

A Village School until 1982, **The Cholmondeley Arms** was elegantly converted in 1988 into one of the truly exceptional pubs in the country. Set in quiet Cheshire countryside adjacent to the parks and gardens of the historic Cholmondeley Castle, The Cholmondeley Arms offers award-winning homemade food from an expansive daily menu, as well as comfortable accommodation, all situated in the peaceful environment of South Cheshire. We use fresh local produce wherever possible and Carolyn Ross-Lowe and her team of chefs take great pride in their work.

This has been borne out over the years by our number of local and national awards such as National Dining Pub of The Year in 1996. You are promised a truly exceptional dining experience here and are sure to return.

Quay, begun in 1545, was completed, it had become useless. Visiting Neston in the late 1700s, Anna Seward described the little town set on a hill overlooking the Dee estuary as "a nest from the storm of the ocean".

The Welsh Borders

Awake or asleep, the medieval Lords of the Marches made sure their swords were close at hand. At any time, a band of wild-haired Welshmen might rush down from the hills to attack the hated Normans who had dispossessed them of their land. A thousand years earlier, their enemies had been the Romans and the centuries-old struggle along the Marches only ended when one of their own people, Henry Tudor, defeated Richard III in 1485 and ascended the throne as Henry VII.

Conflict was to flare up again during the Civil War when the Welsh supported the Royalist forces against mainly Parliamentary Cheshire, but nowadays the valley of the Dee is a peaceful and picturesque area, and nowhere more so than around Farndon on the Denbighshire border.

FARNDON

7 miles S of Chester off the B5130

John Speed · Stretton Watermill

Built on a hillside overlooking the River Dee, Farndon is literally a stone's throw from Wales. Most travellers agree that the best approach to the principality is by way of this little town and its ancient bridge. Records show that building of the bridge began in 1345, and it is one of only two surviving medieval bridges in the county, the other being in Chester. From Farndon's bridge, riverside walks by the Dee extend almost up to its partner in Chester. During the Civil War, Farndon's strategic position between Royalist North Wales and Parliamentarian Cheshire led to many skirmishes here. Those stirring events are colourfully depicted in a stained glass window in the church, although only the Royalist heroes are included.

One Farndon man who deserves a memorial of some kind but doesn't have one, is **John Speed**, the renowned cartographer, who was born here in 1542. He followed his father's trade as a tailor, married, had 18 children and was nearly 50 before he was able to devote himself full time to researching and producing his beautifully drawn maps. Fortunately, he lived to the age of 87 and his 54 maps of England and Wales were the first really accurate ones to be published.

Close to Farndon, and well signposted from the A534, stands **Stretton Watermill**, a working corn mill in a lovely peaceful setting. Visitors see the two waterwheels driving the ancient wooden mill machinery and turning the millstones. The miller demonstrates the whole skilled operation to transform grain into flour. Also on the site are an exhibition, small shop and picnic area.

MALPAS

14 miles S of Chester on the B5069

St Oswald's Church

Cholmondeley Castle Garden

With its charming black and white cottages and elegant Georgian houses, Malpas is one of the most delightful old villages in Cheshire, though its Norman-French name implies that it once lay in difficult terrain – "mal passage". Of the Norman castle that once protected this hilltop border town only a grassy mound behind the red sandstone church survives.

Approached through 18th-century gates attributed to Vanbrugh, **St Oswald's Church** is lavishly decorated with a striking array of gargoyles, but is most notable for the splendour of its interior. The nave roof is brilliant with gilded bosses and winged angels, all created around 1480, and there are two magnificent chapels separated from the nave by delicately carved screens. The Brereton chapel dates from 1522 and contains an alabaster effigy of Sir Randal Brereton, in the armour of a medieval knight, together with his lady.

Across the aisle, the Cholmondeley chapel commemorates Sir Hugh Cholmondeley, who died in 1605. The Cholmondeley family owned huge estates around Malpas and it was they who built the town's attractive old almshouses and a school in the 18th century. They lived at Cholmondeley Castle, a few miles to the northeast. The Gothic-style castle is not open to the public but the 800 acres of **Cholmondeley Castle Garden** are. The gardens are planted with a variety of acid-loving plants including rhododendrons, hydrangeas, magnolias, camellias, dogwoods, mahonias and viburnums. There's a lovely Temple Garden with a rockery, lake and islands, and a Silver Garden planted with distinctive silver-leafed plants as a commemoration of Elizabeth II's Silver Jubilee. The paddocks are home to rare breeds of farm animals, including llamas and African pygmy goats.

Cheshire Peaks and Plains

To the east rise the Peak District hills, while westwards gently undulating pastures and woods drop down to the Cheshire Plain. This is an area of sudden and striking contrasts. Within half a mile you can find yourself travelling out of lowland Cheshire into some of the highest and wildest countryside - acres of lonely uplands with rugged gritstone crags, steep valleys watered by moorland streams. Here, too, is the old salt town of Middlewich, and Sandbach with its famous Saxon crosses, along with a host of quiet, attractive villages. The two major towns of South Cheshire are Nantwich, with a history stretching back beyond Roman times, and Crewe, with no history at all until 1837. That was when the Grand Junction Railway arrived and five years later moved all its construction and repair workshops to what had been a greenfield site.

Cholmondeley Castle Garden

Congleton

The Bridestones | Town Hall
Congleton Museum | Lion & Swan Hotel
Congleton Park

Some residents have dubbed this thriving old market town the 'Venice of the North' because of the number of nearby man-made lakes such as Astbury Mere and Brereton Country Park, both of which offer a wide range of recreational activities. Set in the foothills of the Pennines, Congleton was an inhabited place as long ago as the Stone Age. The remains of a 5000-year-old chambered tomb known as **The Bridestones** can be seen beside the hill road running eastwards from the town.

In Elizabethan times, the townspeople of Congleton seem to have had a passion for bear-baiting. On one occasion, when the town bear died they handed 16 shillings (80p) to the Bear Warden to acquire another beast. The money had originally been collected to buy a town bible: the disgraceful misappropriation of funds gave rise to the ditty: *Congleton rare, Congleton rare, sold the bible to buy a bear.* Known locally as the 'Bear Town', Congleton was the very last town in England to outlaw bear-baiting - the town's emblem is still an upright chained bear.

Congleton's impressive **Town Hall**, built in the Venetian Gothic style in 1864, contains some interesting exhibits recalling the town's long history, including some fine civic regalia. **Congleton Museum** has displays recording the work of such ancient civic officials as the swine-catcher, the chimney-looker and the ale-taster. Another display concerns an aid to domestic harmony called the 'brank' – a bridle for nagging wives, which the town jailer would activate for a small fee. A metal framework was fitted over the 'victim's' head and a metal tongue acted as a gag, making speech almost impossible. Other exhibits include a prehistoric log boat found in 1923 at Ciss Green near Astbury, prehistoric tools and pottery, coin hoards and cannonballs from the Civil War, and more recent acquisitions covering the Industrial Revolution and the World War Two. Congleton did not play a big part in the Civil War (due in part to an outbreak of the plague in 1641), but it was a

The Bridestones, Congleton

THE PLOUGH INN

Macclesfield Road, Eaton, Congleton,
Cheshire CW12 2NH
Tel: 01260 280207
Fax: 01260 298458
e-mail: theploughinn@hotmail.co.uk
website: www.ploughateaton.com

The Plough at Eaton has a long history going back to the 1600s when it was built as a coaching inn. In those days, the beer used to be brought up from the cellar in large jugs and served to travellers in the lamp-lit bar and cosy snug. The inn has been modernised in recent years but the ancient oak beams, small alcoves and blazing open hearth fires are still in place and make this a cosy, intimate place for a quiet drink or a meal. Food is also served in the Old Barn Restaurant which is full of character with its gallery and wealth of exposed timbers. Although it looks as if it has always been here, the barn is originally from Wales where it watched over the Welsh hills for more than 300 years. It arrived at Eaton in hundreds of pieces rather like a huge jigsaw puzzle waiting to be assembled. Since its change of address the barn fulfils a new role as a luxurious restaurant rather than as a winter store for cattle feed.

As well as the popular menu, specials which change regularly, are served in both the non-smoking Old Barn and the pub. It includes traditional favourites such as steak & kidney pudding, and imaginative, original dishes created by the experienced team of chefs. All the dishes are freshly prepared from natural ingredients and served by attentive and helpful staff. In 2004, the restaurant was runner-up in *High Life* magazine's North West Restaurant of the Year Award; made its first entry into the *Good Pub Guide,* and received a four-Diamond rating from the RAC.

If you are planning to stay in this attractive corner of the county, close to the Peak National Park and historic attractions such as Gawsworth Hall, the Plough offers some impressive accommodation. In 1985, the garages at the rear of the pub were converted into eight double en suite rooms. The bedrooms were created by top London designer Michael Priest of Belgravia who also created the interior design for Raymond Blanc's Le Manoir aux Quat' Saisons and Inverlockie Castle. The bedrooms were inspired by traditional Royal Doulton china ranges and feature matching key fobs and door nameplates. A further nine rooms are currently nearing completion, all offering the same sumptuous comfort and some with disabled facilities.

The Plough is also licensed to hold civil ceremony marriages and its delightful garden provides a perfect setting for those all-important wedding photographs.

former mayor of Congleton, John Bradshaw, who was president of the court that condemned Charles I to death; his signature was the first, even before Cromwell's, on the death warrant.

One of the oldest buildings in Congleton is the **Lion and Swan Hotel**, a 16th-century coaching inn on the old Manchester to London route. This grand old building with its superb black and white half-timbered frontage has been fully restored to its Tudor glory, complete with a wealth of exposed dark oak beams and elaborately carved fireplaces, as well as the oldest window in town, dating from 1596. Another ancient hostelry is Ye Olde Kings Arms, whose pink-washed half-timbered frontage leans picturesquely to the left as if exhausted with the weight of years.

During the 18th century Congleton developed as an important textile town with many of its mills involved in silk manufacture, cotton spinning and ribbon weaving. In Mill Green, near the River Dane, part of the very first silk mill to operate in the town can still be seen. Nearby is the entrance to **Congleton Park**, a popular amenity with mature tree-lined avenues set beside the river. Within the park is the Jubilee Pavilion, built in 1887 to celebrate Queen Victoria's Golden Jubilee and now housing a café/bar and restaurant. Another Jubilee, that of Queen Elizabeth II in 1953, was marked by the creation of the Jubilee Gardens (or coronation gardens) to the designs of Edward Kemp.

In the Community Garden, a life-size bronze statue has recently been erected to commemorate Congleton's war hero, Sgt George Harold Eardley, who won the Victoria Cross while serving with the King's Shropshire Light Infantry in Holland in October 1944.

Around Congleton

ASTBURY

2 miles SW of Congleton on the A34

St Mary's · Little Moreton Hall · Mow Cop · Rode Hall

The pretty little village of Astbury, set around a triangular village green, was once more important than neighbouring Congleton, which is why it has a much older church, built between 1350 and 1540. Arguably the finest parish church in the county, **St Mary's** is famous for its lofty recessed spire (which rises from a tower almost detached from the nave) and the superb timberwork inside: a richly carved ceiling, intricate tracery on the rood screen, and a lovely Jacobean font cover.

Just three miles down the A34 is an even more remarkable building. Black and white half-timbered houses have almost become a symbol for the county of Cheshire and the most stunning example is undoubtedly **Little Moreton Hall** (National Trust), a 'wibbly

Little Moreton Hall, Astbury

wobbly' house, which provided a memorable location for Granada TV's adaptation of *The Adventures of Moll Flanders*. The only bricks to be seen are in the chimneys, and the hall's huge overhanging gables, slanting walls and great stretches of leaded windows create wonderfully complex patterns, all magically reflected in the moat. Ralph Moreton began construction in 1480 and the fabric of this magnificent house has changed little since the 16th century. A richly panelled Great Hall, parlour and chapel show off superb Elizabethan plaster and woodwork. Free guided tours give visitors a fascinating insight into Tudor life, and there's also a beautifully reconstructed Elizabethan knot garden with clipped box hedges, a period herb garden, a yew tunnel and an orchard planted with traditional trees of apple, pear, medlar and quince, which blossom in May.

About a mile south of Little Moreton Hall is the Rode Hall estate. It was an 18th-century owner of the estate, Randle Wilbraham, who built the famous folly of **Mow Cop** (now in the care of the National Trust) to enhance the view from his mansion. This mock ruin stands atop a rocky hill 1100 feet above sea level, just yards from the Staffordshire border. On a clear day, the views are fantastic: Alderley Edge to the north, the Pennines to the north-east, south to Cannock Chase and Shropshire, and westwards across Cheshire. **Rode Hall** itself, home of the Wilbraham family since 1669, is a fine early 18th-century mansion standing within grounds created by three of the most notable landscape designers. Humphry Repton drew up the plans for the landscape and Rood Pool in 1790, and between 1800 and 1810, John Webb constructed the Pool, a 40-acre lake, along with the terraced rock garden and grotto. In 1860 William Nesfield designed the formal garden, which remains much as he planned it to this day.

BIDDULPH

5 miles SE of Congleton on the A527

Biddulph Grange Gardens

Biddulph Grange Gardens are imaginatively divided into a series of enclosed areas bounded by massive rock structures, hedges, stumps, roots and moulded banks. A trail leads through a superb Chinese garden to an enchanting Scottish glen, while other areas reproduce the magic of Egypt or the tranquillity of rural America. The shop is packed with gardening books, Victorian plants, cards and quality souvenirs, and a pleasant tearoom serves local specialities and homemade cakes.

SANDBACH

6 miles W of Congleton on the A534, 1 mile SW from Junction 17 of the M6

Saxon Stone Crosses

Sandbach's former importance as a stopping place for coaches (both stage and motor) is evident in the attractive old half-timbered inns and houses, some of them thatched, which line the main street. Sandbach's handsome market square is dominated by its two famous **Saxon Stone Crosses**, 16 and 11 feet tall. These superbly carved crosses (actually only the shafts have survived) were created some time in the 9th century, and the striking scenes are believed to represent the conversion of Mercia to Christianity during the reign of King Penda. A plaque at their base notes that they were restored in 1816 "after destruction by iconoclasts" – namely the Puritans. The restorers had to recover fragments from here and there: some had been used as street paving, some as cottage steps and some in the

walls of a well. Somehow they fitted the broken stones together, like pieces of a jigsaw, and the result is immensely impressive.

HOLMES CHAPEL

5 miles NW of Congleton on the A50/A54

Brereton Heath Country Park

In the mid-18th century, the little village of Holmes Chapel was stirred by two important events. In 1738, John Wesley came and preached outside St Luke's Church. Fifteen years later, on July 10th 1753, a disastrous fire swept through the village. When the flames were finally quenched, only two buildings had survived the blaze: St Luke's Church and The Old Red Lion alongside.

About three miles southeast of Holmes Chapel, **Brereton Heath Country Park** is a popular beauty spot where the heath land and flower meadows are criss-crossed by a network of many footpaths. The former sand quarry provides a congenial habitat for a range of species, details of which can be obtained from the park ranger at the visitor centre. The lake here is used for angling, canoeing and windsurfing.

GOOSTREY

7 miles NW of Congleton on a minor road off the A50/A535

Goostrey Arts Festival

The village of Goostrey is a quiet little place on a minor road just north of Holmes Chapel but famous for its annual gooseberry shows where competitors vie to produce the plumpest berries. The name of the village actually has nothing to do with gooseberries but derives from a personal name, Godhere, and the Saxon word for tree.

Goostrey Arts Festival, which has been affectionately dubbed Goosfest, is a week-long series of events held in October. Involving both professional and amateur practitioners, the festival embraces stand-up comedy, classical, folk or contemporary music, poetry, paintings, photography, pottery and sculpture.

LOWER WITHINGTON

7 miles NW of Congleton on the B5392 (off the A34)

Jodrell Bank

Visible from miles around, the huge white dish of the world famous **Jodrell Bank** (see panel on page 302) radio telescope has a good claim to being the most distinctive building in the county. The Observatory came into service in 1957 and was used by both the Americans and the Soviets in their exploration of space. Jodrell Bank offers visitors a fascinating guide to exploration of the universe with its 3D theatre and exhibition

Jodrell Bank Science Centre & Arboretum

Jodrell Bank, Lower Withington,
Macclesfield, Cheshire SK11 9DL
Tel: 01477 571339
e-mail: linda.bennett@manchester.ac.uk

Jodrell Bank Science Centre is home to the third largest radio telescope in the world, the Lovell Radio Telescope. Take a walk around the base of the telescope on the Observation Pathway with exhibition panels about the work of the telescopes. See the changing seasons in the 35-acre arboretum, with National Collections of Malus and Sorbus. Tour the Solar System or take a Journey to Mars in the 3D Theatre and, when you return to Earth, why not try some of the delicious homecooked food in the café. The shop is full of unusual gifts and souvenirs. In the grounds you will find whispering dishes and picnic areas.

centre. Operated by Manchester University, the telescopes allow astronomers to watch the birth and death of stars, new planets outside our solar system, super-massive black holes at the heart of other galaxies, and trace the origin of the universe in the Big Bang.

Outside, there's a superb 35-acre arboretum planted with 2000 species of trees and shrubs, each one helpfully labelled, and an Environment Discovery Centre, which explains the importance of trees to the natural environment. The site also contains a picnic area, play area, café and shop. A recent addition is an Observational Pathway stretching around the Telescope.

MIDDLEWICH

10 miles W of Congleton on the A54, 2 miles W of Junction 18 of the M6

- Roman Middlewich Trail
- Middlewich Boat & Folk Festival
- St Michael's Church

A bustling market town with good motorway links, Middlewich has doubled its population in the last 30-odd years. The Romans called their settlement here Salinae, meaning saltworks. Excavations have revealed outlines of their long, narrow, timber workshops, brine pits and even a jar with the word AMYRCA scratched on it (Amurca was the Latin name for brine waste, which was used throughout the Empire as a cleansing agent). Middlewich Town Council publishes an informative leaflet detailing the **Roman Middlewich Trail**, a one-mile circular walk that reveals the history and layout of the Roman town and shows how Middlewich would have looked in those days.

In more recent times it was the need for Cheshire's salt manufacturers to get their cumbersome product to markets in the Midlands and the south that gave a great impetus to the building of canals in the county. Middlewich was particularly well provided for with its own Middlewich Branch Canal linking the town to both the Shropshire Union and the Trent and Mersey Canals. Today, most of the canal traffic comprises traditional narrow boats, some of which can be hired for holiday trips. The **Middlewich Folk and Boat Festival**,

TEMPTATIONS

66-68 Wheelock Street, Middlewich, Cheshire CW10 9AB
Tel: 01606 832472

Established some 30 years ago, **Temptations** is a family-owned card and gift shop offering an enticing choice of gifts to suit a variety of tastes and interests. It's not so much an Aladdin's Cave, as a labyrinth of caves with 14 different rooms extending over two levels. Many brands well-known in the industry are represented in these rooms, including Jellycat, Russ Berrie, Born to Play, Hallmark, Toy Workshop, Bomb Cosmetics, Yankee Candles, Minichamps models and many more. One room is dedicated to the famous grey bear 'Me to You' by Carte Blanche and includes the majority of their gifts, ceramics and cards. There's also a fresh flower room, a chocolate and sweets room, a toy room and, the jewel in Temptation's crown, three rooms on the second floor bursting with models and motor-sport memorabilia. Many of the models and other items in this department have been signed by some of motor-sports greatest legends. Temptations is located in the heart of Cheshire, close to Oulton Park, Jodrell Bank, the Anderton Boat Lift and Tatton Park.

held in June each year, is now firmly established on the folk circuit and it is estimated that 30,000 people visit the town during the festival weekend, along with 400 boats.

During the Civil War, Middlewich witnessed two of the bloodiest battles fought in the county. In March 1644, Royalists trapped Cromwell's men in the narrow lanes and alleys of the town and slaughtered 200 of them. A few managed to find refuge in **St Michael's Church**. The church has changed greatly since those days, but still has some notable old carvings and a curiosity in the form of a carved coat of arms of the Kinderton family of nearby Kinderton Hall. Their crest shows a dragon eating a child, a reference to the occasion on which Baron Kinderton killed a local dragon as it was devouring a child. The incident apparently took place at Moston, near Sandbach, and a lane there is still called Dragon Lane.

Crewe

Queens Park · The Railway Age

Lyceum Theatre

Lakemore Country Park Animal Kingdom

Sandbach Flashes · Winterley Pool

In 1837 the Grand Junction Railway arrived, and five years later moved all its construction and repair workshops to what had been a greenfield site. A workforce of 900 had to be housed so the company rapidly built cottages, each one shared by four of the lowest paid workers, and detached 'mansions', which accommodated four families of the more highly skilled. At one time, seven out of every

10 men in Crewe worked on the railways.

Later, in 1887, the railway company also provided the town with one of the most splendid parks in the north of England, **Queens Park**, some 40 acres of lawns and flowerbeds, together with an ornamental lake. Between 1946 and 2002, Rolls-Royce's engineering works brought further prosperity, but it is as a railway centre that Crewe is best known. Its railway station, about a mile from the town centre, is still one of the largest in the northwest with 12 platforms in use. **The Railway Age** museum offers a fascinating insight into Crewe's place in railway history with hands-on exhibits, steam locomotive rides, model railway displays and a children's playground. Also worth a visit is the **Lyceum Theatre**, built in 1902 and with its glorious Edwardian opulence undimmed.

A couple of miles north of Crewe, **Lakemore Country Park Animal Kingdom** is home to a wide variety of animals – wallabies, llamas, miniature donkeys, owls and many other unusual and rare breeds. Children can feed the farm animals, visit the pets corner and enjoy both the indoor and outdoor play areas. Within the 36-acre site are five fishing lakes and a log cabin coffee shop. A pleasant country walk using footpaths, towpaths and old drovers' roads starts at Moss Bridge, on the western outskirts, and takes in **Sandbach Flashes**, one of the best places for birdwatching in Cheshire. Waders and wildfowl gather in large numbers in winter, attracting predators such as merlin and sparrowhawks, and the salty conditions resulting from the local industry are ideal for plants usually only found in coastal areas, such as sea club-rush, lesser sea-spurrey and sea aster. Further along the walk, **Winterley Pool** is a refuge favoured by mute swans. Nearby Haslington Hall (private), a fine black and white Tudor house, was built by Admiral Sir Francis Vernon in 1545. Sir Francis had the task of dismantling ships from the Spanish Armada and some say that timbers from these ships were used in later extensions to the hall. Later, the hall became the home of Mrs Watts, the founder and first President of the Women's Institute.

Nantwich

- Elizabeth I · Churche's Mansion
- Cathedral of South Cheshire
- Rev Joseph Priestley · Nantwich Museum
- Stapeley Water Gardens
- Bridgemere Garden World
- Hack Green Secret Nuclear Bunker

Several disasters have befallen Nantwich down the centuries. In the 11th century the town was totally destroyed except for a single building. King Henry III ordered the destruction to prevent the Welsh using the town as a base and also exploiting the amenity of the salt spring. The most disastrous event fully recorded was the Great Fire of 1583, which consumed some 600 of the town's thatched and timber-framed buildings. Fanned by constant winds, the blaze raged for 20 days and the fire-fighting operations were more than somewhat hampered by the escape of four bears from their cage in the town's bear pit behind the Crown Hotel. (Four bears from Nantwich are mentioned in Shakespeare's comedy *The Merry Wives of Windsor*.) **Elizabeth I** contributed the huge sum of £1000 to the cost of rebuilding and ordered her Privy Council to arrange collections throughout the land to augment the funds; she also donated quantities of timber from

Delamere Forest to assist in the building work. A grateful citizen, a builder by the name of Thomas Cleese, commemorated this royal largesse with a plaque on his new house at No 41 High Street. The plaque is still in place and reads:

God grant our ryal Queen in England
longe to raign
For she hath put her helping hand
to bild this towne again.

The most striking of the buildings to survive the conflagration, perhaps because it was surrounded by a moat, is the lovely black and white house in Hospital Street known as **Churche's Mansion** after the merchant Richard Churche, who built it in 1577. Astonishingly, when the house was up for sale in 1930, no buyer showed any interest and the building was on the point of being transported brick by brick to America when a public-spirited local doctor stepped in and rescued it. The ground floor is now an antiques centre.

The Great Fire also spared the stone-built 14th-century church. This fine building, with an unusual octagonal tower, is sometimes called the **Cathedral of South Cheshire** and dates from the period of the town's greatest prosperity as a salt town and trading centre. Of exceptional interest are the magnificent chancel and the wonderful carvings in the choir. On the misericords (tip-up seats) are mermaids, foxes (some dressed as monks in a sharp dig at priests), pigs, and the legendary Wyvern, half-dragon, half-bird, whose name is linked with the River Weaver, 'wyvern' being an old pronunciation of Weaver. An ancient tale about the building of the church tells of an old woman who brought ale and food each day from a local inn to the masons working on the site. The masons discovered that the woman was cheating them by keeping back some of the money they put 'in the pot' for their refreshment. They took revenge by making a stone carving showing the old woman being carried away by Old Nick himself, her hand still stuck in a pot. A plaque in the church remembers the **Rev Joseph Priestley** (1733-1804), who was a minister here. A writer on education, philosophy, government and science, he is best known today as the discoverer of oxygen.

During the Civil War, Nantwich was the only town in Cheshire to support Cromwell's Parliamentary army. The town was frequently besieged by Royalist troops, and after a particularly long siege the Royalist forces, under Lord Byron, were finally defeated on 25th January 1644. The people of Nantwich celebrated by wearing sprigs of holly in their hair and hats, and the day became known as

Nantwich Museum

'Holly Holy Day'; every year, on the Saturday closest to January 25th, the town welcomes Cromwellian pikemen and battle scenes are re-enacted by members of the Sealed Knot. There are records of the Civil War in the **Nantwich Museum** in Pillory Street, which also has exhibitions about the town and its dairy and cheese-making industries.

Just before Nantwich Lake, on the edge of town, is a memorial linked with a later war. First Lieutenant Arthur L Brown, an American pilot, crashed here in 1944, staying with his blazing Thunderbolt fighter to avoid coming down on the town.

It was salt that had once made Nantwich second only in importance to Chester in the county. The Romans had mined salt here for their garrisons at Chester and Stoke where the soldiers received part of their wages in 'sal', or salt. The payment was called a 'salarium', hence the modern word salary. Nantwich remained a salt-producing town right up to the 18th century, but then it was overtaken by towns like Northwich, which enjoyed better communications on the canal system. But a brine spring still supplies Nantwich's outdoor swimming pool.

Within a few miles of the town are two notable gardens. A mile south, off the A51, is **Stapeley Water Gardens** (see panel below), which attracts nearly 1.5 million visitors each year. The 64-acre site includes the National

Stapeley Water Gardens

London Road, Stapeley, Nantwich,
Cheshire CW5 7LH
Tel: 01270 623868
e-mail: stapeleywg@btinternet.com

Located just south of Nantwich and set within 64 acres, **Stapeley Water Gardens** makes a great day out. It has become the world's leading and largest water garden centre and is a delight to wander around. The ponds and the small lake here are filled with an enormous variety of water lillies, which bloom at their best during the summer months. A range of water fountains accompany them. Everything you could possibly need for your own garden can be found here and experts are on hand to assist.

The Palms is an indoor tropical oasis with exotic flowers, lush foliage and stately palms. Catfish lurk beneath the leaves of the Giant Amazon water lily and Giant Gouramis swim amid the coral reef, whilst, in the Zoo Room you will find macaws, tarantulas and tamarins. There is a changing exhibition of photographs, paintings and poster graphics on wildlife and nature to be enjoyed, along with video and slide shows.

Stapeley is also a paradise for anglers with a vast selection of rods, poles and seatboxes - indeed everything the fisherman could want.

The garden centre is full of products for the home and garden, but be sure to visit the Idea Display Garden created in conjunction with *Garden Answers* magazine. In addition, there are a further two gift shops and a superb restaurant.

Collection of Nymphaea (more than 350 varieties of water lilies), a comprehensively equipped garden centre, an angling centre, a pet centre, a restaurant, two cafés and a gift shop. In The Palms Tropical Oasis are a vibrant fountain and koi pool, blue and gold macaws and Amazon parrots. The Zoo room is home to a family of cotton top tamarin monkeys, water dragons, box tortoises, scorpions, tarantulas and a cayman crocodile. There are frogs of all kinds - poison arrow frogs, tree frogs, South American cane toads - in the World of Frogs, while in the tropical house piranhas, catfish and pacus are shaded by the enormous leaves of the Giant Amazon water lily. The stingray pool, the Tunnel of Underwater Life and the blacktip reef sharks are other attractions not to be missed at this brilliant family venue, which is open throughout the year.

About six miles further south along the A51, and straddling the Staffordshire border, **Bridgemere Garden World** provided the location for BBC TV's *Gardeners' Diary*. This is just one of 22 different gardens, among them a French rose garden, a woodland setting, a cottage garden and a rock and water area. The extensive glasshouses contain houseplants of every description and the garden centre is stocked with everything a gardener could possibly need. There's also an aquatics house with some splendid fish, a specialist food hall, a flower arrangers' centre, a bookshop, HobbyCraft arts and crafts shop, a restaurant and a coffee shop.

A few miles south of Nantwich, just off the A530 Whitchurch road, is **Hack Green Secret Nuclear Bunker**. For 50 years this vast underground complex remained secret, built as the centre of regional government in the case of a nuclear war, but it was declassified in 1993 and is now a unique attraction open to the public. Visitors pass through the massive blast doors into the chilling world of the Cold War, including the Minister of State's office, life support area, communications centre and decontamination facilities. Cinemas show once secret films, and children can have fun as secret agents, following the Soviet Spy Mouse Trail. A trip can end with a visit to the bunker's NAAFI-style canteen to pick up survival rations, and a browse through the shop for a souvenir.

Around Nantwich

BEESTON

8 miles NW of Nantwich on a minor road off the A49

Beeston Castle Peckforton Castle

A craggy cliff suddenly rising 500 feet from the Cheshire Plain, its summit crowned by the ruins of **Beeston Castle** (English Heritage), Beeston Hill is one of the most dramatic sights in the county. The castle was built around 1220 but didn't see any military action until the Civil War. On one rather ignominious occasion during that conflict, a Royalist captain and just eight musketeers managed to capture the mighty fortress and its garrison of 60 soldiers without firing a shot. A few years later, Cromwell ordered that the castle be 'slighted', or partially destroyed, but this 'Castle in the Air' is still very imposing with walls 30 feet high and a well 366 feet deep. An old legend asserts that Richard II tipped a hoard of coins, gold and jewels down the well, but no treasure has ever been discovered. The castle hill is a popular place for picnics, and it's worth climbing it just to enjoy the spectacular views that extend across seven counties and

Wybunbury

Distance: *3.0 miles (4.8 kilometres)*

Typical time: *90 mins*

Height gain: *0 metres*

Map: *Explorer 257*

Walk: *www.walkingworld.com ID: 370*

Contributor: *Robin and Christine Jones*

ACCESS INFORMATION:

Wybunbury is situated off the A500 Stoke to Nantwich road. Parking is available at the rear of the Swan Inn.

DESCRIPTION:

This is quite an intriguing walk, around Wybunbury Moss, which is a nature reserve set up to protect one of the best floating bogs in Europe. A word of warning - please keep to the paths as it is dangerous to enter the Moss. If you are lucky, as we were, on returning to the Tower you may get the conducted tour. Plenty to see in this, one of Cheshire's oldest villages.

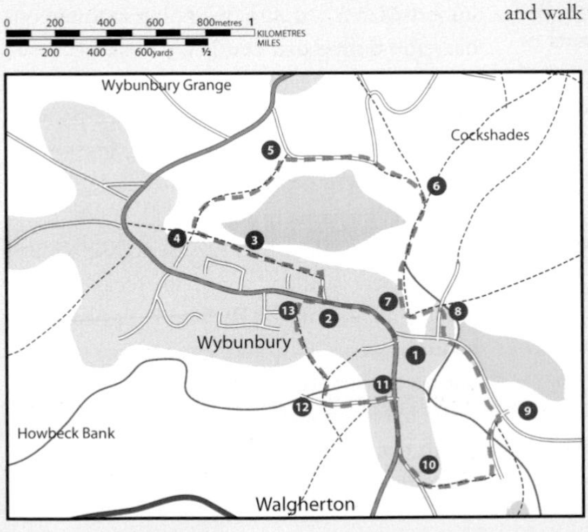

ADDITIONAL INFORMATION:

Please keep to the paths as it is DANGEROUS to enter the Moss. Wybunbury Moss consists of a thick bed of peat floating on water. The peat is covered by sphagnum moss and supports numerous rare bog plants including the insectivorous sundew and several very rare insect species. Wybunbury Tower was built in the 15th century. This is all that is left of the many churches built on this unstable site and eventually moved to a better one. The Tower had a lean but is now stabilised. The Moat is mentioned on the maps of the area and refers to two medieval moated houses, one built by the Bishop of Lichfield. Wybunbury is mentioned in the *Doomsday Book*; the oldest house is the Elizabethan cottage next door to the Swan Inn.

FEATURES:

Pub, Church, Wildlife, Birds, Flowers, Great Views

WALK DIRECTIONS:

1 | Leave the car park, turn right in front of the pub and walk up the main street.

2 | At Kiln Lane, turn right and walk down the drive. At the stile in the hedge, cross, turn left and walk along the field edge. Cross the stile and continue in the same direction. Cross the stile and enter the grounds of a large house. Keep straight ahead, aiming for the round flowerbed on the far side of the drive.

3 | Walk round the circular bed; the path is on the far side.

4 | At this junction of paths turn right to walk round the Moss. At this point take the left-hand gate and continue on the path.

5 | Join the road and continue ahead. As the road turns left, keep straight ahead into the grassy lane. Cross the stile and continue along the defined path, which follows the field edge.

6 | As the path turns to the right, follow it through the gate. Follow the path to the stile, cross it and turn right along the field edge. Cross the stile and follow the path now heading for the church tower. Follow the track leading up to a gate in the wall of the churchyard.

7 | Walk through the graveyard and through the gate at the foot of the tower. Go through the gate and turn left to follow the path round the tower. Go through this gate and descend the steps - take care, they can be slippery.

8 | When the path reaches the lane, turn left and walk along the road.

9 | At this farm drive on the right, turn right and follow the drive round to the left. Cross the stile on the right of the drive (I like it when there is no fence, just a stile). Now walk up the slope towards the hedge. Go over the stile and follow the grassy path up the hill to the next stile. Cross the stile and turn sharp right to follow the path along the field edge.

10 | Cross over the stile and go down a short "green lane" to the road. Go over the stile and turn right to walk down the road. At this junction take the right fork, heading back towards the church tower.

11 | At the lane junction, turn left and walk down the lane towards Brook House.

12 | Just before the gates to Brook House turn right over the stile and descend towards the stream. Cross the footbridge and follow the defined path up the hill over the next field. Go over the stile, ascend the steps and walk along the edge of the playing-field. Walk across the car park and up a short drive.

13 | On meeting the main road, turn right and walk back to the start and the car park.

over to a 'twin' castle. **Peckforton Castle** (private) looks just as medieval as Beeston, but was, in fact, built in 1844 for the first Lord Tollemache who spared no expense in re-creating features such as a vast Great Hall and a keep with towers 60 feet tall. The architect Gilbert Scott later praised Peckforton as "the very height of masquerading". Its authentic medieval appearance has made the castle a favourite location for film and television companies, as well as for conferences and weddings.

WILLASTON

2 miles E of Nantwich between the A534 and A500

World Worm Charming Championships

It was in the village of Willaston that one of the most unusual world records was established in 1980. Some 200 competitors had gathered at the Primary School here for the annual **World Worm Charming Championships**. The prize goes to whoever induces the greatest number of worms to poke their heads above a small patch of playing field aided only by a garden fork. Each contestant is allowed half an hour and the current world champion, Mr T Shufflebotham, charmed 511 out of the ground - a rate of more than 17 wrigglies a minute. The secret of his wonderful way with worms has never been revealed.

WYBUNBURY

5 miles S of Crewe on the B5071

St Chad's Church

Wybunbury Moss National Nature Reserve

South Cheshire's answer to the Leaning Tower of Pisa is the 100ft tower of **St Chad's Church** in Wybunbury. It was built in 1470 above an unsuspected ancient salt bed.

FULL MOON SILVER

Unit 13/14 The Arcade, Dagfields Craft & Antiques Centre,
Crewe Road, Walgherton, nr Nantwich, Cheshire CW5 7LG
Tel: 01270 842879
e-mail: fullmoonsilver@yahoo.co.uk

Part of the Dagfields Craft Centre in Walgherton, **Full Moon Silver** is owned and run by Marian Latham who lived in India and south-east Asia for many years. She realised that she could bring back to the UK many locally-made crafts and, by cutting out the middle man, offer them at reasonable prices. In her shop you will find many unusual silk fabrics and high grade stone along with unique pieces sourced from around the world.

GOLDFINGERS INTERIORS & GIFTWARE

No. 15 The Arcade, Dagfields Craft & Antiques Centre,
Crewe Road, Walgherton, nr Nantwich, Cheshire CW5 7LG
Tel: 01270 841323
e-mail: goldfingers@fsmail.net

Located in the rural Dagfields Crafts & Antiques centre three miles south of Nantwich, **Goldfingers Interiors & Giftware** is a classy shop whose owner has a flair for finding stylish and unusual giftware and occasional furniture. Her selection of beautifully designed table lamps has become well-known in the area. As the name suggests, there is a timeless touch of gold in most of the range. The very competitive prices along with a warm welcome will ensure a memorable visit to Goldfingers. It is open from 10am to 5pm, Wednesday to Sunday.

YUM

Unit 1, The Arcade, Dagfields Crafts & Antiques Centre,
Crewe Road, Walgherton, nr Nantwich, Cheshire CW5 7LG
Tel: 01270 842500

The owners of **Yum** pride themselves on a product range second to none. From their delicious handmade soaps to foot lotions and body butters, from shower gels and aromatherapy massage oils to moisturisers, Yum stocks only the finest products made from the finest ingredients - and none of them has been tested on animals. At any one time Yum will have around 30 varieties of soap and solid shampoos, 25 varieties of bath bombs, creamers and brulees, 25 types of mini-bombs and oodles of other sumptuous yummies.

The shop also stocks exquisite gift bags, baskets and wrappings. For an extra special gift, there's a wide selection of Yum's own 'yummy' gift sets, freshly prepared on site.

Subsidence has been the reason for the tower's long history of leaning sideways by as much as four feet and then being straightened up, most recently in 1989. Once given the title of 'The Hanging Steeple of Wimberie', it now rests on a reinforced concrete bed and is unlikely to deviate from the vertical again. The tower stands alone, surrounded by a graveyard: the body of the church, once capable of holding a congregation of 1600, collapsed on no fewer than five occasions. In 1972, the villagers finally decided to abandon it and build a new church on firmer ground. The tower is still used for bell ringing, with a fine set of bells rung on special occasions. In the fields near the church can be seen the remains of two medieval moated houses that were used as 'safe houses' for visiting clergy. In the 15th century the Bishop of Coventry leased two gardens to a hermit called Nicholas Baker on condition that they were kept only by fit priests or honest hermits.

A pleasant walk from the tower takes in **Wybunbury Moss National Nature Reserve**, where the mossland habitat is home to rare plants such as sundew, bog asphodel and bog rosemary. The boggy area at the western end of the Moss is what remains of the well that supplied the north end of the village in the Middle Ages. At one time Wybunbury Brook was a source of power for corn milling and iron production.

North West Cheshire

The north-western part of the county contains the pleasant rural area known as the Vale Royal, and the more industrial environs of Warrington and Runcorn. It was Prince Edward, later Edward I, who gave the area its name and who founded the great Abbey of Vale Royal in fulfilment of a solemn vow made in dramatic circumstances. He was returning from the Crusades when his ship was struck by a violent storm. The Prince made a pledge to the Virgin that if his life were spared he would found an Abbey for 100 monks. Lo! the ship was tossed ashore, and the Prince and his companions waded through the surf to safety. In 1277, Edward, now King and with his young wife Eleanor of Castile by his side, honoured his vow by placing the first stone of Vale Royal Abbey. "No monastery," he decreed, "shall be more royal than this one in liberties, wealth and honour, throughout the whole world." Vale Royal Abbey, about three miles south of Northwich, indeed became the largest and most powerful Cistercian Abbey in England, a building reputedly even more glorious than Tintern or Fountains. Unlike those abbeys, however, barely a stone of Vale Royal now remains in place. The abuse by the medieval Abbots of their vast wealth, and of their unfettered power of life and death over the inhabitants of the Vale, may partly explain why their magnificent building was so quickly and completely destroyed after Henry VIII's closure of the monasteries. Over the centuries, the county has lost many fine buildings unnecessarily, but the deliberate destruction of Vale Royal Abbey must take prime place in the litany of crimes against sublime architecture.

Northwich

Salt Museum

Dock Road EdwardianPumping Station

The Vale Royal is now a district borough centred on the old salt town of Northwich. Even before the Romans arrived, Cheshire salt was well known and highly valued. But

Anderton Boat Lift

production on a major scale at Northwich didn't begin until 1670 when rock salt was discovered in nearby Marston. Salt may seem an inoffensive sort of product, but its extraction from the keuper marl of the Cheshire Plain has produced some quite spectacular side-effects. In Elizabethan times, John Leland recorded that a hill at Combermere suddenly disappeared into underground workings, and Northwich later became notorious for the number of its buildings leaning at crazy angles because of subsidence. Even today, the White Lion Inn in Witton Street lies a complete storey lower than its original height. The arrival in the 19th century of new processes of extraction brought different problems. In 1873, John Brunner and Ludwig Mond set up their salt works at Winnington on the northern edge of the town to manufacture alkali products based on brine. The ammonia process involved cast an appalling stench over the town and devastated vegetation for miles around. On the other hand, Brunner and Mond were model employers: they paid their workforce well, built houses for them and were among the first firms in the country to give their employees annual holidays with pay.

The long involvement of Northwich and Cheshire with salt production is vividly recorded at the **Salt Museum**, the only one of its kind in Britain. It stands about half a mile south of the town centre in London Road (A533) and occupies what used to be the Northwich Workhouse. Like so many of those dreaded institutions, it is an exceptionally handsome late-Georgian building, designed by George Latham, the architect of Arley Hall. With its unique collection of traditional working tools, and displays that include working models and videos, the Salt Museum recounts the fascinating story of the county's oldest industry. One of the displays, 'Made from Salt' explores some of the 14,000 uses of salt, from mummies to polythene.

The Water Heritage Trail concentrates on the industrial archaeology and water heritage of Northwich, and takes visitors to docks, locks, bridges and warehouses. One of the highlights is the **Dock Road Edwardian Pumping Station**, a fully restored sewage pumping station where the noise and splendour of the working machinery create an atmosphere of power and tradition.

Around Northwich

ANDERTON

1 mile N of Northwich on minor road off the A533

Anderton Boat Lift · Anderton Nature Park

Marbury Country Park

One of the most stupendous engineering

feats of the canal age was the **Anderton Boat Lift**, built in 1875 and recently comprehensively restored. This extraordinary construction - known as the 'Cathedral of the Canals' - was designed by Edwin Clark to transfer boats from the Trent and Mersey Canal to the Weaver Navigation 50 feet below. Two barges would enter the upper tank, two the lower, and by pumping water out of the lower tank, the boats would exchange places. Thousands of visitors come every year to marvel at this impressive structure, and to take a trip through the lift on the *Edwin Clark*, converted from a maintenance craft that once worked on the Leeds and Liverpool Canal. Also here are an exhibition centre and operations centre. A six-mile circular trail - the Victorian Trail - visits the Boat Lift, the Lion Salt Works and Great Budworth, providing an insight into the area's industrial heritage and also into its rural character. For nature lovers, another trail runs through **Anderton Nature Park**. This wildflower trail introduces visitors to the varied plant life that thrives in the prevailing soil conditions (salt, lime, ash clinker), and markers along the trail show the best places to look for particular plants.

Marbury Country Park

About a mile north of Anderton, **Marbury Country Park** was formerly part of a large country estate, but the area is now managed by Cheshire County Council whose wardens have created a variety of habitats for plants, trees and animals. The Park lies at the edge of Budworth Mere and there are attractive walks and bridleways around the site, which also has an arboretum, picnic area and garden centre.

ANTROBUS

5 miles N of Northwich off the A559

Just a couple of miles from the magnificent Arley Hall and its world-famous gardens is the pleasing little village of Antrobus, the only place in Britain to bear this name. Even the *Oxford Dictionary of English Place Names* is baffled by Antrobus: "Unexplained" it says curtly, adding as its excuse, "Hardly English".

CROWTON

4 miles W of Northwich on the B5153

Crowton has many times been voted the Best Kept Village in Cheshire and its 18th-century hostelry, The Hare and Hounds, enjoys a particularly picturesque position in this appealing village.

ACTON BRIDGE

4 miles W of Northwich off the A49

Weaver Valley Way | Hazel Pear Trees

The bridge here crosses the River Weaver, a waterway whose scenic merits have been largely unsung. The Vale Royal Council has developed the **Weaver Valley Way**, which allows walkers to enjoy some lovely stretches, particularly those between Weaver Bridge and Saltersford Locks, and the six mile route from Northwich to Winsford Marina.

During World War One, Acton Bridge made an unusual contribution to the war effort. Near the village was a plantation of **hazel pear trees**, whose fruit is quite inedible but whose juice provided the khaki dye for soldiers' uniforms.

HATCHMERE

8 miles W of Northwich on the B5152

In medieval times the village of Hatchmere was surrounded by the Forest of Delamere, the largest of Cheshire's three major woodlands. It stretched from the Mersey to Nantwich, and although there were small areas of pasture and arable land, its status as a royal forest meant that the prime duty of those in charge of it was the preservation of the 'beasts of the chase'. It was not until 1812 that Delamere was officially 'disafforested' and today Delamere Forest covers little more than an area about two miles long and one mile deep. From Hatchmere attractive trails lead through the woods and around Hatch Mere, the sizeable lake that gives the village its name.

SANDIWAY

5 miles SW of Northwich on the A49

Cheshire Waterlife Aquatic and Falconry Centre

A popular attraction at Blakemere Craft

EDDISBURY FRUIT FARM

Yeld Lane, Kelsall, Cheshire CW6 0TE
Tel: 0845 094 1023 Fax: 0845 094 1024
e-mail: m.dykes@eddisbury.co.uk
website: www.eddisbury.co.uk

Located in the village of Kelsall in the glorious Cheshire countryside, **Eddisbury Fruit Farm** is a family-run business established in 1936 by Leslie Haworth who converted an old dairy farm into a viable fruit farm. After inheriting the farm in 1971, Colin Haworth ran the farm until 2001 when he went into joint partnership with his stepson, Michael Dykes. Along with growing a range of quality fruits and asparagues, the farm also produces Cheshire Apple Juice and Cheshire Cider, as well as homemade liqueurs made from the finest quality fruit, all lovingly grown on rich Cheshire soils and pressed and bottled at the farm.

In the past year the farm shop has been refurbished and is now able to offer customers an extensive range of local produce and speciality foods, along with seasonal fresh fruit and its own apple juice, cider and liqueurs. An even more recent addition is the tearoom offering customers a selection of tea, coffee, homemade cakes, soups, sandwiches, paninis and more. If the weather is being kind, you can also sit out in the sunshine and enjoy the rural scenery.

LITTLERS BUTCHERS

47-49 Mere Lane, Sandiway, Northwich, Cheshire CW8 2NR
Tel: 01606 883146
e-mail: littlersbutchers@aol.com

For almost 90 years, the people of Sandiway and around have been fortunate enough to have the services of an outstanding butchers within easy reach. **Littlers Butchers** was established in 1918, and ever since has maintained a distinguished record of providing high quality meats and outstanding customer service. In the spring of 2007, the shop had a major refit and is now looking very smart and stylish.

Their products consistently receive top awards - Gold for their Cumberland Sausages, for example, and silvers for their plain pork sausages, pork and leek sausages, and Lincolnshire pork sausages. Other products on sale here include beef and lamb, all of which comes from farms within a six-mile radius, and free range chicken and pork products. Littlers occupies a pleasant rural setting and there is car parking outside the shop. Attractions within easy reach include Beeston Castle, the Blakemore Craft Centre, Delamere Forest and the grand house and estate of Tatton Park, which is just 20 minutes drive away.

Centre on Chester Road is the **Cheshire Waterlife Aquatic and Falconry Centre**. Falconers fly several different species of birds of prey, supplying a running commentary on each bird, and visitors can also take a guided tour of the aviary complex - home to several species of rare owls - and take lessons in bird handling and falconry. The centre has a pets corner, with rabbits, guinea pigs, hamsters and caged birds, and also houses marine fish and invertebrates, koi carp and tropical fish.

CUDDINGTON

5 miles SW of Northwich off the A49

Whitegate Way

Cuddington is at the western end of the **Whitegate Way**, a pleasant rural walk of about five miles which, follows the trackbed of the old railway that used to carry salt from the Winsford mines. There is a picnic site and car park at the former Whitegate Station.

COTEBROOK

7 miles SW of Northwich on the A49

Cotebrook Shire Horse Centre

The **Cotebrook Shire Horse Centre** is home to the internationally renowned Cotebrook Shire Horse Stud. In addition to these mighty beasts, the Centre has miniature Shetland ponies, pigs, goats, ducks and hens, foxes, red deer, red squirrels and birds of prey. Open daily all year, the Centre also has a nature trail, picnic area and gift shop.

LITTLE BUDWORTH

7 miles SW of Northwich on a minor road off the A49 or A54

Little Budworth Common Country Park

Little Budworth Common Country Park is a pleasant area of heathland and woods, ideal for picnics and walking. The nearby village enjoys splendid views over Budworth Pool but will be better known to motor racing

THE CHASE

Long Lane, Wettenhall, nr Winsford, Cheshire CW7 4DN
Tel: 01270 528092 Fax: 01270 528449
e-mail: salharding@aol.com
website: www.bestofnantwich.co.uk

Whether you are a keen collector of antiques, or looking for a 'nice run out' head along the A51 towards Alpraham and just 2.7m off this road you'll find **The Chase.** Set in beautiful countryside, this is a superb place to visit. The Chase was established several years ago after BSE and then Foot and Mouth devastated the Harding family farm. Alison had previously worked in the antiques trade for seven years.

Whilst at home with her two daughters, Alison put a simple board at the end of her drive, advertising her antiques. This quickly brought two or three sales a week. Realising the potential on her doorstep, Alison set about turning the barn into a showroom, but realising that the space was far too big for her to fill on her own, she decided to invite other local dealers to rent space for the sale of their antiques. The barn is 'date lined', which means that everything in it is pre-1970s, so that people know exactly what they are buying. It is now filled with beautiful pieces of furniture, pottery, china and works of art.

Moving out of the date lined barn, you come across The Chase Gardeners' Corner, where beautiful hanging baskets, gifts, herbs and plants, including British wild flowers, are available. From here you enter the second barn, which was built by Tim himself. This superb building is packed to the rafters with a huge variety of goods displayed by 16 local dealers - and at great prices, too!

In another part of the barn is The Chase Farm Shop where the shelves groan with delicious gourmet foods that are just too tempting to pass by. A good range of produce is available, including fruit and vegetables sourced locally where possible. Patchwork pâté, Cartmel Sticky Toffee pudding, Cheshire Farm Icecream, local Butlers award winning cheeses and meat supplied by Burrows of Bunbury - a very good local butcher who sources all his meats locally, to name but a few.

You can enjoy tasty snacks, lunches, and daily specials in The Boot and Slipper. They provide a warm welcome, quality ales and excellent food. Alison and Tim's hope for the future is to build a small childrens petting farm, which will utilise the rest of the farm and the fields.

THE RED LION

Vicarage Lane, Little Budworth,
Cheshire CW6 9BY
Tel/Fax: 01829 760275
e-mail: theredlionlittlebud@tiscale.co.uk

The first landlord at **The Red Lion** served his first customer way back in in 1797; many others have succeeded him. One of them, Fanny Worsley, was landlady here for more than 40 years, from 1879 to 1921. The inn stands next to the parish church in the delightful village of Little Budworth and is now in the capable hands of landlady Julie Wardle, a friendly and welcoming host. It enjoys a great reputation for its traditional, freshly prepared home-cooked food with a menu that offers all the popular favourites like steaks or fish & chips along with a selection of vegetarian dishes and salads.

The well-kept ales include real brews such as Robinson's Unicorn. As well as the separate dining room, there's an open plan bar with a snug and open coal fire. This is a lively pub which supports no fewer than three bowls teams and has its own bowling green as well as a secluded beer garden for fair-weather days. A recent addition to The Red Lion's amenities was its quality accommodation – three comfortable guest bedrooms all attractively decorated and with en-suite facilities.

enthusiasts for Oulton Park racing circuit a mile or so to the south.

TARPORLEY

12 miles SW of Northwich on the A51/A49

In the days when most of this area was part of Delamere Forest, Tarporley was the headquarters of the verderers, or forest wardens. It was from Tarporley in the early 17th century that John Done, Chief Forester and Hereditary Bow-bearer of Delamere, entertained King James to a hunt. The chase was, he reported, a great success: *"deer, both red and fallow, fish and fowl, abounded in the meres".* A grateful king rewarded his host with a knighthood.

UTKINTON

10 miles SW of Northwich off the A49 or A51

During the Middle Ages, the verderers had their own courts in which they meted out rough justice to offenders against the forest laws. One such court was at Utkinton, and in an old farmhouse stands a column formed by an ancient forest tree, its roots still in the ground. When the court was in session, the wardens would place on this tree the symbol of their authority, the Hunting Horn of Delamere. The farmhouse is not open to the public but the horn, dating from around 1120, has survived and can be seen at the Grosvenor Museum in Chester.

WINSFORD

6 miles S of Northwich on the A54

Botton Flash

Winsford is another of the Cheshire salt towns that expanded greatly during the 19th century, swallowing up the old villages of

Over and Wharton on opposite banks of the River Weaver. Two legacies of those boom years should be mentioned. One is Christ Church, which was specifically designed so that it could be jacked up in the event of subsidence. The other is **Botton Flash**, a sizeable lake caused by subsidence but now a popular water recreation area for the town.

LACH DENNIS

4 miles SE of Northwich on the B5082

Shakerley Mere Nature Reserve

The small village of Lach Dennis derives its name from the Old English 'laecc', meaning a bog, and the Dennis family who once had an estate here. A mile or so to the east, **Shakerley Mere Nature Reserve** is host to a diverse range of wildlife with Canada Geese, herons, mute swans and mallards a common sight. Cormorants fly here from their breeding grounds on the coast to feast on the fish, and more exotic species arrive at different times of the year.

ASHTON

8 miles E of Chester on the B5393

Delamere Forest

A couple of miles to the northeast of Ashton stretch the 4000 acres of **Delamere Forest**, a rambler's delight with a wealth of lovely walks and many picnic sites, ideal for a peaceful family day out. In Norman times, a 'forest' was a part-wooded, part-open area, reserved as a hunting ground exclusively for royalty or the nobility. There were savage penalties for anyone harming the deer, even if the deer were destroying crops, and household dogs within the forest had to be deliberately lamed to ensure that they could not harass the beasts. By the early years of the 17th century many of the great oaks in the forest had already been felled to provide timber for ship-building – as well as for Cheshire's familiar black and white half-timbered houses. Since the early 1900s, Delamere Forest has been maintained by the Forestry Commission, which has undertaken an intensive programme of tree planting and woodland management. Delamere is now both an attractive recreational area and a working forest, with 90% of the trees eventually destined for the saw mills.

MARSTON

1 mile NE of Northwich on a minor road

Lion Salt Works Museum

In Victorian times, the Old Salt Mine at Marston was a huge tourist attraction. About 360 feet deep and covering 35 acres, it even brought the Tsar of Russia here in 1844. Ten thousand lamps illuminated the huge cavern as the Emperor sat down to dinner with eminent members of the Royal Society. By the end of the century, however, subsidence caused by the mine had made some 40 houses in the village uninhabitable, and one day in 1933 a hole 50 feet wide and 300 feet deep suddenly appeared close to the Trent and Mersey Canal. Happily, the village has now stabilised itself, and at the **Lion Salt Works Museum** volunteer workers keep alive the only surviving open pan salt works in Britain.

GREAT BUDWORTH

3 miles NE of Northwich off the A559

St Mary and All Saints Arley Hall & Gardens

Stockley Farm

A charming small village nowadays, 'Great' Budworth was accorded that designation at a time when it was the largest ecclesiastical parish in all Cheshire, the administrative centre for some 35 individual communities. The imposing church on the hill, built in the 14th and 15th centuries, reflects its importance during those years. **St Mary and All Saints** attracts many visitors to its host of quaint carvings and odd faces that peer out at unexpected corners: some with staring eyes, others with their tongues poking out. A man near the pulpit appears to be drowsing through some interminable sermon. Under the roof of the nave you'll find a man with a serpent, another in mid-somersault, and a minstrel playing bagpipes. The distinguished 17th-century historian, Sir Peter Leycester, is buried in the Lady Chapel, and the Warburton Chapel has a finely carved Tudor ceiling and 13th-century oak stalls – the oldest in Cheshire. During the 19th century, Great Budworth was part of the Arley Hall estate and it is largely due to the energetic Squire Egerton-Warburton, a conservationist well ahead of his time, that so many of the attractive old cottages in the village are still in place.

Cheshire can boast many grand houses and many fine gardens, but at **Arley Hall and Gardens** one of the grandest houses and one of the finest gardens are in perfect harmony. The present Hall was completed in 1845, a few years after Rowland Egerton-Warburton arrived at Arley with his new bride, Mary Brooke. The newly-married couple took possession of a dilapidated old mansion, infested with rats and with antiquated drains from which an unbearable stench drifted through the house. Understandably, Rowland and Mary soon demolished the old hall and in its place rose a sumptuous early-Victorian stately home complete with (bearing in mind those drains) such state-of-the-art innovations as 'Howden's Patent Atmospheric Air Dispensers'. Rowland and Mary were both ardent gardeners and it was they who master-minded the magnificent panoramas of today's Arley Gardens. Rowland is credited with creating what is believed to be the first herbaceous border in England; his descendant, the present Viscount Ashbrook, has continued that tradition by cultivating The Grove, an informal woodland garden planted with spring bulbs, flowering shrubs and exotic trees, a pleasing contrast to the more formal design of the main gardens.

Other attractions at Arley include a tearoom housed in a beautifully converted 16th-century barn, and a plant nursery offering a wide selection of herbaceous and other plants.

Also within the Arley estate, **Stockley Farm** is a 400-acre organic dairy farm that provides a great family day out. A visit begins with a tractor and trailer ride to the farm where there are always baby animals for children to handle and feed. Adult animals include an 18-hand shire horse, Star, a lovely big pig called Olive, and Kate, the Highland cow. There are miniature tractors to ride, pony rides, an adventure play area, a souvenir shop and a Country Café.

PICKMERE

6 miles NE of Northwich on the B5391

Pick Mere

The delightful village of Pickmere commands superb views of the Cheshire Plain, extending from the Dee estuary to the Pennine hills. The nearby **Pick Mere**, from which the village takes its name, is popular with wind surfers and yachtsmen, and boats are available for hire.

Warrington

Town Hall | Museum & Art Gallery

Mad Hatters Tea Party | River of Life

St Elphin's Church | Holy Trinity Church

Victoria Park

Lying at an important bridging point of the

River Mersey, Warrington claims to enjoy Britain's most convenient location. It stands midway between the huge conurbations and ports of Manchester and Liverpool, and on a pivotal point of communications close to where the M6, M62 and M56 motorways intersect, and where the West Coast main railway line links London and Scotland.

Warrington is North Cheshire's largest town – an important industrial centre since Georgian and Victorian times and with substantial buildings of those days to prove it. Its imposing **Town Hall** was formerly Lord Winmarleigh's country residence, built in 1750 with all the appropriate grandeur: windows framed in painfully expensive copper, and elaborately designed entrance gates 25 feet high and 54 feet wide. Along with its 13 acres of parkland, the hall provides a dignified focus for the town centre.

A major Victorian contribution to the town is its excellent **Museum and Art Gallery** in Bold Street, dating from 1857 and one of the earliest municipal museums. "An uncommonly dignified building" was how Pevsner described it. The exhibits are remarkably varied, among them are shrunken heads, a unique china teapot collection, a scold's bridle, Egyptian mummies, a Roman actor's mask and other Roman artefacts discovered in nearby Wilderspool. There are some fine paintings as well, most of which are Victorian watercolours and oils, and a rare Vanous still life. In the Golden Square is a large granite sculpture by Edwin Russell of the **Mad Hatters Tea Party**. This statue was unveiled by the Prince and Princess of Wales in 1984 and commemorates the area's connection with Lewis Carroll, who lived in nearby Daresbury. The **River of Life** in Bridge Street is a memorial to the victims of the 1993 terrorist bomb, which killed two young boys and injured dozens of citizens. Artist Stephen Broadbent worked with local children to design 12 bronze plaques, each with an inscription chosen by the children - self-control, joy, peace, forgiveness, encouragement, reconciliation, patience, justice, love, hope, friendship and faithfulness. There's more public art in Market Gate with its 10 Guardian Pillars and the Well of Light, while in nearby Horsemarket Street are some lively action fountains.

Also worth visiting is **St Elphin's Church** with the third highest spire in the country, a 14th-century chancel and memorials celebrating the Butler and Patten families. **Holy Trinity Church,** built in 1760, is a fine example of a typical 18th-century Georgian church complete with galleries and box pews. It also has an impressive chandelier rescued from the old House of Commons in 1801.

The town's premier leisure site is **Victoria Park**, purchased by the Corporation in 1897 and named to commemorate Queen Victoria's jubilee. The park is a good starting point for exploring the area, following the Mersey Way along the river or joining Black Bear Park and the Trans-Pennine Trail. An interesting curiosity at Bridge Foot nearby is a combined telephone kiosk and letter box. These were common in the early 1900s, but Warrington's is one of the few survivors.

Two well-known names associated with the town are the television presenter Chris Evans, who was born here, and the durable comedian and ukulele player George Formby, who is buried in the Catholic section of the town's cemetery.

Around Warrington

DARESBURY

5 miles SW of Warrington on the A558

Lewis Carroll

There has been a church at Daresbury since the 12th-century and the present church has many interesting features including 17th-century carvings, a 16th-century font and an 18th-century hair picture, a beautifully embroidered picture of the church sewn completely in human hair. The church also has a unique 'Green Man' and a Geoffrey Webb stained glass window in memory of **Lewis Carroll** who was born in the village in 1832 when his father was vicar here. The window depicts Lewis Carroll and many characters from *Alice in Wonderland*. The church is open daily from 9am to dusk and a small gift stall sells cards and souvenirs.

WIDNES

6 miles SW of Warrington on the A557

Spike Island Catalyst Science Discovery Centre

Described in the 1860s as "a quiet industrial village", Widnes now has a population of around 60,000. It stands on the north shore of the Mersey, linked to Runcorn by a remarkably elegant road bridge.

A popular attraction is **Spike Island**, which provides a landscaped walk from where the superstructures of ships passing along the Manchester Ship Canal can be seen gliding past. Widnes has a popular family attraction in the **Catalyst Science Discovery Centre**, where four galleries and more than 100 hands-on exhibits make sense of the world of science and technology.

RUNCORN

7 miles SW of Warrington on the A557

Norton Priory Museum and Gardens

Runcorn is one of Britain's best-known post-war new towns, developed around a much older town bearing the same name.

Norton Priory Museum and Gardens is always an delightful and intriguing destination for a family outing whatever the weather. Despite being located close to junction 11 of the M56, it lies in a peaceful oasis with 16 acres of beautiful woodland gardens running down to the Bridgewater Canal. The Augustinian priory was built in 1134 as a retreat for 12 'black canons', so called because they wore a cape of black woollen cloth over a white linen surplice. Recent work by the Norton Priory Museum Trust uncovered the remains of the church, chapter house, cloisters and dormitory. These finds are informatively explained in an audio-visual presentation in the museum. Also within the site are a sculpture trail, an award-winning Walled Garden, which contains the National Collection of tree quinces, a coffee shop, retail area and temporary exhibitions gallery. A programme of exciting events takes place throughout the year with something for everyone, from medieval festivals to 'make-your-own scarecrow' days.

Norton Priory, Runcorn

DUNHAM MASSEY

4 miles E of Lymm on B5160

Dunham Massey Hall and Park

Dunham Massey Hall and Park (National Trust) has 250 acres of parkland where fallow deer roam freely and noble trees planted in the late 1700s still flourish. A fully restored 17th-century sawmill can be seen in working action, and there are splendid walks in every direction. The Hall, once the home of the Earls of Stamford and Warrington, is a grand Georgian mansion of 1732 with an outstanding collection of furniture, paintings and Huguenot silver.

Dunham Massey Mill

LYMM

6 miles E of Warrington on the A56

During the stagecoach era, Eagle Brow was notorious, a dangerously steep road that dropped precipitously down the hillside into the village of Lymm. To bypass this hazard, a turnpike was built (now the A56), so preserving the heart of this ancient village with its half-timbered houses and well-preserved village stocks. The Bridgewater Canal flows past nearby and the church is reflected in the waters of Lymm Dam. Popular with anglers and birdwatchers, the dam is a large man-made lake, part of a lovely woodland centre linked to the surrounding countryside and the canal towpath by a network of footpaths and bridleways. The village became an important centre for the fustian cloth (corduroy) trade in the 19th century, but is now best known simply as a delightful place to visit.

Lymm stands on the sides of a ravine and its streets have actually been carved out of the sandstone rock. The same rock was used to construct Lymm's best-known landmark, the ancient cross crowned with a huge cupola that stands at the top of the High Street.

HELSBY

8 miles NE of Chester on the A56

There are seven Iron Age forts scattered across Cheshire, but only the one at Helsby, maintained by the National Trust, is open to the public. The climb out of the village along pretty woodland paths to the red sandstone summit is quite steep, but the views across the marshes to the Mersey Estuary and Liverpool repay the effort.

FRODSHAM

10 miles NE of Chester on the A56

Church of St Laurence Francis Gastrell

This is an attractive town with a broad main street lined with thatched cottages and substantial Georgian and Victorian houses.

During the 18th and early 19th centuries, Frodsham was an important coaching town and several fine coaching inns survive. Built in 1632, The Bear's Paw, with its three stone gables, recalls the bear-baiting that once took place nearby.

Of the Earl of Chester's Norman castle only fragments remain, but the **Church of St Laurence** (an earlier church here was recorded in the *Domesday Book*) is noted for the fine 17th-century panelling in its exquisite north chapel.

The vicar here from 1740 to 1756 was **Francis Gastrell,** a name that is anathema to all lovers of Shakespeare. Gastrell bought the poet's house, New Place, at Stratford and first incensed the townspeople by cutting down the famous mulberry tree. Then, in order to avoid paying the Corporation poor rate, he pulled the house itself down. The outraged citizens of Stratford hounded him from the town and he returned to the parish at Frodsham that he had neglected for years.

Knutsford

Elizabeth Gaskell   Richard Harding Watt

Penny Farthing Museum

Knutsford Heritage Centre

Knutsford and its people were the heroes of one of the most durable of Victorian novels, **Elizabeth Gaskell's** *Cranford.* This gently humorous, sympathetic but sharply-observed portrait of the little Cheshire town, and the foibles and pre-occupations of its citizens, was

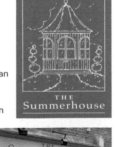

FIBRE + CLAY CRAFT GALLERY AND KNIT STUDIO

11-13 Minshull Street, Knutsford,
Cheshire, WA16 6HG
Tel: 01565 652035
website: www.fibreandclay.co.uk

Fibre + Clay is a very special and unique gallery and knit studio, all in one delightful shop in the heart of historic Knutsford. It's the creation of owners, Riana and Nigel Martin, born out of their passionate love for ceramic and textile arts.

Here you can view and buy pieces hand crafted by some of the leading designers and makers in their field, while upstairs is the knit studio, a warm and welcoming space where you'll find everything you need for your knit or crochet projects – exquisite yarns, patterns and accessories.

The Knit Studio is a space where lovers of knitting and crochet can browse at their leaisure through the latest designer patterns, see, feel and enjoy exquisite yarns from all the leading collections, join in with weekly informal knit gatherings, and learn new skills or revive rusty ones at our regular knit workshops.

The gallery space has an ever changing selection of pieces from leading designers, artists and makers in ceramics and textiles, as well as exciting work by new names. Some are useful, some purely beautiful or decorative, but each one has been chosen because it is unique.

first published in 1853 and is still delighting readers today. Elizabeth was scarcely a month old when she came to Knutsford. Her mother had died shortly after her birth and her father sent her here to be brought up by an aunt who lived in a road that has now been re-named Gaskell Avenue. The motherless child grew up to be both strikingly beautiful and exceptionally intelligent. Early on she evinced a lively interest in the town's characters and its history: she was intrigued, for example, to find that in the house next door to her aunt's had once lived a notorious highwayman, Edward Higgins, hanged for his crimes in 1767, and she wrote a story about him. Marriage to William Gaskell, a Unitarian pastor in Manchester, took her away from Knutsford, although she returned often and for long periods. She died in 1865 and was buried in the grounds of the Unitarian Chapel, where her husband and two of her four daughters also lie.

The Knutsford that Elizabeth Gaskell knew so well and wrote about so vividly has expanded a great deal since those days of course, but in its compact centre, now designated an outstanding area of conservation, the narrow streets and cobbled alleys still evoke the intimacy of a small Victorian town. Two parallel roads, Toft Street and King Street, form a rectangle surrounding the old town. But Mrs Gaskell would surely be astonished by the building erected in King Street to her memory by **Richard Harding Watt** in 1907. A gifted entrepreneur, Mr Watt had made a huge fortune in Manchester as a glove manufacturer, but what really aroused his enthusiasm was the flamboyant architecture he had seen during his travels through Spain, southern Italy and the Near East.

On his return, he spent lavishly on trying to transform Knutsford in Cheshire into Knutsford-on-the-Med. At the north end of the town, he built a laundry complete with Byzantine domes and a minaret. A vaguely Ottoman style of architecture welcomed serious-minded artisans to his Ruskin Reading Rooms. In Legh Road, he erected a series of villas whose south-facing frontages are clearly in need of a really hot sun. And in King Street, as homage to the town's most famous resident, Richard Watt spent thousands of Victorian pounds on the Gaskell Memorial Tower. This tall, blank-walled building seems a rather incongruous tribute to the author who was herself so open and so down-to-earth.

But it is eccentrics like Richard Watt who make English architecture as interesting as it is. He was so proud of his contribution to the town's new buildings that, travelling on his coach to the railway station, he would rise to his feet and raise his hat to salute them. As he did so, one day in 1913, his horse suddenly shied, the carriage overturned, and Richard Watt was thrown out and killed. What other changes he might have made to this grand old town, had he lived, we can only imagine.

An unusual exhibition and well worth visiting is the **Penny Farthing Museum**, located in the Courtyard Coffee House off King Street. These bizarre machines were in fashion for barely 20 years before the last model was manufactured in 1892. The collection includes a replica of the famous Starley Giant with a front wheel seven feet in diameter, and a sign outside the coffee house promises a free tea to anyone arriving on a penny-farthing.

Close by, in King Street, a striking sculpture by Philip Bews of a Green Man greets visitors to the volunteer-run **Knutsford Heritage Centre.** The Centre houses a permanent exhibition, with displays and a video on the story of Knutsford, detailing the town's famous names, areas, associations and periods. The Gallery Exhibition Centre, a separate building to the rear of the Centre, presents a changing array of exhibitions and events.

Knutsford is a town with a long history – Edward I granted the town a Charter in 1262, and at the same time a local landowner, William de Tabley, was given a money-making licence to control the market. The Heritage Centre is housed in a restored 17th-century timber-framed building which in Victorian times was a smithy. During the restoration the old forge and bellows were found in a remarkable state of preservation. The wrought-iron gate in front of the building was specially created for the Centre and depicts dancing girls taking part in Knutsford's famous Royal May Day celebrations – Royal because in 1887 the Prince and Princess of Wales honoured the festivities with their presence. Every May Day the town centre streets are closed to all traffic except for the May Queen's procession in which colourful characters such as Jack in Green, Highwayman Higgins and Lord Chamberlain, Morris dancers, maypole dancers and many others take part. One curious tradition whose origins are unknown, is the practice of covering the streets and pavements with ordinary sand and then, using white sand, creating elaborate patterns on top.

A colourful Knutsford character was Trumpet Major Smith, who sounded the Charge into the Valley of Death at the Battle of Balaclava. He is buried in the grounds of the Georgian parish church.

Around Knutsford

Tatton Park · Tudor Old Hall · Tabley House

Tabley Cuckoo Clock Collection

Sweeping up to the very edge of Knutsford are the grounds of **Tatton Park** (see panel below), 2000 acres of exquisite parkland landscaped in the 18th century by the celebrated Humphry Repton. This lovely park, where herds of red and fallow deer roam freely, provides a worthy setting for the noble Georgian mansion designed by the equally celebrated architect Samuel Wyatt. The combination of the two men's talents created a house and park that have become one of the National Trust's most visited attractions. Tatton's opulent state rooms, containing paintings by artists such as Canaletto and Van Dyck along with superb collections of porcelain and furniture, provided the television production of *Brideshead Revisited* with a sumptuous setting for Marchmain House.

More than 200 elegant pieces of furniture were commissioned from the celebrated cabinet-makers, Gillow of Lancaster. Particularly fine are the superb bookcases in the library, constructed to house the Egerton family's collection of more than 8,000 books. By contrast, the stark servants' rooms and cellars give a vivid idea of what life below stairs was really like.

The Egerton family built Tatton Park to replace the much earlier **Tudor Old Hall**, which nestles in a wood in the deer park and dates back to around 1520. Here, visitors are given a guided tour through time from the late Middle Ages up to the 1950s. Flickering light from candles reveals the ancient timber roof of the Great Hall, supported by ornate quatrefoils, while underfoot, the floor is strewn with rushes, providing a warm place for the medieval Lord of the Manor and his servants to sleep.

There's much more to see at Tatton Park: Home Farm is a working farm, working as it did in the 1930s, complete with vintage machinery. Traditional crafts (including pottery), stables and many farm animals provide a complete picture of rural life some 60 years ago. Tatton's famous gardens include a Victorian maze, an orangery and fernery, a serene Japanese garden, American redwoods, and a splendid Italian terraced garden. There's

Tatton Park

Tatton Park, Knutsford, Cheshire WA16 6QN
Tel: 01625 534400
e-mail: tatton@cheshire.gov.uk
website: www.nationaltrust.org.uk

Tatton Park is one of the most complete historic estates open to visitors. The early 19th-century Wyatt house sits amid a landscaped deer park and is opulently decorated, providing a fine setting for the Egerton family's collections of pictures, books, china, glass, silver and specially commissioned Gillow furniture. The theme of Victorian grandeur extends into the garden, with fernery, orangery, Tower Garden, pinetum and Italian and Japanese gardens. The restored Walled Garden includes a kitchen garden and magnificent glasshouses, where traditional methods of gardening are used. Other features include the Tudor Old Hall, a working 1930s' farm, a children's play area and speciality shops.

also a busy programme of educational activities for children, an adventure playground, shops, and a restaurant. You can even get married in the sumptuous mansion and hold your reception either in the house itself, in the Tenants Hall, which can cater for parties of up to 430, or in a marquee in the magnificent grounds. With so much on offer it is small wonder that Tatton Park has been described as the most complete historic estate in the country.

Tabley House, nr Knutsford

Just west of Knutsford, on the A5033, is **Tabley House,** home of the Leicester family from 1272 to 1975. Mrs Gaskell often came to picnic in the grounds of the last of their houses, a stately Georgian mansion designed by John Carr for the first Lord de Tabley in 1761. This Lord de Tabley loved paintings and it was his son's passion for art, and his hunger for others to share it, that led to the creation of London's National Gallery. His personal collection of English pictures, on display in Tabley House, includes works by Turner (who painted the house several times), Lely, Reynolds, Opie and Martin Danby, along with furniture by Gillow, Bullock and Chippendale, and fascinating family memorabilia spanning three centuries. Through various activities, the Friends of Tabley House raise funds for the restoration and refurbishment of the house; recent undertakings have included the redecoration of the grand entrance hall and the restoration and re-hanging of the 18th-century hall lantern. The 17th-century chapel next to the house looks perfectly in place, but it was originally built on an island in Tabley Mere and only moved to its present site in 1927.

Also in Tabley, at the Old School, is the **Tabley Cuckoo Clock Collection.** Brothers Roman and Maz Piekarski are well-known horologists and clock restorers, and over the past three decades they have sought out and renovated some of the rarest and most notable examples of this 300-year-old craft. Also on display are some mid-19th-century cuckoo clocks, which include complex musical movements to reproduce popular tunes of the day.

MOBBERLEY

2 miles E of Knutsford on the B5085

George Mallory

The main glory of this scattered village is the spectacular woodwork inside the church: massive roof beams with striking winged figures, and one of the finest rood screens in the country, dated 1500. The screen is covered with a rich tracery of leaves and fruit, coats-of-arms, and religious symbols. Two generations of the Mallory family held the rectorship here, one of them for 53 years. He is commemorated in the east window. Another window honours his grandson, **George**

Over Peover

Distance: *4.5 miles (7.2 kilometres)*

Typical time: *150 mins*

Height gain: *0 metres*

Map: *Landranger 118*

Walk: *www.walkingworld.com ID: 214*

Contributor: *Robin and Christine Jones*

ACCESS INFORMATION:

Bus services available from Macclesfield, Knutsford and Northwich to Over Peover (peever). No train services. Access by car from M6 Motorway - leave at Junction 19 for Knutsford town centre; take the A50 South for Stoke and Holmes Chapel for 2½ miles. Turn left into Stocks Lane at the Whipping Stocks Inn. Parking is available on the roadside, just after the road bends to the left, in a small lay-by.

DESCRIPTION:

This walk is in a figure-of-eight, starting at one of the entrance drives to the Peover Hall Estate. The Hall itself dates from 1585, and is still occupied as a residence. To the west is the Jodrell Bank Science Centre, which is open to visitors all year. The river, known as the Peover Eye, gives its name to the village. Peover is an Anglo-Saxon word meaning "bright water". Parts of the Church of St Lawrence featured in the walk are 550 years old, but most was rebuilt about 200 years ago.

FEATURES:

River, Pub, Church, Stately Home, Wildlife, Birds, Flowers, Great Views.

WALK DIRECTIONS:

1 | Walk to the Four Lane Ends junction and follow the lane with the footpath markers. Carry straight on along the drive past the village hall and through the gates. Cross the stile and continue along the avenue of trees. A word of warning: you may find horses and riders crossing this path, where the fences have been modified for cross-country events.

2 | Over the stile, cross the footbridge and through the gate. On the right is Peover Pool, a conservation area. Walk straight ahead following the direction of the yellow Waymark arrows on the gate. On arrival at the main gates of Peover Hall, cross the stile and turn left away from the house.

3 | At the lane turn right - do not go up the path labelled 'Church'. We go to see the church later.

4 | At the stile on the left-hand side of the lane, proceed along the field edge in the direction of the wood. Turn right on reaching the wood and proceed along the

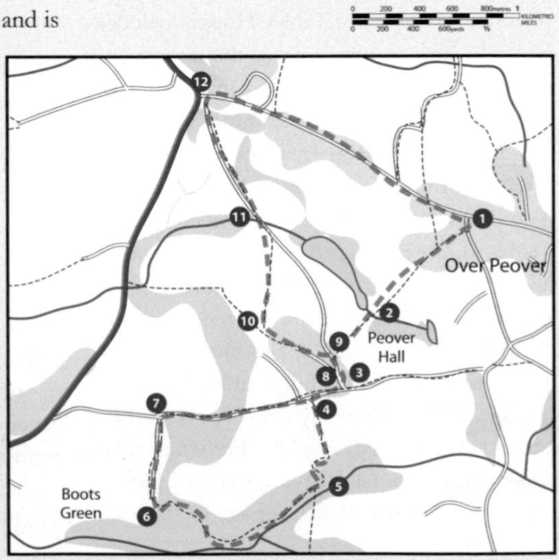

field edge to the corner of the wood. On reaching the corner of the wood, take the marked footpath on the left leading downhill into the wood.

5 | On reaching the river (The Peover Eye), turn right and follow the path along the riverbank. Do not cross the river. As the path ascends into Spinney Wood, follow the path to the left, going in the same direction as before. The path is marked by white spots painted on the trees.

6 | The path will lead you to a white gate. Turn right through the gate and follow the field edge to walk alongside the greenhouses.

7 | Where the farm drive meets the lane at the end of the glasshouses, turn right along a bridleway. Follow the path until it joins the lane again in front of the cottages.

8 | Proceed along the lane passing Waymark 4, to arrive back outside the gates to Peover Hall. Walk to the left of the gates in front of the old stable block. At the end of the stables go through the white gates and turn right.

9 | At the main junction of the path, turn right to go up to the church. Of interest here is the pets' cemetery.

10 | Follow this path up to the church - unfortunately mostly closed - and then turn left to rejoin the main path. Cross the stile and turn left. Go to the next stile and turn right, following the path through the meadow. Follow the path through the old gateway.

11 | Cross the stile and then turn left along the drive, which is more distinct once you cross the cattle grid. On reaching the end of the drive, proceed through the white gates and turn right onto the road.

12 | Refreshments are available at the Whipping Stocks Inn. Now it's just a gentle stroll down Stocks Lane back to the lay-by where the car is parked.

Mallory, the mountaineer who perished while making his third attempt to climb Mount Everest in 1924.

LOWER PEOVER

4 miles S of Knutsford on the B5081

St Oswald's Church · Peover Hall

General George Patton

The village of Lower Peover (pronounced peever) is effectively made up of two hamlets. One is grouped around the village green on the B5081, the other is at the end of a cobbled lane. It's a picturesque little group. There's a charming old coaching inn, The Bells of Peover, which during World War Two numbered Generals Patton and Eisenhower among its customers. The American flag still flies here alongside the Union Jack. Nearby are a handsome village school founded in 1710, and a lovely black and white timbered church, more than 700 years old, with a massive Perpendicular tower built in 1582. **St Oswald's** is notable as one of the few timber-framed churches in the country still standing, and probably the oldest. Inside, there is a wealth of carved wood – pews and screens, pulpit and lectern, and a massive medieval chest made from a single log of bog oak. At one time local girls who wished to marry a farmer were required to raise its lid with one hand to demonstrate they had the strength to cope with farm life.

About three miles east of Lower Peover is **Peover Hall**, very much hidden away at the end of a winding country road but well worth tracking down. During World War Two, **General George Patton** lived for a while at the Hall, which was conveniently close to his then headquarters at Knutsford. There's a memorial to him in the church nearby, but many more to the Mainwaring family, whose fine monuments crowd beside each other in both the north and south chapels.

MERE

3 miles NW of Knutsford on the A50/A556

Dick Turpin

One of the Kilton Inn's more notorious guests, back in the 18th century, was **Dick Turpin.** This intrepid highwayman made the inn the base from which he plundered travellers along the Knutsford to Warrington road (now the comparatively safe A50). After one such robbery (and murder) Turpin, on his famous horse Black Bess, "galloped to the Kilton and, altering the clock, strolled on to the bowling green and proved an alibi by the short time he took to cover the four miles".

Macclesfield

Silk Museum Paradise Mill Museum

St Michael & All Angels

Charles Frederick Tunnicliffe

West Park Museum William Buckley

Nestling below the hills of the High Peak, Macclesfield was once an important silk manufacturing town. Charles Roe built the first silk mill here in 1743, beside the River Bollin, and for more than a century and a half, Macclesfield was known as *the* silk town. It's appropriate then that Macclesfield can boast the country's only **Silk Museum**, where visitors are given a lively introduction to all aspects of the silk industry, from cocoon to loom. The Museum is housed within the Heritage Centre, built in 1813 as a Sunday school to provide education for the children who worked in the silk mills. An award-winning audio-visual programme traces the development of the silk industry in Macclesfield and there are fascinating exhibitions on the Silk Road across Asia, on silk cultivation, fashion and other uses of silk. The Heritage Centre also has some interesting displays on Macclesfield's rich and exciting past.

The silk theme continues at nearby **Paradise Mill Museum**. Built in the 1820s, and in commercial use until 1981, it is now a working museum demonstrating silk weaving on 26 Jacquard hand looms. Exhibitions and restored workshops and living rooms capture the working conditions and lives of mill workers in the 1930s. It is also possible to buy locally-made silk products here.

In pre-Saxon times, Macclesfield was known as Hameston – the homestead on the rock, and on that rock is set the church founded by King Edward I and Queen Eleanor. From the modern town, a walk to the church involves climbing a gruelling flight of 108 steps. **St Michael and All Angels** was extended in the 1890s, but its 14th-century core remains,

Paradise Mill Museum

notably the Legh Chapel built to receive the body of Piers Legh, who had fought at Agincourt and died at the Siege of Meaux. Another chapel contains the famous Legh Pardon brass, which recalls the medieval practice of selling pardons for sins past and, even more conveniently, for sins not yet committed. The inscription on the brass records that in return for saying five Paternosters and five Aves the Legh family received a pardon for 26,000 years and 26 days. The Savage Chapel and other parts of the church contain many memorials to the illustrious Savage family, whose numbers included Sir Thomas, who became Archbishop of York towards the end of the 15th century.

One of the Macclesfield area's most famous sons is **Charles Frederick Tunnicliffe**, the celebrated bird and wildlife artist, who was born at the nearby village of Langley in 1901. He studied at the Macclesfield School of Art (now the Silk Museum) and first came to public attention with his illustrations for Henry Williamson's *Tarka the Otter* in 1927. A frequently changing collection of Tunnicliffe's striking oil paintings, watercolours and etchings can be seen at the **West Park Museum** in a public park on the north-western edge of town. This purpose-built museum, founded in 1898 by the Brocklehurst family, also includes exhibits of ancient Egyptian artefacts acquired by Marianne Brocklehurst during visits to Egypt between 1873 and 1891. The collection features a mummy case, and the afterlife displays examine the process of mummification and the objects buried with the dead. Incidentally, the park boasts what is thought to be the largest bowling green in England.

A less well-known figure is **William Buckley**, who was born in Macclesfield around 1780 and later became a soldier. He took part in a mutiny at Gibraltar against the Rock's commanding officer, the Duke of York, father-to-be of Queen Victoria. The mutiny failed and Buckley was transported to Australia. There he escaped into the outback and became the leader of an aboriginal tribe who took this giant of a man, some six feet six inches tall, as the reincarnation of a dead chief. For 32 years Buckley never saw a white man or heard a word of English. When the explorer John Bateman, on his way to what is now Melbourne, discovered him, Buckley had virtually forgotten his mother tongue. He was pardoned, given a pension and died at Hobart at the age of 76.

Around Macclesfield

PRESTBURY

3 miles N of Macclesfield via the A523/A538

Norman Chapel

A regular winner of the Best Kept Village title, Prestbury is a charming village where a tree-lined main street runs down to a bridge over the River Bollin, ancient stocks stand against the church wall, and old coaching inns and black and white buildings mingle with the mellow red brickwork of later Georgian houses. The Church of St Peter, dating from the 13th century, still maintains a tradition that began in 1577. Every autumn and winter evening at 8pm a curfew bell is rung, with the number of chimes corresponding to the date of the month. Close by is a building known as the **Norman Chapel** with a striking frontage carved with the characteristic Norman zig-zags and beaked heads. Even older are the carved fragments of an 8th-century Saxon cross preserved under glass in the graveyard. Opposite the church is a remarkable magpie timber-framed house, now a bank, but it used to be the vicarage. During the Commonwealth, the rightful incumbent was debarred from preaching in the church by the Puritans. Undaunted, the priest addressed his parishioners from the tiny balcony of his vicarage.

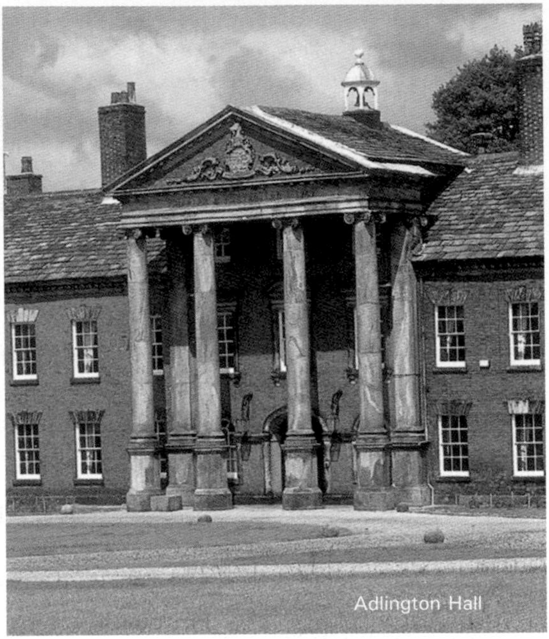
Adlington Hall

ADLINGTON

4 miles N of Macclesfield off the A523

Adlington Hall

Adlington boasts a fine old house, **Adlington Hall**, which has been the home of the Legh family since 1315 and is now one of the county's most popular attractions. Quadrangular in shape, this magnificent manor house has two distinctive styles of architecture: black and white half-timbered buildings on two sides, later Georgian additions in warm red brick on the others. There is much to see on a tour of the Hall, with beautifully polished wooden floors and lovely antique furnishings enhancing the air of elegance and grandeur. The Great Hall is a breathtaking sight, a vast room of lofty proportions that set off perfectly the exquisitely painted walls. The beautifully preserved 17th-century organ here has responded to the touch of many maestros, none more famous than George Frederick Handel, who visited the Hall in the 1740s.

BOLLINGTON

4 miles NE of Macclesfield on the B5091

Middlewood Way White Nancy

In its 19th century heyday, there were 13 cotton mills working away at Bollington, a little town perched on the foothills of the High Peak. Two of the largest mills, the Clarence and the Adelphi, still stand, although now adapted to other purposes. The Victorian shops and cottages around Water Street and the High Street recall those busy days. A striking feature of the town is the splendid 20-arched viaduct, which once carried the railway over the River Dean. It is now part of the **Middlewood Way**, a 10-mile, traffic-free country trail that follows a scenic route from Macclesfield to Marple. The Way is open to walkers, cyclists and horse riders, and during the season cycles are available for hire, complete with child seats if required. Just as remarkable as the viaduct, although in a different way, is **White Nancy.** This sugarloaf-shaped, whitewashed round tower stands on Kerridge Hill, more than 900 feet above sea level. It was erected in 1817 to commemorate the Battle of Waterloo and offers sweeping views in all directions.

DISLEY

10 miles NE of Macclesfield on the A6

Lyme Park Country Park Lyme Park

The small town of Disley lies close to the Macclesfield Canal and little more than half a mile from **Lyme Park Country Park**. At the heart of the spectacular 1400-acre moorland park where red and fallow deer roam freely stands **Lyme Park** (National Trust), home of the Legh family for more than 600 years. The elegant Palladian exterior of this great house encloses a superb Elizabethan mansion. Among the many treasures on show are carvings by Grinling Gibbons, tapestries from Mortlake, and a unique collection of English clocks. The house featured many times in the BBC's 1995 production of *Pride and Prejudice* when it represented the exterior of Pemberley, the home of Elizabeth Bennett's curmudgeonly lover, Mr Darcy. It also appeared in Granada's *The Forsyte Saga*, and some of the costumes from that production are on display.

Amenities at the park include two shops, a restaurant, a tearoom and a children's play area. From Easter to October, Lyme Park hosts a varied programme of events, from plant fairs and outdoor performances of plays to art exhibitions and a Morris Minor Owners Club Rally.

Lyme Park, Disley

SUTTON

2 miles S of Macclesfield on a minor road off the A523

Raphael Holinshed

This small village, close to the Macclesfield Canal, is honoured by scholars as the birthplace of **Raphael Holinshed**, whose famous *Chronicles of England, Scotland & Ireland* (1577) provided the source material for no fewer than 14 of Shakespeare's plays. As well as drawing heavily on the facts in the Chronicles, the Bard wasn't above adopting some of Holinshed's happier turns of phrase.

BOSLEY

6 miles S of Macclesfield on the A523

Macclesfield Canal

To the east of Bosley town centre runs the **Macclesfield Canal**, one of the highest waterways in England, running for much of its length at more than 500 feet above sea level. Thomas Telford was the surveyor of the 26-mile route, opened in 1831, which links the Trent and Mersey and the Peak Forest canals. Between Macclesfield and Congleton, the canal descends over 100 feet in a spectacular series of 12 locks at Bosley, before crossing the

River Dane via Telford's handsome iron viaduct. Other unusual features of this superbly engineered canal are the two 'roving bridges' south of Congleton. These swing from one bank to the other where the towpath changes sides and so enabled horses to cross over without the tow-rope having to be unhitched.

GAWSWORTH

3 miles SW of Macclesfield off the A536

Gawsworth Hall

Gawsworth Hall is a captivating sight with its dazzling black and white half-timbered walls and lofty three-decker Tudor windows. The Hall was built in 1480 by the Fitton family, one of whose descendants, the celebrated beauty Mary Fitton, is believed by some to be the Dark Lady of Shakespeare's sonnets. The Bard would no doubt approve of Gawsworth's famous open-air theatre, where performances range from his own plays to Gilbert and Sullivan operas, with the Hall serving as a lovely backdrop. Surrounded by a huge park, Gawsworth, to quote its owner Timothy Richards, is "the epitome of a lived-in historic house". Every room that visitors see (which is virtually every room in the house) is in daily use by him and his family. And what wonderful rooms they are! Myriad windows bathe the rooms in light, the low ceilings and modest dimensions radiate calm, and even the richly-carved main staircase is conceived on a human scale. The beautifully sited church, and the lake nearby, add still more to the appeal of this magical place. The Hall was the scene - in 1712

HOLLANDS NURSERIES

Garden Centre & Farm Shop, Gawsworth,
nr Macclesfield, Cheshire SK11 9JB
Tel: 01260 223362
website: www. hollandsnurseries.co.uk

Owned and run by the Holland family, **Hollands Nurseries, Garden Centre and Farm Shop** began as a small business selling fresh vegetables grown on the site. It then expanded into selling annuals, herbaceous perennials, shrubs and trees. Today, the extensive site sells just about everything a gardener could require from paving stones to garden tools, from summerhouses to chippings, and from compost to terracotta pots. Hollands is also the franchisee for the upmarket range of Alfresco hot tubs. A recent addition to the site's amenities is the stylish coffee shop, which opened in 2006 and offers customers a range of freshly-made sandwiches and filled baguettes, soups, lasagne and other snacks and light meals. Before leaving Hollands, do have a browse around the farm shop, which sells a wide selection of local pre-packed bacon, pork, beef and lamb chops, along with an appetising choice of cheeses, jams, preserves and much more.

Gawsworth Hall and Gardens

artefacts collected by family members during the course of their Grand Tours throughout Europe, America and the Far East. The Queen Anne Room features a monumental fireplace, while the Box Room has a fascinating collection that ranges from a Victorian oak letter box to antique hat boxes and cigar boxes. In medieval times the head of the Bromley-Davenport family held the post of Chief Forester of Macclesfield Forest, which gave him authority to mete out summary justice to anyone who transgressed the savage forestry laws. As a reminder of their power, the family crest includes the severed head of a felon. One of these crests, on the main staircase built in the 1860s, was commissioned by the staunchly Conservative Bromley-Davenport of the time and the felon's head is instantly recognisable as the Liberal leader of the day, William Ewart Gladstone. In the grounds, near the Georgian family chapel, the 18th-century Italian gates open on to lakeside gardens.

- of a famous duel when Lord Mohun and the Duke of Hamilton fought over the estates; both were killed. The country's last professional jester, a certain Samuel Johnson, lived in the house and is buried in a nearby spinney.

CAPESTHORNE HALL

5 miles W of Macclesfield on the A34

Capesthorne Hall

The home of the Bromley-Davenport family for generations, **Capesthorne Hall** dates back to 1719 when it was designed by the Smiths of Warwick. It was altered in 1837 by Blore and, following a fire in 1861, was remodelled and extended by the celebrated architect Anthony Salvin. The present building presents a magnificent medley of Elizabethan-style turrets and towers, domes and cupolas, while inside the house is a wealth of portraits and

NETHER ALDERLEY

6 miles NW of Macclesfield on the A34

Nether Alderley Mill

Nether Alderley Mill is a delightful 15th-century watermill that has been restored by the National Trust. The red sandstone walls are almost hidden under the huge sweep of its stone tiled roof. Inside is the original Elizabethan woodwork and the Victorian mill

Nether Alderley Mill

machinery, which is still in working order, with two tandem overshot wheels powering the mill. The 14th-century church of St Mary is almost a private mausoleum for the Alderley branch of the Stanley family: monuments to dead Stanleys are everywhere. Living members of the family were provided with an unusual richly carved pew, set up on the wall like an opera box and reached by a flight of steps outside.

ALDERLEY EDGE

6 miles NW of Macclesfield on the A34

Hare Hill Gardens

Alderley Edge takes its name from the long, wooded escarpment, nearly two miles long, that rises 600 feet above sea level and culminates in sandy crags overlooking the Cheshire Plain. In Victorian times, this spectacular area was the private preserve of the Stanley family and it was only

COLOURS AND CRAFTS

61 London Road, Alderley Edge, Cheshire SK9 7DY
Tel: 01625 586100
e-mail: seahorse6259@aol.com

The best art and craft shop for miles around, **Colours and Crafts** is owned and run by Stella and Paul Rowley who moved their shop to Alderley Edge in March 2003. Stella and Paul are always more than happy to help, and pride themselves on the knowledge and advice that they give to their customers. Stella's background is in libraries, but she has always been very artistic and creative and both her and Paul take watercolour classes. The shop stocks a comprehensive range of art and craft materials - whatever your particular interest you can be confident of finding the necessary components here. Also in stock are Colours & Crafts own label beads. Stella also holds workshops in arts and crafts for both adults and children - just call for details.

GRANTHAM'S

68 Heyes Lane, Alderley Edge, Cheshire SK9 7LB
Tel: 01625 583286
e-mail: info@granthamfinefood.com
website: www.granthamfinefood.com

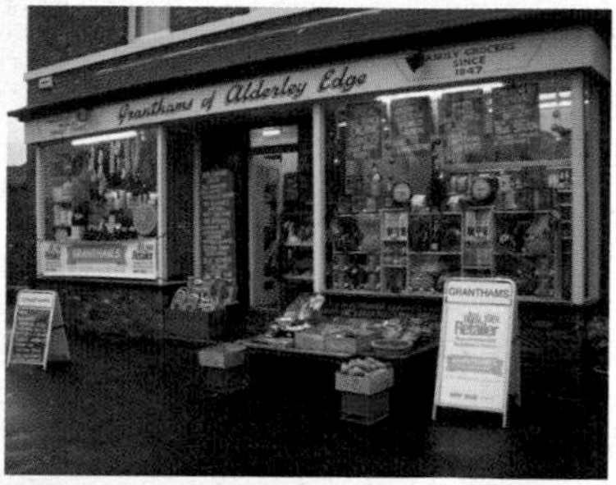

Voted Best Regional Retailer for Cheshire and North Wales 2006 by the Countryside Alliance, the Daily Telegraph and Farmer's Weekly, **Grantham's** is an outstandingly good grocers, delicatessen and wine merchants. The shop takes its name from the family of partners Michael and Gillian Grantham who are often joined by their daughters Rachael, Jessica and Lydia in running the business. The shop was established in the early 1900s and acquired by Michael's grandfather, Percy, in 1947 - local people still fondly refer to the business as 'Percy's'. Michael joined the family business straight from school and now has 32 years experience in the trade.

As you enter the shop, your nostrils are greeted with the aromas of a bygone age - roasting meats and the fragrance of fresh ground coffee fill the air. The shop is renowned for its traditional home-cooked hams, roast ribs of beef and free range pork. It also stocks a wide selection of continental hams, sausages and salamis, including the delicious Pata Negra Iberico ham. There are more than 150 different English and Continental cheeses, mainly sourced from small artisan producers; an ever-expanding range of organic foods, beers and wines, and much, much more.

under great pressure that they grudgingly allowed the 'Cottentots' of Manchester access on occasional summer weekends. Nowadays, walkers can roam freely along the many footpaths through the woods, one of which will take them to **Hare Hill Gardens**, one of the lesser-known National Trust properties. These Victorian gardens include fine woodland, a walled garden themed in blue, white and yellow flowers, and huge banks of rhododendrons.

WILMSLOW

6 miles NW of Macclesfield off the A34

St Bartholomew's Church · Romany's Caravan

The oldest building in Wilmslow is **St Bartholomew's Church**, built between 1517 and 1537, and notable for its magnificent ceiling, some striking effigies, and for the fact that Prime Minister-to-be Gladstone worshipped here as a boy. A hamlet in medieval times, Wilmslow mushroomed as a mill town in the 18th and 19th centuries, and is now a busy commuter town offering a good choice of inns, hotels and restaurants.

Claiming to be the smallest tourist attraction in the country, **Romany's Caravan**, or Vardo, stands in its own special Memorial Garden in Wilmslow. Its interior has been restored to what it was like when used by traveller Romany and his family when on holiday in his beloved North Country. It is open to the public on the second Saturday of the month from May to September.

STYAL

7 miles NW of Macclesfield, on a minor road off the B5166

Styal Country Park | Quarry Bank Mill

Styal Village

Quarry Bank Mill, Styal

Cared for by the National Trust, **Styal Country Park** is set in 250 acres of the beautifully wooded valley of the River Bollin and offers many woodland and riverside walks. The Park is open to the public from dawn to dusk throughout the year, and is a wonderful place for picnics. Lying within the Park is **Quarry Bank Mill**, a grand old building erected in 1784 and one of the first generation of cotton mills. It was powered by a huge iron waterwheel fed by the River Bollin. Visitors follow the history of the mill through various galleries and displays within the museum, including weaving and spinning demonstrations, and can experience for themselves, with the help of guides dressed in period costume, what life was like for the 100 girls and boys who once lived in the Apprentice House. The Mill stages a full programme of events throughout the year. Also within the park is the delightful **Styal Village**, which was established by the mill's original owner, Samuel Greg, a philanthropist and pioneer of the factory system. He took children from the slums of Manchester to work in his mill, and in return for their labour provided them with food, clothing, housing, education and a place of worship.

Cheshire

ALTRINCHAM
Altrincham Tourist Information Centre, 20 Stamford New Road, Altrincham, Cheshire, WA14 1EJ
e-mail: tourist.information@trafford.gov.uk
Tel: 0161 912 5931

CHESTER
Chester Town Hall Tourist Information Centre, Town Hall, Northgate Street, Chester, Cheshire, CH1 2HJ
e-mail: tis@chester.gov.uk
Tel: 01244 402111

CHESTER
Chester Visitor Centre, Chester Visitor Centre, Vicars Lane, Chester, Cheshire, CH1 1QX
e-mail: tis@chester.gov.uk
Tel: 01244 402111

CONGLETON
Congleton Tourist Information Centre, Town Hall, High Street, Congleton, Cheshire, CW12 1BN
e-mail: tourism@congleton.gov.uk
Tel: 01260 271095

ELLESMERE PORT
Ellesmere Port Tourist Information Centre, Unit 22b, McArthur Glen Outlet Village, Kinsey Road, Ellesmere Port, Cheshire, CH65 9JJ
e-mail: cheshireoaks.cc@visitor-centre.net
Tel: 0151 356 7879

KNUTSFORD
Knutsford Tourist Information Centre, Council Offices, Toft Road, Knutsford, Cheshire, WA16 6TA
e-mail: ktic@macclesfield.gov.uk
Tel: 01565 632611

MACCLESFIELD
Macclesfield Tourist Information Centre, Town Hall, Macclesfield, Cheshire, SK10 1DX
e-mail: informationcentre@macclesfield.gov.uk
Tel:01625 504114

NANTWICH
Nantwich Tourist Information Centre, Church House, Church Walk, Nantwich, Cheshire, CW5 5RG
e-mail: touristi@crewe-nantwich.gov.uk
Tel: 01270 610983

NORTHWICH
Northwich Tourist Information Centre, Information Centre, 1 The Arcade,Northwich, Cheshire, CW9 5AS
e-mail: tourism@valeroyal.gov.uk
Tel: 01606 353534

WARRINGTON
Warrington Bus Interchange, Travel & Visitor Information Centre, Horsemarket Street, Warrington, Cheshire, WA1 1TF
e-mail: informationcentre@warrington.gov.uk
Tel: 01925 428585

WILMSLOW
Wilmslow Tourist Information Centre, The Information Centre, Rectory Fields, Wilmslow, Cheshire, SK9 1BU
e-mail: i.hillaby@macclesfield.gov.uk
Tel: 01625 522275

Cumbria

ALSTON MOOR
Alston Moor Tourist Information Centre, Town Hall, Front Street, Alston, Cumbria, CA9 3RF
e-mail: alston.tic@eden.gov.uk
Tel: 01434 382244

AMBLESIDE
Ambleside Tourist Information Centre, Central Buildings, Market Cross, Ambleside, Cumbria, LA22 9BS
e-mail: amblesidetic@southlakeland.gov.uk
Tel: 015394 32582

APPLEBY-IN-WESTMORLAND
Appleby-in-Westmorland Tourist Information Centre, Moot Hall, Boroughgate, Appleby-in-Westmorland, Cumbria, CA16 6XE
e-mail: tic@applebytown.org.uk
Tel: 017683 51177

BARROW-IN-FURNESS
Barrow-in-Furness Tourist Information Centre, Forum 28, Duke Street, Barrow-in-Furness, Cumbria, LA14 1HU
e-mail: touristinfo@barrowbc.gov.uk
Tel: 01229 876505

BOWNESS
Bowness Tourist Information Centre, Glebe Road, Bowness-on-Windermere, Cumbria, LA23 3HJ
e-mail: bownesstic@lake-district.gov.uk
Tel: 015394 42895

BRAMPTON
Brampton Tourist Information Centre, Moot Hall, Market Place, Brampton, Cumbria, CA8 1RW
e-mail: ElisabethB@CarlisleCity.gov.uk
Tel: 016977 3433

BROUGHTON-IN-FURNESS
Broughton-in-Furness Tourist Information Centre, Town Hall, The Square, Broughton-in-Furness, Cumbria, LA20 6JF
e-mail: email@broughton-tic.fsnet.co.uk
Tel: 01229 716115

CARLISLE
Carlisle Tourist Information Centre, Old Town Hall, Greenmarket, Carlisle, Cumbria, CA3 8JE
e-mail: tourism@carlisle-city.gov.uk
Tel: 01228 625600

TOURIST INFORMATION CENTRES

COCKERMOUTH

Cockermouth Tourist Information Centre, Town Hall, Market Street, Cockermouth, Cumbria, CA13 9NP
e-mail: email@cockermouth-tic.fsnet.co.uk
Tel: 01900 822634

CONISTON

Coniston Tourist Information Centre, Ruskin Avenue, Coniston, Cumbria, LA21 8EH
e-mail: mail@conistontic.org
Tel: 015394 41533

EGREMONT

Egremont Tourist Information Centre, 12 Main Street, Egremont, Cumbria, CA22 2DW
e-mail: email@egremont-tic.fsnet.co.uk
Tel: 01946 820693

GRANGE-OVER-SANDS

Grange-over-Sands Tourist Information Centre, Victoria Hall, Main Street, Grange-over-Sands, Cumbria, LA11 6DP
e-mail: grangetic@southlakeland.gov.uk
Tel: 015395 34026

KENDAL

Kendal Tourist Information Centre Addess: Town Hall, Highgate, Kendal, Cumbria, LA9 4DL
e-mail: kendaltic@southlakeland.gov.uk
Tel: 01539 725758

KESWICK

Keswick Tourist Information Centre, Moot Hall, Market Square, Keswick, Cumbria, CA12 5JR
e-mail: keswicktic@lake-district.gov.uk
Tel: 017687 72645

KIRKBY LONSDALE

Kirkby Lonsdale Tourist Information Centre, 24 Main Street, Kirkby Lonsdale, Cumbria, LA6 2AE
e-mail: kltic@southlakeland.gov.uk
Tel: 015242 71437

KIRKBY STEPHEN

Kirkby Stephen Tourist Information Centre, Market Street, Kirkby Stephen, Cumbria, CA17 4QN
e-mail: ks.tic@eden.gov.uk
Tel: 017683 71199

MARYPORT

Maryport Tourist Information Centre, Maryport Town Hall, Senhouse Street Maryport, Cumbria, CA15 6BH
e-mail: maryporttic@allerdale.gov.uk
Tel: 01900 812101

MILLOM

Millom Tourist Information Centre, Station Building, Station Road, Millom, Cumbria, LA18 5AA
e-mail: millomtic@copelandbc.gov.uk
Tel: 01229 774819

PENRITH

Penrith Tourist Information Centre, Middlegate, Penrith, Cumbria, CA11 7PT
e-mail: pen.tic@eden.gov.uk
Tel: 01768 867466

RHEGED

Rheged Tourist Information Centre, Rheged Tourist Information Centre, Rheged, Penrith, CA11 0DQ
e-mail: tic@rheged.com
Tel: 01768 860034

SEDBERGH

Sedbergh Tourist Information Centre, 72 Main Street, Sedbergh, Cumbria, LA10 5AD
e-mail: tic@sedbergh.org.uk
Tel: 015396 20125

SILLOTH-ON-SOLWAY

Silloth-on-Solway Tourist Information Centre, Solway coast Discovery Centre, Liddell Street, Silloth-on-Solway, Cumbria, CA7 5DD
e-mail: sillothtic@allerdale.gov.uk
Tel: 016973 31944

SOUTHWAITE

Southwaite Tourist Information Centre Adress: M6 Service Area Southwaite, Carlisle, Cumbria, CA4 ONS
e-mail: southwaitetic@visitscotland.com
Tel: 016974 73445

ULLSWATER

Ullswater Tourist Information Centre, Main Car Park, Glenridding, Penrith, Cumbria, CA11 0PD
e-mail: ullswatertic@lake-district.gov.uk
Tel: 017684 82414

ULVERSTON

Ulverston Tourist Information Centre, Coronation Hall, County Square, Ulverston, Cumbria, LA12 7LZ
e-mail: ulverstontic@southlakeland.gov.uk
Tel: 01229 587120

WHITEHAVEN

Whitehaven Tourist Information Centre, Market Hall, Market Place, Whitehaven, Cumbria, CA28 7JG
e-mail: tic@copelandbc.gov.uk
Tel: 01946 598914

WINDERMERE

Windermere Tourist Information Centre, Victoria Street, Windermere, Cumbria, LA23 1AD
e-mail: windermeretic@southlakeland.gov.uk
Tel: 015394 46499

WORKINGTON

Workington Tourist Information Centre, 21 Finkle Street, Workington, Cumbria, CA14 2BE
e-mail: workingtontic@allerdale.gov.uk
Tel: 01900 606699

Greater Manchester

BOLTON
Bolton Tourist Information Centre, Central Library Foyer, Le Mans Cres, Bolton, Greater Manchester, BL1 1SE
e-mail: tourist.info@bolton.gov.uk
Tel: 01204 334321

BURY
Bury Tourist Information Centre, The Met Arts Centre, Market Street, Bury, Greater Manchester, BL9 0BN
e-mail: touristinformation@bury.gov.uk
Tel: 0161 253 5111

MANCHESTER
Manchester Visitor Information Centre, Manchester Visitor Centre, Town Hall Extension, Lloyd St, Manchester, Greater Manchester, M60 2LA
e-mail: touristinformation@marketing-manchester.co.uk
Tel: 0871 222 8223

OLDHAM
Oldham Tourist Information Centre, 12 Albion Street, Oldham, Greater Manchester, OL1 3BD
e-mail: ecs.tourist@oldham.gov.uk
Tel: 0161 627 1024

SADDLEWORTH
Saddleworth Tourist Information Centre, Saddleworth Museum, High Street, Uppermill, Saddleworth, Oldham, Greater Manchester, OL3 6HS
e-mail: ecs.saddleworthtic@oldham.gov.uk
Tel: 01457 870336

SALFORD
Salford Tourist Information Centre, The Lowry, Pier 8, Salford Quays, Salford, Greater Manchester, M50 3AZ
e-mail: christine.ellis@salford.gov.uk
Tel: 0161 848 8601

STOCKPORT
Stockport Tourist Information Centre, Staircase House, 30 Market Place Stockport, Greater Manchester, SK1 1ES
e-mail: tourist.information@stockport.gov.uk
Tel: 0161 474 4444

WIGAN
Wigan Tourist Information Centre, 62 Wallgate, Wigan, Greater Manchester, WN1 1BA
e-mail: tic@wlct.org
Tel: 01942 825677

Lancashire

ACCRINGTON
Accrington Tourist Information Centre, Town Hall, Blackburn Road, Accrington, Lancashire, BB5 1LA
e-mail: tourism@hyndburnbc.gov.uk
Tel: 01254 872595

ASHTON-UNDER-LYNE
Ashton-under-Lyne Tourist Information Centre, Council Offices, Wellington Road, Ashton-Under-Lyne, Lancashire, OL6 6DL
e-mail: tourist.information@mail.tameside.gov.uk
Tel: 0161 343 4343

BARNOLDSWICK
Barnoldswick Tourist Information Centre, The Council Shop, Fernlea Avenue, Barnoldswick, Lancashire, BB18 5DL
e-mail: tourist.info@pendle.gov.uk
Tel: 01282 666704

BLACKBURN
Blackburn Tourist Information Centre, 50-54 Church Street, Blackburn, Lancashire, BB1 5AL
e-mail: visit@blackburn.gov.uk
Tel: 01254 53277

BLACKPOOL
Blackpool Tourist Information Centre, 1 Clifton Street, Blackpool, Lancashire, FY1 1LY
e-mail: tic@blackpool.gov.uk
Tel: 01253 478222

BURNLEY
Burnley Tourist Information Centre, Burnley Bus Station, Croft Street, Burnley, Lancashire, B11 2EF
e-mail: tic@burnley.gov.uk
Tel: 01282 664421

CLEVELEYS
Cleveleys Tourist Information Centre, Victoria Square Thornton, Cleveleys, Lancashire, FY5 1AU
e-mail: cleveleystic@wyrebc.gov.uk
Tel: 01253 853378

CLITHEROE
Clitheroe Tourist Information Centre, 12-14 Market Place, Clitheroe, Lancashire, BB7 2DA
e-mail: tourism@ribblevalley.gov.uk
Tel: 01200 425566

FLEETWOOD
Fleetwood Tourist Information Centre, Old Ferry Office, The Esplanade, Fleetwood, Lancashire, FY7 6DL
e-mail: ferrytic@wyrebc.gov.uk
Tel: 01253 773953

GARSTANG
Garstang Tourist Information Centre, Council Offices, Discovery Centre, High Street, Garstang, Lancashire, PR3 1FU
e-mail: garstangtic@wyrebc.gov.uk
Tel: 01995 602125

LANCASTER
Lancaster Tourist Information Centre, 29 Castle Hill, Lancaster, Lancashire, LA1 1YN
e-mail: lancastertic@lancaster.gov.uk
Tel: 01524 32878

TOURIST INFORMATION CENTRES

LYTHAM ST ANNES

Lytham St Annes Tourist Information Centre, Visitor & Travel Information Centre, 67 St Annes Road West, Lytham St Annes Lancashire, FY8 1SL
e-mail: touristinformation@fylde.gov.uk
Tel: 01253 725610

MORECAMBE

Morecambe Tourist Information Centre, Old Station Buildings, Marine Road Central, Morecambe, Lancashire, LA4 4DB
e-mail: morecambetic@lancaster.gov.uk
Tel: 01524 582808

PENDLE HERITAGE CENTRE

Pendle Heritage Centre Tourist Information Centre, Park Hill, Barrowford, Nelson, Lancashire, BB9 6JQ
e-mail: heritage.centre@pendle.gov.uk
Tel: 01282 661701

PRESTON

Preston Tourist Information Centre, The Guildhall, Lancaster Road, Preston, Lancashire, PR1 1HT
e-mail: tourism@preston.gov.uk
Tel: 01772 253731

ROCHDALE

Rochdale Tourist Information Centre, Touchstones, The Esplanade, Rochdale, Lancashire, OL16 1AQ
e-mail: tic@rochdale.gov.uk
Tel: 01706 864928

Merseyside

LIVERPOOL JOHN LENNON AIRPORT

Liverpool John Lennon Airport, Arrivals Hall, South Terminal, Liverpool John Lennon Airport, Speke Hall Avenue, Liverpool, Merseyside, L24 1YD
e-mail: info@visitliverpool.com
Tel: 0151 233 2008

LIVERPOOL '08 PLACE

Liverpool '08 Place, Whitechapel, Liverpool, Merseyside, L1 6DZ
e-mail: contact@liverpool08.com
Tel: 0151 233 2008

SOUTHPORT

Southport Tourist Information Centre., 112 Lord Street, Southport, Merseyside, PR8 1NY
e-mail: info@visitsouthport.com
Tel: 01704 533333

ST HELENS

St Helens Tourist Information Centre, The World of Glass, Chalon Way East, St Helens, Merseyside, WA10 1BX
e-mail: info@sthelenstic.com
Tel: 01744 755150

INDEX OF ADVERTISERS

ACCOMMODATION, FOOD AND DRINK

INDEX OF ADVERTISERS

ACTIVITIES

ANTIQUES AND RESTORATION

ARTS AND CRAFTS

FASHIONS

GIFTWARE

INDEX OF ADVERTISERS

HOME AND GARDEN

JEWELLERY

PLACES OF INTEREST

INDEX OF ADVERTISERS

SPECIALIST FOOD AND DRINK SHOPS

INDEX OF WALKS

Looking for more walks?

The walks in this book have been gleaned from Britain's largest online walking guide, to be found at *www.walkingworld.com*.

The site contains over 2000 walks from all over England, Scotland and Wales so there are plenty more to choose from in this book's region as well as further afield - ideal if you are taking a short break as you can plan your walks in advance. There are walks of every length and type to suit all tastes.

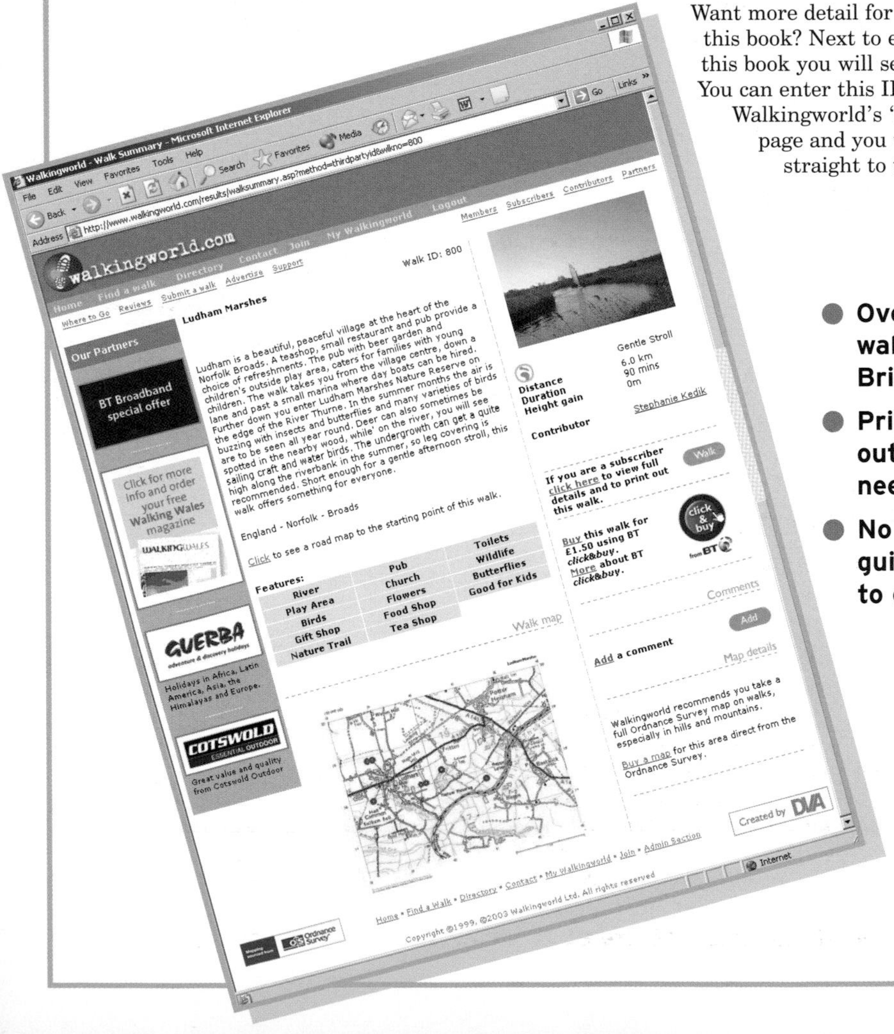

Want more detail for the walks in this book? Next to every walk in this book you will see a Walk ID. You can enter this ID number on Walkingworld's 'Find a Walk' page and you will be taken straight to the details of that walk.

- **Over 2000 walks across Britain**
- **Print routes out as you need them**
- **No bulky guidebook to carry**

ORDER FORM

To order any of our publications just fill in the payment details below and complete the order form. For orders of less than 4 copies please add £1 per book for postage and packing. Orders over 4 copies are P & P free.

Please Complete Either:

I enclose a cheque for £ ______ *made payable to Travel Publishing Ltd*

Or:

CARD NO: ______ EXPIRY DATE: ______

SIGNATURE: ______

NAME: ______

ADDRESS: ______

TEL NO: ______

Please either send, telephone, fax or e-mail your order to:

Travel Publishing Ltd, 64-66 Ebrington Street, Plymouth, Devon PL4 9AQ
Tel: 01752 276660 Fax: 01752 276699 e-mail: info@travelpublishing.co.uk

	Price	Quantity
Hidden Places Regional Titles		
Cornwall	£8.99	....
Devon	£8.99	....
Dorset, Hants & Isle of Wight	£8.99	....
East Anglia	£8.99	....
Lake District & Cumbria	£8.99	....
Northumberland & Durham	£8.99	....
Peak District and Derbyshire	£8.99	....
Yorkshire	£8.99	....
Hidden Places National Titles		
England	£11.99	....
Ireland	£11.99	....
Scotland	£11.99	....
Wales	£11.99	....
Country Pubs and Inns Titles		
Cornwall	£5.99	....
Devon	£7.99	....
Sussex	£5.99	....
Wales	£8.99	....
Yorkshire	£7.99	....

	Price	Quantity
Country Living Rural Guides		
East Anglia	£10.99	....
Heart of England	£10.99	....
Ireland	£11.99	....
North East of England	£10.99	....
North West of England	£10.99	....
Scotland	£11.99	....
South of England	£10.99	....
South East of England	£10.99	....
Wales	£11.99	....
West Country	£10.99	....
Other Titles		
Off The Motorway	£11.99	....
Garden Centres and Nurseries of Britain	£11.99	....

TOTAL QUANTITY ______

TOTAL VALUE ______

READER REACTION FORM

The **Travel Publishing** *research team would like to receive readers' comments on any visitor attractions or places reviewed in the book and also recommendations for suitable entries to be included in the next edition. This will help ensure that the* **Country Living series of Rural Guides** *continues to provide its readers with useful information on the more interesting, unusual or unique features of each attraction or place ensuring that their visit to the local area is an enjoyable and stimulating experience. To provide your comments or recommendations would you please complete the forms below and overleaf as indicated and send to:*

The Research Department, Travel Publishing Ltd, 7a Apollo House,
Calleva Park, Aldermaston, Reading, RG7 8TN

YOUR NAME:

YOUR ADDRESS:

YOUR TEL NO:

Please tick as appropriate: COMMENTS ☐ RECOMMENDATION ☐

ESTABLISHMENT:

ADDRESS:

TEL NO:

CONTACT NAME:

PLEASE COMPLETE FORM OVERLEAF

READER REACTION FORM

COMMENT OR REASON FOR RECOMMENDATION:

....

....

....

....

....

....

....

....

....

....

....

....

READER REACTION FORM

The **Travel Publishing** *research team would like to receive readers' comments on any visitor attractions or places reviewed in the book and also recommendations for suitable entries to be included in the next edition. This will help ensure that the* **Country Living series of Rural Guides** *continues to provide its readers with useful information on the more interesting, unusual or unique features of each attraction or place ensuring that their visit to the local area is an enjoyable and stimulating experience. To provide your comments or recommendations would you please complete the forms below and overleaf as indicated and send to:*

The Research Department, Travel Publishing Ltd, 7a Apollo House, Calleva Park, Aldermaston, Reading, RG7 8TN

YOUR NAME:

YOUR ADDRESS:

YOUR TEL NO:

Please tick as appropriate: COMMENTS ☐ RECOMMENDATION ☐

ESTABLISHMENT:

ADDRESS:

TEL NO:

CONTACT NAME:

PLEASE COMPLETE FORM OVERLEAF

READER REACTION FORM

COMMENT OR REASON FOR RECOMMENDATION:

....

....

....

....

....

....

....

....

....

....

....

....

READER REACTION FORM

The **Travel Publishing** *research team would like to receive readers' comments on any visitor attractions or places reviewed in the book and also recommendations for suitable entries to be included in the next edition. This will help ensure that the* **Country Living series of Rural Guides** *continues to provide its readers with useful information on the more interesting, unusual or unique features of each attraction or place ensuring that their visit to the local area is an enjoyable and stimulating experience. To provide your comments or recommendations would you please complete the forms below and overleaf as indicated and send to:*

The Research Department, Travel Publishing Ltd, 7a Apollo House, Calleva Park, Aldermaston, Reading, RG7 8TN

YOUR NAME:

YOUR ADDRESS:

YOUR TEL NO:

Please tick as appropriate: COMMENTS ☐ RECOMMENDATION ☐

ESTABLISHMENT:

ADDRESS:

TEL NO:

CONTACT NAME:

PLEASE COMPLETE FORM OVERLEAF

READER REACTION FORM

COMMENT OR REASON FOR RECOMMENDATION:

....

....

....

....

....

....

....

....

....

....

....

....

READER REACTION FORM

The **Travel Publishing** *research team would like to receive readers' comments on any visitor attractions or places reviewed in the book and also recommendations for suitable entries to be included in the next edition. This will help ensure that the* **Country Living series of Rural Guides** *continues to provide its readers with useful information on the more interesting, unusual or unique features of each attraction or place ensuring that their visit to the local area is an enjoyable and stimulating experience. To provide your comments or recommendations would you please complete the forms below and overleaf as indicated and send to:*

The Research Department, Travel Publishing Ltd, 7a Apollo House, Calleva Park, Aldermaston, Reading, RG7 8TN

YOUR NAME:

YOUR ADDRESS:

YOUR TEL NO:

Please tick as appropriate: COMMENTS ☐ RECOMMENDATION ☐

ESTABLISHMENT:

ADDRESS:

TEL NO:

CONTACT NAME:

PLEASE COMPLETE FORM OVERLEAF

READER REACTION FORM

COMMENT OR REASON FOR RECOMMENDATION:

....

....

....

....

....

....

....

....

....

....

....

....

READER REACTION FORM

The **Travel Publishing** *research team would like to receive readers' comments on any visitor attractions or places reviewed in the book and also recommendations for suitable entries to be included in the next edition. This will help ensure that the* **Country Living series of Rural Guides** *continues to provide its readers with useful information on the more interesting, unusual or unique features of each attraction or place ensuring that their visit to the local area is an enjoyable and stimulating experience. To provide your comments or recommendations would you please complete the forms below and overleaf as indicated and send to:*

The Research Department, Travel Publishing Ltd, 7a Apollo House, Calleva Park, Aldermaston, Reading, RG7 8TN

YOUR NAME:

YOUR ADDRESS:

YOUR TEL NO:

Please tick as appropriate: COMMENTS ☐ RECOMMENDATION ☐

ESTABLISHMENT:

ADDRESS:

TEL NO:

CONTACT NAME:

PLEASE COMPLETE FORM OVERLEAF

READER REACTION FORM

COMMENT OR REASON FOR RECOMMENDATION:

....

....

....

....

....

....

....

....

....

....

....

....

READER REACTION FORM

The **Travel Publishing** *research team would like to receive readers' comments on any visitor attractions or places reviewed in the book and also recommendations for suitable entries to be included in the next edition. This will help ensure that the* **Country Living series of Rural Guides** *continues to provide its readers with useful information on the more interesting, unusual or unique features of each attraction or place ensuring that their visit to the local area is an enjoyable and stimulating experience. To provide your comments or recommendations would you please complete the forms below and overleaf as indicated and send to:*

The Research Department, Travel Publishing Ltd, 7a Apollo House, Calleva Park, Aldermaston, Reading, RG7 8TN

YOUR NAME:

YOUR ADDRESS:

YOUR TEL NO:

Please tick as appropriate: COMMENTS ☐ RECOMMENDATION ☐

ESTABLISHMENT:

ADDRESS:

TEL NO:

CONTACT NAME:

PLEASE COMPLETE FORM OVERLEAF

READER REACTION FORM

COMMENT OR REASON FOR RECOMMENDATION:

....

....

....

....

....

....

....

....

....

....

....

....

READER REACTION FORM

The **Travel Publishing** *research team would like to receive readers' comments on any visitor attractions or places reviewed in the book and also recommendations for suitable entries to be included in the next edition. This will help ensure that the* **Country Living series of Rural Guides** *continues to provide its readers with useful information on the more interesting, unusual or unique features of each attraction or place ensuring that their visit to the local area is an enjoyable and stimulating experience. To provide your comments or recommendations would you please complete the forms below and overleaf as indicated and send to:*

The Research Department, Travel Publishing Ltd, 7a Apollo House, Calleva Park, Aldermaston, Reading, RG7 8TN

YOUR NAME:

YOUR ADDRESS:

YOUR TEL NO:

Please tick as appropriate: COMMENTS ☐ RECOMMENDATION ☐

ESTABLISHMENT:

ADDRESS:

TEL NO:

CONTACT NAME:

PLEASE COMPLETE FORM OVERLEAF

READER REACTION FORM

COMMENT OR REASON FOR RECOMMENDATION:

....

....

....

....

....

....

....

....

....

....

....

....

TOWNS, VILLAGES AND PLACES OF INTEREST

A

B

TOWNS, VILLAGES AND PLACES OF INTEREST

TOWNS, VILLAGES AND PLACES OF INTEREST

D

TOWNS, VILLAGES AND PLACES OF INTEREST

TOWNS, VILLAGES AND PLACES OF INTEREST

TOWNS, VILLAGES AND PLACES OF INTEREST

TOWNS, VILLAGES AND PLACES OF INTEREST

TOWNS, VILLAGES AND PLACES OF INTEREST

T

U

TOWNS, VILLAGES AND PLACES OF INTEREST